de Jong, Roth, Badini-Kinda, Bhagyanath

Ageing in Insecurity – Vieillir dans l'insécurité

Schweizerische Afrikastudien
Études africaines suisses

Herausgegeben von der
Schweizerischen Gesellschaft für Afrikastudien (SGAS)

Édité par la
Société suisse d'études africaines (SSEA)

Band/Tome 5

LIT

Willemijn de Jong, Claudia Roth
Fatoumata Badini-Kinda, Seema Bhagyanath

Ageing in Insecurity
Case Studies on Social Security and Gender in India and Burkina Faso

Vieillir dans l'insécurité
Sécurité sociale et genre en Inde et au Burkina Faso
Études de cas

Translation: Rose-Marie Ried
Traduction: Chantal-Nina Kouoh

LIT

Cover Picture/Illustration de couverture: Manù Hophan, Zurich
Layout/Mise en page: Christoph Schwager, Zurich

Bibliographic information published by Die Deutsche Bibliothek
Die Deutsche Bibliothek lists this publication in the Deutsche
Nationalbibliografie; detailed bibliographic data are available in the
Internet at http://dnb.ddb.de.

ISBN 3-8258-7846-5

© LIT VERLAG Münster   2005
Grevener Str./Fresnostr. 2   48159 Münster
Tel. 0251-62 03 20   Fax 0251-23 19 72
e-Mail: lit@lit-verlag.de   http://www.lit-verlag.de

Distributed in North America by:

Transaction Publishers
New Brunswick (U.S.A.) and London (U.K.)

Transaction Publishers
Rutgers University
35 Berrue Circle
Piscataway, NJ 08854

Tel.: (732) 445 - 2280
Fax: (732) 445 - 3138
for orders (U. S. only):
toll free (888) 999 - 6778

Contents

Sommaire

Acknowledgments / Remerciements

In the course of the last three and a half years various institutions and many people in India, Burkina Faso, and Switzerland have accompanied us along the way. We would like to extend our heartfelt thanks for their support.

Différentes institutions et de nombreuses personnes nous ont soutenues et accompagnées en Inde, au Burkina Faso et en Suisse pendant trois ans et demi. Nous souhaitons leur exprimer ici notre profonde gratitude.

Sponsors of the book and the research project
Swiss National Science Foundation SNSF, Swiss Development Cooperation SDC, Swiss Society for African Studies SSAS, Swiss Academy of Humanities and Social Sciences SAHS, Institute of Social Anthropology of the University of Zurich, Competence Centre Gender Studies CGS, Zurich University Alumni Association

Bailleurs de fonds du livre et du projet de recherche
Fonds National Suisse de la recherche scientifique FNS, Direction du Développement et de la Coopération DDC, Société Suisse d'Études Africaines SSEA, Académie Suisse des Sciences Humaines et Sociales ASSH, Départment d'Anthropologie Sociale de l'Université de Zurich, Centre de Compétence des Études du Genre, Société Académique Zurichoise

Institutions
Applied Human Science for Development and Evaluation, Bobo-Dioulasso; Centre for Development Studies, Thiruvananthapuram; Centre of Delwendé of Tanghin, Ouagadougou; Community Aid and Sponsorship Programme CASP, Kochi; Institute of Social Anthropology of the University of Zurich; Interpreter Services of the Ministry of Foreign Affairs, Ouagadougou; Loyola College of Social Sciences, Thiruvananthapuram; National Centre of Scientific Research, Ouagadougou; National Institute of Statistics and Demographics, Ouagadougou; Provincial Administration of Social Action and National Solidarity, Ziniaré; Rajagiri College of Social Science, Kochi; Rajagiri Community Development Scheme RCDS, Kochi; Society for African Studies SSAS, Bern; Swiss Development Cooperation SDC, Ouagadougou; University of Ouagadougou; Ziniaré City Hall

Bureau de la Coopération Suisse DDC, Ouagadougou; Caisse du développement Rajagiri, Kochi; Centre Delwendé de Tanghin, Ouagadougou; Centre National de la Recherche Scientifique CNRS, Ouagadougou; Département d'Anthropologie Sociale de l'Université de Zurich; Direction Provinciale de l'Action Sociale et de la Solidarité Nationale, Ziniaré; Institut National de la Statistique et de la Démographie, Ouagadougou; Institut des Sciences Sociales Loyola, Thiruvananthapuram; Institut des Sciences Sociales Rajagiri, Kochi; Mairie de Ziniaré; Programme d'aide et de soutien à la communauté, CASP, Kochi; Science de l'Homme Appliquée au Développement et à l'Évaluation SHADEI, Bobo-Dioulasso; Service d'Interprétariat du Ministère des Affaires Étrangères, Ouagadougou; Société Suisse d'Études Africaines SSEA, Berne; Université de Ouagadougou

Persons / Personnes

Fr. Jose Alex, Kochi; M. P. Antoni, Kochi; Amadé Badini, Ouagadougou; Ludovic Bationo, Ouagadougou; Franz von Benda-Beckmann, Halle; Keebet von Benda-Beckmann, Halle; C. K. Bhagyanath, Kannur; Saguna Bhagyanath, Kannur; Françoise Bourdarias, Tours; Jean-François Bürki, Ouagadougou; Chef du village de Kuila; Jenny Duyne Barenstein, Zurich/Lugano; Peter van Eeuwijk, Basel; Marie Gade, Nantes; Raymond Gade, Nantes; Kamala Ganesh, Mumbai; Katharina Ganz, Zurich; Urs Geiser, Zurich; M. K. George, Thiruvananthapuram; Jawahar Gopalakrishnan, London; Jürg Helbling, Zurich; René Holenstein, Ouagadougou/Sarajewo; Manù Hophan, Zurich; Joseph I. Injodey, Kochi; S. Irudaya Rajan, Thiruvananthapuram; Mary Joseph, Kochi; Fr. M. K. Joseph, Kochi; Fr. Antony Kariyil, Kochi; Helen Judith, Thiruvananthapuram; Karuppan, Kadamakuddy; Eva Keller, Zurich; Blahima Konaté, Bobo-Dioulasso; Juliette Koning, Amsterdam; Sheela Koshy, Thumpamon; Chantal-Nina Kouoh, Neuenhof; Thomas K. M., Thiruvananthapuram; Sumitha P. Kuruvila, Thiruvananthapuram; André Leliveld, Leiden; Sr. Alice Lukose, Alappuzha; Robert Malfait, Paris; Sojan Mathew, Thiruvananthapuram; Lassina Millogo, Bobo-Dioulasso; Jan Morgenthaler, Zurich/Esfahan/Berlin; Hans-Peter Müller, Zurich; Tiéné Nacro, Ouagadougou; Léonard Nana, Kuila; Nadja Ottiger, Zurich; Fatoumata Ouattara, Bobo-Dioulasso/Marseille; Malimata Ouattara-Millogo, Bobo-Dioulasso/Ouagadougou; Mathieu Ouédraogo, Ouagadougou; Thomas Padikkala (†), Kochi; Rajni Palriwala, New Delhi; Paul Parin, Zurich; Sujata Patel, Pune; Fr. J. Prasanth Palakkappillil, Kochi; Fr. Dominic George Puthenpurackal, Thiruvananthapuram; Shalini Randeria, Zurich; Renjini. D., Thiruvananthapuram; Rose-Marie Ried, Zurich; Carla Risseeuw, Leiden; Lilo Roost Vischer, Basel; Anne Roth-Huggler, Paris; Martin Saka, Ouagadougou; Issiaka Sanon, Bobo-Dioulasso; Jeanne Sanon, Bobo-Dioulasso; Odile Sanon, Bobo-Dioulasso; Alain Sanou, Bobo-Dioulasso/Ouagadougou; Sita Malik Sawadogo, Ouagadougou; Christine Schuppli, Zurich; Christoph Schwager, Zurich; Salif Simbre, Ouagadougou; R. Sooryamoorthy, Thiruvananthapuram; Beat Sottas, Fribourg; Susi Staub, Zurich; Anna Straub, Zurich; Celine Sunny, Kochi; Tessy Thomas, Kochi; Alassane Traoré, Ouagadougou; Silppa U. J., Kochi; Seena U. J., Kochi; Fr. Varghese K. Varghese; Vincent Thomas Varghese, Kochi; Nisha Vikraman, Kochi; Robert Vuarin (†), Marseille; Sabine Wunderlin, Zurich

We would also like to thank all the informants who participated in our studies, hosted us in their homes and shared their life experiences with us. Without their cooperation our studies would not have been possible.

Nous tenons également à remercier toutes les personnes qui nous ont renseignées pendant notre recherche et nous ont accueillies les bras ouverts chez elles et ont partagé leurs expériences de vie avec nous. Sans leur aide précieuse, notre recherche n'aurait tout simplement pas été faisable.

Ageing in Insecurity
Case Studies on Social Security and Gender in India and Burkina Faso

Preface

When colleagues asked me what I was working on twenty years ago and I would tell them I was studying social security in a developing country, the reaction was anything between commiseration and disbelief. Who would want to study a subject that was so clearly related to the modern, western world, in particular the West-European welfare state? That was something for sociologists to study in the north, but certainly not for anthropologists studying in developing countries. Since the pioneering work of 1984 by James Midgley, "Social Security, Inequality, and the Third World", in which he pointed at the lack of empirical studies in developing countries, a number of interesting monographies have appeared focussing on social security and contributing to the theoretical understanding of the field. Social security is, under different labels, a main theme in the sociology of development, in development studies and in social anthropology. Besides, the international and bilateral donor communities have put the issue on the agenda. Social security is, thus, an accepted yet still under-researched topic.

There are two sets of reasons that I can think of for this blind eye that the social sciences still turn on the subject in poor countries, especially countries with weak states. One is that social security remains generally associated with state policies. And since nothing can be expected of the state in poor countries, there is no point giving it further thought. That was the cliché and it persists for some researchers. Of course, this is a distorted point of view. Nowhere in the world is social security confined to what the state provides. Even in the most extended social welfare systems of the wealthy countries public policies are only part of the total picture. In the specific history of western industrialization the political struggle has been to create solidarity circles large enough to carry the main risks related to industrial production: loss of income due to sickness, disability, dismissal, old age. At the height of social welfare, the focus had come to lie almost entirely on the state and its policies. But any woman who has taken care of children or an aged parent will know that support by the state may at best make her task lighter. In addition, social security would be far less effective without the huge amount of volunteer aid.

A second reason why it took social scientists and policy makers so long to start thinking seriously about social security in poor countries is that social security has been associated almost entirely with income. This may be adequate for countries where lack of wage is the most important reason for poverty. In poor countries lack of wage is of course a major problem as well. However, exclusively focussing on money seriously limits our understanding of social security. For a full understanding of social security we have to look at labour, both for production and for care, and at the availability of resources as well. Fortunately, policy makers have come to realise that the field of social security requires a more inclusive approach. Reports from the ILO, the World Bank and the major donor agencies nowadays acknowledge this, though it seems to be difficult to draw conclusions from this insight.

Similarly, social scientists have come to understand that social security involves more than state policies. Many social scientists have approached the theme from a perspective of poverty or livelihood studies. These have pointed at the central importance of social relationships, nowadays often discussed under the trendy notion of social capital, and of the importance of education and of health, in particular reproductive health. These studies have also generated important insights into the specific risk profiles of the poor, profiles that differ from those who are better off. While these issues are all of crucial importance for an understanding of social security, poverty and livelihood studies have been weaker on another point: they look predominantly at adult, able persons and perhaps at children, but they do not deal extensively with the sick, the weak, the old or the disabled. The assumption is that the poor in principle can work and make a living, if only access to credit, market, education and health would improve. While those who cannot work, or only very reduced, are not completely excluded from livelihood and poverty studies per se, and they usually remain rather marginal. Categories of persons who are least visible in production processes also remain relatively invisible in livelihood and poverty studies. But unless we consider them as well we will miss important aspects of social life, aspects that reach far beyond these categories: Understanding social security is crucial for understanding social life in general.

The research of which this volume is the result takes a broad perspective of social security. To study social security in a meaningful way it is necessary not only to look at the institutions made specifically for social security, but also to consider the whole spectrum of ways in which the needy may be supported. It comprises social security provided by the state, by the market, by voluntary organisations and by kinship and communities. Societies have normative structures defining what is considered ordinary behaviour and what constitutes need and what are grounds for legitimate claims for support. These normative structures also define circles of solidarity and their internal social differentiations, but the official legal system of the state may have different notions of need and obligation for support than customary legal systems or religious law. In actual life, the provision of social security is negotiated within these different normative frameworks and people create mixes, drawing on various sets of rules and regulations, and various types of social security, based on religion, customary law and state legislation.

While the number of monographs is steadily increasing, there has been relatively little comparative work of the type presented in this volume. The research project is important for several reasons. First, it is an attempt to design research in close collaboration with people from the areas to be researched, instead of hiring research assistants for the empirical work while leaving the theoretical framework for researchers from the North. Secondly, it takes considerable courage to attempt to make comparisons between countries that are as totally different as India, or rather Kerala, and Burkina Faso. Anthropologists, if they embark on comparison at all, tend to make comparisons within relatively small regional boundaries, and there is much that speaks for such confined comparisons. But a comparison that crosses the usual regional boundaries has its own advantages, especially if the comparison is built into the research design from the onset. It allows researchers to ask questions that one might not ask if staying within one country or region, and to question some of the things that are usually taken for granted.

Though this volume does not focus on migration, looking at urbanisation and comparing rural and urban situations would allow analysing circles of solidarity that extend over longer distances, and by doing so change and become internally more differentiated.

While Western Europe, and to a lesser extend the USA, has responded to urbanisation and new production methods by state systems of social security, poor countries have not developed a robust state social security system. They do not have the resource basis and often refuse to decide to allocate the meagre means they have to social security. Where this has been done, social security funds are notoriously corruption ridden. On the other hand, in contrast to Western Europe, state institutions in general play an important role in social security, not in their official capacity, but on the basis of their unofficial parallel order. Retrenchment programmes on the basis of structural adjustment therefore not only mean the threat of losing one's job; it has far deeper implications for social security. It is because of this double threat that these policies cause such deep anxiety, insecurity and disappointment.

This research is particularly important because it questions the idea that family in developing countries is a firm basis for social security. By looking at the situation of poor elderly people, the research has shown that family does not always offer the circle of solidarity that policy makers believe it to be. Though the circles of solidarity based on kinship are in many cases virtually the only form of social security available, they are very fragile indeed and offer little security. This becomes notably clear because the researchers focussed in this book on perhaps the most vulnerable sector of society: the elderly poor. Many of the poorest elderly do not have a strong set of kin that could take care of them. Indeed, lacking close kin, in particular children, seems to be a main factor for the elderly to be living in poverty. This is exacerbated by the fact, as the studies in this volume also show, that living in poverty also means that one cannot engage in the necessary exchange to entertain meaningful kin relations. The poor, therefore, have a smaller circle of support, even though there may be a larger kin group that potentially could be mobilised for support. Given the rapidly growing incidence of HIV/AIDS, and given the high rates of migration, relying on family as the major provider of social security turns out to be a decidedly problematic strategy. The contributions to this volume give us an empirical basis to look at just how precarious kinship networks of social security are. The research, therefore, is as important for those having a theoretical interest in social security as it is for policy makers and development agencies designing social security networks.

Keebet von Benda-Beckmann
Halle, October 2004

Introduction: A Comprehensive Perspective on Social (In-)Security

Willemijn de Jong

The Subject, the Project, the Case Studies

Old Age and Insecurity

"Ageing in insecurity" – the statement that poor people in countries of the South such as India and Burkina Faso age in insecurity seems to be a truism. However, what their ever-changing support networks at present look like and how secure or insecure they are is less well known. If questions about "social security" are addressed among academics, perceptions of public, often governmental provisions dominate the imagination. If questions of "informal safety nets" are addressed, perceptions of the coverage of needs by "the family" come to the forefront. In the South a pervasive public image about "the family" as the institution that provides full protection and a safety net for its members cloud the actual practices of social support in old age, as "the state", despite retrenchment, does in the North.

We researchers of the North were also susceptible to this perception. During the research process we changed our view in that in the beginning, by investigating both low-income and middle-income classes, we concentrated solely on security. In the end and focusing particularly on the low-income classes for this book, we increasingly discovered that security with regard to the life phase of old age is a delicate achievement for the poor population and the result of continuous struggles against insecurity within structures of social inequality. Part of the poor population does not live in security in old age. They lack "the capability to perform certain basic functionings", which are the "capabilities to be adequately nourished, to be comfortably clothed, to avoid escapable morbidity and preventable mortality" (Drèze and Sen 1991: 7, 8).

The aim of the book is to present specificities of the support networks, or social security arrangements, of poor elderly with regard to
security and insecurity in a rural and an urban context in India and
Burkina Faso. This knowledge can be useful for community development, especially in times in which anxieties about the care of growing
numbers of elderly people increase. Thereby, the gendering, and possibly degendering, of their security networks is of special interest.[1]

Our point of departure is a recently developed, comprehensive approach to social security, which also opens up new ways for looking at
poverty. We have connected this with gender approaches in the fields
of new kinship studies as well as citizenship studies. The people represented in the four case studies mainly belong to the social category
of small farmers and casual workers who subsist on irregular incomes.
Brief comparisons with the conditions of wealthier middle-class
groups will be made with the intention of giving clearer contours to
the situation of the poor.

Local Social Security and Gender in India and Burkina Faso

This book is the result of a research project entitled "Local Social Security and Gender in India and Burkina Faso" (July 2000 until December 2003) which was conducted within the "Research Partnership
with Developing Countries" programme of the Swiss National Science
Foundation and the Swiss Development Cooperation and consisted of
four subprojects. The choice of our Southern partners from India and
Burkina Faso and the focus on these countries resulted from previous
research experiences and contacts of the Northern partners in Asia and
Africa who also initiated the project. The project had an interdisciplinary character because the Southern partners are sociologists, whereas
the Northern partners are anthropologists.

An article by Keebet von Benda-Beckmann (1991) on Indonesian
migrant women and their changing patterns of "social security" in the

---

[1] "Gendering" means that social entities, domains or processes become differentiated
according to gender; "degendering" means that they become less differentiated according to gender.

Netherlands inspired us to conduct a project on this subject. We were attracted by the approach which she developed together with Franz von Benda-Beckmann in a number of other publications. They established social security as an "inclusive" field of study. With their approach they were influential in the Netherlands and beyond. For the studies in Africa, the work by Robert Vuarin (2000) on "social protection" in Mali was additionally important. Concerning the link between social security or "circles of support" on the one hand and kinship and gender on the other, the publications by Rajni Palriwala and Carla Risseeuw (1996), as well as Carla Risseeuw and Kamala Ganesh (1998), were a model. With all of these scholars we communicated personally.

Within India the focus is on the state of Kerala which offers a stark, yet challenging, contrast to Burkina Faso. Kerala, in Southwest India, and Burkina Faso, in West Africa, represent opposing poles with regard to postcolonial development. We presumed that this difference would have an impact on social security. In Kerala, social reform movements and other factors caused a decline in agriculture and a formation of public welfare that led to improvements in education and health as reflected in quality of life indicators comparable with developing countries. Burkina Faso's modernity can be characterised as principally based on subsistence agriculture, with little public welfare and ample foreign development aid. With regard to income per capita, however, the difference between the two countries is less marked (see appendix). As we also expected differences between the rural and the urban areas in Kerala and Burkina Faso that would influence social security, we conducted comparative studies in both contexts.

The aim of our project was to generate new insights into the local conditions of social security in Kerala and Burkina Faso with a special focus on gender, which could also serve as a basis for new development efforts. Our main research questions were: How supportive are existing social security networks? What kinds of practices do people pursue with regard to family, kinship, community and state to prevent a decline in living standards, and what are their ideas in these respects? Also, what are the effects of market and governmental structures as well as of historical processes?

During the first year we tried to obtain an overview of the conditions of social security in the four localities. Subsequently, we concentrated on old age, a topic which two of the research partners had already worked on previously. The issue of care in old age has recently become of particular interest for scholars and policy makers due to the awareness and anxieties concerning the increases in the ageing population as a result of higher life expectancy. This is applicable in the North as well as the South (e.g. Irudaya Rajan et al. 1999, Makoni and Stroeken 2002). We gave special attention to the limits of family support, as we had indications in the literature and in our own data that not only does public support leave the poor elderly in insecurity, but more importantly, family support is also a delicate and uncertain resource. This focus on kinship also made sense because state-based social security is mainly restricted to the small minority of civil servants in the countries of the South.

We carried out nine months of fieldwork in 2000, 2001 and 2002 and each year we deepened our knowledge of the subject matter. About thirty semi-structured interviews with narrative components were carried out during each fieldwork phase. Most of them were individual interviews with low-income and middle-income elderly people and their children concerning social security efforts. Some of the interviews included a biographical perspective and some were with representatives of organisations (e.g. caste organisations, old age homes, charity and social welfare organisations). For empirical convenience we defined "being old" as being a grandparent of fifty-five years and older. Explorative data were also elicited from focus group interviews. Participant observation was used as a complementary method, including information from numerous informal conversations. Moreover, in the Indian subprojects a quota survey with males and females of average education and occupation and belonging to the middle generation was carried out at the end of the fieldwork. The survey comprised 80 questionnaires in the rural area and 120 questionnaires in the urban area. Thereby certain key issues such as financial resources, support relationships and housing were checked.

Regarding the collection and analysis of the empirical data, we basically followed the methodological principles of the "grounded theory" developed by Glaser, Strauss, and Corbin (1994, 1998 [1967]). Considering the different research backgrounds of the project partners, this procedure was most feasible for us. We began with hypotheses to the research questions mentioned above, however, by collecting and analyzing the data we differentiated the hypotheses on the one hand, and generated new hypotheses on the other. Correspondingly, we carried out the first steps of evaluation during fieldwork. The process was time-consuming but due to this "constant comparative method" (Strauss and Corbin 1994: 273) we were able to quickly get a deeper understanding of the research subject.

During the nearly five years of the project, the research team worked very closely together during parts of the fieldwork phases, at three workshops in Zurich after phases of data evaluation, and via email for the preparation of several working papers and for this publication. André Leliveld and Juliette Koning, participants in a research circle on social security by Keebet and Franz von Benda-Beckmann in the Netherlands in the 1990s, coached us during two workshops in Zurich. We worked with Peter van Eeuwijk, a Swiss scholar in the field of health and old age, during the third workshop.

The official part of our research project was concluded with an international conference titled "South-North Debates: Social Security Relations and Gender" in December 2003 in Burkina Faso. There we discussed with about fifty scholars and practitioners, the majority from Burkina Faso and some from India and from Europe, the issue of social security and the main results of our research. Keebet von Benda-Beckmann and Robert Vuarin delivered the key speeches.[2] The research team's conference papers have been revised and are now presented as case studies in this book.

---

[2] A website containing the results of the conference and the papers presented is available until the end of 2005 (www.northsouth.ch).

Limits of Family Support in Old Age

As already indicated, dominant public and academic discourses in countries of the South often suggest that social security arrangements with regard to old age can more or less be equated with "the family", whereby the support of "the son" is stressed. In case the family is not able to carry out this normative expectation, in particular required by the state, public support should at least be provided to family caregivers so that they could fulfil their task (e.g. United Nations 1994). Although we also think that family and kin relations play an important role, we were forced to question these general assumptions after we analysed the field data following our first year of research. From then on the limits of old age support by the family and resulting insecurities became important research concerns.

To obtain clearer answers with regard to our doubts concerning the myth and/or the norm of "the family" as the security providing institution *par excellence*, and concerning the image of "the son" as the ultimate support-giver for elderly parents, we dealt with the following questions in the case studies:

– To what extent are people of poor social groups able to mobilise support from family and kin members in old age, according to prevalent ideas and practices, and what kind of alternatives do they have?
– To what extent is old age security of people of poor social groups gendered, and what are the consequences?

Issues of food, housing and care in everyday life are of primary interest in the case studies, whereas health also figures as an important issue. Thereby we mainly concentrated on security networks and kinship, with a look at citizenship.

We began with the same research questions in the four subprojects and used the same qualitative methodological procedures and question guides. In the case studies presented here we placed different emphases depending on the most striking findings in the different localities. Moreover, as this book is the result of a North-South project, we did not try to even out but intentionally left scope for the different kinds of research experiences of the scholars, with regard to training, duration of fieldwork in the locality altogether, representation of findings and academic culture (cf. de Jong 2002). In the two brief chapters that precede the case studies of India and Burkina Faso, we outline crucial social, economic, political and historical aspects with regard to both countries. This structural and historical contextual information should give clues to a better understanding of the old age (in)securities of the people with whom we worked. In the last chapter we draw some conclusions with regard to the most important comparative issues that resulted from the case studies.

Theoretical Background

The Concept of Local Social Security

Many studies about social security embark from a Euro-American institutional and policy-oriented perspective with a focus on the state and other public organisations as the main agencies for providing support in specific situations of personal need and distress. This approach is strongly influenced by international organisations such as the International Labour Organization (ILO) which has been responsible for the standardisation of public social security in both developed and developing countries since the 1940s. In a recent ILO publication social security is defined as "benefits that society provides to individuals and households – through public and collective measures – to guarantee them a minimum standard of living and to protect them against low or declining living standards arising out of a number of basic risks and needs" (van Ginneken 2003: 11). The World Bank also concentrates on "public interventions" (World Bank 2001: 9). With these institutional approaches the large realm of support provided by kin and other more or less institutionalised personal relationships in the South and in the North remains invisible, and the small realm of public support for people in the organised sector is unduly emphasised.

In the 1980s Franz and Keebet von Benda-Beckmann, specialised in the anthropology of law, began to develop an "inclusive" social security approach based on their research with different groups of Indonesian people.[3] The term "inclusive" refers to their focus of study which is not only on institutions or organisations which supply public support, but also on the individuals and groups of individuals who are the recipients of public support. Scholars of different disciplines who conducted studies on social security in Asia and Africa have followed their approach.[4] The manner in which the authors and their colleagues construct social security as a field of study is exemplified in particular in the edited volumes "Between Kinship and the State: Social Security and Law in Developing Countries" (1988) and "Coping with Insecurity: An 'Underall' Perspective on Social Security in the Third World" (2000 [1994]).

In the essay "Coping with Insecurity", which is most programmatic with regard to their work on social security, the authors expose their dynamic model of social security based on a new view of social organisation. Their use of social security in a wider sense, although the term has emerged with regard to governmental social security, is evidently epistemologically motivated in that they consider insecurity as the pivot of social organisation instead of conflict or disruption (F. and K. von Benda-Beckmann 2000 [1994]).

Following Franz and Keebet von Benda-Beckmann, we consider social security as an integral aspect of social and economic life and as central to the understanding of social organisation and change. With this the dual nature of social security as both a social and an economic phenomenon is also indicated, whereas in institutional approaches the economic aspects are often overemphasised. Of central importance is the conversion of economic resources into social security needs at any level of poverty or wealth.

With regard to the empirical dimension of social security we adopted the following definition: "Empirically, social security refers

---

[3] Cf. F. von Benda-Beckmann 1988, K. von Benda-Beckmann 1988, K. von Benda-Beckmann 1991, K. von Benda-Beckmann and F. Leatemia-Tomatala 1992, F. and K. von Benda-Beckmann 1998, K. von Benda-Beckmann 2004, and F. von Benda-Beckmann and R. Kirsch 1999 concerning Africa.

[4] Cf. e.g. Vel 1994, Leliveld 1994, 2004, de Bruijn and van Dijk 1995, Hirtz 1995, Biezeveld 2002, Nooteboom 2003, Koning and Hüsken 2005.

to the social phenomena with which the abstract domain of social security is filled: efforts of individuals, groups of individuals and organisations to overcome insecurities related to their existence, that is,
concerning food and water, shelter, care and physical and mental
health, education and income, to the extent that the contingencies are
not considered a purely individual responsibility, as well as the in-
tended and unintended consequences of these efforts" (ibid. 14).

This approach concentrates especially on the social practices of individual and collective actors with regard to social security. They are
also related to the general cultural ideas and the individual notions of
social security as well as to the institutionalised rights and obligations,
and to the actual social relationships of givers and receivers of social
security. Moreover, the consequences of the practices are also of interest. What comes less explicitly into focus in their model, however,
are the structural and historical contexts of the social security discourses and practices as well as its genderedness. In their publications,
however, they reflect on these dimensions, in particular on the state.

When social security is achieved, it can be inferred that the related
social relationships contain a security quality due to "security mechanisms" which enable natural, economic and social resources to be
converted into actual social security provisions. The authors stress that
these resources alone do not provide social security. With statements
such as "One cannot eat rice land" and "Money does not cook" an
informant in Indonesia enlightened them about the importance of
"chains of conversions" (ibid. 22).

The French sociologist Robert Vuarin (2000, 2004) also concentrates on the constitution and the use of support networks with regard
to what he calls "social protection", and he additionally looks at the
reconstruction of those networks under the present conditions of globalisation. In his model of a "protection system" he distinguishes in the
first place four structural and legitimizing poles of collective protection with their different group constellations, i.e. the state with its
formalised social security and social assistance provisions, religion
with its institutionalised charity, the market with its institutionalised
insurances and civil society under which he subsumes kinship and

other personal relationships and voluntary organisations. Additionally, at the level of individual interactions he conceptualises an "elementary relationship of protection". This relationship has to be negotiated in practice. With regard to support systems in urban Mali in West Africa, he is particularly interested in the potential of civil society to provide sociability and protection, meaning networks of reciprocal support among kin and friends, relationships between patrons and clients and voluntary organisations. He sees most potential for relationships of protection in cooperative voluntary organisations with membership on the basis of equality, as the hierarchies of power that exist in other kinds of social relationships can thus be ruled out because of a depersonalisation of redistribution and because of an institutionalisation of altruistic aims. In the end, he advocates an institutionalisation of social protection that prevents hierarchies and inequalities, whether in the form of a formalised governmental arrangement or a formalised civil arrangement (Vuarin 2004: 10).

Local social security efforts are responses to insecurities rather than risks. The term risk is closely connected with insurance. Ulrich Beck who has coined the term "Risikogesellschaft" (risk society) remarks, for example, "Risks concerning modernisation are *big business*. They are the needs which are searched for by economists but which cannot be settled. Hunger can be appeased, needs satisfied. Civilisation risks are a tub with needs without a bottom, not to be settled, without an end, self-producing" (Beck 1986: 30, translation WdJ). From this perspective, risks are created and in the subsequent processes securities are produced. At the same time power is exerted and profits are made. Accordingly, old age can be seen to range as a risk in current public discourses in countries in the North and in the South. However, when the poor people, who are the focus of our case studies, talk about old age it is mainly with respect to threatening insecurities and expected securities.

The key terms used in our case studies are formulated as follows. With the term "local social security" the functional approach that we pursue is stressed. In our conception, the term implies the discourses and practices of people in a specific locality, as well as the conditions of social security in that locality, with reference to the context of the regional market, the nation-state and global economic and cultural influences. When we talk about "social security arrangement" we mean the whole complex of security efforts or the social security mix of an individual, a group of individuals or an organisation. We conceive of social security arrangements of certain social groups of people as consisting of a network of social relationships which can be mobilised for support. Thus, social security arrangements of the poor elderly consist of those social ties that they are able to mobilise in situations of need, be it relationships with certain family members, with certain members in the local community or with organisations. The social security arrangements of the different groups together constitute the "social security system" of a societal entity. As Franz and Keebet von Benda-Beckmann we try with our perspective to overcome the usual dichotomies such as traditional and modern social security, informal and formal social security, or private and public social security.

Uses of Kinship and Citizenship

Kin and kin-like relations with neighbours and friends are of the utmost importance for social security in societies that lack sufficient public provisions. Therefore, in addition to studies on social security, we based our research on kinship studies. We particularly refer to the anthropologists Sylvia Yanagisako and Jane Collier (1987) who developed a highly influential "unified analysis of gender and kinship". With that analytic model, which presupposed that constructions of kinship and gender are closely related, they aimed to overcome analytical dichotomies such as sex and gender, nature and culture, production and reproduction as well as private and public (cf. de Jong 2001). Their publication initiated the "new kinship studies", a revival of studies on kinship and family issues that formerly were at the core of anthropological concerns. They base their model on the theoretical stances of both David Schneider (1972), famous for the study of cultural meanings of kinship and family, and Pierre Bourdieu (1977,

1990), who strongly promoted integrated actor and system oriented studies.

The analytic procedure followed by Yanagisako and Collier relates the social world of actors, their ideas, perceptions and actions to societal structures of inequality and to historical developments. We also assume here, in accordance with that approach, that social security like other societal fields of study is structured by social inequality, in particular by gender and class which impacts on individuals. At the same time, we have to take into account that individuals reproduce and transform the structures through their agency. An important point of this approach, and contrary to the women's study approach, is that no preclusive assumption is made that male and female individuals think and act differently. Thus, they also take a "non-gendered system of inequality" (ibid. 40) into consideration, as for example in societies of hunters and gatherers. However, if the analysis shows that the cultural values or social processes discriminate between females and males, then it has to be explained with the gendered character of their social spaces of action. Interestingly, the authors also hint at insecurity or ambivalence in kinship and gender systems related to historical processes when they say: "We can see how aspects of ideas and practices which in our systemic models seem to reinforce and reproduce each other, also undermine and destabilize each other" (Yanagisako and Collier 1987: 47).

Carla Risseeuw, Rajni Palriwala, Kamala Ganesh and other scholars apply the combined kinship and gender approach of Yanagisako and Collier in studies on "shifting circles of support" in several countries in South Asia and Sub-Saharan Africa.[5] They focus on changing kinship relations under colonialism, on changing educational and legal systems and the family, changing economic conditions and kinship, as well as on the negotiation of (in)security in changing societies. The Indian scholars Rajni Palriwala and Kamala Ganesh also conducted research on changing family relations and the welfare system in the Netherlands as well (cf. Palriwala 2000). The authors criticise the often static ideological and policy constructs of the family, and under-

---

[5] Cf. Palriwala and Risseeuw 1996, and Risseeuw and Ganesh 1998.

line the transformations of family and kinship relations and the negotiated character of networks of support. They also include citizenship
in their analysis, which they mainly associate with legal systems of the
colonial and postcolonial state. We have adopted their classification of
security systems on three levels: domestic, community and state.

One of the most crucial suggestions made by Risseeuw and Palriwala (1996) for our case studies touches upon the issue of insecurity
or ambivalence. They state: "Marriage, family and kinship are social
domains characterised by a duality. They carry elements of control –
even oppression – limiting people's options to realise their own welfare and interests or of those for whom they take particular responsibility. The interests of the socially and economically most powerful
members of a network as well as group interests can and do create
forms of oppression from which the more vulnerable and dependent
cannot extricate themselves easily, if at all. Yet these structures continue to be the main social arenas providing care in the regions covered here" (ibid. 39).

In the same vein, as the categories kinship and gender, the category
age, along with other categories such as class, caste, race, ethnicity,
and nationality, are all analytically conceived of as socially and culturally constructed in current social science approaches.[6] Rubinstein
(1990) explicitly refers to the approach of Yanagisako and Collier and
advocates that a "unified analysis of gender and kinship" should include generation and age. This is a valuable perspective for our study
as well. The literature on the life phase of old age states that women
achieve more decision-making power during their life-course but that
the asymmetry between genders is only slightly diminished with age
(e.g. Albert and Cattell 1994). Thus, it can be inferred that the structuring principle of age is subordinate to gender and that it is important
to analyse gender as a changing category with regard to the life-course
and generation.

In this context, it is also important to stress that old age has a different meaning in different societies. In particular, "being old" is a
relative concept dependent on the social and cultural context (cf. Sok-

---

[6] Cf. e.g. Rubinstein 1990, Sokolovsky 1990, and Cohen 1994.

olovsky 1993). It is mainly related to chronological age in governmental discourse, e.g. in Kerala the official retirement age is fifty-five,
and in academic discourse, e.g. in India it is equated with 60+ and
"being old-old" with 70+ (cf. Irudaya Rajan et al. 1999). However, the
elderly themselves may not use chronological criteria but rather refer
to changing social and economic roles, which may be a gradual process, e.g. becoming old in the sense of becoming unable to earn
money. Often, the category of the elderly is differentiated according to
the healthy and unimpaired elderly and the ill and feeble. Those most
likely to be neglected are elderly people who are infirm and weak (e.g.
E. and L. Holmes 1995). These practices with regard to the elderly
relate also to the dimensions of insecurity or ambivalence regarding
social order, kinship and family. The fact that neglect and ambivalence of kinship, with respect to the elderly in Non-western societies,
may go unnoticed is linked to the fact that social scientists often report
cultural ideals of filial piety regarding elders rather than the actual
practices. Like the informants, they tend to construct myths of a
"Golden Age" or of "Golden Isles", as has already been criticised in
gerontology for some time (Nydegger 1983).

In our case studies we use the term "being old" as synonymous
with "being elderly" and "elderliness" (cf. Makoni and Stroeken 2001:
5), whereas we use "old age" to refer to the last phase of life. Although old age and being old is often associated with illness and decline in Western societies, this is no reason for us to substitute these
terms by euphemistic ones such as elderliness, being elderly, or senior
citizens, terms that blur social realities.

Kin relationships also play an important role for the elderly in the
North, as the scarce studies about this issue illustrate (e.g. Cantor
1980). The study by Janet Finch and Jennifer Mason (1993) on kinship and family responsibilities in England, which also includes elderly people, is interesting because they examine the negotiation of
support relationships within family and kinship networks very precisely. It also gave us important clues with regard to the conceptualisation of "social support", or "care", in a wider sense. With regard to
support systems in the South, we constructed a simpler, threefold clas-

sification of "material support" (including providing money, food and accommodation), "physical support" or "care" in a narrow sense (i.e. domestic work and the physical care of children, the elderly and the sick), and "emotional support" (including socializing and giving advice).

A great number of publications on the issue of "care" (family and community care) have appeared in recent years, also with regard to citizenship and welfare (e.g. Waerness 1987, Fraser 2000, Ungerson 2000). These cannot, however, be applied to the poor in countries of the South due to the very limited welfare provisions in these countries compared with the North.

In the course of our research, we became increasingly aware of the fact that national and also transnational issues of social security can favourably be analysed from new perspectives on citizenship. Nira Yuval-Davis' work is particularly useful in clarifying issues of citizenship and gender. In accordance with recent debates on citizenship, based on the work of T.H. Marshall, she sees it "as a multi-tier construct, which applies to people's membership in a variety of collectivities – local, ethnic, national and transnational" (Yuval-Davis 1997: 68). Thereby, she considers these collectivities as ideological and material constructions, whose boundaries, structures and norms are a result of the continuous processes of struggles, negotiations and social developments. Citizenship also has individual and collective dimensions. The lower castes in India, for example, experience collective rights through positive discrimination by the state, through benefits in education and jobs in the civil service sector.

With regard to women, Yuval-Davis claims that women's citizenship should not only be considered in contrast to men's, but also in relation to women's affiliation to dominant and subordinate groups, their ethnicity, origin and urban or rural residence, as well as with regard to global and transnational issues. From an individual perspective, attributes such as gender, class position, religion, origin, ability and phase in the life-course determine one's citizenship, to the extent that "[m]ost members of most families, usually the children, the sick, the elderly and women, can determine very little of their lives even within the family, let alone outside it" (ibid. 91). To overcome the limitations of the analytic private and public dichotomy, the author distinguishes three spheres: the sphere of family relations, i.e. "social, economic and political networks and households which are organised around kinship or friendship relations" (ibid. 14), the sphere of civil society and that of the state.

Issues of citizenship are also dealt with in the following case studies, although not centrally. They are more important in the Indian case studies than in the one's pertaining to Burkina Faso.

A Functional Gender Approach

Theories, whether they are more or less explicit, influence the way we interpret our data. This is why we pointed out ways in which our study was theoretically and empirically influenced by previous studies about social security, kinship, citizenship and gender. Following these elaborations we are now in a better position to formulate our gender approach. Basically, we do not consider elderly women and men mere "victims" of their social conditions, although we are aware of the fact that their room for agency may not be very broad. We look at the issue of social security in old age from an actor and gender oriented approach, with a focus on the uses of social relationships by the elderly and their children as both receivers and givers of social security.

In the discursive and practical interactions of the actors we distinguish more or less marked dimensions of "doing gender", i.e. the production of gender in everyday activities (West and Zimmerman 1987). Within these more or less gendered interactions, certain relationships with other individuals and with groups of individuals are used to obtain security in old age.

Furthermore, the societal structures and processes can also be conceived of as more or less gendered, i.e. they are institutionally and ideologically imprinted by gender, which causes social exclusion. On the one hand, gender is a key structuring principle in the distribution of labour, property and other valued resources in a society, and often results in women having less access to income, as well as land and other property. This is the political-economy dimension of gender. On the other hand, gender is a key structuring principle in the "range of harms" that women suffer in different societies, such as trivialisation, disparagement, demeaning representations of "feminine" things, attitudinal discrimination, sexual harassment, domestic violence and denial of full citizenship rights. This is related to the cultural or value oriented dimension of gender (Frazer 1997, Kabeer 2000). Regarding old age security, this means that the, mostly, gendered uses of relations of kinship and citizenship lead to more or less secure arrangements, depending on the economic and cultural structures and processes and their degree of genderedness.

Gender positionality should be looked at in relation to other social categories, in particular ethnicity, race, class and age (cf. Moore 1994, Anthias 2002). For example, we found that in India and Burkina Faso gender positionalities similarly differ according to occupation or income-class, and class is again to some extent related to ethnicity. Gender is also related to age, but differently in the two research contexts, as we will show.

The social security functions or uses of social relationships should not be confused with their causes, as in functionalist approaches. In accordance with practice theory, we take the interests of the individual actors into account and ask why, for whom, to what extent and under what circumstances certain social relationships provide social security (cf. Bourdieu 1977, 1990).

Pursuing such a functional gender approach contributes to a more comprehensive understanding of social security (cf. de Jong 2005). The focus of such investigations is on the more-or-less gendered actions of individual and collective actors and their relationships aimed at the achievement of social security both in the domestic sphere and in the public sphere of civil society and the state, and not mainly on the actions of collective actors in the public sphere as in institutional approaches. It also includes an awareness of the specific modernities of the research contexts as the results of the mostly gendered transformations through global economic and cultural impacts.[7]

---

[7] Cf. e.g. Stivens 1998a, 1998b with regard to modernity and gender in Asia.

Kerala as a Model?
Context of the Case Studies in India

Willemijn de Jong

The Indian case studies deal with poor, mostly unskilled casual workers of the Pulaya caste in Central Kerala. They are compared in some relevant issues with middle class employers belonging to the Nayar caste.[1] We focussed on them because demographically they represent rather large groups of the population of the low- and middle-income classes in Kerala, they were formerly occupationally related in that the Pulayas worked as agrestic slaves for the Nayars, and both groups are well documented in the literature.[2] The elaborations in this chapter are necessarily concise and would need differentiation elsewhere.

Concerning the caste system, people are classified into categories of wealth and status, justified by concepts of "purity" and "pollution".[3] In general, the highest castes were the richest who had the power and were ritually "pure". The lowest castes were poor, powerless and "untouchable". Kerala had the most rigid and elaborate caste system in India. Brahmins, Nayars and Syrian Christians are the most important highest castes of former landlords, whereas the Pulayas are the most numerous lowest caste of former slaves. In between are the Izhavas, Muslims with low-skill occupations and Latin Catholics.[4]

---

[1] We are well aware that castes are not static or homogeneous entities, and that caste and class cannot be equated. For our case studies class criteria are more important than caste criteria. We use the caste names for convenience, but we mean the particular occupational groups of mostly unskilled workers and middle-level employers respectively.

[2] Important publications about the Pulayas are from Iyer 1981 [1909], Alexander 1968, Saradamoni 1980, and den Uyl 1996, 2000. Relevant publications about the Nayars are among others from Iyer 1981 [1912], Gough 1962, Fuller 1976, and Saradamoni 1999.

[3] Although the analytical concept of caste has necessarily been deconstructed (cf. Fuller 1997), it still has importance empirically (e.g. Srinivas 1997, Osella and Osella 2000).

[4] Contrary to public opinion, not only Hindus, but also Muslims and Christians are included in the caste systems in the Indian states (cf. Fuller 1976, Srinivas 1997). The percentages of the castes are estimates because census data do not include caste

The Nayars, comprising about fifteen percent of the population in Kerala, are now often middle and higher employees. Their kinship system is matrilinear, however, their matrilinear inheritance rules have changed. As a dominant caste, the Nayars had a major impact on Kerala's society and culture. The Pulayas, who make up about eight percent of the population, are mainly unskilled day-labourers in agriculture and services. Only part of the younger generation has acquired job skills. It is contested whether this caste is patrilineal or matrilineal. From a governmental perspective, the Pulayas belong to the so-called Scheduled Castes (SC), i.e. they are registered and they benefit from quotas in education and civil service and have other facilities. Although their educational level has increased, this does not correlate to the attainment of higher occupations (Franke 1996).[5]

According to the 1991 census, Kerala has a population of approximately thirty million, 57 percent Hindus, 24 percent Muslims, and 19 percent Christians.[6] Kerala's social indicators are outstanding; more precisely it has higher literacy and life expectancy rates, higher age at marriage, lower birth and infant mortality rates, as well as greater accessibility to drinking water, electricity, roads, schools and health centres than other Indian states and other developing countries (see appendix). As a result of its developmental achievements, Kerala's modernity is often characterised as "rurban", i.e. there are no considerable differences between rural and urban areas.[7] Due to its high quality of life, also in regard to education and the health status of women, and despite low economic growth, Kerala has become "a

---

membership today (Fuller 1976: 37). People with a tribal background, i.e. those belonging to the so-called Scheduled Tribes (ST) who are positively discriminated by the government, are only a small minority in Kerala, viz. 4,940 people according to the census of 1991.

[5] In pre-indepence times they were called *harijans*, but today the Pulaya politically identify themselves with other lower castes that struggle for a better social status as *dalits* (cf. Webster 1999). There are 241,750 people belonging to the Scheduled Castes in Kerala according to the census of 1991.

[6] In all of India Hindus constitute by far the majority with 82 percent, Muslims 12 percent, and Christians 2 percent.

[7] The term "rurban" is used for example by Ramachandran (1997) and Kurien (2000).

model" for development from which "lessons could be learnt". Whether this model is sustainable is now contested (Parayil 2000).

Public action and state policy are mentioned as the main reasons for Kerala's development, in addition to its matrilineal history, a strong Christian influence, as well as its global trade and colonial economy.[8] Franke and Chasin (2000) argue that the latter produced a modern rural proletariat and they suggest: "More sharply than any other part of India, Kerala experienced a rupture of traditional ties of kinship, caste and locality, creating the potential for intensified class consciousness" (ibid. 26).

In 1957, one year after the state of Kerala was established, social movements made up of peasants and workers effected the election of a Communist government. Since then, Communist governments have alternated with those led by the Congress Party. As a result of public pressure, trade unions were formed and the government initiated social reforms. The important Kerala land reform of 1969 contained a ceiling on absolute size of holdings, the abolition of rice land tenancy, and the abolition of tenancy in house compound land, of which the two latter measures have effected a considerable redistribution of land rights. Prior to this, the poor had to pay rent to the landlords for the land where their huts were located, which also affected the Pulayas. The anthropologist Franke (1996) concludes in his detailed village study in Central Kerala on inequality and redistribution that although the Pulayas and the other poorest people continued to lack resources, "Land reform struggles reinforced the leverage of these lowest caste groups and allowed them to move upwards economically" (ibid. 149).

In addition to the land reforms, welfare measures were also enacted. Education was strongly promoted, and this included promoting education for girls. Schools and colleges remain "Kerala's greatest industry" (Jeffrey 1992: 150), for which government and Christian and Hindu organisations competed. Governmental primary education

---

[8] Important references with respect to public action and state policy are Drèze and Sen (1991), Franke (1996), Kurien (2000), and with respect to other factors Jeffrey (1992), Gulati et al. (1996), Ramachandran (1997) and Franke and Chasin (2000).

is free of charge today. With regard to health provisions, nursing was developed, governmental health centres for mother and child opened, and family planning was propagated.

Christian organisations had already founded medical centres, orphanages, and refuge homes in Kerala during the nineteenth century, and they remained active in educational matters. Caste-based Hindu welfare organisations, such as the Kerala Pulaya Maha Sabha (KPMS) and the Nayar Service Society (NSS), followed their example at the beginning of the twentieth century. These civil society organisations developed strong organisational structures and conducted welfare activities according to their means (Jeffrey 1992, Kariyil 1995).

National social security schemes, e.g. contributory provident funds for governmental industrial staff, were implemented in India in the 1950s. Pensions for civil servants were already initiated at the end of the nineteenth century, but today about 90 percent of the work force is employed in the unorganised sector and receive low wages. The National Social Assistance Programme (NSAP), social assistance mainly for elderly people without adult sons, was designed with them in mind (Jain 1999). In the context of the national Public Distribution System (PDS), items of daily need such as wheat, rice, sugar, palm oil and kerosene are provided at a cheaper rate in ration shops for people with a ration card. This implies that they live "below the poverty line" (BPL), equivalent to an annual income of less than Rs 21,000 (about $ 420)[9] in 2001 (cf. Kannan and Francis 2001).

In Kerala, more than thirty social security schemes were created since 1960; the Kerala Destitute and Widow Pension Scheme, as well as the Agricultural Workers Pension Scheme being the most important. Statistics indicate that about 25 percent of the aged population benefit from these schemes (Irudaya Rajan et al. 1999: 200). Franke found that welfare payments had only little effect on social inequality but the payments constituted a large portion of the incomes of many of the poorest households (Franke 1996: 183).

---

[9] In 2002 one US$ was almost Rs 50, viz. Rs 48.

Moreover, in 1972 the government embarked on the "one *lakh*[10] housing scheme", which was the most extensive programme for housing construction for poor people in India. It was meant for those poor people who had not benefited from the land reforms. Although the goal was only partly achieved, housing is now a permanent issue on the governmental agenda (Jeffery 1992, Franke 1996).

Of interest with regard to old age is that Kerala has a high number of old age homes, more than one hundred in all. Most of them are run by Christian organisations and thirteen are run by the state. The majority of people in old age homes are poor Christians and more than 60 percent have no children. Destitute people can live in these homes free of charge (Irudaya Rajan 2000).

Particularly since the recession of the 1990s, the Kerala model has experienced a crisis and has come under severe scrutiny. Profound societal transformations have been gradually occurring since the 1970s: The agricultural sector is declining, rice is imported and the industrial sector is stagnating. The service sector has most potential for growth at present. Employment is largely informal. In 1987-88 only 17 percent of workers were regularly employed, nearly 40 percent were self-employed and 43 percent were casual workers (Prakash 1999: 35). The already high unemployment rate is increasing and is especially high in the urban centres due to the higher population density. Therefore, urban poverty is also much higher than rural poverty in Kerala (Retnaraj 1999: 158). With regard to gender, unemployment is much higher for females than for males, particularly in urban Kerala (Gulati et al. 1996: 32). Moreover, many migrants from the Gulf countries have returned. Prior to this, migration contributed much to the alleviation of poverty (Zachariah et al. 2002). Due to a lack of financial means and pressures from structural adjustment programmes, social welfare programmes and spending on education and health are threatened. Nevertheless, there are voices, which remain optimistic. They hope for stronger economic growth induced by the new decentralisation policy, without losing the welfare gains and the democratic

---

[10] Measure of quantity, 1 *lakh* = 100,000.

achievements attained. These same voices, however, express anxieties about Kerala's internal power relations and its dependence on national and global developments.[11]

---

[11] Among the optimists are Franke and Chasin (2000) and Véron (2000) for example, whereas Thomas Isaac (2000) shows in cooperation with Franke the achievements of the decentralisation policy.

On the Verge of Insecurity:
The Poor Elderly in Urban Kerala

Willemijn de Jong

"The elderly can be happy, if they adjust well with society and their family and if they maintain harmony. It is like threading beads. You need a lot of patience. And once you have done it, you must hold it together, otherwise the string will break." (Kanan, an elderly worker, 2001)

In Kerala, in contrast to other Indian states and in contrast to Burkina Faso, due to social reform movements a whole variety of social security measures and schemes were developed by the government as well as by civil society organisations during the twentieth century, as pointed out in the preceding chapter. These public provisions also aimed at the elderly. The questions to be addressed in this case study are: To what extent can poor people in urban Kerala mobilise support with regard to old age not only from their families, but also from the state and other public agencies? And to what extent is old age security gendered? Based on literature in the field of development and social policy in Kerala, it can be assumed that the poor urban elderly not only mobilize kin-based support, especially from a son, but also public support (e.g. Irudaya Rajan 1999). Further, it can be assumed from the literature on gender that social security is especially problematic for elderly widows (e.g. Gulati et al. 1996, Gulati 1998).

The aim of this chapter is to show that due to economic and social reasons the social security arrangement of the poor working class elderly in urban Kerala is much more complex than national and local imagery on support in old age suggest. Thereby, it will be revealed that because of the limits of both public and family support these working class elderly live on the verge of social insecurity in that most of them experience a fragile security, and the poorest widows and other women without near kin experience critical insecurity.

Research on old-age security of poor populations is still scant in India (cf. Cohen 1998). The focus here is on poor Hindus, who in relevant aspects are compared with Muslims of the low-income class and with middle-class Hindus of the Nayar caste. We also include Muslims in this case study because they represent a large part of the population in the research area.[1]

The Field Site

Fieldwork for this case study was conducted in the industrial suburb of Kochi, called Kalamassery.[2] With about one million inhabitants, Kochi is the largest and most important commercial city of Kerala. The municipality of Kalamassery has grown enormously since the 1960s in terms of inhabitants and industries. In 1961 it counted about 17,000 people.[3] According to the 2001 census, the population increased to 63,106, of these 31,196 females and 31,910 males. There were 14,023 households, 812 (about six percent) of which belong to the scheduled castes (SC). Together with other poor people they live in thirteen so-called "colonies". The main problems in Kalamassery are the settlement of landless people, the educational backwardness of a large part of it inhabitants and a lack of employment opportunities.[4]

The main industrial enterprises produce steel, chemicals, rubber and electronics. In 1981 there were sixty industrial units employing altogether more than 7,000 workers. Air and water pollution have also become a problem (Kuruvilla 1989). However, since the 1990s the development of the manufacturing industries has been stagnating

---

[1] A survey in the slum settlements of the research area reports 54.35 percent Hindus, 29.38 percent Muslims and 15.92 percent Christians (Rajagiri 1996: 3).

[2] About 100 qualitative individual interviews were carried out in Thiruvananthapuram in 2000 and in Kochi in 2001 and 2002 (cf. de Jong 2003). Furthermore, a quota survey with 120 quantitative questionnaires (40 working class Hindus, 40 working class Muslims, 40 middle class Hindus) was carried out in Kochi in 2002. Additional data were obtained by participant observation, some focus group interviews, and numerous informal talks. The results presented here are analysed with regard to the whole body of ethnographic data. For my fieldwork in Kochi I received invaluable help from Rajagiri College of Social Science and its related community development organisations CASP and RCDS, as well as from two research assistants who also translated as I did not master the language in this case.

[3] Source: Municipality of Kalamassery on August 16, 2001.

[4] Source: Kalamassery at a Glance: 10th Five Year Plan 2002-2007. Decentralisation Plan Report. Kalamassery Municipality.

(Mathew 1999). In fact, during the last years several factories have halted production.

As already mentioned in the previous chapter, the people focussed on in this case study belong to the Pulaya caste.[5] They live in a settlement called a "slum pocket" (Rajagiri 1996) with one hundred and twenty Pulaya households. The other eighty households mainly belong to the "communities" of Izhavas, Muslims and Latin Catholics. Most of the Pulayas were squatters who settled in Kalamassery in the 1960s. But by and by many of them were able to have their small house plot officially registered.

The Pulaya males and females in the settlement are mostly un-skilled day-labourers, formerly working in the domain of agriculture, today mainly in the domain of construction and cleaning services such as grass cutting and domestic work. Only a minority, mostly of the younger generation, are permanently employed in the factories and are skilled workers. Most of the elderly Pulaya informants were illiterate or had gone to school for only a few years. The elderly women were all illiterate. The younger generation, however, had completed six to ten years of schooling. I assume that the situation of the Pulayas can be considered as representative for people of other low-income classes in urban India who are also unskilled labourers without permanent income.

The Fragile Security of the Poor Elderly

Public Support: Housing and Health Care

Starting from the fact that the literature concerning Kerala's develop-ment emphasises the important role of public welfare, we first will ask to what extent the Pulayas make use of public support from the state and from voluntary organisations with regard to social security in old age. Many Pulayas associate the state in the first instance with Kerala, and not with India, and they connect it in particular with governmental

---

[5] In fact, this group calls itself "Pulayar" to distinguish themselves from the "Pu-layan".

provisions such as ration cards, pensions and house loans. Moreover, they are well aware of the fact that they have special benefits as members of a scheduled caste.

Elderly people benefit to some extent from the ration shops which are part of the national Public Distribution System (PDS). They buy products such as kerosene, and some also buy rice, which was Rs 10 (about $ 0.20)[6] instead of the normal price of Rs 12 (about $ 0.25) in 2002. But some consider the rice quality inferior and do not buy it there. Studies confirm that there is little demand for wheat and inferior rice varieties, including among the poor (e.g. Mohandas 1999).[7]

Receiving social assistance, so-called "pensions", is dependent on having no adult sons and a very low household income. Furthermore, receiving such assistance is linked with high administrative hurdles and having the right connections with the authorities.[8] The data contained in the quota survey showed that approximately 25 percent of households had access to the Kerala Destitute and Widow Pension Scheme and the Kerala Agricultural Workers Pension Scheme.[9] But these amounts were said to be small, Rs 100 per month and Rs 125 per month (about $ 2 to 2.5) respectively, and they were paid irregularly. On average, these pensions amount to one day's wage of Rs 150 (about $ 3) (cf. Irudaya Rajan 2001: 615). This is equivalent to ten to fifteen kilogrammes of rice. The old widow Vallothi (example 4), however, commented her pension with: "That is not even enough to buy coconut oil for my hair."

The government housing policy seems to have been most beneficial to the Pulayas. Many of them possess a piece of land of three to ten cents.[10] Several elderly male household heads obtained their land from the government related to the land reforms in the 1960s. Men of the

---

[6] In 2002 one US$ was the equivalent of almost Rs 50, viz. Rs 48.

[7] Like other authors Mohandas (1999: 90) shows that PDS is important for the poor in Kerala, but he also cautions: "There is virtually no demand for coarse cereals and even inferior varieties of rice in Kerala. If these are distributed it would further reduce cereal consumption in the state, which is the second lowest at present (...)."

[8] This is also stated by I.S. Gulati and L. Gulati (1998).

[9] Widow pensions n = 11 and agricultural pensions n = 6, of a total quota survey sample of 40 Pulaya households.

[10] 1 cent equals 40.5 square meters.

younger generation often received three cents of land from their fathers in order to build next to the family home. Not all have official
land titles. Some have not yet managed to have their land registered
and are still squatters. Moreover, many of the Pulayas have received
"loans" for their houses from the government (up to Rs 35,000, i.e.
about $ 700), which they were not obliged to pay back, or only a por-
tion had to be repaid.

The housing policy in Kerala also includes old age homes, as mentioned in the preceding chapter. The criteria for access to governmental old age homes are age above fifty-five, good general health and
lacking financial support from children. If an elderly person becomes
bedridden, she or he is transferred to a Christian geriatric centre. The
main aim is to provide a home for elderly people who have no children or have been abandoned by them. The Pulayas would only resort
to such facilities if they have no children, and thus no care. However,
no one had had this kind of experience.

For health care, the Pulayas can consult a local organisation called
Rajagiri Community Development Scheme (RCDS).[11] The tradition of
Christian welfare in Kalamassery goes back several decades and much
longer in Kerala (Kariyil 1995). According to this programme, a
medical doctor and a nurse visit the settlement weekly and the people
themselves can also go to the organisation's office for medical check-
ups. Most people spend Rs 25 to Rs 100 (about $ 0.50 to 2) per month
for medicines. For the elderly, consultations and medicines are free.
The Pulayas make extensive use of these services.

Moreover, the Pulayas can mobilise several kinds of support from
the local caste organisation, called Kerala Pulayar Maha Sabha
(KPMS). In the settlement there is a small KPMS building with a
board. This local branch was founded in the 1960s and builds on the
tradition of welfare activities of its umbrella organisation in Kerala

---

[11] Both RCDS and CASP, which among others offer educational support for poor
children, are related to Rajagiri College of Social Sciences. This institution was
founded in 1955 by the Carmelites of Mary Immaculate (CMI), an indigenous
Christian society. In 1967 the college moved to Kalamassery. It is now part of a
bigger complex of the prestigious Rajagiri educational institutions and related social
service organisations.

present since the beginning of the twentieth century, as with other caste organisations (Jeffrey 1992). In this eastern district of Kochi (Kannayannur Taluk) there are thirty-five branches, which demonstrates how well organised the Pulayas are. The KPMS in the settlement helps with housing, hospitalisation, marriage, death and family conflicts. It also requires a membership fee of Rs 2 per month from each household. Many important governmental affairs are in fact administrated by the caste organisation such as the registration of births, marriages, deaths, as well as applications for housing subsidies and for hospitalisation. It also carries out the ceremonies and formalities for cremation. If someone in the community dies, a fee is collected from every Pulaya household to cover the expenses. Additionally, the organisation provides entertainment through yearly feasts and it conducts pilgrimages, for which fees are also collected. The Pulayas believe that such an organisation cannot replace family, but they consider its activities helpful. With respect to old age, its assistance with subsidies for housing and hospitalisation are most important.

We can summarise that although there are many public support schemes in Kerala, its impact on the poor elderly in the settlement is less visible than expected. As citizens, the Pulayas are most strongly involved in the different activities of the local caste organisation, which is well integrated in the settlement and in Kerala society. This Hindu welfare organisation is most important as a mediator between the Pulayas and the state, especially with regard to housing and hospitalisation. In the field of health care, the Christian welfare organisation plays an important supplementary role. However, these religion-based welfare organisations leave the poor population in insecurity with regard to long-term daily needs for food, money and care. A problematic issue is also that strong caste-based collectivities reinforce communal cleavages. This contradicts the democratic and secular principles of the Indian state.

National Imagery of Support: "The Family" and "the Son"

In addition to the emphasis on public support in the development literature about Kerala, in the social science literature and official documents about Kerala and India we find a strong emphasis on support by the family.[12] As the issue of family support and its limits is the main focus of our study, it is useful to have a closer look at the imagery behind this national discourse. Thereby we will restrict ourselves to some examples.

Urged by United Nations resolutions and by other forums on ageing issues, in 1999 the Indian Ministry of Social Justice and Empowerment published a document on the "National Policy on Older Persons". The document presumes that "family ties in India are very strong and an overwhelming majority live with their sons or are supported by them" (Government of India 1999: 3). The right of parents to be supported by children is also legally established. Since families in the cities increasingly seem unable to care both for children and elderly parents, a number of "action strategies" for the support of the elderly by governmental and non-governmental organisations were proposed in the fields of financial security, health care and nutrition, shelter, education, welfare, as well as protection of life and property. By promoting a sharing of responsibilities for elderly parents between sons and daughters, the state also intends to degender caring norms, although eligibility for social assistance is further dependent on having no adult son. The general tenor of the paper is that "Family is the most cherished social institution in India and the most vital non-formal social security for the old. Most older people live with one or more of their children, particularly when independent living is no longer feasible. For them it is the most preferred living arrangement and also the most emotionally satisfying. It is important that the familial support system continues to be func-

---

[12] Cf. e.g. Chowdhury 1992, Gokhale et al. 1999, Rajagiri 1999, Shah 1998, 1999 with regard to academic discourse, and Government of India 1998, 1999 with regard to national discourse on old age support and the family.

tional and the ability of the family to discharge its caring responsibilities is strengthened through support services" (ibid. 19).

A similar line of argument can be discovered in many Indian
studies on old age. Often, a past Golden Age of support of the elderly
in joint families is explicitly or implicitly presented without temporal
and spatial specificities. At the same time, many scholars complain
that today's nuclear families are no longer able to care adequately for
the elderly and that therefore the status of the latter decreases (e.g.
Irudaya Rajan et al. 1999). Lawrence Cohen (1998: 103) has poig-
nantly called this discourse the "narrative of the Fall into the Bad
Family", and he critically comments that the diversity of families both
in the past and in the present has thus faded out.

One of the outstanding critics of the family concept in India is the
Indian sociologist A.M. Shah. Since the middle of the 1960s he has
been advocating a differentiated and contextualised analysis of kinship
and family categories. He shows for example that the joint family has
been conceptualised very differently in social science research in India. If you look at it as a household or a co-residing unit, as he proposes, it was a widespread ancient Sanskritic ideal indeed, but practised mainly by the high castes and classes. The average household
was of the nuclear family type (Shah 1989). With regard to old age
research, Shah cautions against the popular discourse of the disintegration of the joint family and against glorifying the past. This type of
household was never free from tensions and conflicts. He shows that
today more elderly people reside in joint family households than fifty
years ago. But it does not mean, he adds, that all elderly people are
well cared for. Nevertheless, in the end he also advocates the vision of
old age security by the family, i.e. the joint family household, which
should be adjusted to modern requirements (Shah 1999).

As already pointed out in the introduction of this book, Indian
scholars in the field of new kinship studies still take another stance in
that they include the issue of gender.[13] They stress that the naturalised
links between tradition, family and women have to a large extent been

[13] Cf. e.g. Palriwala 1994, Dube 1997, 1998 and Ganesh 1998, as wel as Agarwal
1991 who also deals with the issue of family relationships and insecurity.

created by state intervention in the sphere of personal law reform, particularly since Indian independence.[14] In addition, they conceptualise the family explicitly as a changing, ambivalent and gendered social entity. A similar perspective is applied in this study in that shifting conditions of support-giving and support-receiving in kin-based relationships are considered.

We can summarise that ideas about support for the elderly in India are constructed in a globalised context in which international organisations are important actors.[15] The dominant discourse on support in old age by the nation-state and by academics emphasise strongly, if not solely, "the family" and often consider it as a natural and ahistorical, i.e. fixed category, without specifying its many varieties according to class, caste and locality. Instead of addressing support of "the family", it makes more sense to ask which kin relationships, differentiated according to gender and generation, are meaningful and useful to old age security for certain social groups at a certain time and place, and why this is so.

Support by Kin: Daily Needs for Food, Money and Care

Among the Pulayas, "family" means in the first place "all living harmoniously in one house" and cooperating together. This household-based notion of family consists of parents and their unmarried children, i.e. a nuclear family household. With regard to elderly parents it is a household with one married son, his wife and children, i.e. a "joint family household" (cf. Dube 1997, Shah 1998) or an extended family household, as I will also call it.[16] The first people from whom an eld-

---

[14] Cf. e.g. also Collier, Rosaldo and Yanagisako 1982 and Bourdieu 1996 with regard to the creation of the family by the state.
[15] Part of the debate on old age and the family by the United Nation is for example published in the proceedings "Ageing and the Family" (1994). Cf. Stivens 1998b for a more recent account of global impacts on the construction of the "Asian family".
[16] In anthropology, "joint family" mostly designates a family built on connections between brothers or sisters, whereas an "extended family" is built on parent-child connections. A household is a co-residing unit of consumption, and in certain contexts also of production (cf. Keesing and Strathern 1998). As the relevant Indian literature uses the term joint family also for a three-generation unit built on parent-

erly person expects daily financial and physical support in old age are the co-residing family members.

The role of the father is "to guide the family in the right way". The mother should "care for the family". Childcare is exclusively the responsibility of women, moreso than among the Muslims and Nayars according to the quota survey. If males are unskilled workers, females are also expected to contribute to the household income. If they are skilled workers with a permanent job, the female will generally take on the role of housewife. Males are supposed to manage financial matters outside the family, females inside.

Providing children the best possible care and investing in their education and marriage is considered a basic rule for old age security. Fosterage of children other than one's own biological children is not appreciated. Children should not marry too late; for sons marriage should take place before the end of their twenties so that they will be settled and able to support the parents by the time they reach old age. Characteristically, an elderly man said: "My real savings are my children." In conformity with national imagery, the dominant local idea with regard to old age security is that "the son", who in a metonymic manner often is "the family" or "the children", provides support for his elderly parents. Preferentially, the youngest son should provide financial care, whereas his wife should deal with physical needs. As a counterprestation, the son providing support is entitled to inherit the house. Further financial and physical help is expected from a daughter "in case of need" and "according to her capability", although she will "go away" to live in her husband's place of residence after marriage.

According to women's views, support from children is uncertain in the end. An elderly wife said for example that children care more for the parents as long as the father is alive. She associated this with the authority and respect he enjoys in the family. This would imply that widows are more insecure, which is confirmed in a statement by an elderly widow that "God is the only being who cares for you. If He

---

child connections, I will use the terms joint family and extended family synonymously here. In national and local contexts in India the term "family" often means "household" in anthropological terms.

thinks that you should be cared for, then your children will care for you."

Interestingly, the imagery of the actual security by children is often contrasted with a past Golden Age of affluence in which landlords provided material security and children social security through care and respect. In this context, "landlords" and "children" are often mentioned as complementary providers, as are "the son" and "the daughter-in-law" today. It was noted that "Earlier, the landlord provided food and took care when you were old. Your children and your relatives also would care for you." As far as the parents were concerned, this was backed by the belief that they were God-like and could put dangerous curses upon their descendants. One elderly woman even said: "Earlier, hunger did not exist, the people slept on a bed of rice. We were dedicated to our parents, and we believed that they were God in a human form. So we respected and loved them, and we listened to their advice and followed them." These statements indicate that the norm of financial responsibility for the parents by "the son" has only emerged since the 1960s among this group.

To what extent can children really be considered "savings" today? The youngest son is often assigned the role of main material support-giver for his parents. Additionally, other sons and daughters help financially and physically, as well as the spouses about whom will be talked in more detail further on. This is also substantiated by the quota survey.[17] Today the number of children in most of the Pulaya families is not very high: two or maybe three,[18] but among people over seventy the number of children is higher. This low number of children reinforces the insecurity of the poor elderly, if access to jobs is difficult.

The limited financial support of parents by only one son is evident if we look at the household income of the middle generation. Accord-

---

[17] The most important related person providing financial help for the mother is the son (n = 23 of 40), then the husband (n = 13). The second important person is again the son (n = 14), then the daughter (n = 10), then the brother (n = 9), and further the husband (n = 3) and the daughter's husband (n = 3).

[18] The anthropologist den Uyl (1996: 180) who worked in a village in Kerala with many Pulayas, found that many couples practiced sterilisation due to government campaigns.

ing to the quota survey a man may earn between Rs 2,000 and Rs 3,000 (about $ 40 to 60), and a woman between Rs 500 and Rs 2,000 (about $ 10 to 40) per month. The figures in the qualitative interviews on average monthly wages for unskilled, mostly irregular work are still lower: Rs 1,500 for a male and Rs 1,000 for a female (about $ 30 and 20 respectively).[19] In more than half of the cases of the survey two people, most often a husband and wife, contribute to the household income. Almost twenty percent of the interviewees live in households with a yearly income below the poverty level of Rs 21,000 (about $ 420). They will also be the ones who say they consume only two meals per day, and thus hardly able to support parents sufficiently. Seventy percent of the interviewees live in households with a very moderate yearly income. The income of these households would suffice to care financially for elderly parents, but only if the "middle generation squeeze" (cf. United Nations 1994) is not too strong, i.e. that there are no additional expenses for the elderly (e.g. hospitalisation), for the children (e.g. education, marriage), and for the middle generation themselves (e.g. house, hospitalisation). In the ten percent of the households which have a somewhat higher income, there most probably is an earner with permanent work.[20] These households are most able to support parents financially. Moreover, a little more than twenty percent of the households have some savings, mostly at the bank and a few through insurances, but almost seventy-five percent of the households have debts.

An earlier study of the "slum settlements" in Kalamassery complements the picture of the population's socio-economic conditions

---

[19] In 2001 and 2002 day-labourers earned Rs 175 to Rs 200 as a male, and Rs 100 to Rs 125 as a female. To be able to spend one US $ a day a household had to have a monthly income of at least Rs 1,500. In the quota survey we distinguished three categories of household income per year: less than Rs 24,000, between Rs 24,000 and Rs 60,000 and above Rs 60,000.
[20] Although Pulayas aspire to be permanently employed, because of the labour market conditions this is possible only for a small minority of them. As mentioned in the preceding chapter, 43 percent of the total workers in Kerala were casual workers and only 17 percent were regularly employed (Prakash 1999: 35). Payment of daily wages is not taxed, so that employers have few incentives to engage permanent workers.

(Rajagiri 1996), which is extenuated slightly by the quota survey. Of the target population of 6,728 people (or 1426 "families"), 38 percent were dependents (below 18 and above 65 years of age), 28 percent were unemployed, 19 percent performed unskilled labour and only 10 percent did skilled labour. Furthermore, one percent was active in agriculture, two percent did petty business, and three percent were lower level employees. Of those individuals who earned an income, only 13 percent earned an annual income above Rs 25,000 (about $ 500), most likely including the skilled workers and the lower employees. The unskilled earners and the others will have earned about Rs 2,000 (about $ 40) or less per month. This corresponds with our findings in the qualitative interviews. If a husband and a wife both earn as unskilled, irregular workers, they will have a yearly household income of between Rs 30,000 and Rs 40,000 (about $ 600 and 800). Pulaya males who were permanently employed earned twice as much, similar to the Muslim males of the low-income class. The middle class male Nayar employees with higher educations earned on average eight times as much.

Although the unskilled work the Pulayas do is not strongly gendered, and the productivity of women is not very different from that of males, women earn only about two-thirds of men's wages. In the households of the middle generation, in almost half of the cases the wife contributes to the household income, which seems less than among the older generation. On the other hand, it is more than among the Nayars and much more than among the Muslims.

Care in the narrower sense of physical support for the elderly is mainly provided by "the daughter-in-law", but if needed sons, daughters, and the husband also help.[21] The relationship between the mother-in-law and the daughter-in-law is structurally tense in India because of their potentially conflicting interests in the son's resources. It is assumed that the strains in this relationship are increasing because conjugality has gained in importance (Palriwala 1994, Dube 1998).

---

[21] The first person who gives physical support to the mother is the daughter-in-law (n = 31 of 40) or the husband (n = 6), and the second person is a son (n = 20 of 40) or a daughter (n = 8).

Physical care depends on proximity, and thus on the living arrangements. According to the quota survey, one-third were joint family households in which children and elderly parents were cared for, and two-thirds were nuclear family households without elderly parents. Some of the elderly covered by the qualitative interviews, however, lived in nuclear family households or the remainder of these families, when the youngest son was still unmarried. In these cases there was no immediate help by a daughter-in-law with regard to housework, but the elderly female did this work herself with the help of a daughter, or else the son. For instance, the unmarried son of the widow Kali (example 3) cooked food and cleaned, if his mother did not feel well. In all these cases, married sons and daughters-in-law were also living nearby. Only one elderly woman lived in a single household, as she had been deserted by her husband and had no children. The elderly Muslim lived almost without exception with one or two married sons, whereas the elderly Nayars mostly lived only with a son or daughter when one parent was ill or had died. With respect to care, it is an advantage for the elderly Pulayas that their children seldom migrate, probably because the expenses are too high. This strongly contrasts with children of wealthier sections of the population in Kerala (cf. Zachariah et al. 2002). The following example illustrates the intergenerational support relationships.

Example 1: Kunjappan, his Wife and his Mother-in-law –
Support from Children
Kunjappan (62), born in 1940, is already "old" in the local sense. He is a grandfather, but he is still able to earn money. For the past forty-five years he has been performing all kinds of manual work in a nearby Catholic convent led by sisters. With his unskilled, but in this case permanent job, he earns Rs 100 (about $ 2) per day. He lives slightly above the poverty line, but not very comfortably, he says. His income is used for daily household expenses and for the care of his wife's mother. He has no savings for extra daily needs or for old age, but he also has no debts. The convent sisters helped him to pay school fees. He also borrowed money from them to build his tiled house, and they assisted him in saving money for his part of his daughter's dowry. He thinks that the people in his "community" do respect him, but that getting respect from higher castes is difficult.

He grew up and went to school for two years in nearby Eloor where he learned to read, but not to write. At that time school classes were still separated according to caste. Before he married in 1966, at the age of 26, he worked as an agricultural labourer for seven years. His father fell seriously ill with TB in the mid 1960s. Kunjappan took care of him in the hospital and at home, and also bought medicine for him. After the death of his father, his mother was taken care of by his elder brother, and the brother inherited the paternal house after her death. Due to disagreements with his brother, Kunjappan left the paternal house, renounced his share of the inheritance and moved to Kalamassery. There he occupied four cents of wasteland owned by the government and built a small thatched house.

His children, a daughter (36) and a son (26), attended school for ten years. Both are married and, exceptionally, have permanent jobs. The daughter has just married and is living, as is the norm, in her husband's nearby place of residence. His son, a skilled worker in a factory, is living with his Christian wife and their two-year-old son together with Kunjappan in a joint family household. The son provides for additional household expenses. The daughter-in-law does the housework. Contrary to his wife, Kunjappan has already adjusted to his daughter-in-law: "She cares for me like my daughter."

Kunjappan's wife is temporarily living with her mother in her native place because the mother has been bedridden for two years due to a "brain illness" and her mother's daughters-in-law are neglecting her. Now Kunjappan's wife is paying back the help her mother gave her earlier when the children were small and she had to earn money.

As far as the future is concerned, Kunjappan is convinced: "I cared very well for my children in their childhood and youth, sent them to school, gave them love, food and everything. So I think that my children will continue to take care of me. And in case of need, the daughter will also come and give care, financially and emotionally." In return for their old age support he has decided that the son will inherit the house and the land, but the equivalent in money of half of the land (two cents) he has to give to his sister. This will only happen after the death of both parents, Kunjappan asserts, and thus he will retain some bargaining power in the relationship with his children.

Kunjappan's old age is rather well secured because of his participation in former and actual exchange relationships, in the sense of generalised reciprocity, with his son. He cannot live in security without his son's financial support for non-daily expenses, such as a dowry, and the physical support of his daughter-like daughter-in-law. For additional help, financial and physical, he can also rely on the long-term exchange with his daughter. Therefore, the daughter is also endowed with a part of the inheritance.

Relationships between the mothers-in-law and daughters-in-law are strained in this kin network. Kunjappan's mother-in-law cannot rely on the physical help of her daughters-in-law, as the official rule would require. Kunjappan's wife provides intensive physical care in her role as daughter, which is legitimated with the help her mother gave her with childcare, i.e. also generalised reciprocity. If elderly people, especially elderly females, become disabled or bedridden, physical support from a daughter-in-law is not always guaranteed (cf. also Shah 1999). This may also negatively influence the relationship between the son and the mother, or vice versa, e.g. it is unclear whether the son of Kunjappan's mother-in-law still provided financially for her; at least Kunjappan as a son-in-law did. Theoretically, elderly people can call in the support from children through the mediation of the local caste organisation, and backed by national law.

Kunjappan's wife is financially secure due to her husband, son and daughter. To what extent she will later receive physical care from her daughter-in-law is uncertain. It depends on how they negotiate their exchanges in this delicate relationship.

It can be assumed that Kunjappan will further live in security, provided that the economic situation of his son and daughter does not decrease and that he is able "to maintain harmony" in his family and beyond (cf. initial quotation). As far as his wife is concerned, this is less certain.

In contrast to support from "children", intragenerational support in old age is subordinate in national and in local imagery. However, marriage is generally associated with security among the Pulayas. This corresponds with the importance of the conjugal bond in India, and in Kerala today (cf. Palriwala 1994, Busby 2000). Men stressed "lifelong companionship", which implies mutual help and love; some also called it a sacred relationship. Nevertheless, sometimes husbands may leave their wives because of "insincere hearts" as the deserted woman said. Women consider marriage as important both with regard to financial security and companionship. Wives protect their husbands. An elderly woman remarked that a wife has to be strong. Her husband was not mentally well anymore, but she should never show that in public in order not to damage his reputation. Widowhood is thus connected with increasing insecurity. One of the elderly widows said: "As long as your husband is alive, you have no worries because of his additional income and his companionship." Another elderly widow resented the death of her husband, although he used to drink and beat her. But he was a support, she said, in that he always gave half of his earnings to her for household expenses. And a third one remarked with bitterness: "Married life is forgotten, marriage has no meaning for me in old age."

Spouses benefit reciprocally from their income, if he or she is still working in old age. But females benefit more from the earnings of males than vice versa because men earn more. Elderly females also benefit from the relationships which the spouse has built up during his life-course. Elderly males particularly benefit from the children, especially sons, their wife had borne and brought up, and the physical support she is able to give because she is younger and will probably live longer. It can be suggested that the conjugal relationship is important for old age security as well, but in the end, women can rely less on marriage for social security than men because they often survive their husbands and are then dependent on their children.

No regular support in old age is expected from "relatives", i.e. married siblings and affines, or in-laws, because "They also are all poor". But they should participate in life-cycle ceremonies and visit in case of illness. In these ceremonial contexts relatives can also be called "family", but then the term is used in a wider sense. As a last resort, brothers do help financially and physically, which the quota survey also confirmed with regard to financial aid from a woman's brother (cf. footnote 17). This also applies to sisters' husbands, especially if they are not married yet and if they are living nearby. This kind of help was mostly directly reciprocated within a certain time span.

In summary, the economic conditions of the children who have to provide financial care for the elderly are in large part insufficient. In the majority of households it would be very difficult for a son to be

the only provider for his elderly parents, even when his wife also contributed to the household income. Thus, the elderly necessarily have to
mobilise relationships with other sons and daughters, and sometimes
other kin, to be able to survive. The living arrangements generally
enable good conditions for physical support for elderly parents, and
also the fact that in the middle generation women are more often
housewives than among the older generation. Financial support giving
by children is not as strongly gendered as existing ideas make us believe. However, receiving support in old age has a gendered character,
which means that the security of women, especially as widows, is
more in jeopardy than that of men. This may relate to the generally
ambivalent relationships with the daughter-in-law, and consequently
with the son.

*Support by Neighbours and Employers: Non-daily Needs
for Food and Money*

Unexpectedly, and not represented by national or local images, neighbours are also important providers of material and physical support for
many Pulayas. They complement the support of kin. To some extent
they resemble kin relationships, and sometimes neighbours are considered as "relatives". In times of need, female neighbours contribute
to daily needs for food and small amounts of money, whereas male
neighbours contribute to non-daily needs for larger amounts of money.
Moreover, employers, often called "patrons", provide non-daily material support such as food and sometimes clothes at the annual feasts,
money or gold jewellery for dowries and financial contributions for
houses. It is also believed that former landlords – who are attributed
ideal kin-like traits of a father or a son – were better support-givers
than the employers today. Males in particular consider neighbours,
friends and employers as important support givers in old age. The

survey data, and the following example as well, confirm the importance of support by neighbours and employers for the Pulayas.[22]

Example 2: Kumaran – Support from the Wider Neighbourhood

Kumaran (75) was born in 1927. He had two children, a son and a daughter, but the
son died twelve years ago at the age of thirty-three and left a wife, a daughter and a
son behind. Kumaran is living in a joint family household with his wife, his daughter-in-law and his grandson. He was an agricultural labourer and gets an "agricultural workers pension" of Rs 125 (about $ 2.5) per month, the amount of which is
transferred to him every half a year. His wife and his daughter-in-law are both domestic workers and earn up to Rs 1,000 (about $ 20) per month each. The grandson
who is twenty-one gets training and is working as a mechanic in an auto workshop
and earns Rs 750 (about $ 15) per month.

The death of his son due to heart problems caused a crisis in Kumaran's life. His
wife, daughter-in-law and near kin helped him. Moreover, the neighbours supported
him. "These people are trustworthy." Kumaran thinks that there are some differences between women and men in handling crises: "Women easily handle problems
inside the house because they are more attached to the children. But men should get
support from their wives. Then they can contribute to problem solving. Men are
more familiar with people outside the house."

One year later Kumaran also became seriously ill and had heart surgery. The expenses were Rs 5,000 (about $ 100), but because he had no money, he went to a
government hospital where a relative of his was a doctor. As such, all the facilities
and medicines were free. Moreover, he received free medicines from the local
Christian welfare organisation (RCDS).

On the role of unrelated local people Kumaran remarks: "If relatives do not live
nearby, then the neighbours give support. The neighbours can also help at ceremonies or in case of illness. If there is poverty, the neighbours give food and money.
Patrons give mainly financial support." He goes on to specify: "On my children I
can rely any time. On my relatives and neighbours I can rely in times of need."

Kumaran has a dense social network indeed. He has been living in Kalamassery
more than fifty years. For eleven years (1989 until 2000), he was a guard in the
house of a man who was working abroad and who had left his wife and children in
Kerala. That employer gave him money and clothes and visited him when he was ill.

In his spare time he used to socialise with neighbours, and he continues to do so.
"The neighbours next door are like relatives." In addition, he was also a fervent

---

[22] Neighbours are mentioned first among the unrelated persons who give support to a
mother (n = 35 of 40), next to employers (n = 4 as the most important unrelated
person, and n = 17 as the second important unrelated person).

member of the Communist Party. He particularly admired the agrarian policies of
the Communist government in the 1960s.

Kumaran's example shows that the support of children is delicate: his
only son died. The grandson substitutes for the son, but so far more in
a moral than in a material way. Due to his illness, Kumaran himself
can no longer contribute to his old age security with an income, but he
can rely on the financial support of his wife. Additionally, the neighbours help, as he emphasises: "If there is poverty, the neighbours give
food and money." Kumaran has a dense and widespread network of
relationships with "relative"-like neighbours. It also comprises relationships with political aims, which is more a concern of males. For
widows, the support of neighbours is important for sheer livelihood, as
the following example shows.

Example 3: Kali – Support from the Surrounding Neighbourhood

Kali (75) was born in 1926 and has nine children, four sons and five daughters. She
married when she was sixteen years old and she did construction work and cut grass
for her livelihood until two years ago. Her husband died fifteen years ago. Kali is
living in a tiled house with her second-to-last son. He is thirty-six-years old and the
only son who is not yet married.

The son earns about Rs 1,500 (about $ 30) per month with unskilled irregular
work. He takes care of his mother by giving her money and also helping her with
cooking and cleaning when she is not feeling well. First, he spends his money for his
own needs, and then he gives an amount to his mother, sometimes Rs 50, sometimes
Rs 100 (about $ 1 to 2). One of her daughters and that daughter's children also sup-
port Kali with money and cloth. The employer of that daughter also supported Kali
with the dowry, plus the savings for jewellery by the daughter herself. Kali's sister
also used to help with money before she died.

Kali has not been able to save anything for her old age. She does not have any
assets. The house is still in her husband's name. She has always earned just enough
to meet her daily needs. Nevertheless, she thinks that an elderly person should be as
independent as possible. She hopes that she does not become so old that she can no
longer do housework. Otherwise, she expects that the son who is living with her and
her daughters will help her. She hopes that her son will soon marry "a good girl" so
that she also has a daughter-in-law to care for her. As an improvement in the situation of the elderly she proposes that they get medicine and money: "It is important to
have money to be considered as a respectful old person."

In case of need, she can ask several neighbours for money or food: "My neighbours in front and behind help me with food if I am hungry or with money if I don't have any. We also give food, if they do not have enough."

Kali is supported financially and physically by the only son who is still unmarried, and thus has no other obligations yet, and financially by a daughter. The other seven children are not able or not willing to help. Kali is very much in need of the additional support of her neighbours, especially for food. In contrast to Kumaran's, Kali's neighbourhood network is more concentrated on exchange relationships for her basic daily needs. It has to be considered, however, that neighbourhood support is only given on terms of balanced reciprocity, as in relationships with "relatives".[23] This means that the goods and services have to be paid back within a reasonable span of time. Thus, only people with a minimum of economic resources can participate in this kind of relationship. Kali can participate because on those days that the son is working she will have at least a small amount of money, and thus food which she can share with others. Both examples also show the importance of support by employers.

Personal Contributions of the Elderly: Money, Care and Housing

Lastly, the elderly themselves contribute to their old age security. This fact is, however, not symbolised in the national and local imagery. What do the elderly think about old age and how do they contribute? Being old is associated for both men and women with a change in economic and social roles. Most important is the lost capacity to earn an income rather than the chronological retirement age of fifty-five common among the middle class. Furthermore, being old means becoming grandparents and caring for grandchildren, particularly for elderly women. The latter are also expected to perform housework as long as they can. Insecurities with regard to old age are mainly voiced with regard to lacking money and having no support from children.

---

[23] Cf. Sahlins (2004 [1965]) with regard to the terms generalised, balanced and negative reciprocity.

Many elderly Pulayas, such as Kali (example 3), had little security throughout their life. This is why they sometimes have no particular notion of insecurity, nor much interest in talking about it.

The general opinion is that an elderly person should work and be independent as long as he or she is healthy and able. Self-support is thus considered important. Moreover, the elderly person should behave well, i.e. be helpful, sociable and not quarrelsome. Respect is said to relate to having money and good individual behaviour. Therefore, elderly Pulayas try to earn money as long as possible, and be friendly. Many elderly people, however, no longer have the physical strength or the health conditions to perform the tough kind of wage labour they did earlier. Some men and women who are strong enough and who have indulgent employers, still work until the age of eighty and above, but their earnings are very low. For example Kunjappan (example 1) and a colleague of his who was in his eighties earned in the convent about half of the average daily wage for males, and Vallothi (example 4) in her eighties earned only Rs 500 (about $ 10) per month as a sweeper in the temple. With such a monthly income it is not possible to cover all the daily needs, let alone additional needs.

Next to taking good care of one's children, old age planning for the Pulayas also consists of building a house, as the example of Kunjappan illustrated. The most important material resource which most of the elderly were able to acquire during their life-course, due to public support as we have seen above, is a house with a monetary value of about Rs 100,000 (about $ 2,000), including three cents of land. These houses are made of bricks, have three tiny rooms and a kitchen, no running water, often not even a latrine, hardly any furniture, but subsidised electricity. Males mostly owned the plot and the house. This was confirmed by the survey data.[24] But because of political problems and corruption, not all of them were the legal owners of their house plots, although they were entitled to the land. Although many Pulayas

---

[24] They show that in almost 75 percent of the cases (n = 28 of 40) a male owns the house, whereas among the Nayars and also among the Muslims it is much less (n = 22 and n = 20 respectively of 40 each). Cases of female house ownership, alone or together with the husband, were least among the Pulayas (n = 12), more among the Nayars (n = 18) and, interestingly, most among the Muslims (n = 20).

started to build their houses with public support, they often had to take on additional debts to finish these dwellings, for example by having the wife pawn her gold jewellery.

Women generally do not possess houses, and thus have little bargaining power to oppose the authority of their husbands or sons who formally represented the household.[25] Only some women own land as daughters in their natal place, not as wives in their husband's place.[26]

Ownership of a house among the working class is thus an important resource and leverage in authority relationships between elderly parents and children, especially between fathers and sons. It is rather a new phenomenon as these elderly are the first generation which does not live in the much simpler thatched huts.

Finally, savings are mentioned as important for old age planning, but only skilled workers with a permanent job can save about Rs 250,000 (about $ 5,000). Elderly Nayars had at least bank savings of that amount, as well as some form of inheritance in addition to a house worth about Rs 1,500,000 (about $ 30,000). Day-labourers are not able to make savings for old age. This is especially due to the high expenses for their daughters' dowries, which is about Rs 100,000 (about $ 2,000) per daughter, and thus similar to the cost of a house. The amounts had not reached these levels at the time the elderly married, and non-existent when their parents married.[27] Most of the elderly live from hand to mouth, and cherish the notion that their children are their savings.

To be able to live at least in fragile security, it is important that an elderly person can still participate in interactions of exchange with a minimum of goods or services, or that he or she has invested sufficiently in exchanges with the spouse and children so that at least the

---

[25] In several cases the house was still registered in the name of the husband, although he had already died. A renewed registration is probably arranged only after the wife has died because unnecessary costs need to be avoided.
[26] According to the survey data, in six of forty cases the wife owned a house. In four cases the mother is mentioned as the house owner, which probably means that the house is still registered in the name of the dead husband.
[27] Dowries must have emerged in the 1960s among the Pulayas. Kunjappan (example 1) said that he received something for his wife, although he had not asked for it. At the time of his parents' marriage, in the 1930s, dowries were not given.

basic needs for food, clothing and shelter are provided. Personal contributions to old age security are gendered. Elderly women are not
able to earn as much money as men and they mostly do not have their
own assets such as a house, but they provide household services and
childcare as long as they can. Interestingly, elderly women are often at
the same time receivers and givers of support.

The Critical Insecurity of the Poorest Elderly Women

Besides the majority of the elderly Pulayas who live in fragile security, there is a minority of women who live in critical insecurity. They
are neglected to the extent that their basic needs for food are not met.
This concerns women without husbands and those who have no children. Since they receive too little support from kin they also cannot
participate in reciprocity networks with neighbours. They belong to
the poorest Pulayas, such as Vallothi, the old widow in the example
which follows.

Example 4: Vallothi – Waiting for Food

Vallothi (about 85), a widow for most of her life, was born about 1916. She had five
children: three sons, one of whom died early, and two daughters. Her husband died
when she was only in her thirties and her children were still very young. She cared
for her youngest son who was handicapped and unmarried until 2002 when he died.

Vallothi never attended school. She worked as an agricultural labourer and later
as a sweeper in the nearby temple. She stopped earning money only two years ago.
In her last job as a sweeper she earned Rs 500 (about $ 10) per month and received
cloth. When she retired, because she became too weak, she received a lump sum of
Rs 2,000 (about $ 40) which she gave to her eldest son. That same son provided her
with one or two meals a day. Vallothi remarks that she feels hungry in the morning.
People say that the daughter-in-law is neglecting her and that she only gives Vallothi
food because the son forces her. He, again, cannot afford large expenses for his
mother because he himself is already about sixty years old and works irregularly.
But fortunately he has three sons.

Vallothi also receives a small widow's pension totalling about Rs 500 (about $
10) a year from the state, according to her information. She commented: "That is not
even enough to buy coconut oil for my hair". Moreover, she receives free medicines
on a weekly basis from the Christian welfare organisation (RCDS).

During the time that she had to bring up her children alone, she regularly received food and money from a Christian employer in her natal place. That employer also contributed to her daughters' dowry.

She is living on her own land of three cents, in a small brick house with a simple cot as the main furniture. The house, in her name, was newly constructed with a "loan", but still looks incomplete. Her eldest grandson arranged the loan (without repayment) with the help of the local caste organisation (KPMS) at the municipality. As a return he will inherit her house upon her death. Vallothi is not able to decide for herself on house matters. Her eldest son and two of his sons are her immediate neighbours and her daughters also live nearby.

Vallothi thinks that the elderly in the settlement are generally satisfied, and despite the fact that she does not have enough to eat, she seems in fairly good condition mentally, physically and socially. Her only wish is to get a daily breakfast. To find solace she still visits the temple daily.

Most of the Pulayas think that the elderly in their locality are satisfied, although there are cases of social insecurity as well as of neglect and concomitantly of social exclusion. However, in the cases we know of, it was not a matter of complete neglect or exclusion. Possibly, the purported lack of discontent among the lower class elderly resulted from partial neglect or exclusion only, in tandem with an acquiescing "image management" (cf. Sokolovsky 1993) of insecurities in old age. Vallothi had three sons and two daughters, but two of her sons have already died. Her only remaining son has an irregular income. But he and his wife are also needy to some extent because they are already old. In this difficult situation, not least due to Vallothi's longevity, the relationship between Vallothi and her daughter-in-law seems to be fraught with ambivalence, so that the latter does not seem willing to pay much for Vallothi's care. Her daughters could give some additional help, but it is not their responsibility to provide food on a daily base. Thus, Vallothi suffers from a lack of food, and the only insufficient capital she still can use in exchange relationships is her friendliness.

The last example is about a deserted and childless woman called Devu.

Example 5: Devu – Begging for Food

Devu (60), born in 1941, has worked as a manual labourer since she was eight years old. Because her father was seriously ill and could no longer work, she and her mother used to cut and sell grass to run the household. Later she did construction work. As she had no brothers, she also helped to finance one of her two sister's marriage.

Her husband also did construction work. Eight years ago, at the time her mother died, he abandoned her. On marriage she remarks: "Marriage is security, but some husbands leave their wives. They do not have a sincere heart, so they abandon them. As an old woman you have to be prepared when the husband looses interest in you and looks for a young girl to be his wife. You have to have a house to sleep in and money to buy food." Neither of these were easy to arrange for her. She adds that males do not experience such crises because they can remarry. She experienced the abandonment by her husband as a major crisis in her life.

She moved back to her natal place in Kalamassery where she had some land. Earlier she had bought three cents of land from the local government for her mother who settled there, later together with Devu's first sister and her sister's son. Devu built herself a small, windowless room as an annex to her mother's house where she lives now. Since her mother's death she still owns one cent of the compound land. She goes to her cousin's house to bathe and watch TV.

Devu continued to earn money until she was fifty-five. Then she began to have health problems with her arms becoming swollen. Since then she goes to her niece or to her cousins to ask for food, or else she begs, mainly outside the settlement where the people do not know her. One of her nearest kin relationships is with the daughter of her youngest sister. Devu helped to finance the marriage of this niece and she will bequeath the remaining patch of land (one cent) to her. Muslim women help Devu to wash her clothes which she cannot do herself due to her illness.

"My whole life is a big crisis", Devu points out. As a girl she had to support her mother and as a wife her husband, and now she is alone. The worst thing she says is to have no children. Earlier she had wished to adopt children, but her husband did not agree. One of her urgent wishes is that the elderly poor get external support, particularly money and medicine.

She is one of the few informants I met who would like to go to an old age home, as she has nobody to care for her. But she needs the consent of her cousin's sons and they will unlikely agree as it would harm their reputations she guesses. So she continues to live as she does. Should she become seriously ill, she imagines that she will drag herself out of her room to the road, and ask people there to take her to a government hospital. "Then it is sure that I will die. That is the way I will end my life."

Devu was one of the few informants who thought that the elderly living around her are unhappy. Her narrative exemplifies in a striking way the critical insecurity of poor women without "family". She can only rely on more distant, and still more insecure kin relationships. She is not eligible for governmental support through the "destitute and widow pension" because she is not officially divorced. She would be eligible to go to an old age home, but her nearest male relatives do not agree for fear of their reputation.

The examples of Vallothi and Devu illustrate cases of critical insecurity in which neither kin nor neighbourhood relationships provide sufficient support when it comes to the most basic daily necessity – food. Their narratives are not a complaint discourse with which an elderly person tries to ensure support from kin (cf. Rosenberg 1990, Cattell 1997). Although both have a patch of land, and Vallothi even has a house, this does not give them enough bargaining power with regard to their daily social security. Gender imagery and power relationships contribute to the fact that elderly males often get more support from their children and from their spouses, and that elderly females without husbands are dependent on the decisions of younger males.

These are not unique cases. Chen (1998) found in her study on widows in Kerala and six other Indian states that "Few (if any) widows living on their own receive 'maintenance'– that is, food on a regular basis – from other households. Moreover, if a widow lives as a dependent in a household headed by her son, more so in households headed by others, she is likely to be subject to neglect unless she is seen to contribute something important to the household: for example, domestic services, land or other property, wage earnings, or a pension" (Chen 1998: 39).

Kinship and Insecurity

The imagery of family support has to be questioned. As we found in several cases among this working class group, the elderly are not sufficiently supported by their families, let alone by solely one son. The insecurity of intergenerational relationships is largely hidden by national and local imagery. The family can become a space of insecurity for the elderly, on the one hand because of a lack of economic resources, and on the other hand because of ambivalence in kin relation-ships. Old age security has to be negotiated continuously through the agency of the elderly in their exchange relationships with the support-givers. Former and possibly future investments in the generalised ex-change with spouse and children are of the utmost importance, as one of the elderly impressively narrated (cf. initial quotation).

An interesting topic in the new kinship studies is the ambivalence of kinship relations, which so far has only been elaborated to a slight degree, theoretically and empirically.[28] With loose reference to this literature, I use the term ambivalence in the sense of a conflicting at-titude and related practices in kin relationships due to divided interests which are not only economically motivated but also symbolically, when for instance prestige is an issue. The latter is the case if in an extended family household near or even below the poverty line for prestigious reasons the daughter-in-law is a housewife. Thereby household earnings are forsaken, which impacts on the basic needs of the elderly. The ethnographic material presented here strengthens the argument that kinship relations not only provide security and support, but they can also produce insecurity and neglect. The latter is also in-dicated in a recent empirical study about the abuse of elderly people in the capital of Kerala (Merlin 1999).[29] The issue of ambivalence may lead to ruptures or just distance in support relationships, particularly with regard to elderly women.[30]

Conclusions

The questions addressed in this chapter were to what extent can the poor elderly in urban Kerala mobilise support from public agencies and from the family, and to what extent is old age support gendered.

---

[28] Cf. Risseeuw and Palriwala 1996, Ganesh 1998, Faubion 2000, Böck and Rao 2000, and Peletz 2001. In the literature on old age there is some discussion about intergenerational conflicts, but mainly from a functionalist approach, e.g. Foner 1984.
[29] Cf. also Rosenblatt and Antoni 2002.
[30] These insights with regard to kinship ambivalence which result from a longer process of data evaluation and in-depth analysis of contextualised examples need more elaboration elsewhere.

Public support of daily needs is less secure than assumed. Most important are governmental provisions in the realm of housing. Here, the local caste organisation (KPMS) is of significance with regard to mediation between workers and the state as far as subsidies for housing are concerned. With regard to health, the Christian non-governmental organisation of Rajagiri provides basic care. Thus, citizenship relations with these Hindu and Christian welfare organisations are of direct importance for the elderly. The relationships with the state are often indirect.

What makes old age more insecure, however, is that even the joint or extended form of "the family" does not play the protective role which the Indian state and Indian social science scholars often presume or require. The discourse on the support of "the family" should be reformulated. Relations with children and conjugal relations provide support only under certain economic and social conditions. The social security arrangement of the Pulayas is strongly diversified. Husbands play an important role with regard to financial and sometimes also physical support. Daughters provide subsidiary support, both financial and physical. Financial support is less concentrated on only one son than expected. Male siblings and in-laws may also play a subsidiary role.

Security in old age requires that the elderly mobilise sufficient means for daily and non-daily needs in their kin network. It further requires that the kin relationships in question are not affected by ambivalence, in the sense of negative attitudes and practices resulting in some kind of neglect. This again implies intact relations of reciprocity (generalised reciprocity with household members, balanced reciprocity with other kin) with ongoing contributions by the elderly to the household or childcare services.

Unexpectedly, relationships with neighbours play an important complementary role with regard to having daily needs met. They can only be maintained, however, if the provisions received, such as money and food, are reciprocated within a certain time span (balanced reciprocity). Moreover, relationships with employers provide assistance with non-daily needs such as housing and dowries as a counter-prestation for already invested surplus labour.

Due to the importance of an extended local network of support among the poor working class elderly, I suggest coining the term "extended neighbourhood" which comprises all kinds of relations of kinship and citizenship that are used with regard to old age security in the locality.

Except the elderly who live in fragile security, i.e. those whose satisfaction of their daily needs can change any time because of financial adversities or familial tensions, there are elderly people who live in critical insecurity. Their daily needs for food are not satisfied. These are widows and other women who neither have enough economic capital nor social capital.

The case study has thus shown three modes of daily living in old age: 1) support by household members is sufficient in cases in which household income is sufficient and familial ambivalence is neutralised, 2) support by household members is complemented with support by neighbours and other locals in cases in which household income is temporarily sufficient and familial ambivalence is acted out, and 3) support by household members is insufficient and cannot be complemented by more distant kin, neighbours and other locals (actual or former employers) in cases in which both household income is insufficient and familial ambivalence is acted out.

Support-giving by children is not strongly gendered. Daughters also contribute with money, and sons also contribute with physical help, if necessary. But care-giving by elderly women is more elaborate than that provided by males, for instance with regard to grandchildren and sick kin. Thus, the elderly are sometimes both receivers and givers of support. Neighbourhood support is gendered in the sense that sons and other local males tend to provide financial support, whereas females provide food and physical support.

The receiving of support is strongly gendered. Elderly women are disadvantaged and have less bargaining power because of less access to resources (lower education, lower income, no house) and because of lesser authority than men, even if they are much older. The poorest elderly women without near kin particularly suffer from insecurity. Although women are said to adjust more easily to old age than men, they adjust less easily to daughters-in-law. The dependence of mothers on son's decision-making is much stronger than of fathers, especially when a mother no longer has the backing of a husband. In such cases, she has to cope with the possibly divided interests of the son between his wife, his children, his mother and himself. This can become a greater problem as a result of the increasing longevity of women.

Neither "the state" nor "the family" provide for the social security of these working class elderly. Low-income Muslims with permanent work seem to be able to rely more exclusively on family members, whereas middle class Nayar employees may rely on a governmental pension, their own assets, and on physical support by domestic workers, home nurses and family members. Social security in old age among the mainly unskilled Pulaya workers is, more or less successfully, based on a complex, patchwork-like network of specific and changing relations of kinship (as a spouse, a mother, a father) and citizenship (as a neighbour, an worker, a member of an organisation, municipality, state or nation-state), and that means on the continuous efforts of the elderly themselves to maintain their flexible network within the existing structures. Such a social security arrangement can be called an "extended neighbourhood network", which in the end seems to be more important for the security of poor people than the joint or extended family. In the case of the poor working class elderly, I therefore suggest focussing rather on the maintenance of support relationships of that extended neighbourhood network than on the extended family or any other family, be it imagined as good or as bad.

The following case study about rural Kerala confirms the major findings of this urban case study. Interestingly, we discovered fewer differences with respect to the social security of the poor elderly than we expected, but certain issues do contrast.

Limited Social Security of the Poor Elderly in Rural Kerala

Seema Bhagyanath

By the year 2001, the United Nations predicted one of seven elderly persons in the world would be Indian.[1] India will progress from a "mature society" to an "ageing society".[2] The changing demographic profile of the country poses questions concerning the care for the elderly. Within India, it is interesting to examine the social security of the elderly in Kerala for two reasons: Firstly, because Kerala has completed the demographic transition to an "ageing society", with the aged population comprising 8.77 percent in 1991 and projected to reach 11.74 percent by 2011 (Irudaya Rajan et al. 1999: 45). Secondly, because Kerala is well known for its widespread social security schemes from which the elderly can benefit, as already elaborated in the preceding chapters.

This study concentrates on the social security relationships of the working class elderly in rural Kerala belonging to the Pulaya caste. In relevant aspects they are compared with middleclass employees belonging to the caste of the Nayars. In the course of this chapter, I will address the following questions: Firstly, what kind of insecurities do the elderly experience? Secondly, which economic resources and social relationships are accessible to them for their support? And lastly, to what extent is old age gendered? The main result of this case study corresponds with the previous one on urban Kerala. In rural Kerala, the elderly of the working class also depend on a diverse support network for their social security.

---

[1] According to the Central Statistical Organisation (2000:1) the aged population in India, which was 56.7 million in 1991, is expected to increase up to 137 million by 2021.
[2] A society with an elderly population between 4.7 and 7 percent of the total population is called mature, whereas a society with an elderly population more than 7 percent is called an ageing society.

Research Location

The village where I conducted my fieldwork for a total of six months between 2001 and in 2002 is Kadamakuddy, located in the district of Ernakulam in Central Kerala.[3] This village was selected because of the concentration of Pulayas (Rajagiri 1991). The population of the village is 14,668.[4] Christians, both Syrian Christians and Latin Catholics, represent the majority and there were no Muslim families. There are several Hindu castes, i.e. Izhavas, Kudumbis, Pulayas, Kanakas and a minority of Nayars. According to local experts, in 1995 there were about 278 Pulaya households in the whole of Kadamakuddy. My fieldwork was done on one of the islands with about 120 Pulaya households.

Until 2001 the only way to reach the island was by boat. In recent years, as a part of a new National Highway, the government has also been constructing a bund that would connect the island to the mainland. By 2002, the bund was almost finished. The roads in the village are still narrow beaten earth tracks, so within the village the people mostly go on foot. Some villagers have bicycles and very few have motorised two-wheelers. Women always walk. Reaching facilities, such as the hospital, can take up to an hour. The people of the island believe that once they are connected to the mainland by road the island will develop more vigorously.

Until now the tax income of the village is one of the lowest in Kerala because there has not been much scope for business due to its inaccessible topography. For development funds the village is therefore depending on subsidies from the state government. Agriculture was a major source of employment in the village but now it has de-

---

[3] The case study is based on qualitative data collected from 52 persons, i.e. 40 individual interviews and 12 from experts on caste, community and elderly issues. Additionally, to get a clearer impression of the population under study, a quota survey covering 80 households was carried out, viz. 40 Pulaya and 40 Nayar households. Most informants are Hindus, the largest religious community in Kerala.
[4] Source: Department of Economics and Statistics 1995.

clined because it is no longer profitable.[5] Other sources of employment are prawn cultivation, fishing, clay manufacturing, manual labour, such as construction work and digging trenches for sewage, as well as teaching. There are also many inhabitants who live on the island and work on the mainland, such as government employees, teachers, shop assistants, clerks, automobile mechanics and manual labourers. Commercialisation in the village was only recently stimulated as a result of the private purchase of land by an enterprise seeking to build cottages to run a backwater resort.

The waste affluence of a chemical industry in the larger area causes problems for the villagers. The pollution adversely affects fishing and also causes respiratory problems for the inhabitants. To provide a picture of the living conditions of the elderly Pulayas, I will present some general socio-economic facts about this social group in the village.

Socio-economic Background of the Pulayas

All the elderly Pulaya men and women formerly worked as agricultural labourers. Due to the seasonal nature of this occupation they also performed other kinds of manual labour to earn their livelihoods, including preparing coconut husk for coir making, carrying head loads of brick, sand and earth for construction, and digging. In the past, jobs in agriculture were often poorly remunerated, often in kind. For the harvesting and chaffing of 100 kg of rice, a worker would get 10 kg and the landlord 90 kg. For other kinds of manual labour, wages were also low. Thus, the labourers were not able to save any money.

Most of the elderly Pulayas no longer work because of poor health and also because agriculture has lost its importance in the village. In certain cases, the elderly work irregularly in wealthier households; men do small jobs, such as cleaning the compound from weeds and

---

[5] After the land reform the agricultural landholdings have become small. Moreover, the cost for preparing the land for cultivation is high and the yield from the small landholdings is not enough to make it profitable.

grass and chopping wood for cooking[6], whereas women perform domestic work. The only fixed income that the elderly Pulayas can hope to get in old age in the village is a social assistance benefit or a "pension" of Rs 110 (about $[7] 2) per month. All the elderly who participated in the qualitative interviews receive this type of social assistance. However, the quota survey showed that about half of the interviewees did not receive such a pension.[8]

The economic situation of the middle class elderly Nayars looks quite different. Only the men are employed, whereas the women are housewives. The men work as teachers or as employees in the governmental or private sector. Thus they are able to save for their old age. Those in government employment have the privilege of getting an average pension of Rs 5,000 (about $ 100). In one case an elderly Nayar received a pension of Rs 12,000 per month (about $ 240).

As the elderly Pulayas receive nearly no income, it is important to examine whether their children have one. The middle generation Pulayas mostly work as semi-skilled labourers. Many of them work on a contract basis for a certain period of time and are paid daily wages. They are better remunerated than those who work on a daily basis only. But as they are not permanently employed, they have no secure working conditions.[9] According to the quota survey, males mostly earn a small monthly income between Rs 2,000 and Rs 3,000 (about $ 40 to 60). The females mostly earn between Rs 500 and Rs 2,000 ($ 10 to 40) per month, but many younger married women did not earn any wages and were housewives.

If we look at the household incomes, to which more than one person may contribute, then almost all of them are placed above the poverty line (BPL), i.e. above a yearly income of Rs 21,000 ($ 420). But as there is no official record of their income and as they visibly live in

---

[6] Wealthier households sometimes use firewood, as they believe that the food becomes tastier. For heating water and cooking rice, which fuel consumption is more, they generally use firewood. Firewood, mostly from fallen coconut tree branches, is also easily available.
[7] In all cases Rupees are converted to US dollars.
[8] n = 21 of 40.
[9] A man earns about Rs 150 (about $ 3) as a day labourer, a woman Rs 120 (about $ 2.5) for the same kind of work.

poor conditions, they nevertheless get the BPL benefit of a ration card. As already mentioned in the preceding chapters, with such a card they can procure rice and other basic provisions at a subsidised rate. These conditions contrast with the urban case where a larger proportion of the households have incomes below the poverty line. Moreover, living in the village is cheaper than living in town. Land and housing taxes and prices for commodities such as fish and vegetables are cheaper.

The Pulayas are proud that they attended school. All the elderly had about two years of formal education in the island village and some a little more. Most of them had to discontinue school after some years due to family constraints. They either had to start working in order to supplement family income or they had to look after a younger sibling while the parents went to work. The middle generation, irrespective of gender, attended up to ten years of school, and the youngest generation has at least ten years of education. Similarly as in the village study by Franke (1996) in Central Kerala, however, school education does not guarantee a permanent job among the Pulayas. For example, one man exceptionally studied physics but works in construction for Rs 225 a day (about $ 4.5).

Nearly all the elderly of the working class have a house. This is a result of the land reform that was implemented in Kerala in the 1970s. Everyone who had worked as an agricultural labourer was entitled to ten cents of land in a specific area, but by the time the land was divided, they only received about six cents. They were able to build a house on that land with a loan. In general, the men own the houses, but women often own houses after the death of their husbands. In the quota survey, in seventy-five percent of the cases males owned the house, in twenty-five percent females.

The house was mostly a cemented three-room structure with a tiled roof. Many houses have electricity. In some houses they were not able to afford windows and so they used huge plastic sheets. Several houses were built on low-lying areas on the waterfront, which meant that during rains the water could come up to the house. Generally, the houses do not have running water. For bathing purposes, the Pulayas collect water from the river, but for cooking and drinking they have to collect water from the public taps. During summer, when there is shortage of water, the village government supplies water from tanks ferried to the village in boats. The responsibility of collecting water rests solely with the women.

From this brief description, we can infer the contribution that the elderly Pulayas make themselves with regard to their old age security: they have a house for shelter and a small pension. Sometimes they even have some kind of irregular work, which provides them a small income of their own, but this it is insuffient for their livelihood, meaning that the elderly Pulayas generally depend on their children. The question is to what extent and how.

Fear of Insecurity in Old Age:
No Money, No Food, No Health Care

Elderly Pulayas regard old age as a phase of decline, a period when they are unable to walk properly, unable to do much work and their health is deteriorating. In general, the elderly link the concept of security in old age to having someone to support them, i.e. to look after their needs. The responsibility was usually perceived to fall on the children, mostly sons, and in the absence of sons, daughters. As the elderly hardly have any income, having no money to fulfil basic needs for food was a significant concern for them. However, food did not seem to be a real problem. One of the elderly women remarked that getting food was not so difficult because in the household in which she lived with her married son food was cooked anyway. The second biggest worry of the elderly is obtaining the necessary medicines. There is no guarantee that they would be able to buy medicine if they are completely dependent on their children.

Issues regarding health are a cause of anxiety among the elderly. Particularly with regard to becoming bedridden, the elderly fear being considered a burden and being neglected. Most of the elderly express a desire to die before reaching this point because for them this would mean depending on others for all of their functional needs. The elderly do not want to become an encumbrance on their children.

The health status of the elderly has an impact on their quality of life in that in certain cases it could lead to less mobility, which adversely effects the social interactions of the person. In my sample, two elderly women whose sight was impaired stayed at home. One elderly man who suffered from high blood pressure did not go out alone for fear of fainting from dizziness. Another elderly man who was recovering from an illness also remained at home. In all these cases, their only opportunity for interaction was with the family members who stayed in the house or with people who visited them. This confirmed the finding of the study by Willigen, Chadha and Kedia (1996) that the elderly with poor health have a small social network. Lack of social interaction can also lead to feelings of loneliness and exclusion. A few of the elderly Pulayas complained that nowadays life was so busy that the younger generation did not have time for the older generation.

Another factor that the elderly considered important, with regard to their security, was to have fulfilled all of their responsibilities. Most important was the marriage of their children. Finding a suitable match for their children is crucial because their security in old age depends, in the first place, on a good relationship with the daughter-in-law or son-in-law. Related to marriage is the question of dowry. To marry a daughter, a dowry has to be donated. The dowries among the Pulayas in the rural area ranged from Rs 24,000 to Rs 41,600 (about $ 480 to 832).[10] This is much less than in the urban area where it is about Rs 100,000 (about $ 2,000). Most of the elderly Pulayas had managed the dowry for their daughter's marriage by taking a mortgage on their house and by borrowing from others. It is possible to repay the debts only if they are earning, thus marrying their daughters during their working age is important for the elderly.

---

[10] More exactly, the dowries amounted from Rs 5,000 plus 5 *pavan* gold to Rs 15,000 and 7 *pavan* gold, whereby one *pavan* was eight grammes of gold with a value of Rs 3,800 in 2002.

Relations and Resources for Support in Old Age

We now turn to the question of what kind of economic resources and
social relationships do the Pulayas have access to for support in old
age. We can break it down in terms of support from kin, from the
community and from the state.

Support from Kin

Patricia Uberoi (1993) notes that the definition of family in India
changes depending on the context in which it is used. In the context of
a two-generation household, one speaks of the family in terms of the
parents and children; in the context of a three-generation household, it
encompasses parents, children and grandchildren; and in ceremonial
contexts it includes siblings, aunts, uncles and cousins. Here we break
up the unit of the family and we especially examine the support relationships of the elderly with their children, with the spouse, as well as
with kin beyond their own household.

It is presumed in the writings of many scholars that in the past the
joint family system provided the aged with the needed security, love
and affection, and that its disintegration is problematic for the aged
(e.g. Bose 1988, Mohanty 1989, World Bank 1994). In Indian society
the norm that the elderly should be cared for in the family is culturally
informed through written Hindu texts and socially enforced. The notion that children owe their parents a tremendous debt for giving them
birth, feeding and caring for them throughout infancy and childhood is
axiomatic. The parent-child relationship in the Indian context is thus
conceptualised as a life-span relationship. In her study of the elderly in
the northern Indian village of Rayapur, Vatuk (1980:127) asserts:
"Old age is seen as a period of rightful dependency with security contingent upon the support of an extended family (especially an adult
son)."

In the case of the Pulayas, the elderly expect that their children will
look after them. They believe that if they have a son, the son should
care for them, and in his absence it should be the daughter. The gen-

eral perception is that once a daughter gets married she goes to her husband's place and her ability to help will depend on the husband's willingness to allow her to do so. In the words of one of the elderly men: "If you look after your children and take care of their needs when they are young, then the children will look after you in your old age." One of the younger men said: "It is the duty of every child to look after one's parents. It would be sinful to neglect or abandon them." His words echoed the opinion of most people of the middle generation who felt that it was the duty of the children to look after the parents. Children who live away from their parents feel a sense of guilt. One of the younger men had moved to a new house and, despite the distance, he still cared for his widowed mother. He pays the tax for her house and he visits his mother regularly to make sure if she is all right. His younger brother stays with her permanently. This demonstrates that it is not only the youngest son who gives financial support to the elderly parents.

Most of the elderly Pulayas who were interviewed live in three-generation households with a son or a daughter, his or her spouse and their children. According to the quota survey, all the elderly live together with family members; no one lives alone. The proportion of extended families is even much larger than in the urban case. As far as the support of the elderly women is concerned, the person primarily responsible for providing physical support is the daughter-in-law. The support from the husband, daughter, son and other kin are also important. For financial support, the elderly women mainly depend on the son and to some extent on the husband. In certain instances, daughters and brothers also help.[11] Thus, physical and financial support are provided mainly by the daughter-in-law and the son respec-

---

[11] The first related person who gives physical support to the mother: daughter-in-law n = 30, husband n = 5, daughter n = 5; the second related person who gives physical support to the mother: son n = 20, husband n = 9, daughter-in-law n = 7, son-in-law n = 3.
The first related person who gives financial support to the mother: son n = 30, husband n = 8, daughter n = 1, son-in-law n = 1; the second related person who gives financial support to the mother: daughter n = 12, brother n = 10, son n = 8, son-in-law n = 6, husband n = 4.

tively, but other kin within the own household and from other households also help with physical and financial assistance in certain cases.

The following example highlights an elderly married woman
named Tilotamma who emphasises the relationship with her son with
regard to security in old age. Her son takes care of her daily material
needs and provides for her medicines. But in fact, Tilotamma's old
age is also secured due to her husband's and her daughter-in-law's
support.

Example 1: Tilotamma – Supported by her Son and Daughter-in-law

Tilotamma (61) was born in 1940 in a village called Puttampally. Her family moved
to Kadamakudddy, the native place of her mother, in her childhood when her father
died. She went to school until the third class, after which she started working. She
mostly worked as an agricultural labourer, and she dehusked coconuts and prepared
the husk for coir making. She married at the age of sixteen. Her husband was an
agricultural labourer as well. Formerly, he was the head of the labourers on a field in
the neighbouring village. She used to accompany her husband there for agricultural
work. Together they built a house, which is owned by him. Neither she nor her husband works now due to health reasons. The husband suffers from asthma and she
from high blood pressure. Being casual labourers they have not been able to save
any money, but both she and her husband receive an "agricultural workers pension",
which gives them some income in their old age. They have only one son aged thirty-
three. He, with his wife and two children, lives with them. For Tilotamma the support of her son, who is a bricklayer, is most important: Her prayer to God is that he
should look after her until the day she dies. Her daughter-in-law also looks after her
well, but sometimes there are conflicts between the two women. However, Tilotamma thinks that in times of need she can depend on her, as happened when she
was ill. Tilotamma shares the housework with her daughter-in-law and if needed she
also looks after the grandchildren.

When she was seriously ill due to high blood pressure and was on bed rest for
many weeks her husband and her daughter-in-law took care of her. She takes homeopathic medicines for her ailment. This is not provided for free by governmental
health care, but has to be bought. Her son pays for her treatment. She believes very
deeply in God and believes that prayers will protect her from all harm.

The ideas that are related to care in old age do not always correspond
with practice, and the practices are less gendered than it seems at first
sight. There were two cases in which the daughter and the son-in-law
were providing care. In both cases the daughter and her husband were

staying with her parents, and the son-in-law was looking after the financial needs of the elderly. In one case, the son-in-law did not have surviving parents, and in another case his widowed mother was staying with the younger son. Being married thus did not hamper the caregiving ability of the daughters, as is often said. An older Pulaya woman, who has two daughters who are unmarried, mentioned that she has to look for suitable grooms for them. For one of her daughters she will try to find a groom who will stay in the elderly woman's house after the marriage. This will ensure that her daughter and son-in-law will care for her when she is older and no longer able to care for herself. Support from children cannot be taken for granted, as the following example shows.

Example 2: Vallom – In Sudden Insecurity
Vallom (75), born in 1927, travelled all over Kerala and worked in many places as an agricultural and manual labourer. Since his marriage at the age of twenty-four he has lived and worked in Kadamakuddy. He has a married daughter of forty and a married son of thirty-two. Vallom and his wife built a house in 1985 when they were still working. They saved on the construction by doing it themselves, but they had to take a loan for materials. He owns the house.

It has been more than eight years since he stopped working. He suffers from high blood pressure and dizziness and thus does not go out anymore. He has become a recluse, spending all his time sitting on the veranda, watching people go by. Vallom's son and daughter-in-law stayed with them and looked after them. His son worked in construction. Then in 2001, the son had a serious accident and suffered multiple fractures in his leg. For more than a year, his leg was in a plaster with plates and screws. In September 2002, when I last met Vallom, his son's leg was still in a plaster. As the son has to go for regular check-ups, he has moved to his wife's parents' house located near the city hospital.

Vallom mortgaged his house for Rs 5000 for his son's medical expenses. He has no idea how they are going to repay this amount because neither he nor his wife work regularly anymore. However, his wife occasionally works in a neighbour's house and receives a small wage. They also have another debt of Rs 1000 from the time of Vallom's illness. They each receive a small monthly pension of Rs 110 (about $ 4.5). The money they have at least prevents them from starving, but it is not enough to repay the loans. For months they have not paid anything and they are worried that they would be asked to vacate the house. Their daughter lives nearby, but she is not in a position to help as she is not earning money and her husband who is recovering from a heart attack is currently unemployed. Moreover, they have two children to care for.

Vallom and his wife suddenly came to live in insecurity. Their children, even with the best of intentions, cannot support them anymore. Vallom believes that if they had had more children then probably one of them would have been able to help.

Nowadays the longevity of the elderly has increased. In 1961, life expectancy at birth in Kerala was 46.2 years for men and 50 for women. By 1991, it had increased to 60.5 for men and 62.1 for women. At the same time, birth rates have decreased. The fertility rate for Kerala was 4.1 in 1971 and fell to 1.8 in 1991 (Irudaya Rajan et al. 1999). As a result, there has been a drastic reduction in the number of caregivers available for the elderly in the family, at a time when the duration of care for the elderly has increased. Just because parents live with the children, one should not assume they are well looked after. Economic constraints on the family can lead to insufficient care of the elderly. The Ministry of Social Welfare (1987:10) states a trend of greater investments by families in the education and upbringing of the children. This trend affects the intra-family distribution of income in favour of the younger generation.

The quota survey showed that the proportion of the Pulayas who cared for both parents and children was high. Though none of the elderly informants ever mentioned neglect, some did mention that they could not always get the medicine they required due to a lack of money. In certain cases the financial dependence of the elderly on their children can lead to a kind of social exclusion. An elderly Christian woman at the Day Care Centre (DCC) in another part of the village said that she is living with her son and daughter-in-law. As long as she was earning everything was fine, but since she stopped working two years ago the situation worsened. She gets food but nobody speaks with her. She feels lonely and thinks that she has become a burden for her family.

Several scholars have noted that if the elderly parents who co-reside with their children have some economic resources, then they have a better status in the family due to their bargaining power (Reddy and

Rani 1989, Vatuk 1990). The resentment of children, with respect to the economic dependence of their elderly parents, has been pointed out in village studies in South India by Marulisiddiah (1966) and by Reddy and Rani (1989). Mahajan (1992) found in his study on the lower class elderly in a village in northern India that economic dependency is one of the chief instigators of abuse.

Whereas the Pulayas say they expect support from the children, at the same time they reciprocate in any way they can because they do not want to be considered as burdens. The house with the land is left to the child who looks after them in their old age. The elderly women help with housework. Sometimes the elderly men run small errands and do small repair work on the house. Their pension is added to the household income. Once I witnessed an older woman who received her pension money order. Immediately she and her daughter-in-law went to buy rice in the ration shop with that money.

In the middle class, the children often live in the city and sometimes even abroad because of scarcity of employment in Kerala. Thus, though the elderly would prefer to spend their last years with the children, they were living on their own, sometimes with the help of a domestic worker. Geographical distance does not necessarily mean emotional distance, as it was noted that children maintained contact with parents through regular visits, letters and phone calls and also sent them remittances. In the West, this pattern of interaction has been called "intimacy at a distance" (Treas 1975).

Studies have shown that having a living spouse positively affects satisfaction in life in old age.[12] The general notion among the elderly Pulayas is that in a conjugal relationship, in times of need one has each other, there is companionship and therefore one does not feel lonely. For the elderly Pulaya male, the support of the wife is significant. The elderly woman in her role as a wife does most of the personal chores for the husband, like washing his clothes, heating his water for a bath and taking care of his needs. For elderly women, however, the importance of the spouse, especially in terms of financial support, is uncertain. These women who still sometimes work and

---

[12] Cf. e.g. Raj and Prasad 1971, and Gurudoss and Lakshminarayanan 1989.

earn an income and who receive a pension are not entirely dependent on the husband and children for financial security. One of the elderly woman said: "If you have a good relationship with your spouse then you have something to look forward to in sharing your life with your husband." She said that her husband previously would drink a lot and squander all the money, but he had stopped drinking and she feels that in her old age she is having a better relationship with him. In another example the woman said: "My husband in his old age spends all his time doing nothing. At least previously he used to earn something to contribute to the running of the household." Leela's situation shows that the support from the spouse is dependent on the quality of the conjugal relationship.

Example 3: Leela and her Insecure Old Age

Leela (58), born in 1943, is married and has four daughters and one son. The eldest daughter is thirty-three and the youngest son is nineteen years old. Leela did not have an easy childhood. Being the eldest of twelve siblings, she had to drop out after two years of school to supplement the family income. Marriage did not make things easier. In the initial years of marriage, her husband spent all his earnings on alcohol and tobacco. He even beat her at times when she asked for money. But over the years he has improved. Nowadays, he sometimes contributes to the household income. They have built a house, which he agreed to keep in her name. All her life she has been working as an agricultural or manual labourer, and she still does. Currently because jobs in agriculture have decreased, she works as a labourer on construction sites. All her children are formally educated and two of her daughters are married. There are still two more to be married and this she thinks is a big responsibility, especially as she has to shoulder it mostly on her own. Getting the second daughter married was expensive. They spent almost Rs 100,000 (about $ 2,000). They mortgaged their house for Rs 30,000 (about $ 600). Her younger brother and the husband's elder brother contributed an amount and they also used some money from the provident fund of the daughter who married. Leela said that until the mortgage is repaid she could not think of marrying another daughter.

Her son is a bright student and his education was sponsored by an NGO called CASP. He did vocational training to become an electrician, but because of financial difficulties, he dropped out and is now working in a bakery. Leela feels guilty about this but there was no other way. Her husband gets an old age pension. He also does small jobs to earn some money, but his contribution to the household income cannot be depended on. She has many questions concerning her future old age: Will she be able to get her daughters married? Will she be able to repay the mortgage? Will her son be able to finish his course and get a good job? She wonders how things will be when she gets older and cannot work, but she hopes that her son will be there and will provide security in her old age.

Leela comments that her husband is not contributing as much as he should because he still spends money on alcohol. Her security solely depends on the support from her children, mainly her son.

Among the middle class elderly, as in the working class, the wife takes care of all the needs of the elderly male. Unlike the elderly Pulaya women, however, the middle-class elderly women are more dependent on their husbands. They are generally housewives, and therefore they completely rely on the husband for the daily expenses. In most cases the women owned assets, but it was fixed in terms of land, house or jewellery and would be sold only in financial crises. Whereas most of the middle-class elderly men are graduates, the women have little formal education and not much exposure to the outside world, making them dependent on their husbands for advice. Companionship and emotional support from the spouse are important for both men and women.

The elderly Pulayas also turn to their "relatives", i.e. married siblings or in-laws, for support in times of need. This is mainly during illness and at the times of weddings of daughters. Help received from such "relatives" must be reciprocated. It has been aptly pointed out by one of the elderly men: "There has to be some closeness with one's relatives so that there is some emotional bonding before one can expect any assistance." The example of Thangamma, who is not married, shows that ties of exchange and affection between not-closely-related kin, such as nephews, can in certain cases also lead to a secure support relationship.

Example 4: The Unmarried Thangamma and her "Created Children"

Thangamma (63) was born in 1939. She had two elder sisters, and one elder and one younger brother. Today only she and her two brothers are alive. She attended school for eight years and then dropped out as she failed. She did not marry because of family responsibility. Her elder sister, who had two sons, became a widow at a very young age. Initially Thangamma did not even go to work; she looked after the two children when her sister went to work. When she started earning money herself, she decided not to marry but to continue to help her sister in raising the children. She does not regret having done this because today her nephews are like her sons. She and her sister jointly built a house. The sister was the owner and since her death the owner is the younger nephew. That has not been a problem for Thangamma as her nephew has always acknowledged her sacrifice. So she can continue to stay with him and his wife. During most of her lifetime, Thangamma has worked as an agricultural labourer. The strenuous work has affected her back and she had also fractured her arm at work, but it was never set properly. Now she cannot lift heavy items anymore. Her eyesight has also become weak. Due to all of these infirmities she has not worked for the past seven years. Her nephew who is a manual labourer and his wife provide for most of her support. Her elder brother who lives nearby also helps her. Her younger brother, who is a primary school teacher, helps her once in a while. She has been receiving an "agricultural workers pension" since 1999. She feels good about this as she can use it to buy her homeopathic medicine and also contribute to the household. Because of her health, she does not participate in any housework. In her opinion the best way the elderly can contribute to secure their old age is to be satisfied by what they receive and avoid being a nuisance.

Thangamma does not regret having had no children of her own. She says that her nephews treat her with respect, especially her younger nephew with whom she is living. Even his wife looks after her well. It is also good for her that her brother and his family live nearby; if the people at home are busy she goes to their place if she needs company or wants to talk. Thus, it becomes clear that mainly the children, and in certain cases the children of siblings, play the most important role in the support network of the elderly as regards physical support.

Support from the Community

When needed, the elderly also seek assistance within the village community. This is mainly in case of material needs like food and medicines that are not fulfilled by kin. In the community, the elderly have access to neighbours, friends, employers and also local organisations that can play a support-giving role.

For the Pulayas there is often a relationship of give and take with the neighbours, who mainly provide food and money, and occasionally companionship. In Kadamakuddy, with the land reform the Pulayas were entitled to land in a specific quarter of the village called

Korampadam, where they are now settled. Most of them have been living in Kadamakuddy for years and are well acquainted with each other. Their familiarity and the spatial proximity favour support relationships. In the words of one of the elderly women: "If we are on good terms with the neighbours, we have some security because in case of an emergency the neighbours would be the first people that we would contact." She recounted the incident when her husband suddenly had a paralytic stroke. None of her children were at home at that time. It was the neighbour's son who carried him to the boat and took him to the hospital. For elderly men friends are particularly important. They spend time together and share their thoughts and feelings. Their bonds are strong, as they grew up together and have lived in the same village nearly all their lives. For elderly men socializing almost daily is a must. The example of Bava shows how friends besides children can be a source of support.

Example 5: The Widower Bava – Supported by his Children and Friends

Bava (87) was born in 1914. He made a living as an agricultural labourer. He worked until about ten years ago. Due to cataracts and an accident that injured his arm and knee, he had to stop working. He has three daughters and three sons; the eldest daughter being about fifty and the youngest son being twenty-eight years old. His wife died about twelve years ago. Bava built a house in his working days so he has a roof over his head. He receives an agricultural workers pension from the government of Rs 110 (about $ 2) per month. From this small amount he keeps some small change to spend on tea and tobacco, and contributes the rest to household expenses. His youngest son and family live with him and look after him, but in times of necessity all his children help. For instance, at the time of his accident his children pooled their resources to pay his treatment of Rs 2,000 (about $ 40). They have also filed a case to claim compensation, but court proceedings are slow and the decision can take more than five years.

His son works as a manual labourer and his daughter-in-law as a domestic worker. While they manage a day-to-day living, there are many unfulfilled needs. Bava has been advised to have a cataract operation, but it is too expensive. The house is dilapidated and could fall apart at any time. When it rains heavily, he cannot sleep for fear that the roof will collapse. Bava has four friends with whom he went to school. He and his friends used to meet regularly at the teashop to chat, drink tea and read the newspaper together. Recently, ill health has restricted his mobility so his friends come to Bava's place to chat. At times, they even come to accompany him to the teashop. In Bava's opinion, his children and his friends are his biggest support. The support of his friends is important because in the daytime when his son and daughter-in-law go to work and his grandchildren go to school he is alone at home. Then his ill health becomes a handicap, as he cannot go out on his own. Bava worries that because of his age and poor health something could happen to him when he is alone at home, but if his friends are there they can immediately call for help. Apart from this, he also looks forward to the visits from his friends for the companionship they provide.

Women, on the other hand, lose contact with their friends once they move to their husband's house after marriage. Moreover, they become so involved with their new family that they do not have much time to socialise. Therefore, they have greater support from their neighbours than from friends.

Employers formerly played a significant role in providing support for the older generation of Pulayas. In times of need, the landlord with whom they worked as agricultural labourers, gave them rice and money, and during festivals he donated clothes. At their children's marriages, the employers also helped with money. But now the employers are old themselves and are no longer in a position to give much help. Many of them transferred their assets to their children and the children think that with the land reform the Pulayas received their share of land and should not make any further claims on them. Today, the labourer and the employer have a contractual relationship and the dealings are impersonal and do not provide much support.

The elderly can also make use of the long relationships with the people in the village in that they can buy on credit essential commodities such as vegetables and fish in the local shops. Recently, a new trend has emerged that people buy things and pay on instalments. Usually clothes are bought in this manner. The elderly Pulayas also make use of loan facilities from the bank and the cooperative society in the village. Loans are usually procured against a mortgage on the house or land, or both.

The local religious and caste-based organisations also provide some assistance to the elderly. It is mainly in health care, and in certain cases, also material support such as money and food grains. Though the Pulayas are mostly Hindus, some of them also believe in

Jesus and Mary. Those who regularly pray in a Roman Catholic way receive benefits such as food grains from the church. Now and then, the Hindu sect Satya Saibaba Trust and the Izhava caste organisation, the Sree Narayana Dharma Paripalana Trust (SNDP), organise health camps in the rural area and the elderly take advantage of these. For instance, an elderly woman who had cataracts in both her eyes visited with her son an eye camp organised by the SNDP in a nearby village. She underwent surgery and can now see with the aid of thick spectacles. Thus, in certain cases the welfare activities of religious groups are beneficial for the poor elderly.

In Kadamakuddy, there is also a local branch of the Kerala Pulaya Maha Sabha (KPMS), the caste organisation of the Pulayas. All Pulayas are members of this organisation. The caste organisation generally helps out at funerals by paying Rs 1,000 (about $ 20) for ceremonial expenses. Previously, they had a fund for medical expenses. One of the informants received Rs 100 (about $ 2) from the fund when she was ill. This fund has now been discontinued due to a lack of funds. The KPMS also has a programme of giving a scholarship to one female and one male Pulaya student who secure the highest marks at school. While the organisation lacks funds, it has plenty of manpower so any kind of physical assistance can be mobilised, such as for example for a wedding or a funeral ceremony.

However, the KPMS in Kadamakuddy was not an organisation on which the elderly and the Pulayas in general could rely. One reason was the lack of strong leadership. There was no transparency with regard to the utilisation of funds. This gave the people the impression that the funds were being diverted for personal use. In 2002, there was a change of leadership in the KPMS. A highly respected senior man who had just retired from government service is now president of the organisation. He hopes to make the KPMS a beneficial organisation again, as the KPMS is supposed to work for the well being of the entire Pulaya "community".

Kadamakuddy is a village that is unique in the sense that it has a Day Care Centre (DCC) for its senior citizens. The centre is located in Kothad, a part of the village which is mostly inhabited by Christians.

In 1997, the DCC was established as a joint project of the people's organisation, Kothad Grama Vikasana Samiti, and the main funding bodies Rajagiri College of Social Science and the Community Aid and Sponsorship Programme (CASP).[13] The village government allotted the land for the building. Local people contributed with donations and with free labour. The DCC functions on the basis of donations from individuals and subsidies from the village government. The elderly meet there twice a week. They begin with prayers, read interesting new articles and play some games. They also get lunch. The DCC also has a Health Centre which is open one afternoon per week for all of the villagers. Consultations with a doctor and basic medicines are free. Most of the elderly Pulayas of the sample were not interested in joining the DCC, however. They found the concept of elderly people getting together to play games and sing songs strange, and it was also too great a distance for them to walk.

The village community of Kadamakuddy thus supports the elderly in their basic needs. Neighbours and friends provide material support and companionship, whereas the caste organisations and religious groups mainly provide health care. However, this assistance is episodic and cannot be sustained over a long period of time.

For the middle class elderly, the support from neighbours in the community is crucial, especially when they live without children. But in most other matters they did not need the support from the community. One last point that I would like to mention, related to community support, is the increasing awareness among the middle class elderly that they can form groups to help other elderly people in need. There is such a senior citizen organisation in the village next to Kadamakuddy. Some of the middle class elderly had formed a senior citizen

---

[13] In close cooperation with the people's organisation in Kothad, i.e. based on a participating model of development, the CASP-Rajagiri community development organisation has conducted several projects, e.g. with regard to education and sanitation, since 1992 (cf. Antoni 1996).

organisation called "Sauhridum" with the aim to give help to those elderly in their village who are poor and needy.[14]

Support from the State

Kerala has implemented several social security and assistance schemes. It is thus pertinent to examine the support that the Pulaya elderly receive from the state. The elderly in the village associated citizenship in the first place with being a Malayalee, a citizen of Kerala. Due to a generally high political awareness, the Pulayas take voting seriously, and in their opinion they are carrying out their duty as citizens by casting their vote. At the same time, they believe that corruption in the government is widespread and, furthermore, they think that whoever participates in the government tries to increase their own benefits, without much concern for the people. Worries are expressed about the strategy of opposition parties to bring down the ruling party to gain power for themselves. The common man would be the one to suffer in this process.

As already mentioned in the introductory chapter on Kerala, there are three major social assistance schemes that directly provide pensions to the poor elderly. They are the Kerala Agricultural Workers Pension Scheme, the Kerala Destitute and Widow Pension Scheme and Special Pension Scheme for the Physically Handicapped and Mentally Retarded (cf. Irudaya Rajan 1999). The Kerala Agricultural Workers Pension Scheme is a good example to illustrate that the active role of the people in demanding welfare, also with regard to old age, has been fruitful. The agricultural workers in Kerala have been in the forefront of the trade union movement since the 1920s. Their demand for social security dates back to 1960 (Gulati 1990). After many years of agitation, the pension for the agricultural labourers came into effect in 1980. It is statistically estimated that 345,000 people bene-

---

[14] At the national level there is a senior citizen movement that tries to act as a pressure group in order to get some benefits from the government, but the movement is still in its infancy.

fited from this pension in 1993, of which 58 percent were women (Irudaya Rajan et al. 1999).

As already mentioned, many elderly Pulayas in Kadamakuddy receive a "pension" of Rs 110 (about $ 2) per month. This type of social assistance is paid once every three months by money order. The old-age pension schemes occupy an important place in the governmental social security provisioning in Kerala. It is estimated that in 1991 its coverage was around sixty percent of the aged poor in Kerala (Kanan and Francis 2001: 423). According to the Kadamakuddy village records,[15] there were 351 elderly getting the agricultural workers pension, 90 elderly receiving the disabled and handicapped pension, 84 elderly women getting the widows pension and 61 elderly getting an old age pension[16]. The public distribution system (PDS) is another important social security programme in Kerala. It covers 92 percent of the population (Kanan and Francis 2001: 432). The availability of food from the PDS has been a major factor in providing nutrition to the poor and the elderly.

However, if we assess the adequacy of the social security schemes provided for the elderly in Kerala, then serious doubts in terms of its sufficiency can be raised. To what extent can the pensions meet, for example, basic food needs and other requirements? The underlying assumption of this type of governmental social assistance is that care of the elderly is the responsibility of the family, mainly the children. What the pension is supposed to do is reduce the burden on the family, thus making the elderly more acceptable.[17] One of the elderly Pulaya women said in this regard: "In former times there also were wants but the government was indifferent to the needs [of the elderly] and did not consider giving them any help."

---

[15] Unpublished records of the Kadamakuddy village government, noted in September 2002.

[16] This is a pension scheme introduced by the central government under the National Social Assistance Scheme in 1995.

[17] Cf. Gulati 1990, Gulati and Gulati 1995. In a study conducted by P.K.B. Nair, 97 percent of the people who received "agricultural workers pension" stated that it did increase their acceptability (Nair 1987, quoted in Gulati 1990).

The elderly Pulayas in my study are grateful for the pension they received because it gives them some source of income in their old age. It must be added, however, that the bureaucracy encountered in processing the application form made it a tedious and difficult procedure for the elderly to obtain assistance. In one case, the elderly woman who applied for the pension was refused because she had a son who earned an income. Fortunately for her, she had done some work for the civil servant in the village office so with her help she got the pension the second time she made the application.

Since most of the Pulayas are literate they read the newspapers, listen to the radio and discuss politics, making them well aware of the fact that the state of Kerala has a funding problem. They hope that the government will increase the pension, but they know it is not possible.

They also express a desire for the health care facilities to be improved. The nearest medical help is the governmental Primary Health Centre (PHC) in the neighbouring village which is accessible only by boat. The drawbacks are that it is open only for a few hours in the daytime, medicines required are often unavailable and facilities for conducting tests are lacking. Furthermore, there are no beds so for any illness that requires hospitalisation the patients have to go to the government hospital which is in the town. The distance to the hospital becomes a problem not only for the elderly who are ill, but also for their caretakers.

Gender and Old Age

In Kerala, life expectancy at birth and life expectancy at the age of sixty both indicate that women live longer than men (CSO 2000: 35). On average men marry younger women which means that in most cases elderly men will typically have a wife who is capable of caring for him into his old age. On the other hand, the large majority of women will remain widows in old age, without the companionship and support of a husband.

The impact of old age on women is also different from that on men because they hold another status and role in Indian society. The gendered roles established earlier in life have their impact on life in old age. It discourages females from assertive social engagement outside the private domain of the house and any related interaction. There is a general attitude that women must be protected and therefore restrictions are imposed on them for their own benefit (Bali 1997). The elderly respondents in my study have also internalised this attitude and they do not go out alone, unless related to work. This attitude has an impact on the support network of elderly women, as it becomes limited to the family, the immediate neighbourhood and the employer.

Moreover, elderly women do not have any authority in the family. It is usually the male member who makes most of the decisions. One of the elderly women, Thangamma (example 4), had been keen to join the DCC but her nephew, who is supporting her, was not in favour of and thus prevented her from going. In Kadamakuddy, elderly men live mostly idle lives, but the elderly women are expected to contribute to the household duties. Most of the elderly Pulaya women continue to be involved in preparing food, washing clothes, cleaning and sweeping, caring for children and to some extent collecting water and firewood.

Chadha, Aggarwal and Mangala (1990) show that the social network is larger for those aged whose spouses are still alive. I found this to be particularly true in connection with the elderly women in my study. They would not attend social functions unless accompanied by their husband or their children. For these women, widowhood meant not only an emotional loss but also a curtailing of their opportunities for social interaction.

The biggest difference between rural and urban Kerala is the situation of the widows. In urban Kerala the poorest widows live in critical insecurity, i.e. their basic needs for food are not provided for (see de Jong in this volume). Other studies have also shown that widowhood is accompanied by neglect (e.g. Marulisiddiah 1966, Sahayam 1988). However, my study does not confirm this. The reason could be that all the elderly women of the working class have some financial resources of their own. As they are working, they were able to contribute their earnings to the construction of the house they were living in. In their

old age, they received pensions, which allowed these women to contribute to the household expenses. In some cases, especially when they
were widowed, the house and the land was in the name of the elderly
female. Those who had the capability also contributed to the household tasks. All this ensures that elderly women are not marginalised in
the family. I would like to mention the examples of Tara and Kunni
(example 6 and 7) to exemplify this point. They were both widowed at
a young age and managed their lives and the lives of their children
with their own resources and with help from kin. In their old age their
children are looking after them.

Example 6: The Widow Tara and her Fear of Being a Burden

Tara (83), born in 1918, was one of the oldest women I interviewed. She attended
school until the fourth class. She worked most of her life as an agricultural and manual labourer. Due to failing health and weak eyesight she has not earned money for
the past ten years. She married at the age of seventeen but her husband died within a
year so she came back to Kadamakuddy, her natal village. She did not have any
children from that marriage. At the age of 27 she married again and had five children, four boys and one girl. The eldest daughter is now fifty-four and the youngest
son is forty-two. Her second husband died twenty years after marriage. Once again
she returned to Kadamakuddy and lived there with her parents. After a few years,
she built her own house with the help of her elder and younger sister. By then her
eldest son also earned an income and was able to contribute to the household. Her
elder sister's husband, a carpenter, helped her with the construction of her house.
Her sorrow in life is that two of her sons died, one in childhood and the other five
years ago, and that her daughter became a widow at a very young age. At present
she lives with her youngest son, who is a daily wage labourer, the daughter-in-law
and the grandchildren. Age has bent her back and she walks with great difficulty.
She suffers from high blood pressure, which makes her feel dizzy if she stands for
too long. She had cataracts in both eyes, which she had operated in an eye camp in
1996. For the five days she was in hospital her daughter-in-law cared for her. She
can see now but her sight is slightly hazy and she has to use some medicinal eye
drops every day. Since this medicine is expensive, she often manages without it
because they cannot afford to buy it regularly. She receives an agricultural workers
pension, which she contributes to the household income. She feels bad that she cannot manage on her own and is dependent for many things on her daughter-in-law
and son. She still tries to do as much as she can on her own because she does not
want to be considered a burden.

Although the widow Tara is well cared for by her youngest son and his wife, she does not really feel secure, probably because her son's economic situation is delicate, in contrast to the widow Kunni in the next example.

Example 7: The Widow Kunni and her Secured Old Age

Kunni (80), born in 1922, went to school for four years. She started working at about the age of fourteen. She mostly worked as an agricultural labourer and stopped working only ten years ago when she lost her eyesight. She married at the age of twenty-four. She has three sons and two daughters. All her children have formal educations. Her husband died in 1977 and she had the responsibility for the marriage of her youngest daughter. She got together some money, rice and coconut from her former employer and the rest she managed with help from her sons and a brother. She has her own house that was built just before her husband died. At present her youngest son, daughter-in-law and grandchildren live with her. This son works as a stonecutter and earns Rs 225 to Rs 250 a day (about $ 4.5 to 5). Her first son works in a shipyard, and as it is a governmental enterprise she gets concessions for hospital treatment. A few years ago, she suffered from high blood pressure and was hospitalised for some time. Her second son paid for the treatment. Back home, her daughter-in-law looked after her and made sure that she took her medicines and that her food was not salty or oily. Today, she also takes some Ayurvedic medicine. She is totally blind and thus completely dependent on her daughter-in-law. She says that she is lucky to have such a wonderful person around her. She cannot go out on her own, so she mostly stays indoors listening to the radio that her second son bought for her. Her daughters live in town so she does not expect any support from them.

The examples of Tara and Kunni show that although they are old and widowed, their near kin does not neglect them. This is because they can bargain for care on the basis of former and actual assets. In certain respects however, their needs are not fulfilled: for Tara her need for medicine and for Kunni companionship. Another gender aspect related to ageing is the issue of care giving. Women are considered as the principal caregivers in the family. They are expected to meet the simultaneous demands of children, spouse and ageing parents. It is shown that if women work outside the home, these care relations are adversely effected (Panda 1998, Kumar 2000). If women are limited to acting as caregivers, the consequence is that they will lack the financial resources, which they could use as a bargaining tool for support. Without such resources these women could face neglect in their old age.

Conclusions

The crucial factors for social security for the elderly Pulayas relate to the issues of who will care for them in their old age, who will be able to meet their daily requirements for food and medicines, and will they be healthy enough to perform their daily activities independently. They fear being considered a burden. For the working class elderly Pulayas, support from the children is vital. The fact that their children do not migrate for work is an advantage for the elderly. They hope that their children will provide most of their material needs in terms of food and medicines and any physical support. However, it must be realised that caring for ageing parents does not merely depend on bonds of affection, but is also influenced by financial constraints such as low wages, unemployment, inflation, education of their children, and other competing interests.

The elderly try to manage the relationships with their children well. Particularly noticeable is that the elderly themselves opine that the older generation is much less authoritarian now than before. The elderly take care not to antagonise the younger generation because they understand that if this happens, it can lead to unpleasantness and tensions in the family. There is a change in the intergenerational power relations with the old being more acquiescing to the young.

In certain respects old age support is gendered. For example, within the extended family household the idea of support-giving is gendered in that it is considered as the sole duty of the female to give physical support, and the male is considered the sole financial supporter. Even if the wife formerly worked and contributed financially to the household income, care giving in a narrow sense is her sole responsibility. In practice, for the majority of the elderly, the son is most important for financial support and the daughter-in-law for physical support. There are some examples, however, of daughters living with their parents and providing physical support. In these cases, the son-in-law looks after the financial and material needs of the daughter's parents. Elderly males also get emotional and physical support from their wives, whereas elderly females can rely less on such care from their husbands.

Within the wider kin group, the elderly exchange monetary support with male siblings on a reciprocal base. In certain cases daughters may also contribute with money. The elderly further rely on support from non-kin such as neighbours, friends and past employers. Help from these sources is irregular and only short-term, however.

As long as the elderly women have some economic asset or their labour power as a resource for bargaining, they do not face neglect. Compared to the women, the men are in a better position because they have better access to work than women and they earn higher wages for the same type of work. This gives them more economic independence. But if the men are no longer earning and only receiving a pension, then there are no income differences as the pension amount is the same for men and women. Moreover, due to cultural notions elderly men have more authority and decision-making power in the household than women, and the latter have limited access to the wider society. Therefore, in times of need women can only turn for help to their immediate surroundings, thus putting them at a disadvantage as compared with the men.

This case study also shows that the children, although they are an important element of social security in old age, are not the sole agents. The elderly Pulayas practice what Willemijn de Jong (in this volume) calls a "patchwork arrangement" of social security; they do not lean on any kind of family, such as the extended family, but on the "extended neighbourhood". The children are able to provide care and support to the elderly parents only in conjunction with various other agencies. Along with the children, the welfare provisions made by the state of Kerala, the role of social welfare organisations, the assistance given by the former employers, the role of wider kin, neighbours and friends represent the spectrum that when put together shows the extent of the social security network of the working class elderly. Based on this study, I would say that the working class elderly of Kadamakuddy have social security, but a limited one – it rests on a fine line. While no one suffers from hunger as might happen in town, a break down in any aspect of their network can jeopardise their social security.

Burkina Faso: A Donor Darling?
Context of the Case Studies

Claudia Roth

Burkina Faso is one of the poorest countries in the world (cf. appendix). The structure of the economy in Burkina Faso has barely changed since achieving independence in 1960 (Lachaud 1994): Approximately ninety percent of the country's estimated thirteen million inhabitants, including a part of the city dwellers, still live from subsistence farming. Due to irregular rainfall and the exhausted soil farmers in the dry northern part of the country, such as in the village of Kuila (rural case study), work under the most arduous conditions in order to meet their own needs. The farmers in the fertile and water-rich southwest, where Bobo-Dioulasso is located (urban case study), on the other hand, are able to produce also for the national and even the international markets. Cotton is the most important export product for Burkina Faso, followed by cattle and gold. Industry, with its total 15,000 employees, remains in the embryonic stage and is limited to producing a small range of consumer goods (Lejeal 2002). Women are affected by poverty more so than men, and rural dwellers are disadvantaged compared with the city dwellers (Kinda 1998, Nioumou et al. 1997).[1]

For the French colonial power the ancient Upper Volta was a labour reserve with the consequence that their developmental efforts were not focussed on the country itself, which is arid and poor in natural resources. Also after the abolition of forced labour[2] in 1946, migration to the Ivory Coast and to Ghana continued. Till the civil war in

---

[1] Progressive impoverishment is a result of the oil crisis (1970s), debt crisis (1980s), Structural Adjustment Programmes (1990s), FCFA-devaluation in 1994 as well as the general tendency towards economic globalisation and its consequence: Africa takes part in the world market with symbolic 2 % (Rogerson 1997) and 46.4 % of the Burkinabe live below the poverty level of 82,672 FCFA per year (about € 130) (cf. Nioumou et al. 1997, Somda/Sawadogo 2001).
[2] Public works, plantation work, road and railway construction in the Ivory Coast and the Gold Coast.

the Ivory Coast in 2000 approximately two to three million Burkinabe lived there (Hagberg 2001: 17-18). Furthermore, there is a developed internal migration from the dry north to the fertile southwest as well as from the countryside to the cities.

Since its political independence, Burkina Faso has had a long tradition of strong civil society organisations, above all trade unions and organised student groups, and political struggles. These organisations, their members belong to a small and highly educated elite, continue to be an influential force in all important political events. The charismatic Thomas Sankara, president from 1983 till his assassination in 1987, with his revolutionary programme of self-reliance and anti-corruption represented a new Africa: "politically radical and morally good" (ibid. 19). Since the beginning of the 1990s, parallel to the imposed Structural Adjustment Programmes, a process of democratisation has been underway, however, to the exclusion of the poor who cannot write or understand the French officiallese (ibid. 18-21).[3]

Over sixty ethnic groups, speaking an equivalent number of languages, live together. The Moose in the north, the region of the capital of Ouagadougou, represent the majority with over forty percent of the population. In pre-colonial times, a large part of Burkina Faso was under the control of various Moose kingdoms (ibid. 15). The Moose distinguish themselves by their strong hierarchical organisation, in contrast to the many small societies in the western and south-western parts of the country (region surrounding Bobo-Dioulasso), which in their majority are decentralised in their organisation. Accordingly, the gender relationships also differ in the respective societies.

In 1995 twenty-five percent of Burkina Faso's population lived in cities with 5,000 or more inhabitants (IRD 2000: 2). Throughout the country, only few benefit from the statutory welfare system: In 1996, 3.5 percent of the population was employed in the formal sector, which is mostly concentrated in the cities (Kinda 1998). For example, in Bobo-Dioulasso the formal sector comprises 25 percent of the working population (IRD 2000: 29). Old age pensions are insured

---

[3] In Kerala the poor can take part in the political process due to their access to basic education (see "Kerala as a Model?" in this volume).

through the Caisse Nationale de Sécurité Sociale (CNSS) and the Caisse Autonome de Retraite des Fonctionnaires (CARFO).[4] Every three months the beneficiaries receive twenty percent of their average salary over the last five years. This means that even the living standard of those working in the formal sector declines drastically following retirement, in case they have not prepared for their old age otherwise.

For all other Burkinabe, the social security provisions are comprised of activities of the Action Sociale, the social welfare office. For example in Bobo-Dioulasso, just under 0.5 percent of the municipal budget was reserved for social programmes in 2000.[5] Employees of the social welfare office advise, inform, sensitise, mediate and support women, young mothers, street children, orphans, handicapped, the elderly, and also associations, but they do not dispose of any financial means. In the countryside such as the village of Kuila, the social welfare office is inexistent. The rural population has to address themselves to the next nearest municipality; the dwellers of Kuila therefore go to Ziniaré.

In Burkina Faso numerous international donors are active. In addition to UN organisations, the World Bank, the IMF, the European Union as multilateral donors, there are also many states as bilateral donors and about 150 NGOs (Hagberg 2001: 21). Burkina Faso – a donor darling? In Bobo-Dioulasso only a few of the many NGOs and religious associations very selectively engage in welfare tasks, without being specifically focussed on the needs of the elderly. And the example of the village of Kuila makes evident that development aid creates expectations, but ultimately however, the aid does not reach the poorest and therefore also not the elderly.

About ten locally and nationally organised associations are committed to the interests of the elderly (Besana 2001: 27). The basic problem with these associations is that they were founded by retired

---

[4] National Office of Social Security and Autonomous Office of Civil Servant Pensions.
[5] 0.5 percent of the 2000 budget: FCFA 8,800,000 (about € 13,400). Interview in 2002 with Drahman Ouattara, Director of Administration and Finances of the Municipality of Bobo-Dioulasso.

civil servants and therefore tend to be geared to their own old-age needs (cf. also Ministère de l'Action Sociale 2001: 18). To sum up, there is no effective support for the elderly provided by either the State or society.[6] As consequence, family and kinship are also today crucial for the social security of the elderly, both in the countryside and in the cities of Burkina Faso. To what extent the "extended family" really cares for its old men and women will be illustrated in the two following cases studies.

---

[6] Cf. also survey review in Besana (2001).

Threatening Dependency:
Limits of Social Security, Old Age and Gender in Urban Burkina Faso

Claudia Roth

In Bobo-Dioulasso it is widely believed that the "extended family" cares for the social security needs of its members. The myth of "African solidarity" (Vidal 1994) conceals the fact that many women and men age in a state of constant insecurity and that many run the risk of living out their old age in great poverty, often not knowing whether there will be anything to eat the next day. Such poverty also means not being able to fulfil any "socially admired actions" (Hagberg 2001: 59), and it implies becoming dependent on others resulting in social marginalisation and loneliness.

As stated above, Burkina Faso is not a welfare state. Therefore, kin and other social relations actually do play a crucial role in elderly people's lives. Research in Bobo-Dioulasso, however, has shown that the number of social relationships a person has is proportional to the amount of material resources available to them. Solidarity is based on reciprocity, and reciprocity requires financial means. The fewer resources a person has, the smaller their social network inside and outside kinship, and the more limited that person's social security. This social phenomenon also impacts the elderly. The poor cannot save sufficiently during their working lifetimes to ensure their old-age security. Therefore, the question is: How do men and women build up relationships with people that will feel responsible and thus care for them in the last phase of their lives?

The local social security in Bobo-Dioulasso is based on a highly complex network of social security relationships comprised of relatives, neighbours, friends, work colleagues, patrons, religious fellows and members of associations of all kinds. Social security results from the "structural redundancy", as Elwert (1980) defines the overlapping of the various security relationships: "At times the same people are linked among one another through differing connections, and at other times the same kind of support can be expected from different people due to different relationships" (ibid. 689, free translation).

In this chapter, I will begin by illustrating the limits of the social security arrangement of the poor elderly. This leads to the question of what constitutes the core of social security in old age. Our study shows that living in security means preserving one's independence even in old age. This includes having an income, being married and having children that are obliged to care for their parents. Ageing is a process in which men and women as actors are constantly engaged in trying to influence the present situation to their advantage. The various options available to elderly men and women to avoid threatening dependency in their old age will be discussed further on.

The Research Site

Bobo-Dioulasso, with its approximately 400,000 inhabitants, is the second largest city in Burkina Faso. Ethnic diversity has been an important aspect in this area for centuries; about twenty-five different ethnic groups live there together.[1] Due to the draught in the north many Moose, as well as other ethnic groups from the southwest, have moved to the city in search of work.[2]

Thanks to its advantageous geographical location, Bobo-Dioulasso was once a pivotal point for long distance trade and the centre of Islamic belief. Under the French colonial power, as the industrial centre, Bobo-Dioulasso became the "economic capital" of the country and thus a prosperous city. The slow but continuing economic decline began in the 1960s. Today approximately fifty percent of the local wealth is generated in the informal sector, including agriculture, which employs over seventy percent of the population (IRD 2000: 3-7). Furthermore, the Structural Adjustment Programmes of the 1990s

---

[1] Altogether I spoke to members of twenty-one ethnic groups, of which the Dafing, Zara, Bobo (all three Mande societies or influenced by the Mande culture), Senufo and Moose make up the main groups.
[2] In 1990 22 % of the "heads of family" were born in Bobo-Dioulasso, all others inmigrated (Ministère de l'Equipement 1990: 37-38).

led to dismissals and company closures. The result is that today many young people are unemployed.

Koko, with its 10,000 inhabitants, is a small neighbourhood and, following a 1929 French survey, determined to be one of the oldest neighbourhoods in the centre of Bobo-Dioulasso. From the beginning, both the social and political life of the neighbourhood was shaped by two locally important lineages: the Dagaso and the Kassamba Djabi. Today, the Kassamba Djabi is one of the three large Marabout families of the city, and they own three of the five mosques in Koko. They define religious life and the religious community in the neighbourhood. Families belonging to the Zara, Bobo, Dyula, Peul, Dafing, Senufo, Moose, Gurunsi and other groups have lived for generations in Koko and own family compounds; relatives who in-migrated between the 1940s and 1960s established residence there.

Koko has a relatively unvarying social structure. The family-owned compounds have hardly changed hands and remain in large part collective property, occupied by progeny and tenants. Everyone knows each other. Economically Koko is a modest neighbourhood. Many of those earning wages move away to other neighbourhoods or cities. Those remaining are generally old men and women with their unemployed children and their grandchildren, in other words people with a limited income or no income at all. Therefore, two opposing forces are at work in Koko. On the one hand, kinship, neighbour and religious relationships overlap and strengthen each other: the "generational depth" – a characteristic of the social relationships in old neighbourhoods (Vuarin 2000: 187) – slows down the marginalisation process which was set in motion by impoverishment. On the other hand, the youth with earning potential further it by leaving the neighbourhood.

In Koko I was able to interview a good five percent of the elderly belonging to the middle and lower socio-economic classes on the topics of ageing and social security.[3] The twelve middle-class men and

---

[3] Thirty-six people correspond to approximately five percent: According to a census in 1996, 9098 people lived in Koko, 669 men and women were 55 and older (Données de base de INSD/RGPH 1998). Between 2000 and 2002 I conducted over one hundred qualitative research interviews, with among others 52 old and 24 young men and women of the town, of which thirty-six old and twelve young people were

women were once well-earning civil servants with old-age pensions or were successfully self-employed. In contrast, two thirds of the twenty-four poor elderly with whom I spoke are living precariously or socially marginalised. Among other things, this means many were not certain they would be eating the next day. These people did not always live this way, however. They belong to the generation that were young in 1940s, 1950s or 1960s. Politically, this was a time of hope due to the independence of Upper Volta in 1960. Economically it was a prosperous time of growth with an increase in employment and earning potential in the city. Two thirds of those I interviewed migrated at that time from nearby villages to Bobo. Socially it was a time of transition. The extended families that still lived in collective communities in Koko began to split up into individual households. The monetarisation and the modernisation slowly began to change the social structure (Marie 1997). Up until that time more than half of marriages were arranged by the family elders, and about half were polygamous. Women had up to twelve children, but only half survived to adulthood. The men worked as ironers, moped mechanics, bricklayers, farmers, muezzins or drivers; the women as petty traders, clothes washers, soap producers, cotton spinners, farmers or hairdressers. With their incomes they were able to feed their children and send them to school. They were also able to participate in ceremonies and cultivate relationships. In short, they were able to maintain their position in society. However, they were not able to save money, buy land or build a compound – for this they did not earn sufficiently. They were poor, but they did not live precariously. They were counting on the fact that their children would care for them in their old age. The reality turned out otherwise. Today, many of these men and women feel bound to care for their adult children and their grandchildren,

---

living in Koko, as well as repeated focus group interviews with old and young men and women. The numerous conversations with key people in the neighbourhood and the city, with local experts of the older generation in Koko, spontaneous conversations and participant observation allowed me to put the research interviews in their proper context. The fact that I am familiar with Koko due to my fifteen-year connection to the neighbourhood simplified this work for me (cf. among others Roth 1996).

even though they themselves do not know where their next meal is coming from.

Diversified Social Security and Its Limits

The basic model of solidarity is generalized reciprocity, which is anchored in the ancient societal order. This normative model also influences behaviour in urban conditions. Elwert (1980: 684), in accordance with Polyani and Sahlins, defines generalized reciprocity as "a gift which is not directly repaid, but one which a person in similar circumstances can receive in the same way" (free translation). Contrary to balanced reciprocity[4], where an equitable exchange is expected within a specific time period, in generalized reciprocity the expectation of a return in kind is undefined. There exists a subtle obligation to return the favour when the giver needs it (Sahlins 2004 [1965]: 193-195). This understanding becomes evident in the comments made by many of the elderly men and women, as in the example of Ami T. (example 2).

Looking at the continuum developed by Sahlins covering the various forms of reciprocity[5], besides generalised reciprocity a development toward balanced reciprocity is becoming apparent in the urban conditions of Bobo-Dioulasso. In fact, equivalents are not exchanged but the magnitude of the gift should be largely commensurate. In practice the time horizon is given by the necessity of keeping up relations without interruptions so as not to lose the social security embodied therein. Thus, for example, at ceremonies where generalised reciprocity is the norm, it is more often carefully noted who gave what, resulting in poor relatives being excluded from future ceremonies or being fed worse than their wealthier relatives.

The gift creates the debt which circulates and on which protection relationships, not only those with relatives, are based. "Protection re-

---

[4] "Perfectly balanced reciprocity" means the simultaneous exchange of equivalents (Sahlins 2004 [1965]: 194).
[5] Continuum between generalised – balanced – negative reciprocity (cf. Sahlins 2004 [1965]).

lationships are overall no more than the activation of this debt"
(Vuarin 2000: 38, free translation). Giving is in everyone's interest
because one day every gift will be repaid. One's own debts are recog-
nized as a result of the honour code which appeals to solidarity, generosity and respect for the other's request for repayment. "For both the
solicitor and the solicited the honour code is therefore the normative
benchmark for assistance proceedings (between a superior and a subordinate) and mutual aid (between statutory equals), whether its expression is positive, fulfilment of the duty, or negative, the shame, a
sanction due to a breach of this obligation" (ibid. 149).[6]

The social security relations at the level of kinship and community
are numerous. In Vuarin's (ibid.) terminology they range from the
"civil pole" (relatives, neighbours, friendships, work colleagues, patrons, religious communities, associations) to the "economic pole"
(including savings groups, private insurances) to the "religious pole"
(alms). The social security arrangements of the middle class and the
poor are equally diversified. What distinguishes them, however, is the
number of different security relationships which are determined by the
existing resources. Whereas the middle class can simultaneously accumulate economic and social capital due to the acceleration of the
reciprocal conversion, the poor simultaneously lose it for the same
reason, and the men and women become further impoverished (Vuarin
1994: 269). The structural redundancy of their social security arrangement decreases. The consequences of social stratification on the
social security arrangement of the elderly poor will be discussed further on. Below, I will elucidate firstly on the diversified social security
independent of age in order to demonstrate the situation of elderly
men and women on this basis.

Conditional Kin Relations

It is certain that kin relations are the foundation of social security.
Whoever cannot count on relatives cannot count on anyone else ac-

---

[6] For a detailed analysis of the complex of honour, duty and shame cf. Vuarin
(2000).

cording to the research in Bobo-Dioulasso. However, it is not accurate to say that relatives are the symbol of African solidarity and automatically care for their elderly, poor and sick (cf. also Apt 1996). Therefore, the question is: What relationships determine who takes care of whom? Kin relationships must be differentiated between one's own relatives and that of the in-laws, between relatives on the father's side or on the mother's side, whether as a result of polygamy siblings are of the same father *(fadenya)* or the same mother *(badenya),* and the parent-child relationship and the marriage relationship must also be considered. Each of these relationships is characterised by different rights and duties as well as by differing norms and values, which results in different degrees of social security.[7] Furthermore, it is important to discern whether kin is to be considered as a group or as individual members.

Kin as a group is present when a "problem" *(kunko)* arises. Further inquiry into the meaning of "problem" showed that it was a reference to ceremonies, i.e. funerals, but also to weddings and baptisms. Of these, burials are the most important ceremonies; "only kin can bury a corpse," which means the presence of relatives at funerals is unalterable. Social stratification plays the least significant role at funerals, whereas at baptisms and weddings of the poor, fewer wealthy relatives participate and fewer poor are invited to these occasions by rich relatives. The transformation in the direction of balanced reciprocity is elucidated by distancing mechanisms.

In the case of a "personal problem" *(i yere ta kunko),* one can count on specific, individually created relationships ranging from relatives to persons outside the family circle. Membership in a collective of kin[8] is socially determined by the line of descent and associated to specific relations and values. Kinship as a collective, therefore, creates a specific general framework. However, it is dependant on the individuals and their investments, their efforts, their manner and, above

---

[7] For an analysis of the *badenya* as a central element of an individual's social security arrangement and the "badenyanisation" of relationships as a means to procure social security cf. Roth (2003b).
[8] In a patrilineal society affiliation with a specific lineage is determined through the paternal line.

all, their material situation how kin relationships will develop in practice. It all depends on how the individual will realise the reciprocity, which is the foundation of social life and one's own social security. Though kin does not lose importance, as it remains the reference point, it is realised individually and not collectively and automatically.

Relationships with neighbours have many similarities with kin relations. Many of those interviewed commented that in the city neighbours are more important than relatives because they are the first ones on hand in case of a misfortune such as a funeral. Reciprocal help plays a particularly important role at ceremonies. Whoever participates in ceremonies is integrated into the neighbourhood. The neighbours, like the relatives, are rarely asked for help because it is shaming. In addition, individual relationships within the neighbourhood are as fundamental as within kinship.

Close friendships are one of the few relationships where no shame is to be feared.[9] A man or woman's intimate friend is also called *gundonyogonfokela*, referring to a person with whom one can exchange secrets, talk about one's own desperate situation and also ask for help. The poorest in the sample have no friendships. "Without money you can't cultivate friendships," says one old woman.

That which Sahlins (2004 [1965]: 193-194) refers to as the "extreme solidarity" of generalised reciprocity is tied to great social closeness which connects poor elderly men and women in Koko with their children and their spouses. These are the sole two kin relationships that impart a claim to regular support in old age.

Consequences of Social Stratification in Old Age

Often I heard from old men and women that they had no relatives, at least no relevant ones. "When you are poor you cannot count on relatives," says one poor elderly man in the focus group. But even they attend relatives' funerals, however reluctantly since they are treated as unworthy, receive no greeting and are hardly fed. In the course of so-

---

[9] Vuarin (1993: 309-310) analysed the intimacy axis which goes from neighbour *(siginyogon)* to confidant *(lemineyasira)* to persons of hope *(jigi)* to friend *(teri)*.

cial development, monetarisation contributed to the apparition of so-cial stratification and with it to a change in the extended family[10]. Conversations with local experts[11] about their childhood and youth allow us to comprehend this process: Till the 1950s in Koko the mem-bers of a family lived in the classical form under the aegis of the old-est family member who administered the earnings of his sons. One was a civil servant, the other a farmer and all ate from the same bowl. Accentuating differences was frowned upon. In the 1960s differences in earnings manifested themselves, however, and those that earned more money no longer wanted to limit themselves for the benefit of the extended family. As a consequence, individual households multi-plied within the extended families. "It was said at that time that you had to leave the family in order to become somebody, otherwise you would get nowhere," explains a 63-year old man of the middle class. Due to the separation of the extended family into individual house-holds, today it is not unusual for individuals with highly differing in-comes and earning potential to live close together without a redistri-bution of money or goods.

The research in Koko shows the following dynamic: The more a person has the possibility to live financially independent, the higher their tendency to abandon the cycle of generalised reciprocity by nar-rowing the definition of who is worthy of support. Subtle distancing mechanisms are adopted, e.g. the person asked for assistance regret-fully says: "If only you had come yesterday, I would have been able to help you!" – and the one asking for help must realise full of shame

---

[10] In patrilinear and patrilocal organised societies the extended family is comprised of brothers and their spouses as well as married sons and daughters-in-law, unmar-ried sons, daughters, grandchildren and under some circumstances a nephew, a niece or the widowed older sister who returned to the family compound. If the living and economic conditions permit, they live together patrilocally in the family compound, often, however, spread out throughout the city in smaller groups, without therefore becoming nuclear families of the western type (cf. Le Bris et al. 1987, Vuarin 2000: 74–75).

[11] We define local experts as people who as a result of their activities as Griots, Marabouts, activists in women's organisations or in the neighbourhood and their social engagement and interests reflexively deal with the social and historical condi-tions in Koko. We had repeated conversations with five men and women of both socio-economic classes.

that no more help can be expected.[12] Additionally, those who want to curb the reciprocity cycle represent increasingly modern values oriented to the "autonomous subject" such as for instance individual success or the prospective logic of concern for the future of offspring (cf. Marie 1997b). Stahl (2001: 200) also ascertained that the well-to-do members within a kin group often withdraw from the system of generalised reciprocity ("traditional solidarity"). On the opposite side are people who, due to their economic situation, find it increasingly difficult to keep up with the cycle of reciprocity. These people's social connections decrease until their total disappearance. Increasing financial means therefore allow the withdrawal from the cycle of reciprocity, while shrinking financial means lead to exclusion.

The stratum of the poor can be differentiated between those that are poor, those that live precariously and those that live socially marginalised. The poor elderly still have access to economic, social or symbolic capital such as knowledge of indigenous healing plants or the Koran and can therefore keep up kin and other relationships. Whereas the elderly living precariously do not know where their next meal is coming from, their contributions to ceremonies are not assured and their social network is small. Many of them say they have "no relatives", and they see themselves as poor. Their poverty is revealed in the words of Hagberg (2001: 59) "by inferior social performance; the poor person is lonely and without family. Adding to the lack of capacity to work the poor person is perceived as someone unable to perform socially admired actions." The third segment of the elderly poor are the socially marginalised who in turn live outside the system of reciprocity and survive from begging.

On an individual level, ageing is a phase of impoverishment (decreasing strength, decreasing income) and threatening social ruptures such as widowhood, unemployed or deceased children, as well as personal traumas like chronic old-age illnesses. Every economic crisis on the global level that brings with it impoverishment reduces the economic independence of the household and the individual. This compels the elderly to decide between their vital livelihood and the main-

---

[12] Cf. also a pertinent statement in Hagberg (2001: 57).

tenance of their social relationships. Sacrificing these relationships leads to a weakening of one's social affiliations, the right to collective support and accelerates the process of impoverishment and social isolation (Vuarin 2000: 191). The number of those living precariously and socially marginalised appears to increase dramatically with age. Of the twenty-four poor elderly we interviewed, two-thirds lived precariously or socially marginalised.[13]

New Forms of Solidarity I: Associations

In Bobo-Dioulasso there are 400 associations of all types (cf. IRD 2000: 62). In Koko itself the ethnic associations are currently of most importance to the elderly. The informal get-togethers of believers at the mosque, of old men at tea and old women in their reciprocal house visits make up an integral part of social life in the neighbourhood. Members of the ethnic associations are immigrants from villages. The associations serve in the first place to guarantee a proper funeral, still viewed as the most important event even for the poor. In the case of a death, all members contribute an agreed-upon amount.

Like the young men who meet daily for tea, the old men also gather for their tea round. Examples of these men's gatherings are the two groups of old and young men with whom we conducted focus group conversations. In the first one, the men grew old together. Even those who moved away return to these daily get-togethers in Koko. They talk about the world, visit sick friends, participate in ceremonies and help each other make useful connections with people. In a one-on-one interview, one man assured me that in an emergency it is possible to get help within this group, such as in the case of illness, but it is taboo to talk about food problems.

In the 1970s and 1980s there were many women's associations in Koko, and in the early 1990s I myself experienced the numerous women's savings groups, "tontine". Today, there are no savings groups left. I asked a local woman expert why this is the case: "It is

---

[13] Text examples: "poor" – examples 2, 6; "precarious" – examples 3, 4, 5; "socially marginalised" – example 1.

the weariness. Today, people have no money and therefore many don't join in. In the morning you have 200 Francs[14] (about € 0.3) and have to buy millet porridge for the children. But even without the association you still go to baptisms and funerals. We pool the money together, everyone gives 50 Francs (about € 0.07), for example, or whatever is possible. (...) The 'tontine' still exist on the compound. Before they were organised in the neighbourhoods, but no longer because too many women vanished once they received their portion of the money. This is not possible in a compound." The poor old women do not have the money to participate in these savings groups.

New Forms of Solidarity II: Charity

Koko is an Islamic neighbourhood and, as stated earlier, from the beginning was dominated by the powerful Marabout family of the Kassamba Djabi lineage. Islamic institutions offer, contrary to the state, a certain security for people in need (de Bruijn and van Dijck 1994). Begging is not bound to a personalised network which needs to be kept up daily through sociability and money, but rather to unknown believers who give alms and expect nothing in return since the gift of charity already carries with it God's blessing. It is about unilateral, anonymous relations (Vuarin 2000: 150). From the statements made by the elderly it becomes clear that they view faith as a reciprocal relationship: faith as a gift to God who in turn sends a helper in times of need as a countergift.

Barely any of those interviewed gives the *zakat* – a yearly tax on accrued income – to the needy. Whereas many in the middle class and some of the poor give the *zakat-el-fitr* – a per capita pre-determined quantity of grain – at the end of Ramadan to selected poor individuals whom they know, mostly elderly relatives or neighbours. Depending on the size of the family, this can be up to one or two sacks of millet.

Many people make offerings *(saraka)* in order to ensure the success of a project or to appease the omen of a bad dream. To achieve this, one goes out to the street at the crack of dawn and gives a poor person

---

[14] € 1 = FCFA 655.95.

an oblation of a millet cake or rice, as prescribed by a Marabout, for which the giver receives a blessing. "Early in the morning, between five and six-thirty, when the sun is rising, the poor can go into the street for a stroll. People make their offerings at this time and search out poor people to give them to," says one of the local experts. These gifts, however, barely cover their daily needs.

Offerings are also given at ceremonies: A portion of the meal and set sum of money is set aside for the poor. On these occasions many elderly find something to eat. Eight of the poor men and women indeed relied on these offerings for their survival, but did not consider it worth mentioning. An old man who takes care of his great-grandson alone says, "The disregard of the poor is also evident at the ceremonies, the manner in which certain old people are treated. The distribution of the offerings always begins with those who are most respected. And so it happens every time that the plate is empty by the time it reaches the poor people. Maybe there are still 25 or 10 Francs left. You see the other elderly that are being treated like you. You see who is sitting next to each other; those that have and those that have nothing!"

It is also possible for beggars to ask for help via the Imam who asks everyone to give alms, but due to the shame of asking publicly for help, only outsiders coming from other neighbourhoods make such requests. The residents of Koko for their part go to other neighbourhoods or to the large old mosque in the city. Many elderly men and women wander as beggars through the city and in front of the various mosques.

In the mosque community reciprocal and unilateral relations coexist. The members of these communities visit each other in the case of illness and make collections for ceremonies (reciprocal and personalised), and they give alms to the needy (unilateral and anonymous).

Example 1: The Giving of Alms for God's Mercy
Salimata K., around mid-fifty, moved as young married woman from a village to the Koko neighbourhood in Bobo-Dioulasso. She was the second wife of her husband's three wives. She bore two daughters and a son. Today she cares for her oldest handicapped daughter who became ill with meningitis as a child. Her daughter is blind

and mute, but can still hear and listens attentively to our conversation. Salimata K. also cares for her seven-year-old grandson who was brought to her by her second daughter, who lives in Ouagadougou, when her husband died. The youngest, a son studying to be a carpenter, lives in Ouagadougou with relatives of her first husband who died seventeen years ago. At that time, Salimata K. moved into a small room on a large compound. She still occupies this room and shares it with her handicapped daughter and her grandson. She pays a monthly rent of FCFA 1,200 (about € 2). There is no electricity and no running water. Salimata K. collects water in a barrel during the rainy season, but during the dry season she has to buy it.

Her first husband was a Marabout. At that time, Salimata K. tilled a field on the outskirts of Bobo-Dioulasso during the rainy season and during the dry months she spun cotton. Today she has to beg. She goes to all of the ceremonies where she can get offerings *(saraka)* of millet, cola nuts or money, and she goes begging on the street every Monday, Thursday and Friday with her daughter. She says, "No, we don't go to the large mosque. The old men are there and they don't want the old women there." On the street Salimata K. receives alms and on her early morning walks she receives *saraka* of clothes and fabric, millet cakes, a packet of sugar – depending on what a Marabout has prescribed as an offering.

Eleven years ago Salimata K. married again. Her husband begs too. He lives with his second younger wife and eats there. "Every once in a while he comes by and gives me FCFA 150 or 200 (about € 0.3)."

Salimata K. is alone and dependent only on herself. I asked her who washes her and cares for her, who washes her clothes and cooks for her when she is ill. "I do it myself!" she says. "There is no one to help me. Everything stays dirty until I am fit enough again." When she is ill, she buys an amphetamine named "the old women who plays football" *(musokorobabalantonke)* at the street pharmacy for FCFA 25 (about € 0.04).

Her relationships with her kin are very distant or inexistent. She explains, "It is very difficult to have a relationship with relatives when you have nothing. You can't go to see them. And they don't come to visit you. If what I earn is just enough to feed my daughter, my grandchild and myself, what is left over to keep up a relationship? Nothing! Also, the fact that I beg in order to eat makes it hard for me to get close to my relatives. But my relatives beg too – all of them who live here in Bobo. Everyone lived from the fields on the outskirts of the city. Now all of the fields have disappeared. That's why we are all in such difficulty."

The Basis of Security in Old Age: Income, Children and Marriage

Despite the differing societal definitions of protection relationships, according to Vuarin (2000: 38-40) it still remains a universal constant that the right to support is linked with "the duty to autonomy". This means in the first place that a person must work – they participate in the societal division of labour and therefore assume their responsibility. For this reason, the person is not responsible for the misfortune that befell them.[15] This duty to be self-supporting is contrary to old age, which is generally a phase of dependency. Considered from the perspective of society, poverty and ageing have a shared characteristic – dwindling strength.

A local expert of the middle class explains the social understanding of poverty: "In Dioula poverty *(fantanya)* means without strength *(fangatan)*. *Fangatan* is a person without strength. (...) *Se t'a ye* means the ability [to do something] is absent. He is not able. *Se t'a ye* is said of those who live in poverty. Poverty is therefore not about a material deficiency, but rather about the inability to do what is necessary to live. Those who are healthy are not considered poor because they have the strength to do something. And those who can count on the support of their children or other people are also not considered poor. Being poor is not having anything and not being able to do anything about it and on top of that having no people who can – people who are bound by duty such as children. (...) Dependent and poor are those who are at the mercy of others' good will. They live in insecurity."

This social concept of poverty was also described by Hagberg (2001: 44-45/106) who, in a study on poverty conducted in Burkina Faso, refers to "the lack of agency" and "the lack of ability to perform socially valued actions". In fact, people do not exclude structural explanations for poverty, he writes, "But poverty is still seen as a deeply personal experience of not having the capacity to improve the situation." The elderly also view ageing as a highly personal experience – as the "result of life lived". This includes having a "good attitude" *(kewuali nyuman)*, successful children who feel duty bound to their parents, a marriage and a good network of social relations.

---

[15] Theft is another form of helping oneself and remaining autonomous (ibid).

Work in Old Age

All old men and women make efforts to earn income as long as they are able (cf. also Schoumaker 2000: 387). Poor elderly women often work as petty traders selling coal, porridge, spices or *lemburuji*, a ginger-lemon flavoured drink. Others work as soap producers, hairdressers or cotton spinners. The men are generally bricklayers, muezzin, mechanics or net artisans. Among these efforts to earn an income I also count ceremony attendance and the early morning walks, where old men and women like Salimata K. (example 1) walk the streets in search of oblations, and begging. Old-age incomes can be highly diversified as the example of Ami T. illustrates (example 2).

Example 2: The Diversified Old-Age Income

Ami T. (60) returned to her father's compound, where she spent her childhood, twenty years ago. Till the death of her first husband, who was a civil servant, Ami T. was a successful wholesaler who traded in oxen, mopeds and cigarettes between the cities of Bobo-Dioulasso, Ouagadougou, Lome and Abidjan. She has five children. A son with a wife and two children, as well as a daughter with two children live with her and eat from her bowl. "I carry the children on my shoulders," she says. "Every day I get up at four in the morning in order to feed everyone when it should be me getting fed! I don't live in security. I invested everything in my children's schooling believing that when they became successful they would take care of me. But it didn't work out that way." Ami T. gave up her business twenty years ago when her husband died, and up until the death of her sick mother ten years ago she cared for her as well. Today she and her daughter run a small retail operation selling porridge. The morning's earnings of FCFA 500 (about € 0.8) belong to Ami T. and the evening's earnings go to her daughter, which she uses for her small personal needs. If sales are slow, the daughter asks her mother for money.

Ami T. married her second husband "in order to receive support from a man". But she goes on to say, "one cannot say my husband provides support. He pays for the electricity and that's all!" He eats lunch at Ami T.'s, otherwise he lives in another compound with his two first wives, nine of his seventeen children and three of his seven grandchildren. He is therefore in the same situation as Ami T. – he feeds his adult children and grandchildren.

How does Ami T. support her family of about ten members? Her income is diversified. It is made up of a small widow's pension of FCFA 19,655 (about € 30) she receives every three months, her daily earnings of about FCFA 500 (about € 0.8), the rent from the two foyers in the family compound and her husband's regular contribution for the electricity. Additionally, she gets support from a good friend of her unemployed son's, "He helps me a great deal. He comes by to visit, sees a problem and solves it. Also my nephews, my older sister's sons, help me often with FCFA 5000 (about € 8) or FCFA 2500." And occasionally her son in Lome sends money. Ami T. says, "If someone asks me for help, then I help. And if I have nothing, I make an effort to get it somehow. I'm in bad financial shape today because I always give. But I'm ashamed of not being able to give. It's still that way for me today. I share everything I have." She adds that this was all in preparation for her old age. "If as a young married woman you care for other people's children and their success, you will benefit when you get older. If you don't help others, you should not be surprised if no one comes to your aid in old age and no one is there for you. Today, I live quite well because I always had good relationships and always helped when I could. You can only ask for help from relatives you have helped in the past. I helped many including the many children of my mother's sisters and brothers. Today I can turn to them."

Earnings alone do not allow the elderly poor to secure their old age. Impediments include their dwindling strength as well as the young people who compete for the same jobs. Additionally, expenses do not decrease, but may stay the same or even increase if the elderly have to care for their offspring, as in the case of Ami T. (example 2). For women there is the added aspect of an accumulation of lifelong economic discrimination giving them limited access to and control of resources such as income, possessions, property and thus setting them up for a greater risk of poverty than men (cf. Cattell 2002, Lachaud 1997). Additionally, the poor cannot directly accumulate material wealth for their old-age provisions during their working lifetime as can the members of the middle class who may put money aside in banks, invest in a herd of oxen – the traditional form of saving, build compounds, purchase fields or fruit gardens, or open a retail business. The income of the middle-class elderly is diversified and comprised of for example a pension, revenues from rentals and agriculture, as well as savings. The members of the middle class own compounds, whereas in general, the poor do not: half of them live in their father's compound or their father's relatives' compound, and one on his mother's brother's compound. Three are renters and five live "for free", which means the rent was waived by a well-meaning landlord after years of cohabitation.[16] The patrilocal rule of residence in the collective compounds accords a certain security of a place to live. For the elderly poor housing itself is less of a problem than the maintenance of the house.

While the poor may not be able to save as directly as the middle class, indirectly they have the possibility of making material provisions by raising their children well and by cultivating their social network. The socialisation process based on the concept of *mogoya*[17] – humanity – including solidarity and generosity, enables them to do so. Ami T. (example 2) exemplifies this self-image.

The Implicit Intergenerational Contract[18]

Today, children are the only ones with the obligation to take care of their ageing parents' livelihood (cf. also van der Geest 2001: 20), but what originally applied exclusively to sons nowadays includes daughters as well. Sons-in-law are responsible for covering certain aspects of ceremonies. Both young and old accept this concept which draws upon the "law of debt" (Marie 1997a: 68-80). The actual practice, however, is contradictory. If only physical support of elderly parents is considered, then the intergenerational contract appears to be fulfilled nearly one hundred percent. At least one daughter or one son, often more than one child, lives with their parents on the compound. Three-fourths live in a three-generational household. Both men and women emphasise how important physical proximity to their children is, not only as the basis for the social respect they receive from those

---

[16] "Free lodger" is a corresponding category in the census: in 1996 they comprised 23 % in Koko (cf. INSD 1998).

[17] For an explanation of the *mogoya* concept cf. Vuarin (2000: 100-101). Bambara-/Dioula-expression: *mogo* = human being, *-ya* = suffix, the abstraction expresses: *Mogoya* ≈ "politeness, social relations, generosity, helpfulness" (Bailleul 1996). Cf. also Marie (1997a: 70) on the habitus, which is influenced by the principles of solidarity, hierarchy, collective identity and suppression of individual tendencies (primary socialisation in the ancient society).

[18] Following Cattell (1997: 159) I use the term "implicit contract" for the intergenerational relationship, to be understood as implicitly shared understanding, values, customs and required behaviour as regards relationships and commensurate exchanges.

around them, but also due the assistance available in the case of illness or the help provided for house repairs.

For the poor, a look at the financial support, however, shows a different picture of the intergenerational contract. Only one woman in twenty-four people has her livelihood assured ("fulfilled intergenerational contract"). Four women and four men are being supported by a son or daughter, but their livelihoods are not secured, meaning they still have to make an effort to earn a daily income ("intergenerational contract fulfilled without securing livelihood"). Half of the elderly poor, and half of the middle class as well, live in a "reversed intergenerational contract" – they care for their adult children and/or grandchildren.[19]

Example 3: The Son as the Last Refuge
Sibiri G. (71) was born in 1931 in a village and moved to Bobo-Dioulasso to live with a sister of his father's when he was fifteen. He later married and had six sons with his wife. Only two of his sons are still alive. One is ill and lives in another town. The other twenty-seven-year old son lives with Sibiri G. in a compound, which thanks to one of Sibiri's father's "inherited" relationships, they have occupied for decades for free. Today, the compound is run-down and desolate. Sibiri's son says, "My father lives in a state of crisis. This weighs greatly on me. I fight and fight and don't have the least bit to show for it. He gets up in the morning to eke out a living. I do the same... I should be able to support my father. But now I have to do everything at the same time: take care of my father, look for a compound, find work and I would like to have a family of my own – I'm supposed to manage this all! "

Sibiri G. worked as a farmer to support his family. His wife sold the millet and corn on the market in Bobo-Dioulasso. He says, "I couldn't think about the future at that time. I had no possibility to put something aside. Surviving each day and having food to eat were my only thoughts."

Sibiri's wife died many years ago. "That is the big crisis in old age. You have no support. There is no one else there to help you," he explains further. "If my wife were alive, she would be my source of security. When there is a wife around, nothing can go wrong. She would help me to live my life. If the wife has children, the children help their mother care for the father. Without financial means it is impossible to find a wife now." Sibiri G.'s wife had good relationships in Koko and during

---

[19] Intergenerational contract: "fulfilled" – example 6; "fulfilled without securing livelihood" – examples 3, 4; "reversed " – examples 1, 2, 5.

Thomas Sankara's time (1983–87) she was the head of a women's group. He stood
in her shadow Sibiri G. says, and today none of these relationships remain.

His son, a carpenter with little chance to find a job, works at a kiosk and earns
FCFA 500 (about € 0.8) per day, of which he gives his father 250 every morning to
buy his food. Yet Sibiri G. needs FCFA 300. From a street vendor he buys a plate of
rice with sauce three times a day which costs him FCFA 100 (about € 0.15) a plate.
Weak and ill due to lung problems, he often sits on a stool in front of the compound.
Passers-by give him alms and occasionally young people ask him for a blessing
"because they know that this is good for their future," he says. "If there is a ceremony somewhere, I go. Even if I don't feel well I force myself to go and then I may
get 100 or 200 Francs." His son takes care of him. He washes his clothes, cleans his
room and nurses him when he is ill. Sibiri G. can count on his son. Otherwise he
would have no one. "In town I have no relatives, none that I can count on in any
case. And those in the village, my brother's children, they think of me but they have
no means. They have their own problems to survive as farmers." He can't ask his
neighbours. And he has a friend who is not really a friend. "He doesn't think, my
own son is successful, so I'll help my friend by bringing him a sack of rice. These
thoughts don't occur to him."

In regards to the intergenerational contract, the following conclusions
can be drawn from the research conducted in Koko:

The intergenerational contract is a security relationship created and
moulded by the parties concerned, much as for other security relationships as well. The right of the parents to support in old age is based
upon their having fulfilled their duty of helping their children to a
decent existence as adults. For city dwellers this means having sent
their children to school and having helped them to take up a profes-
sion and get a job. Whether they achieved this or not is in urban settings a negotiable matter – the absolute debt has become conditional
and relative (cf. Marie 1997b: 436). If a child has the impression that
their mother or father did not do enough for them, they may refuse to
assist their parents in old age.

Elderly women can count on the support of their children because
as mothers they have generally given everything they have – emotionally, materially and financially. Marriages, however, have become
uncertain (cf. below) and, therefore, women completely count on their
children for their social security. Mothers also routinely receive more
than fathers, even if it is in secret because open favouritism would put

into question the authority of the father, the power figure in a patrilinear structured society. On the other hand, it is more often mothers rather than fathers who care for their "unsuccessful" adult children. Polygamist fathers can hardly count on the support of children whom they formerly neglected or whose mothers they treated badly.[20]

It is not only insufficient means which make it difficult for young people to fulfil the intergenerational contract. They also have their own desires and needs, different life goals from the elderly, and they try to retreat from the pressure of having to solve every family problem with their earnings without breaking off from their kin (cf. also Rosenmayr 2002). Sons with incomes often move to other neighbourhoods or other cities, and they invoke the fact that they have enough expenses with their new families. Married daughters, who are not *per se* duty bound like the sons to care for their elderly parents, are doing so more often. In addition to practical support, provided they live nearby, the daughters also give gifts of cloth or clothes and increasingly considerable amounts of money (degendering of gift-giving). According to the statements made by the interviewees, the daughters give more, more often and are more reliable than the sons.

In view of the uncertainty marriage provides, married women pursue two security strategies: As mothers they put everything into their children to secure their old-age provision, and as daughters they strengthen the relationships to their own kin. Through gift giving they create a social position for themselves and therefore the possibility to return to their relatives in times of crisis. These actions also help provide for their own social security.

The reversed intergenerational contract is an urban phenomenon: The elderly cannot leave any land for the young to work as they would in the villages, where sons largely fulfil the intergenerational contract – admittedly without securing the elderly person's livelihood (cf. Badini-Kinda in this volume). The high unemployment in the cities and the mortality rate among young people due to AIDS partly explain the reversed intergenerational contract.

---

[20] Van der Geest (2001: 29) observed the same in a small town in Ghana.

The question remains, however, why are the elderly willing to provide for their grown children? One reason is the patrilocal extended family which is culturally anchored in southwestern Burkina Faso. Married sons used to live out their entire lives with their families on the father's compound, so adult children are rarely pushed out onto the street. On the one hand, their presence fortifies the authority of the eldest as administrator of the extended family. On the other hand, based on their own self-image the eldest have the responsibility for the economic and social reproduction of the patrilocal extended family during their entire lifetime (cf. Roth 1998). Therefore, the elderly men and women feel obliged to care for their adult children. "You can't reject your child!" says Ami T. (example 2). Her daughter, who with her two children lives with Ami T., agrees: It is the duty of the parents to feed their young and to help them find jobs. Thus, the "unsuccessful" children waver between the shame of not having fulfilled their duties and the perspective of the elderly which says that parents have to help their children find jobs. The most blatant reversed intergenerational contract is the household where grandparents (mostly women) raise their orphaned or illegitimate grandchildren alone – both penniless and without strength (cf. example 1).

Marriage in Old Age

In addition to the implicit intergenerational contract, the marriage contract is the second most important social security relationship in old age. Basically, marriage provides women, as well as men, the social recognition of being a respectable person. With this social integrating effect marriage is the basis of all other security strategies. Marriage is a source of security, as long as the resources suffice, if both the man and woman fulfil their obligations and cooperate with each other. They can mutually accord each other their income and indirectly participate in the social security arrangement of the other. Should parts of the partner's social security arrangement collapse, the other partner's security arrangement is still available and *vice versa* (cf. also Leliveld 1994: 270). A further security aspect of marriage lies in the fact that it conjoins four patrilineages together and increases the social capital of both the man and the woman.

The marriage contract is gendered inasmuch as it does not offer the same security for men and women due to the differing social position and the values[21] associated with the gendered division of work and separation of property. For an elderly man, a wife offers social security on several levels. Firstly, she is the one who cares for him on a daily basis; she cooks, cleans, does laundry and tends to him, with the help of a daughter-in-law if she lives on the compound as well. Secondly, she is the one that can provide access for him to his children, since the man's role as the head of the family generally implies a distanced, respectful and somewhat formal relationship with their offspring. One man commented, "If a woman has suffered because of you, then she will tell her successful and income-earning child not to look after the father and his other wives." Thirdly, it is the wife who will stand in for her husband if he falls ill, loses his job or becomes too weak to care for the family. She takes over his duties without a word – it is one of the secrets of marriage – a *furugundo* (cf. Roth 2003a). Half of all elderly women of the lower and middle class live with this secret and take over all of the household costs. Consequently, the security which a marriage can offer a man could become a source of insecurity for his wife. Marriages have become increasingly conflictive. Economic crises are reflected in marriage crises. A former female wholesaler feeds her entire family with the income from a small grocer's shop because her husband went bankrupt. She says, "Men want to accomplish big things but when it doesn't work out, they have trouble starting from zero. They prefer to do nothing rather than something small. They are embarrassed – contrary to women. Even the young men don't want to start something small, whereas as a young woman can start her business with 1000 or 5000 Francs (about € 8). No man that was once successful wants to go back.

---

[21] In many societies in southwestern Burkina Faso women as mothers are ranked in first place, and as wives they are ranked in second place, whereas men are ranked first as husbands, but second as fathers. This corresponds to a "hidden transcript", as named by Koné (2002: 22) for this criticism of backstage patrilinear authority in Mande societies (cf. also Hoffman 2002).

He prefers to sit around and do nothing." The literature is full of references depicting this tendency in men; during economic hard times they relinquish their tasks and their responsibilities to the women who meanwhile expand, intensify and diversify their work with which they feed their families.[22]

Example 4: Security in Marriage

Siriki C. (65) was born in 1937. He first came to Bobo-Dioulasso as a twenty-year-old and settled down in Koko in 1965. He has been living on the same compound since 1970 – today with his third wife and their four-year-old daughter. Two of their sons died in infancy. One of his two adult daughters from his second marriage also lives with him. They all share two rooms. Previously, Siriki C. paid FCFA 4000 (€ 6) in monthly rent, but since he became ill many years ago he has been living for free on the compound. "The compound owner and his sister consider me a big brother." Siriki C. differentiates whom he considers kin and whom he does not consider kin. "A person with the same mother and the same father is not your relative. A relative is someone who helps you. The compound owner and his sister were previously my neighbours. Today they are my kin." They assist him in times of difficulty and provide money or medicine such as Nivaquine when his indigenous remedies don't bring relief.

Siriki C. became a healer like his father. His earnings are erratic and small. "If I have clients, I can feed my family. I give my wife 150 Francs (about € 0.25) per day. With this she can buy millet flour for 100 and ingredients for the sauce for 50 Francs. Sometimes I have no money. Then my wife feeds the family from her earnings – she sells peanuts in front of the compound. Oftentimes she covers the cost of feeding her relatives or her kin's children come and eat with us."

His grownup daughter occasionally gives him money from her earnings as a hairdresser, but it is already a relief if she can support herself, says Siriki C. His wife and the compound owner ensure his old age security. "No, I've never chased away a woman," he says in relation to his third marriage. "They leave on their own. A wife brings security to the marriage if she is good humoured and lives with her husband in harmony."

Similarly, poor widowed men and women live precariously. Only the children remain as possible consistent supporters, but they often live in the same poverty (cf. example 3, 5). Admittedly, many more

---

[22] Cf. among others Baerends (1998), Bop (1996), Endeley (1998), Lachenmann (1994, 1997), Risseeuw and Palriwala (1996).

women than men are widowed.[23] On the one hand, women have longer life expectancies[24] than men. On the other hand, the women of the present generation of elderly are often five to ten years younger than their husbands. In addition, one-fourth of my female dialogue partners live alone because their husbands live with a younger co-wife. Often, the man no longer even contributes to her household costs as is the case with Salimata K. (example 1). Schoumaker (2000: 385) points out that because of polygamy and their more frequent marriage men have more opportunities to live married and be supported by women in old age.

Example 5: Widowhood as Social Relegation
Bintou S. is in her mid 50's. She was the third of three co-wives and has been a widow for five years. Her husband was in the retail trade selling millet. He left her and their children the possibility of living on his kin's compound for free. He left nothing else. Bintou S. has five children between the ages of fifteen and forty. From her bowl she feeds two daughters, her oldest long time unemployed son and his wife, three grandchildren as well as her old mother. "She lived alone in a hut on a field," explains Bintou S. "She sees badly, can barely hear, has a crooked back and can no longer cook. That's why I took her in two years ago." Bintou S. is alone in caring for the four-generation household. "I wish my children had work, not for me but so that they could care for themselves."

Bintou S. was born and raised in Bobo-Dioulasso. She attended the Koran school for a short while. As a young woman she moved to her in-laws' compound in Koko. For her entire life Bintou S. has produced and sold soap. Today she trades potash and oil which she buys from the Citec factory. With her small income she feeds her family. "You can't count on relatives when you're ill. The medicine is too expensive so you have to buy it yourself," explains Bintou S. In such cases, she takes out a credit which she later pays back. "Getting care is possible though. If I become ill, then my younger sister takes care of me."

"The biggest risk in life is to become a widow," emphasises Bintou S., "you have no one to help you, you have to help yourself. This applies to both young and old women: what your husband did for you, after his death no one else will do for you."

---

[23] Ex. Mali 1987: 5 % of men and 46 % of women over the age of 60 were widowed (Schoumaker 2000: 386).
[24] 20 % more women than men reach the age of 60 and older; 60 % more women than men reach the age of 80 and older (Schoumaker 2000: 385).

An Element of Social Insecurity: Old Age and Illness

None of the old people I spoke to was bedridden, but one man went
blind many years ago and several others are frail or suffer from aches
and pains. Traditionally, fragile elderly men and women are well
cared for, people say, because they are closer to the ancestors. The
actual circumstances, however, barely permit young people to provide
the elderly with the necessary medical supplies. Illnesses increase with
old age, but in relation to the standard of living medical costs are high
– too high to ask kin to pay for them. Treatment in health facilities
such as hospitals, dispensaries or clinics are expensive and must be
paid before any service is rendered.[25] For this reason, the biggest insecurity feared by elderly men and women is becoming ill and bedridden (cf. also Kinda 2003). A local expert of the middle class explains,
"You will see no sick person answer the question 'ça va?' with 'ça ne
va pas aujourd'hui!' This is due to social expectations: When someone
is ill, the neighbourhood has the duty to assist him. And the sick person has the duty not to show his suffering in order not to demoralise
the others – it is a subtle duty. If the illness lasts one, two, four, six
months, if it lasts for a long time, it becomes bothersome because the
children can't come by everyday and they can't absorb all of the costs
as they should. Therefore, if it has to happen, many old people wish
for a short illness and then death so that the children don't have to
suffer. The risk that the children will make themselves scarce increases with the length of the illness. In fact, this happens not because
the children don't want to take care of their parents, but because they
can't. The burden is too big."

The poor elderly take pains not to burden either their children or
the neighbourhood because of their self-image as the elders of the
extended family who are expected to act as autonomous and responsible individuals. They conceal their ailments and many even go in

---

[25] On 1st March 2001, on the initiative of a French psychiatric male nurse and with
French financing, a clinic was opened in Bobo-Dioulasso specialising in geriatrics.
In addition, two health insurance funds ("mutuelles de santé") were launched, one
local and one from the French development assistance programme.

search of their own healing plants. A sixty-two-year old widow[26] with six children, who live far away or have no earnings, says, "You know you have no means and you know that your children or your grand-children are no better off either. When you are sick, you are obliged to hide it, to do everything so they don't realise it because if they find out, they will be uncomfortable since they don't have the money to help."

Women take over the physical care of the ill – much as they do all over the world (Albert and Cattell 1994). For the elderly this refers specifically to daughters-in-law and daughters, a crucial reason why it is important to have children in local proximity. But vigorous old women also tend to the ailing.

Agency, Age and Gender

The elderly men and women of Koko regard the question of their old age as a question of how they have lived their lives, what they have done to prepare for their old age needs and lastly what kind of reputa-tion, relationships and resources they have accumulated. Ageing is a process in which irrespective of age it is important whether a person is still productive or can be active in some form. This includes being able to preserve a certain level of independence, maintain relation-ships and participate in continuous exchanges through visits, advice giving, problem solving or gift giving (cf. Finch and Mason 1993: 173-174). In this regard, men and women follow different approaches.

Ageing proves itself to be on the one hand a process of degender-ing: In old age, in many of the decentrally organised societies of southwestern Burkina Faso, women's situation is becoming more comparable to that of men. They gain influence, decision-making power, and authority over younger men and women, and they contrib-ute to familial and neighbourhood matters in a determining manner as the case of Awa T. shows (example 6). Men on the other hand when

---

[26] In 2001 the research assistant Blahima Konaté conducted one interview each with a 72-year-old married man and a 62-year-old widow in Koko (both poor elderly) on the topics of ageing and illness.

they can no longer be the breadwinner but must instead depend on their children or their wives, become weaker and withdrawn, as Koné (2002) aptly ascertained.[27]

Ageing is, however, gendered in that women on the one hand are impaired in their agency due to the lifelong economic discrimination they experience, as previously mentioned. On the other hand, women dispose of skills due to the gendered division of work and their role as mothers, and the values associated therewith, allowing them other possibilities in maintaining relationships which differ from the options open to men. As wives women have at their disposal household and nurturing skills which permit them to participate in reciprocal exchanges till an advanced age, thereby entitling them to support and social security (cf. also Cattell 1997: 172-173).

The research in Bobo-Dioulasso shows that women count on their children for their old-age provisions and do everything for them so that in the best case the children will later care for them and in the worst case, the women will sustain their adult children. The men, on the other hand, count on marriage as their sole possibility for continuing access to household help, nurturing and support.[28] In addition, during their lives women take care of children that are not their own in the hope that these children will later look after them as in the case of Ami T. and Awa T. (examples 2, 6).

Example 6: "Created" Children

Awa T. (51) was born in 1951 and considers herself an old woman. She has fourteen "grandchildren". She bore no children herself, but helped raise her brothers' and sister's sons and daughters. She is in a polygamous marriage, but never moved to her husband's village. She has lived on her father's family compound from the day she was born.

As a child Awa T. attended the Koran school and later earned her money selling vegetables. In the early 1990s she went bankrupt and had to give up her business. It

---

[27] Women, respected as mothers in the husband's family and as the older sister in the family of origin, can play a considerable role as they age. On the ambiguity of women's social position in different African societies cf. Baerends (1998), Udvardy and Cattell (1992), and in Mande societies cf. Hoffman (2002), Koné (2002).
[28] Håkansson and LeVine made the same observations among the Gusii in Kenia (1997).

was the period of democratisation and many new parties were founded. Awa T., already a key person in various associations since the 1970s, became very active politically. She still benefits from the connections she made during her political activities.

"I have no children and this could have led to my being neglected in old age," says Awa T. "But I managed the situation well. I helped raise my nieces and nephews and that is why they take care of me today." In her everyday life one nephew in particular is important to her. She was instrumental in helping him become a chauffeur. He supports Awa T. and his mother equally by financing meals and medical care. If Awa T. needs money, she can also turn to her other nieces and nephews. "It always depends on the children's situation, whether they have work, money or other problems to resolve. If they can't help, they go ask others for money for me. I avoid this though because it is humiliating for me." Awa T.'s daughters-in-law take care of her when she is ill.

Awa T. feels that old age is the most difficult phase in life. "You don't know how everything will end. The moment could come when my nephew the chauffeur, whom I can count on so much, says: She is a burden for me. Under the influence of his wife he could say that one day because they have children, and as they get older, their needs will grow, so the question could come up whether he has enough means for everyone. What will happen if one day he doesn't help me anymore? That's why ageing is difficult. A lot can change – there are so many things you don't control, you don't know what is ahead. Today, I regret a bit the fact that I don't have my own children. I ask myself how long the support will continue."

Conclusions

Dependency, and thus social insecurity in old age, threatens men and women who have no earnings, possessions or savings, nor children who will care for them. Their social security arrangement loses structural redundancy, and relatives, neighbours and friends retreat. The complex and comprehensive local social security requires having at one's disposal a minimum of resources with which reciprocal relationships can be kept up. As Vuarin (2004: 4) already ascertained, the "redistributive strength" of the social security system is weak, hence economic disparities are reproduced rather than alleviated. The impoverishment process of the elderly poor is thereby furthered. This thus confirms that today "African solidarity" is a myth. The main reason is that solidarity under the present socio-economic conditions can hardly function. The increasing life expectancy means that the number of years an elderly person lives in dependency continues to increase, and this under steadily deteriorating economic conditions.

As with all collectives, the kin collective also began to become socially stratified in the 1950s leading to a dramatic decrease in the redistribution of wealth within the extended family. Accordingly, the elderly poor can be differentiated by whether and to what degree they can still participate in the reciprocity cycle, and whether in their opinion they still have relatives. Admittedly, in patrilocal societies the extended family assures a place to live.

The core of old-age security for the poor, in addition to individual earnings, includes the implicit intergenerational contract and the marriage contract because one's own children and the marriage partner are the only people who are actually duty bound to help in old age. According to the generalised reciprocity principle, the children have to care for their parents; originally it was the sons who performed this duty, but today daughters have increasingly taken on more responsibility for providing material support (degendering of giving). However, today more than ever, it is uncertain whether the elderly will receive back what they once invested. Whether the children can comply with their duty to care for their parents and whether they even want to is debatable in today's urban context. "Debt" has become a relative term and is negotiated by the parties involved. Whether the husband is still alive, and moreover has earnings, leaves women exposed in view of longer life expectancies and the challenging economic situation. Widowed men and women live precariously for several reasons including the loss of the social security relationships of the deceased partner. However, for reasons previously mentioned there are more widows; significantly it is still easier for men to remarry.

Due to the gendered division of work and the role of the mother, women seek their old age security with their children, which moulds women's actions throughout their lives. Men seek social security in marriage, where the wife acts as the intermediary in their relationships with the children. For women, the ambivalence of both these security relationships becomes evident in that the relationships become a source of common destiny for them. If the children find work, mothers often receive more than fathers, but if the children have no income, the women care not only for their adult children and grandchildren, but also for the husband. The research in Koko shows a strong concurrence between the reversed intergenerational contract and the "reversed marriage contract".

Ageing with dignity and retaining respect includes being independent and active, being influential and giving advice, but it also includes the right to be cared for because the children as "dependents" are obliged to – there is no shame in having to ask for help. This is a benefit denied to the men and women who live precariously or socially marginalised. As a result of economic developments in Burkina Faso poverty is steadily on the rise, a situation which cannot be compensated for by the children (cf. also Cattell 2002). It is becoming particularly evident that elderly men and women in Koko are increasingly burdened with the threatening dependence on others, the danger of not being able to maintain relationships due to a lack of resources and the consequence of being socially marginalised. Ageing without dignity is as equally agonising as not having enough to eat.

The Gap Between Ideas and Practices: Elderly Social Insecurity in Rural Burkina Faso

Fatoumata Badini-Kinda

"Kinship is obligation" goes a saying among the Moose,[1] which means that the individual has the obligation to assist and support his or her parents. Do the elderly poor living in the village really benefit from familial and community support today? What is the logic of these types of assistance and social security, as well as their limits? Under what conditions can an aged person expect support? The results of the research conducted in the village of Kuila reveals a significant gap between ideas and practices as regards family and community support of the poor: According to the conceptions, the network of family relations represents the principle network of support for the elderly through conjugal relationships, intergenerational relationships and relationships within the extended family. Yet in practice the possibilities for recourse among family and extra-family relations are limited and inconsistent for the elderly poor, thereby leaving the majority living precariously and in misery. In Kuila, there are many who live in extreme poverty and who find themselves without a daily meal.

Kuila, a Village of "Contrasts"

Situated thirty-five kilometres from the capital of Ouagadougou, Kuila is a Moaga village with 1357 inhabitants.[2] Despite its proximity to the capital, Kuila remains all the same a traditional village with clay shanties, straw granaries, but above all a social organisation which is

---

[1] The Moose (singular Moaga) represent the majority ethnic group among the about sixty groups present in Burkina Faso.
[2] Cf. INSD 1998 (National Institute for Statistics and Demographics). From 2000 to 2002 we realised a total of more than one hundred interviews (individual interviews, focus groups, interviews with local and institutional key persons and local experts) in addition to the collection of statistical data and participant observation. We spoke to 44 elderly people and 22 young people of the middle and lower socio-economic classes.

still that of traditional Moaga society, highly organised and hierarchical. Thus, Kuila has at the top of its population a village chief and other customary leaders, including a religious leader. The rules of life are those of a highly hierarchical and centralised patrilinear society. One of the distinctive features of Kuila is that all of the members of the village are directly related or related by marriage, meaning that neighbours are at the same time relatives.

From the perspective of religion, Kuila is 80 % Christian, 14.1 % Muslim and the remainder are animist.[3] Nevertheless, one often speaks of syncretic religion since the animistic rituals are not completely abandoned by those who have converted. For example, there are many individuals who have two first names (i.e. Noaga Jean-Pierre, Guelbo Mahamoudou) of which the first is a symbolic and protection name and the second is the conversion name. The population of Kuila remains attached to ancestral beliefs and continues to practice numerous traditional and habitual rites which accompany life events: birth, marriage, funerals, initiation rites and atonement and protection rites such as the *basga*[4].

The illiteracy rate in Kuila is 66.5 %.[5] In terms of socio-economic activities subsistence agriculture is minimally productive and diversified. The cash crop culture is underdeveloped and growing vegetables suffers from an irregular water supply. The breeding of animals associated with agriculture consists mainly of small ruminants and fowl, with the exception of some proprietors who deal in livestock. Handicraft and petty trade are practiced in the village, but without great distinction. Salaried work is nearly inexistent in the village, as is the myriad conspicuous manual work in the informal sector common in African cities.

---

[3] Cf. INSD 1998 (National Institute for Statistics and Demographics). The importance of the catholic religion in Kuila could be explained by the fact that it neighbours the village of Guilingou where a catholic church has been located since colonial times.
[4] The *basga* (in the Mooré language) is a traditional ceremony held following the harvest to thank the ancestors and to honour nature for having provided rains during the agricultural season.
[5] Cf. INSD 1998 (National Institute for Statistics and Demographics).

Kuila represents a zone of over-population and demographic pressure on the arable land: The good land is the source of envy and conflict. In addition, the village does not escape the phenomenon of migration of its sons. In general, the rural exodus of the Moose is a tradition which drains the workforce from the village leaving only women, children and the elderly behind. In effect, the proportion of people 55 years old and older reaches 13.6 % of the total population of Kuila, which is above the national average of 8.88 %.[6] We could attribute this over-representation of the aged population on the migration phenomenon.

If Kuila is a village where traditional social forces remain strong, this does not mean that the population is not confronted with modernity, as evidenced by the educated children or by new values such as individualism which have infiltrated the village (cf. also Marie 1997). In Kuila one can find young people who are more well-off than the elderly and men who are wealthier than the chief.

In Kuila the rich and those belonging to the middle class have enough to eat while the poor look on. Of course, it is not always easy to make a distinction between the middle class and the poor. We were required to consider visible clues for classification purposes. Those of the middles class were the villagers who disposed of more or less modern means of production to work the land (plough, oxen, donkeys) and the use of modern production techniques (seedbeds in rows, fertiliser, selected seeds). The wealthy in the village also count on livestock. Agricultural revenue is dependent on rainfall but is also enormously influenced by the exploitation of the technical means of working the land. For the local experts, the quantity harvested can range from a little to a lot, partly contingent on one's technical possibilities. In referring to these criteria, only a small minority reach the middle-class status in Kuila. For our purposes, the middle class includes those that are immune from nutritional insecurities, those whose granaries are full and have reserves from previous years, a sign that they can cover the needs of their families with cereals in the period prior to the next harvest. The middle class has access to modern

---

[6] Cf. Ministère de l'Action Sociale et de la Solidarité Nationale (2001: 9-10).

consumer goods: mopeds, houses with corrugated-iron roofs, modern clothing,[7] nourishment including products such as bread, milk, bouillon cubes in the sauces, pasta and industrially produced beverages. In this socio-economic class we observe their recourse to the dispensary or the maternity ward for their healthcare needs. The young of the middle class particularly value monogamy and the freedom to choose their own spouse.

The poor are defined as those who are still reduced to farming with rudimentary tools such as the hoe *(daba)* and who are unable to harvest enough to last them throughout the year. In the period prior to the harvest, on a daily basis they are compelled to buy cereals in small quantities at relatively higher prices for their family's consumption. If breeding is practiced by this group of people, it is conducted on a much smaller scale. Individuals living precariously are those who have an insufficient harvest and lack of money to purchase goods at the market. They are obliged to solicit help from others or to borrow cereals to assure the survival of their families during the period prior to the harvest. Of the forty-four elderly (men and women) with whom we conducted in-depth interviews, thirty-one are poor.[8] To illustrate, of the thirty-one poor more than 90 % in this category, or twenty-eight people, eat only one warm meal a day, generally in the evening. About a dozen of the poor live in a state of precariousness. They state that there are even days without a proper meal and they have to content themselves with nibbling. Housing conditions are also insecure even if those concerned are owners. The poor elderly live in more or less dilapidated shanties made of clay, and sleep on the floor on woven mats, cardboard boxes or rags. A house with a corrugated-iron roof is their

---

[7] Often this refers to second hand clothing called "goodbye Europe".

[8] The poor can be categorised into three groups: 1. the poor, 2. those who live precariously and 3. those who are socially marginalised (cf. Roth 2003a). Based on the 44 interviews 31 are poor.
a. Of the 31 poor, 28 (or 90 %) have one meal a day; they live in fragile security.
b. Of the 31 poor, 11 (or 35 %) occasionally have days without food; they live precariously.
c. Of the 31 poor, 4 (or approx. 13 %) resort to institutions to request food; they live socially marginalised.
Thus, of the 31 poor, 15 (or 48 %) live precariously or socially marginalised.

dream and they hope to sleep in one before dying. Their clothing situation is not much better: They have rags, second-hand clothes or go shirtless during the day. As regards healthcare, the situation is even direr. The majority do not have access to modern care and some go so far as to refuse such care. Money offerings to the elderly are rare or minimal – FCFA 100 (€ 0.15).[9] Do these elderly men and women receive support from the family or community?

The Gap Between Ideas and Practices of Family Support

For the aged men and women of Kuila, the family is principally a framework for life, of belonging and of reference. It is at the heart of the family that relationships between spouses, between parents and children, and between generations are defined and organised. It is also here where important decisions concerning its members are made and where the satisfaction of their essential needs are expressed and realised. Today in the rural context of Burkina Faso, like in Kuila, the concept of the family as the guarantor of social security of its members remains strong. For the elderly we interviewed who are integrated into their families, their security and support relations essentially take place through kin relations. For them, being a parent "is to be sensitive to the problems of others and to assist them". This means that if on the one hand one can expect everything from kin – help, assistance, rescue – on the other hand there is the duty and the obligation to help the parent in times of need. Generally speaking, in the popular imagery lending assistance to family members is perceived as an incontrovertible obligation (Eloundou-Enyegue 1992: 8). "The obligation to help a parent" in its application introduces rules of reciprocity, of "gift in return for gift", which indicates that the individual who receives assistance acquires a social debt he is expected to repay one day in one way or another. To illustrate the concept of reciprocity, our informants evoke a Moaga proverb which says that "Kin is a piece of wood that deserves to stay in contact with another to keep the hearth of kinship

---

[9] € 1 = FCFA 655.95.

lit", which means that kin relations require being looked after and are maintained thanks to the regular exchanges at work.

The guarantee of a minimum of social security rests on the capacity of the individual to take responsibility for him or herself. Counting on oneself in the first instance is a sign of relative autonomy and at the basis of family support. "When someone washes your back you must be able to wash your face," goes another Moaga saying. From this same perspective Vuarin (2000) speaks of the importance of taking responsibility for oneself and notes that "the first condition of receiving support from others is the effort which tempts the victim to grab the lion by the head: Help yourself and others will help you" (ibid. 39-40, free translation).

In Kuila, people consider that preparation for old age requires a lifetime. Every adult has to have foresight and work without ceasing to contemplate their old age. In practice, preparation for old age is difficult for the poor due to the limited nature of their resources. The revenues obtained from working the land are insufficient to cover the daily needs of the poor elderly. They estimate their harvest at ten or fifteen sacks of millet to nourish a family of about ten people for one year, whereas it takes twice as much to provide two meals a day. In spite of the burden of age, elderly men and women, with the exception of those who are disabled or bedridden, keep their fields and clear the land and work on it with the help of their children; the field of the patriarch being considered the familial field. Breeding represents the principle source of savings, most notably for the men, but is limited for the poor to chickens, guinea fowls and in the best of cases sheep, goats or pigs. Women save through their kitchen utensils, their jewellery, and traditional cloth; all objects which are losing their value in today's marketplace.

Historically, the forced labour during colonial times negatively influenced the lives of the elderly we interviewed. Some of them had to build roads or worked on plantations without receiving any compensation either at that time or today. Migration was developed during this colonial period and the Moaga, considered a "hard worker", greatly interested the colonisers. Since then, the migration process has continued, but nowadays people go in search of money. However, due to the gravity of the economic crisis, migration is no longer synonymous with success and some elderly migrants have returned to the village empty-handed following the exactions.[10]

In summary, the ability of the poor elderly in Kuila to take responsibility for themselves is limited due the daily pressure exacted on their resources, and their lack of savings and investments. Extreme poverty is synonymous with a lack of foresight because life moves ahead and the present weighs on the future. For the majority of men and women of Kuila social insecurity marks their daily existence. They suffer from hunger their entire lives and therefore require assistance in their old age. Family support can come from various types of relations such as marital, intergenerational and those at the heart of the extended family. We will now look at the gap between the ideas and the practices of family support in Kuila.

Marital Relations: Between Paradise and Inferno

Marital relations are supposed to be security relationships in old age in terms of social respect, mutual support and labour sharing. Vis-à-vis society, marriage guarantees men and women social status which inspires respect. In Kuila unmarried elderly people are rare. Widowers systematically remarry or already have other wives because of the accepted practice of polygamy. Divorce is uncommon and the levirate system[11] returns widows, whatever their age, to the marriage circuits (even if sometimes it is just a matter of a symbolic husband where the widow's spouse is a child within the lineage). The practice still in effect today (of the forty-four enquiries six women are in this situation) permits widows to remain in the marital family and avoid social pressure, suspicion, and serious accusations which sometimes lead to marginalisation and social exclusion. According to the conceptions, marriage responds to a social necessity. "Aging without marriage means dying without a funeral," declares an eighty-four year-old man of the

---

[10] Consequences of the war in the Ivory Coast since 2000.
[11] Levirate: custom obliging the brother of the deceased to marry his widow.

middle class. More than a union of two people, marriage is the union of two families, two lineages, and forms a supplementary network of social relations through which are interwoven relationships of support and assistance. "It is always a system of exchange which we find at the origin of marriage rules" (Zimmermann 1972: 39, free translation).

From another perspective, marriage infers social obligations: Husband and wife owe each other succour and assistance. Through marital duty the burdens and responsibilities are shared and the fact that each does his or her part is a source of security for the other. For the family consumption, the head of the family is responsible for providing the cereals and the women supply the different ingredients for the sauce. Beyond material support, social and moral assistance are also greatly appreciated. The spouses have to give each other mutual support. According to an elderly woman of the middle class: "The old vultures pick at each other... The older we get, the more we talk together, something which was not doable before. We exchange ideas. It helps to pass the time and to combat loneliness and the thoughts of death. It helps to live." If these points cannot be generalized, we still have here a sign of the increase in status woman attain with ageing.

In practice, marriage becomes a source of insecurity when marital conflicts multiply or when problems arise with the in-laws. The cases of widows in the village who want to withdraw from the levirate are sufficiently evocative of conflicts with the in-laws. One of our interviewees, who is fifty-eight and poor, explains, "From now on I have to take care of myself and practically raise my children alone, the last one of which was born in 1990. My problems don't really interest my husband's family any more. When there is a social event in my family of origin no one is available. All because I refused to stay with my deceased husband's brother." Therefore, when familial responsibilities are not assumed as required by the social norm, the balance of the household is threatened. Particularly if the head of the family is unable to provide the necessary quantity of cereals for the family consumption, he is perceived as a good-for-nothing (cf. example 6). However, the wife avoids bringing her husband's failures to public attention even if she is suffering. Also among the Moose, the honour of the spouse consists in covering up her husband's incapacities and to take over his responsibilities – tacitly. It is one of the secrets of marriage – a *furugundo*[12] (Roth 2003a : 21). Among the Moose the most valued woman is one who knows how to cover up the difficulties within the household and knows how to swallow suffering. In fact, the women we interviewed all said that there is no ideal home; one has to know above all how to stay. It is in this regard that we can consider the fact that elderly men have young wives who actively work in their fields as a strategy to avoid lacking cereals (as is the case of the couple in which the husband is nearly seventy and the wife is twenty-six). Women turn to their family of origin to request help even if this proves to be socially devaluing. On the other hand, polygamy as practiced in the village (16 of 44 cases)[13] is considered a source of security for both men and women. For the men it signifies hands to work the fields. For the women it means a sharing of domestic chores. However, polygamy is increasingly becoming a source of conflict between spouses and co-wives, which often results in repercussions on the children. Indeed, polygamy poses more problems than it resolves. In general, if marriage provides security there are social costs which the husband and wife have to pay. The husband has to be worthy of his status as head of the family by assuming family duties (above all nourishment) and the wife has to maintain the household, accept being subservient and know how to protect her husband's honour.

Old Age Support: Intergenerational Relations

Intergenerational relations represent the centre of gravity of social security for the elderly poor. This is due to the contract between the generations which reflects this more or less tacit accord of support between the old and the young generations, and particularly between parents and children. According to the conceptions, the progeny constitutes the first line of old-age support. The wealth of the poor lies in

---

[12] The secret of marriage in Dioula: *furugundo*, in Mooré: *ya banguin zindi.*
[13] 7 cases of polygamy of 13 in the middle class and 9 of 31 cases among the poor, even if there is a high proportion of Catholics, a religion emphasising monogamy.

their progeny goes a saying in the village. Among the Moose the intergenerational contract appears to be natural. A proverb says: "You bring a child into the world, you take care of him until he gets his teeth in the hope that he will care for you when you lose yours." In other words, parents care for their children from birth on and in return the children should take care of their parents till death. A notion of intergenerational solidarity, reciprocity and mutual obligation exists between parents and children. It is thus the duty of the young to provide for the needs of the elderly who in turn have to confer advice, lavish blessings for their social accomplishments and share their experiences, their wisdom and their secrets to life.

In practice, in Kuila the contract between the generations is adhered to in the majority of cases (36 of 44 cases). Meanwhile, it also displays considerable limits in regards to meeting the basic needs of the poor elderly. As explained above, the majority of these aged people in the villages live in pronounced insecurity as regards their nutritional needs. The example of Jean Michel (example 1) clearly demonstrates the importance of the intergenerational contract both in terms of conception and practice.

Example 1: Jean Michel's Secure Life
Jean Michel was born around 1940 in Kuila. When a school opened in Guilingou, the neighbouring village, his parents enrolled him but it was difficult to attend regularly, so Jean Michel ran away from school and went to stay with his maternal uncles in Zitenga, a village not far from Kuila. From Zitenga he continued to Ouagadougou before beginning on his adventures outside the country. He left for the Ivory Coast in 1961 in search of a better life. He began by working on a banana plantation for FCFA 4000 (€ 6) per month. Work proved to be unprofitable so he tried masonry which he in turn abandoned to take up other small jobs. Jean Michel returned to the village for the first time in 1966. He returned to Kuila permanently in 1973, married in 1974 and turned to working the land. He also began making bricks and collecting old shoes so he could sell them in Ouagadougou. But little by little old-age made itself known. Jean Michel realises that his only old-age insurance will come from his children. "Those you have brought into this world will be the first to care for you. Someone else from your lineage may help you but that will always be something occasional." Jean Michel adds, "Everything one does for the children when they are little is so that when they grow up they will in their turn care for us until our dying days." Jean Michel, father of six children, believes his four sons will help him work

the fields. His oldest son and his daughter live with an aunt in Ouagadougou where they went to school. Lacking money to continue his studies, his son has been unemployed for two years. For her part, his daughter learned to read and write in Moore but without any positive outcome. "I've heard that she is presently living with a Gurunsi friend[14] in Ouaga, whom I don't know." Getting money is a problem he says. Neither he, nor his wife, nor their children have any. Sometimes, it is even difficult to come upon FCFA 100 (€ 0.15). One of his sons tends the herd of one of Jean Michel's older brothers. He gave him several goats in compensation. "When we have serious difficulties such as a health problem, I sell one of the goats (FCFA 7,000 to 10,000 or € 10 to 15) to solve the problem." Jean Michel's compound includes round shanties, a hangar and granaries made of straw. There are no houses with corrugated-iron roofs in his compound but despite this he doesn't consider himself poor. "Being poor means having no children and being obliged to count on the children of others," he comments.

Jean Michel's story (example 1) illustrates that the intergenerational contract can work despite the many limits. The support of the children for the parents is the most determinant aspect for security in old age. The only problem is that even the most conscientious of children can only give their parents what they have.

A handicapped elderly person is even more dependent on the family and children as the story of Tinga shows (example 2). Increasingly blind, Tinga is always in need of assistance to move around or to get his food. His wife and his children feel obliged to look after him. "He gave us life," says his oldest son.

Example 2: (In)Security in Old Age Due to Disability

Tinga was born in Kuila a little more than seventy years ago. He always worked the land, and raised small ruminants and fowl. When he was much younger he went to Ghana and worked for a year on a cocoa plantation, but since his return he has never again left Kuila. Tinga considers himself an animist and attaches great importance to ancestor worship. In his opinion, nothing can totally erase tradition. Tinga practised polygamy and had two wives, one of whom died. He also lost many children, about ten or so he says. Today, besides his wife, he still has three sons and one daughter. His children have given him six grandchildren. No one in his family had the opportunity to go to school. Tinga has been blind for about twenty-five years and is totally dependent on his family. "My wife and my sons take care of me but unfortunately

---

[14] Gurunsi: one of the ethnic groups in Burkina Faso.

they are destitute. I have to content myself with the minimum they can do for me. I am disabled and can no longer cultivate the land. They take care of the fields in order to get food for us and everything else. Occasionally, I braid chord which the children resell at the market but it's only for FCFA 100 to 200 (€ 0.3). They make their own bricks in the dry season and sell them in order to ensure the most minimal of needs of the family." Neighbours and friends sometimes think of him and visit him. Some bring him cola nuts or millet beer *(dolo)*. For them Tinga is one of the elders of the village and deserves to be honoured. The mission sometimes distributes food to the needy and handicapped and in the past Tinga occasionally benefited from this help. According to our latest information, Tinga died in March 2004.

Thirty-six of forty-four elderly men and women in Kuila are supported by their children; among the poor it is twenty-nine of thirty-one. In comparison to the urban situation in Bobo-Dioulasso, we can say that the intergenerational contract is practiced. Some children say they would like to do more and to better support their parents, but can't because of financial constraints. Their contribution is limited to working the fields. In thirteen[15] of forty-four cases, daughters-in-law and grandchildren live with elderly people, mostly due to cases of force majeure, which are becoming more and more common such as the death or departure of a son on an adventure. The daughters-in-law and grandchildren work in the family fields. "The reversed intergenerational contract" as a consequence of unemployment among the young – striking in Bobo-Dioulasso (cf. Roth in this volume) – is more unusual in Kuila: four of forty-four cases, of which three are from the middle class. This can be explained by the fact that in the village the land is managed by the eldest like in the past, and that working the land and the Moaga social organisation give responsibility to youngsters very early in life by providing them with fields of their own to cultivate. In fact, within families there are more and more children who disobey and provide minimal or no support at all to their elderly parents. It is about young people that refuse to work the land, like the four mentioned cases of the "reversed intergenerational contract", in which the young generation does not support their parents, as expected, but is still dependent on them. Some dispossess their parents

---

[15] Of these 13 people 9 count on other children who support them.

by stealing their goats, mutton and fowl to resell them at the market where they spend all of their time drinking millet beer and eating kebabs, thus resulting in tension between parents and offspring. During the group interviews we were told about a case in 2001 in which an old man in Kuila stabbed his own son when he tried to steal a goat in the middle of the night. Obsessed by modern consumer goods, these young people no longer fear the magical powers of the elderly and seek to obtain money by any means possible.

Example 3: The "Reversed Contract" According to Old Man Benoît

For old man Benoît, who was born in Kuila in 1939, he belongs to the middle-class and is the father of nine children; the reversed contract is also a reality in the village. He's speaking from his own experience. One of his sons went to school in Ouagadougou and Benoît had to spend FCFA 60,000 (about € 92) for his studies. The son played hooky for the entire year and didn't pass at the end. Presently the son is in Ouagadougou but doesn't visit his Benoît because he is afraid of his father's temper.

Old man Benoît believes that young people today want different things than the elderly want: "They don't accept working the land, they smoke cigarettes, consume alcohol and play mini-football. Young people today don't take care of old people anymore but are more concerned with their own stomachs. It's only when they have a problem that they come back to you. Also, some sons find a woman they care more for than for their own father. But it is worse," he says, "when children hope for your death in order to inherit and benefit from all of your work without having had to slave away." According to Benoît "we have children today just to liberate the uteruses of our women."

The opinion expressed by Benoît (example 3) is shared among many of the elderly, men as well as women. If we look at the numbers from the sample on Kuila, about twenty people affirm this. We must emphasise that it is still a matter of a "discourse of neglect" (Cattell 1997) and not a prevalent fact throughout the village.

Differential Support by Sons and Daughters:
The Tree Often Hides the Forest

In Kuila, generations cohabit and it is not unusual to find three or four generations living in one compound.[16] The virilocality results in married sons installing themselves next to their fathers thereby allowing them to contribute to the perpetuation of the family and to provide practical support: working in the fields, carrying out tasks, providing moral support – which makes more visible the support from the sons. However, cohabitation does not always guarantee the support of the elderly. The fragmentation of the fields – each married son disposes of his own field in the vicinity – implies that some sons work less and less for their aged parents. It happens that sons eat without sharing their food with their elderly parents. In these cases, in addition to the family meal, small tastier dishes (bettered with meat in the sauce) are also consumed by young people who don't share them with the aged. Some even go to the market to eat appetising foods while the elderly go to bed hungry (5 of 31 cases among the poor). Such cases demonstrate blatant neglect of aged men and women.

Daughters on the other hand are required to marry outside the village and to only return occasionally. According to the conceptions, their support appears less evident because it is mostly occasional, but in reality the elderly recognise more and more the important contribution of daughters to their social security. Some send food, money and various types of gifts. When they return to the village, they replace their mothers in their domestic chores. In Kuila daughters help their parents with the support of their husbands. Due to arranged marriages, tradition imposes on sons-in-law the duty and obligation to look after their in-laws in old age. That is why the Moose say "We bring a girl into the world to exchange for a son" in reference to the son-in-law.

---

[16] 11 of 13 cases of the middles class and 19 of 31 cases of the poor. Traditionally this type of cohabitation is a sign of wealth and prestige. In effect, wealth was also measured by the number of people one has under his responsibility and dependence. It becomes evident that fewer poor live in households with multiple generations.

In practice, there are differences in the amount of support given by the children to fathers or mothers. In the traditional Moaga milieu, material assistance provided by the children to the father is generally more substantial than that accorded the mother. This is confirmed in the statements made during the interviews. The norms and social principles require that the support accorded by the children, above all if it is considerable, is transferred to the father. This practice would have a tendency to make the contribution to the mother less than or equal to that of the father. In fact, giving assistance or hidden gifts to mothers exists but only in a circumstantial manner. In addition, beyond the affective capacity of the children, their material and financial capacities can influence the security relations with the parents. It occurs that a child who earns sufficiently may support his stepmother as well as his mother. Those who have higher means can give the stepmother more than her own children.

In conclusion, we can state that gendered support of the offspring tends to disfavour mothers.

Absent Children: The Extended Family, Neighbourhood and Friendship

In the village the notion of family or kin remains considerable and goes beyond the nuclear family to encompass collateral members and other members of the lineage, and of the in-laws. The support of the extended family is viewed as circumstantial or supplementary and is most present at social events. The rituals represent occasions for family reunions: marriages, baptisms, but above all funerals where the families of both lineages are always invited and can express their solidarity through an exchange of offerings. On occasions such as funerals there exist symbolic rules for contributions. As a case in point, each son-in-law must provide a goat or sheep, a rooster, a clay pot of millet beer (dolo) and cola nuts for the traditional funeral ceremonies of a father-in-law. These ceremonies and sacrifices are generally conducted by the elders of the lineage. Beyond social events, the support from the extended family occurs occasionally in the case of some elderly people facing certain life circumstances. In the village elderly people who never had children or no longer have offspring are taken care of by the extended family, contrary to what is observed in the city.

Example 4: The Widow Tennoaga – Supported by the Extended Family

Tennoaga was born around 1930 in Guieoghin Tinga, a village not far away from Kuila. She didn't go to school and worked in agriculture during the rainy season, while during the dry season she produced and sold millet beer *(dolo)* and karite butter. Married at the age of seventeen, she has been a widow for more than twenty years. With her two co-wives, they remained in the marriage compound in the bosom of the lineage *(buudu)*. Only her husband's fourth and youngest wife remarried with one of his favourite sons as a result of the levirate. Tennoaga had a total of seven children but one by one they have all passed away. The oldest were the last two to die in 1995 and 2001. Now she only has her seven grandchildren. Tennoaga feels like an orphan without her children: "If I had my seven children, my life would be pleasant and would have meaning. But without them I can't be happy. Growing old without children is a hardship. Who will take care of you? Who will stay near you?" It is the sons and daughters-in-law of her lineage *(buudu)* who ensure Tennoaga's daily needs. As to the question of who takes care of her today, there is a long silence, then a deep sigh, and then she tells us, "In the court yard the women serve me food and when I need cola nuts or tobacco the youngsters buy it for me. That's it." After another bit of silence she concludes, "Yes, I'm taken care of!"

Tennoaga continues to work. At the first sign of rain, she goes out like everyone else, using the little strength she has left to work her small piece of land with her hoe *(daba)*, which is worn down from use. At the end of the season she doesn't have a big harvest: a few baskets of sorghum and millet, some peanuts and green beans, and above all leaves to use as condiments. For her money needs Tennoaga figures it out. Her eldest son had entrusted her with several of his goats. Occasionally, she sells one of them to cover the costs of some of her needs. The members of her birth family visit her but above all on the occasion of ceremonies. They bring her cola nuts, tobacco and sometimes millet or some money – FCFA 100 or 200 (€ 0.3), but not more. From her neighbours – actually her deceased husband's brothers and their wives and children – Tennoaga occasionally receives traditional dishes or food in small quantities.

The associations in the village are not her affair. "This concerns younger people and those that can still hope for something from this world," she says. She does remember, however, having received twice in a row assistance from the Catholic mission, consisting of a few plates of cereal.

In the neighbourhood, other members of her lineage sometimes give her little gifts but she is wary of asking for anything. Soliciting assistance would be interpreted as if no one took care of her within her own direct family. She adds, "If you regularly seek help, you end up getting accused of things. It's enough that a child becomes ill somewhere for someone to suspect you of being the cause or of knowing about it. It's better to stay in one's shanty."[17] In her social life Tennoaga has a tendency to isolate herself because since she lost all of her children she is afraid of being treated as a witch: "I avoid chitchat for fear of hurtful or antagonising words. Always cloistered, I spend my time between my shanty and the shadows of the hangars, the walls or karite trees." Tennoaga lives practically without expressed needs or rather she represses her needs. She is satisfied with what she is given. She says she no longer needs food, water or sleep. Her stomach and her heart are filled with "memories" and "sufferance". In Mooré, she used the word *sountoogo*[18]. She is counting on her husband's kin to give her a proper funeral so that she can join her ancestors and her children in the after world.

We should note that on the central Moaga plateau the phenomenon of sorcery is greatly feared by the elderly, particularly by the poor. In fact, such accusations are more often directed at the poor who have no support and no defence, such as old women who are alone and have no children. According to a Moaga proverb, "No one would dare accuse the mother of the chief of being a sorceress". If the phenomenon of witchcraft is tied to ancestral beliefs, isn't it in fact a consequence of the impoverishment of the individual? Faced with insufficient resources, it constitutes a means of ridding oneself of the social burden represented by the implicated person. This bias in turn legitimises non-assistance to those concerned.

Under the burden of age, Tennoaga (example 4) can no longer care for herself. She receives her nourishment from her co-spouses' offspring. However, her minimal needs are far from being met. The sup-

---

[17] In an implicit manner Tennoaga is making reference to accusations of sorcery vis-à-vis the old women, a topic still pertinent today in Kuila. Four cases were being dealt with by the chief in 2002. The affected parties, often old women, are considered "eaters of souls". Victims of social exclusion, these women end up dying all alone in their shanties if they are not chased from the village. The services of the Social Action in Ziniaré informed us that they treat one or two cases per trimester and the Centre Delwendé de Tanghin in Ouagadougou took in seven women from the Department of Ziniaré in 2001.
[18] *Sountoogo*: bitterness, moral and psychological sufferance.

port provided by the village community, if not totally inexistent, remains exceptional and limited. Tennoaga is marginalised and an outsider in the solidarity circuit of the employer, civil society, the State, and international aid. We have here an example of familial assistance of an elderly person, and, however minimal, we have to ask ourselves what would have become of Tennoaga, lost in that village, without support from her kin?

The levirate is traditionally a social security mechanism for widows, but more and more widows and orphans find themselves despoiled by this bias. The support given by the extended family can also come from cousins, nephews or the in-laws living in town, as told by the widow Pauline (example 5).

Example 5: The Widow Pauline – Supported by Her Sister's Husband

Born near Kuila in the village of Oubriyaoghin, Pauline is in her fifties. Widowed in 1991, her husband left her with ten children. Three children are married and can manage for themselves but Pauline worries a great deal about the remaining seven who live with her, the youngest of whom was born in 1990. Pauline is more than anything active in agriculture and is affected by the same conditions as everyone else: "If it doesn't rain, it's as if I hadn't sown any seeds. There will be nothing to harvest. The periods before the harvest are difficult. Once there is no more food, there is great misery waiting until the new harvest." In addition to agriculture, Pauline contributes to the production of millet beer *(dolo),* an activity organised in the village and assured on a rotational basis among the female producers, which can bring in between FCFA 2000 to 2500 (about € 3 to 3.8) for each batch prepared every nine days.

Pauline lauds the support given by her sister's husband who lives in Ouagadougou and has regularly provided help since her husband's death. "Every month he asks me to send one of the children to pick something up and when the child returns with five or six plates of food I can only thank God for this. In 2000 he became ill and had to have surgery. Since then his own responsibilities have multiplied."

Her roof has been leaking for eight years but her means are lacking so repairing it is impossible. Pauline has enrolled her last two children in school but it is not always easy to assume the costs alone. Some think that a widow should not send her children to school, believing she is overzealous in enrolling her orphaned children in school like the other children. She does it in the hopes that they will pull through so as to help her forget her suffering. When the holy days come nearer it is another nightmare for Pauline because her children risk not having new clothes or special meals, but that is the way life is she says. And her kin, do they assist her through all of this? For Pauline, "when you are rich everyone recognises you as their relative. They are happy to refer to you as a relative and to count you as one of them, even if you are a very distant relative. But when you are poor as we are and you have nothing that interests them, you are neglected." Pauline finds comfort in church. She is a member of the association of Catholic women of Kuila and is in charge of maintaining order in the church. For her efforts, from time to time she receives plates of food and clothing from the mission. According to Pauline, when the State offers food, it is the inequality in the distribution that poses problems. Often the food is pilfered and does not reach the most destitute. If she died and was reborn, she would like to come back as a man, she says, because men have rights and power that women do not have.

Beyond the conceptions, the practice of support by the extended family brings numerous limits for the poor. If the extended family provides support for those who have no children, as in the case of Tennoaga (example 4) or for those who experienced a tragedy like Pauline (example 5), this type of sustenance is nearly inexistent for the poor. In the local context it is said, "Rich or poor, each person's pain is enough to fill them." Being constrained to openly asking for help within the locality covers the person with shame. In Kuila, as in many other places in Africa, social values such as shame, dignity and the honour code impede the social agents from systematically soliciting family support (cf. Vuarin 2000: 143-166). This is even truer for elderly people, particularly the heads of family (example 6). In this regard, if the extended family is very big, paradoxically the possibility for recourse is in practice rigid and limited. Due to the physical proximity of the families, it is difficult to say that one has no kin in the village; however, the elderly person may still find themselves without real sustenance. On the other hand, the requirement for reciprocity in human relations and the law of debt lead to the marginalisation of the most destitute. As stated by Eloundou-Enyegue (1992), "People have the tendency to decrease the assistance provided to those who can give them nothing in return. In the long-term this leads to the marginalisation of the poorest and a rise in inequality".[19] There is a proverb in

---

[19] Cf. also Anspach (2000).

Kuila which says, "It's the millet which causes the hatchlings to come running". Thus, the poor benefit less from kin relations.

Example 6: From Nutritional Insecurity to Suicide

Michel was born around 1950 in Kuila. He said he had a difficult childhood. As the eldest child, he saw his father suffer famine. He must have begun working very young. He helped some people cultivate their land and in return he received food which he took home. He did various small jobs to gather enough money to leave Kuila. He left for the Ivory Coast the first time in 1968 and began by working as a labourer in carpentry, then as a mechanic, and then as a labourer transporting wood. During this period, things went better for him and he was able to look after his parents in the village by sending them money. Following the death of his mother in 1990, Michel returned to the village and met up with his wife and his first son who was born in 1988.

Following his return, things began to rapidly degenerate. Since that time he was no longer able to buy himself a bicycle. In the meantime he wanted to leave again for the Ivory Coast but he had no way to pay for the trip. He asked for help from a friend living in Ouagadougou, but because Michel's father didn't want him to leave, his friend refused to help. Having lent him the money for the trip would have meant the friend sanctioned his departure and would have made him an accomplice. So Michel's friend convinced him to stay. Occasionally, he would send him small amounts of money to the village.

"Today things are difficult for me," Michel would say. "I work the land but without a plough or a donkey so I won't harvest much. During the dry season I go into the bush to cut wood I can sell. I also make baskets and *seccos*[20] to sell so I can feed my family." Regarding support, Michel says, "A parent, an acquaintance, a friend could come to your aid but you can't bet everything on that. It's occasional. I don't get regular support." What support is he referring to? Above all, he is referring to nourishment, food but rarely money. In Michel's household they follow traditional medicine. There isn't enough money to go to the dispensary. For his two children who go to school, each year he sells the school supplies from the year before in order to cover the costs of the new supplies required. "If you are the head of the family and have no resources it is difficult. If I were a woman, I would be with a husband. Women depend on their husbands, but as a man the responsibility for my family falls on me." Nevertheless, Michel would not have wanted to be a woman. He prefers to stay what he is. "For the ceremonies, a neighbour or a relative who has more means helps us. They can kill a pig for Christmas and send us a piece of meat for the family." In spite of these occasional signs of support, Michel was unable to stop himself from the irreparable. In 2001 he hanged himself and left his wife with

---

[20] *Seccos:* braided straw used to cover roofs, make hangars or granaries.

six children, the youngest of whom was a newborn. Still bearing the pain of this tragedy, his wife remains silent on the matter.

As regards family support, elderly women are even more disadvantaged due to the rules of the patrilinear society which is highly hierarchical. If in general it is considered shaming to solicit help, for a woman the disgrace is even greater when she asks her family of origin because this exposes the incapacity of the husband's lineage. As such, women only turn to their natal families in the case of force majeure since it is socially demeaning for her and her husband's family.

Bonded by kin relations, the common traditions and the attachment to the locality, neighbourhood relationships contribute to the social proximity in Kuila. Neighbours supply above all immediate needs: embers for a fire, ingredients for a sauce or for a service. Such support is based on proximity. They are gendered and structured by class like the kin relations. For example, when a neighbour goes to work in the field during the collective activities, the *sissoaga,* the female neighbour helps with the preparation of the meal and the millet beer *(dolo).* Community neighbour relations and kin relations are gendered and obey the rules of reciprocity, to the detriment of the poorest.

Friendships are equally important to the social security of the aged. The people of Kuila sometimes build friendships outside the village which can be more intense than kin relations. A good friend sometimes does more than a close family member for the security of an individual, even if this is not said in front of the family. As with all other relationships, friendships also adhere to the law of reciprocity and debt. In old age some friendships suffer from the difficulty imposed by distance. Friendships are also gendered. In fact, the elderly women of Kuila state that they have a smaller network of friends than the men. Their childhood friends are more often dispersed among the marital homes in different localities whereas the men have been building up their networks since childhood due to virilocality.

The process of distancing oneself or the withdrawal of wealthy kin, which is emerging in Kuila, contributes to the abandonment of the poorest. Some poor elderly comment, "The wealthy become more and more greedy – which once put a blemish on the village". In conclusion

we can say that the poor elderly who are in most need are the same
ones who benefit the least from familial support.

Community Support – Disadvantages for the Poor

Kuila can be characterised by the fact that nearly everyone is related –
either directly or by alliance. So the neighbours, members of the different age groups, members of associations, and members of religious
communities find themselves to be kin. Community support also en-
tails an individual dimension and a collective dimension placed under
the responsibility of the village chief who is charged with organising
symbolic protection rites against famine and epidemics. For the chief
of Kuila his reputation depends on his ability to assure the collective
security. The elderly who adhere to animist beliefs generally rely on
these rites and their symbolic protection. During periods of drought,
they gather around the village chief and the ritual leaders to conduct
these rituals. The Christians and the Muslims also pray for rain.

Beyond symbolic protection, collective work *(sissoaga)* exists at
the village level, including work on the fields and the repairs to roofs.
It happens more and more frequently that these services require a significant investment in foodstuffs, millet beer *(dolo),* cola nuts, tobacco, or even money in return, things which the most destitute and
the needy cannot afford, thereby depriving them of such aid.

Ceremonies such as funerals, harvest rituals *(basga)* or marriages
reunite the entire village and are occasions for the manifestation of
community solidarity through the exchange of goods or services. The
offerings are divided among the eldest and the parts are more often
redistributed based on hierarchical status (i.e. position in family,
wealth). On the occasion of funerals the rich often receive a sheep or a
goat, whereas the poor have to satisfy themselves with chickens or
maybe only a small piece of chicken.

The works of charity conducted by the Church should not be ignored. The Catholic and Protestant missions occasionally offer clothing, mats and food to the poor elderly of Kuila during periods prior to

the harvests or after catastrophes. The *zakat-el-fitr*[21] instituted in the Muslim faith permits a redistribution of foodstuffs to needy elderly people.[22]

Example 7: Survival Thanks to Diversified Gifts

Boureima was born in Kuila in 1920 according to colonial documents. As a young man he was a forced labourer working on the railroad in Bamako, then he went to Kumasi in Ghana, this time in search of money. He spent more than ten years in Ghana working on cocoa plantations. After leaving Ghana he spent about ten years in the Ivory Coast. In total Boureima spent more than fifty years migrating. In the Ivory Coast he worked on coffee plantations with his wife Bibata and their children. The harvests were divvied up into three parts: he kept one-third and the owner of the land received the other two-thirds.

Due to political strife in the Ivory Coast in the last few years many were expelled and Boureima returned to Kuila, his birth village, in 2001 with his wife aged 56 and four of his nine children. Boureima didn't return empty handed. He had saved about FCFA 150,000 (about € 230) and his wife FCFA 100,000 but he says everything was spent on installation expenses and the purchase of food. Upon his return, Boureima first occupied a shanty in the family compound and with the help of his deceased elder brothers' children and other members of the lineage; they produced bricks and managed to build three shanties and a house with a corrugated-iron roof to house his family. Boureima says he had no difficulty obtaining a field to cultivate, but against all expectations the 2001 season was particularly bad. His lot was allevi-ated thanks to the support of his family but above all thanks to the *zakat-el-fitr* and the distribution of food made by the Ziniaré authorities. "What helped me the most were the alms, the *zakat-el-fitr* from the Muslims. The Muslims from Touma sent me white sorghum and millet, as did those from Goughin and Kuila. What I received from the *zakat-el-fitr* was two times what we were able to harvest. It was this which allowed us to hold on till now. To that we have to add what the government gives to the needy: two to three plates of food from time to time. My wife goes to stand in line every ten days which helps us out. At Antoinette's[23] it's enough to go there with your plate. But as the head of the family, I'm ashamed to line up over there."

On this subject, his wife Bibata says: "Not having a granary for millet upon our arrival, we spent all of our time buying food with the little money we had. And when it's like that, if the money is spent and not replaced, it runs out very quickly. From

---

[21] The *zakat-el-fitr* are the alms offered by the head of the household based on the family's resources and the size of the family during the Islamic fasting period.

[22] Regarding social security obtained by Islam cf. Roth (in this volume).

[23] Antoinette, the sister of President Blaise Compaoré of Burkina Faso who lives in her residence in Ziniaré, receives food from him for the local needy.

time to time I go to my family (her natal family) and I use the money that they give me to buy food and return home. One of my brothers works in a bank in Ouagadougou and he occasionally gives me money."

Boureima doesn't minimise the aid given by his kin, the support of his lineage *(buudu)* in the village. "At the beginning of the season, it was our kin who gave us the seeds to cultivate: sorghum, millet, beans, peanuts, everything... In the past, when I returned from the Ivory Coast, I took care of them and gave them things and money. Today, they realize that I have nothing: no chickens, no goats, no sheep, much less a donkey or an ox. My nephews (his brothers' children) give us food from time to time, but never money. In the village, they are incapable of helping you settle a debt for FCFA 10,000 to 15,000 (about € 15 to 23). How could they help you buy a donkey and a carriage to cultivate the land? They themselves don't have these things." Today, Boureima's dream is to buy a donkey and a carriage so that he and his wife and children can better cultivate the land and maintain it till the end of his days, but he doesn't know who to turn to for help. And his wife Bibata notes that due to the almost exceptional situation,[24] kin and neighbours have not abandoned them and have promised them solidarity. Even the village chief helps them with food. However, it proves to be very difficult to ensure the daily needs of an entire family in this way.

The story of Boureima and Bibata (example 7) illustrates the difficulties of migrants who return home. Since migration did not allow people to save sufficiently or to invest in the village, when they return in old age they have to start from zero, create a framework for their lives, build a house with roof over their heads, find a field and begin working that field. With their savings quickly depleted, the couple is able to hang on thanks to the help of the family. Before Boureima also helped some of his kin – and that is the basis of support which he receives today (generalised reciprocity). We have here in addition to family support an example of support by the Muslim religious community through the *zakat-el-fitr*. Not without shame, the couple, and particularly the wife, finds itself constrained to solicit assistance from the authorities. Migration is becoming less and less synonymous with social ascent.

---

[24] Exceptional situation because they returned from the Ivory Coast following the exactions.

Civil and Governmental Organisations: A Drop in the Bucket

On the local level, organisations such as age groups and cultural associations form the framework of an identity reference, of support, rescue and assistance. These associations are created in the spirit of mutual support. It is in this way that the association of youngsters should show itself useful to the elderly: It is their duty to help work the land, look after the environment, put roofs on houses, dig wells and graves. Besides them, the class of the elders and the elderly represent the advice of the wise. If certain tasks are imposed on the young in the village, for example digging graves, other tasks are becoming more and more rare – notably for the elderly who are destitute. The work done in the fields is done through the collectives (*sissoaga*), which as mentioned previously require means beforehand, which in turn deprives the poor elderly from receiving assistance from the community. At the base of the elder generation, support remains dictated by the rules of reciprocity, which implies having the necessary resources to be able to participate.

In Kuila, associations of a more modern nature are slowly emerging, as is the case with the association "Nimb gninga". Created in 2000, the founder and president of which is a former émigré of Gabon, the association is essentially made up of relatives from the village and those living in town. It operates on the basis of dues and accords loans or provides food to its members. The president comments, however: "Since it's between us, some take money and don't reimburse it, and we can't say anything because it's you and your kin." In the past, creating village groupings was attempted but without success. On the matter of savings groups, the "tontines", the elderly of Kuila consider themselves too destitute with aleatory revenues to take the risks associated with them. One old women comments: "Experiences have not resisted poverty." The system of credit remains informal and based on the immediate entourage. On national and international levels, the efforts developed by the associations do not affect the whole of the villages and are not directly focussed on the aged. In Kuila the aged poor do not draw attention to their poverty. The existing local associations are gendered in the sense that they are more the product of men than of women. Elderly women are for all practical purposes absent from these associations.

Overall, in Kuila support provided by associations to the elderly is less diversified and shows the same limits as family support. The support of the aged by governmental organisations is the least visible and most sporadic in our context. In Kuila many elderly people do not know who the state is or what the state does for their social security. In the village, contributions made by the state are limited to punctual operations in which they distribute offerings or sell foodstuffs at social prices to the most destitute during periods of catastrophes or drought: According to the Director of the provincial "Action Social", this can include approximately seven kilos of food per person in the difficult period prior to the harvest.[25] Overall we can affirm that the community networks are less diversified than in the urban context.

Conclusions

In Burkina Faso the question of social security for elderly people represents a thorny issue long kept silent. According to conceptions, family support through marital relationships, intergenerational relationships or extended family relationships represents the principal source of social security for the elderly in the village. These different relations have as a goal to provide the aged with succour, aid and assistance. Progeny remains the old-age insurance for the poor elderly.

In the meantime, the ambivalence of familial and community support shows itself in the numerous limits. Support does not always satisfy the basic needs of those concerned. This is due to the general lack of resources, particularly in villages of the North of Burkina Faso such as Kuila. This lack of resources creates the gap between imagery and practice concerning support of the aged. Kin for example, the source of support, shows itself capable of exclusion, neglect and marginalisation even if the Moaga proverb says that "We wouldn't know how

---

[25] In 2002, an international donation arrived in Kuila: 50 kilos of cereal for heads of family, which created a considerable problem with its distribution.

to wash kinship like laundry", which means one cannot detach oneself from these connections. Thus, marital kin relations include protection and support, but also control and conflict (Risseeuw/Palriwala 1996:16). Familial support in its present form is in fact limited to the poor because they are unable to adhere to the "law of debt" (Marie 1997). The poorer the person, the less they are able to honour this social debt and the less they are able to benefit from kin relations.

The migration of sons, in regards to its ambivalent character, can have as a consequence the neglect of parents. On one hand, sons can skirt their duty of caring for their parents. On the other hand, those who have not succeeded have difficulty returning to the village because they will no longer be respected.

As in other localities, old women in Kuila are also the poorest and the least assisted. Their possibility for recourse through associations and organisations is more limited than for men. The most pitiful are those women who are accused of sorcery and become victims of social exclusion. Not satisfied with ignoring their basic needs, this tactic allows society a "legitimate" way to rid themselves of these poor elderly who represent a social burden.

Community support shows the same ambiguity as familial support and is in the process of eluding the poor. Old forms of community support are becoming more and more "costly" by more often adhering to the principle of balanced reciprocity and new forms of community support do not reach the most destitute. Works of charity emanating from religious and state institutions or NGO's, if at all present, are destined by their very nature to the most needy. However, in order to receive these benefits needy people have to be willing to "publicise their poverty" and bear the social disgrace. For those who are willing to follow this course, these charity contributions nevertheless are not guaranteed as they are often diverted to the benefit of the more affluent who are not in need.

Based on the numerous limits imposed by the practice of familial and community support, where is the capacity for the elderly poor to act? Where is their agency? In the village, their principal security net functions through the intergenerational contract. Economic power through possessions, the administration and control of land, notably by aged men, maintains to this day a real and symbolic power over the younger generations. Additionally, the elderly of Kuila can count on the members of the extended family. Moreover, the place of the elderly in the core of the family cells represents a power and manoeuvring space for the interested parties. This allows them to avoid living on the street and begging as is the case in town. It also sets up an opportunity for engagement in family and social life, while also entailing certain conditions: The aged person must be sociable and above any suspicion of sorcery. Sorcery in this case becomes a significant tool of social control which requires the elderly to be modest and obliging. The strategies implemented by the poor elderly remain, among others, establishing harmonious relationships and demonstrating good character.

Conclusions
Ageing in Insecurity – Differences and Similarities

Claudia Roth and Willemijn de Jong

Based on the joint and parallel research conducted in the four localities in India and Burkina Faso, we discovered existing differences and similarities in old-age security. Below we will compare our most prominent results.

Burkina Faso: Old and New Forms of Solidarity

In Burkina Faso close ties exist between the village and the city: Children from the village attend school in the nearest big city; the sick of the village stay overnight with relatives when they need to go to the municipal dispensary, while in the city those suffering from psychological or physical ailments remember the indigenous treatments of their ancestors in the village. City dwellers go to the village for funerals, as do the village dwellers who travel to the city for the same reason. Young people seek their luck finding work in the city, while those stranded in the city as migrants return to the village to start over. The elderly also often return to the village since it is easier to live there without money. During more prosperous economic times, village dwellers could provide their city kin with millet, but today this kind of support is only symbolic: They make offerings for their kin in the city for the successful outcome of a venture. On the other hand, the material support provided by city dwellers to their village relatives has also declined (cf. Potts 1997).

Migration of the young is more common among the Moose in the northern part of the country than among other ethnic groups in the southwest – the area where Bobo-Dioulasso is located; "to go on an adventure" is also part of becoming a man among the Moose. In today's conditions, however, the migration of the young has created uncertainty for the elderly. It has created a shortage of manpower in the village. It is also unclear whether a young man will find work in the city thereby allowing him to send money back to the village, or whether he will disappear for years on end due to the shame of having failed. In the village of Kuila, like in the city of Bobo-Dioulasso, elderly men and women report of migrated children who barely stay in contact – the "circles of solidarity that extend over longer distances" (see preface) are overburdened.

Despite the close connections between the city and the surrounding villages, the rural and urban situations in Burkina Faso differ considerably. The social change and the decade-long persistent economic crisis have impacted the city and countryside differently. In regards to the social security of the elderly, the principle difference is that old men in the village of Kuila still dispose of the crucial means of production, namely land. This difference shapes intergenerational relationships. The access to land allows the elderly to provide their sons with a livelihood while simultaneously allowing them to maintain power. City dwellers have lost this possibility. For this reason, the implicit intergenerational contract is ninety percent lived up to in Kuila, even though as a result of lacking resources the livelihood of elderly men and women is not assured.

In Bobo-Dioulasso, in contrast to Kuila, the young earn their livelihood independently from the elderly thus allowing them to negotiate the intergenerational power relationship. The loosening of the age hierarchy provides the young with a certain level of autonomy, which in turn is limited by the difficult economic situation and the resulting high unemployment – an ambivalent situation for both sides. The young adults, including unemployed children and unwed mothers, who actually should be responsible for themselves live according to the reversed intergenerational contract, i. e. they furthermore stay as dependents in their father's compound. In fact, for their part elderly men and women occupy their habitual social position and manage the "extended family", but without the benefit of getting back what they once invested.

Another important difference between the city and the village includes new forms of solidarity: the "'secondary' sociability" as a result of social change in urban conditions, that means voluntarily created relationships, sought by the individuals, chosen and constituted day by day through encounters and social situations such as the associations or the savings groups (Vuarin 2000: 187, cf. also Neubert 1990). In contrast, in Kuila, despite newly created associations, the "primary sociability", which is preordained by affinity (lineage, clan, village), determines the solidarity relationships: on the one hand the vertical and hierarchical ones, thus the age and gender hierarchy; on the other hand the horizontal and egalitarian one between those of equal status, thus the age groups. The social security arrangements of elderly men and women in the city are accordingly more diversified, but in practice limited by socioeconomic stratification.

In the village, as well as in the city, lacking resources place narrow limits on kin and non-kin security relations. Kinship is not a given, but rather created by individuals who have to continuously cultivate it. The paradox of this crisis is that the resources, i.e. the means of solidarity, are decreasing although they are simultaneously more necessary than ever (cf. Marie 1997). This fact creates tension and conflict between young and old, men and women, daughters and mothers-in-law, and between younger and older siblings. Differing interests with increasingly scarce resources lead to relationships which can be highly ambivalent and conflictive, since no one can dare to disassociate themselves from their social relations because social security cannot be found outside kin and community relationships.

As a result of AIDS life expectancy is once again beginning to sink in Burkina Faso (cf. appendix). In both the village and the city, elderly men and women complain of having to bury their children. The elderly, in many cases the women, assume the care of their orphaned grandchildren. AIDS strongly impacts the social security of old men and women as well as of the children (cf. also Leliveld 2004). One of the ancient forms of solidarity, namely the levirate, is still lived in villages such as Kuila, but is disappearing in the cities as a consequence of AIDS and also poverty.

Bobo-Dioulasso is also historically a multi-ethnic city. The many ethnic societies differentiate themselves not according to socio-economic levels, but according to language, customs and social organisation. In the Moose society the adult children give their support by turning over their contribution to their fathers, not to their mothers – contrary to the practice in many of the societies in the Southwestern part of the country, where Bobo-Dioulasso is located (cf. also Besana 2001). This is in equal measure due to the social organisation and social change. In Bobo-Dioulasso and in Kuila both social aspects are gendered but to a different degree. In the village of Kuila the sons give more than the daughters to the elderly parents, making them as expected the social security for parents in old age, and thereby fathers receive more than mothers. In contrast, in the Koko neighbourhood of Bobo-Dioulasso, daughters are often more reliable givers than the sons, and the mothers receive more than the fathers. We interpret this as a characteristic of the urban situation, in which for women their natal family is more reliable than their husbands' and where women consider their children as their old-age security, as opposed to men who seek this in marriage. We also see it as an expression of the more or less hierarchically structured society in which age and gender are to a different degree structuring principles and thus affect relationships between men and women and the agency of the women differently.

Kerala: Different Qualities of Social Security Relationships

Much of the Indian literature on old age presumes a worsening of the support conditions of the elderly which is often attributed to an undifferentiated "modernisation" and "urbanisation". How is this evident in the case of Kerala? On first sight the working class people in the town of Kalamassery and the village of Kadamakuddy hardly show any differences with regard to old age security. The social security arrangements in both cases are highly diversified and can be characterized as a "patchwork arrangement" in which the "extended neighbourhood" is important, i.e. relationships with local people in addition to those of the extended family. Particularly in times of crises and difficulties, the working class Pulayas try to obtain every possible resource in that they mobilise help from kin, neighbours, (former) employers, civil organisations and the state.

These similarities can be explained in the first place by Kerala's specific modernity, meaning its "rurban" character. Towns there have a village-like character, compared to similar house compounds, from which only city centres clearly differ (cf. also Kuruvilla 1989). On the other hand, life in a village does not differ much from life in town due to the widespread developments in the field of education and health. In particular, the formal education of the working class Pulayas is similar in both case studies. The elderly generally attended school for two to three years, which was often insufficient to be able to read and write the Malayalam language script, whereas the younger generation had about ten years of schooling.

Furthermore, in both contexts agriculture previously was important. Today, agriculture has lost its importance in both localities, but especially in Kalamassery since the process of industrialisation of the 1960s. But even in Kadamakuddy jobs in agriculture have diminished and have been replaced by work in construction and cleaning services partly in the village but more outside. Thus the elderly in both contexts additionally performed other low-paid manual work; those in Kalamassery to a larger extent. With household incomes just above the official poverty line or below it, it is not surprising that the elderly and their children leave no stone unturned to meet their needs. The diverse social security arrangements in both contexts are thus largely conditioned by poverty.

The urban-rural similarities can also be explained by Kerala's social structure, or rather our focus on the Pulaya caste. In both case studies we concentrated on members of the same class within the same caste who have a kinship system, and family and household structures which are similar throughout the country. For example, the majority of elderly Pulayas in both the rural and the urban context live with a married son, wife and children in a joint or extended family household. In both contexts the composition of the extended family household is rather stable because these people do not have the means to migrate abroad as wealthier people in Kerala do.

Nevertheless, in looking more closely we noted interesting issues that do contrast to some extent and which need further elaboration and explanation. With regard to the daily need for money, households with elderly members seem to be in a slightly better economic position in the village than in town. Food security is therefore not a problematic issue, as it is among the poorest elderly in town, but often there are not enough means for medicines. The elderly in the village less frequently earn some small income than in town since there are fewer job opportunities available to them. Prices for daily products, and housing and land taxes are lower in the village, however. At the same time, household incomes are somewhat higher in that nearly all of them are just above the poverty line, whereas in town there are more households below the poverty line. Fewer people therefore live in thatched huts in the village. The higher household incomes in the village may be due to the fact that many males of the middle generation do contractual work in the nearby town. This kind of work at least guarantees an income during certain periods of time and is therefore better paid than the usual casual day labour, which is still more insecure.

Moreover, the elderly are able to obtain governmental social assistance more easily in the village, in particular "agricultural workers pensions" and "destitute and widow pensions", although if they have sons, they would become ineligible. In the rural context, the long-term familiarity with persons in government offices is an advantageous factor. These connections also facilitate the renewal of housing registrations following the death of a male and make them less costly than in town, so that in the village Pulaya widows more often own homes and thus have increased bargaining power.

In both the village and town, basic health care is provided by a civil organisation, and basic governmental health care is also available in the village. Access to special medicine is a problem in the village, however, as there is no chemist's shop, and access to a hospital in cases of emergency is difficult. In 2002 the trip took one hour due to the isolation of the village.

Besides the economic condition of the households, the quality of the support relationships is slightly different in the village compared with the town. Children, both sons and daughters, are somewhat more supportive in the village, whereas in town the giving of support by the children is somewhat less reliable and also less gendered. In general, both working and kinship relations have undergone significant changes, or even ruptures, during the last century. Particularly the landowning and the landless classes, such as the Pulayas, were involved in these changes. Landlords no longer provide for the social security of the Pulayas, as they did previously, and thus single sons have had to start to begin providing economically for their parents according to the general norm in India. This kind of support is more difficult the poorer the household and the stronger the claims for economic and also symbolic capital (e.g. prestige through having or being a housewife) from different household members are. In general, the elderly Pulayas in the extended households have interests and needs that compete with those of their children and grandchildren, and females have interests and needs that may compete with those of males. In the urban situation, in addition to increased consumer needs (cf. Sooryamoorthy 1997), the middle generation seems to be more interested, and also forced, to favour the needs of their children and thus their own needs for preparing old age, against the actual needs of the elderly parents.

The conjugal relationship has gained clout and has developed a more supportive character today, both socially and emotionally, and particularly in town. The death of a husband may thus cause more insecurity for women than previously and may be an additional reason why widows in town live more insecurely than widows in the village. The increased significance of marriage is also reflected in the amounts of the dowries which are sometimes four times higher in town than in the village. The use of the dowry only came into existence among the Pulayas in the last two generations. At the same time, women seem more mobile in town than in the village.

Furthermore, due to the fact that there is more poverty in town (cf. also Retnaraj 1999), the use of relations of citizenship is more important than in the village, in addition to the use of kinship relations. For example, neighbours play a more important role for exchanges of food and small amounts of money. Non-daily needs for money for houses or dowries can be more easily required from employers because the elderly living in town often have changed their job more frequently and work longer. The social services provided by civil organisations and the state have also taken on greater importance, but governmental services are less accessible to the elderly because their relationships with civil servants are more impersonal. Therefore, the caste organisation's role as a mediator between the people of the working class and the municipality is particularly relevant.

Kerala and Burkina Faso:
Different Uses of Citizenship and Kinship – Similar Insecurities

Kerala's modernity is very different from Burkina Faso's, although both are developing societies. This becomes apparent if we look at the quality of life indicators (see appendix). Income per capita is less in Kerala than in India as a whole, but it is higher than in Burkina Faso. Whereas in Burkina Faso people have to live with less than one dollar a day on average, in Kerala daily income is a little more than one dollar and in all of India it is even slightly higher. This corresponds with the fact that the majority of the informants in Kerala live in fragile security, whereas the majority of those in Burkina Faso live precariously, meaning that their daily food is not ensured.

There are extreme differences, however, with regard to education and health, which is shown by the literacy and life expectancy rates respectively. Literacy rates for males and females are higher in Kerala than in all of India, but compared with Burkina Faso more than twice as high for males and even more than five times as high for females. There are also considerable differences between Kerala and Burkina Faso with regard to life expectancy. The issue of support for the elderly, particularly of elderly widows, is thus more urgent at present in India than in Burkina Faso which has more basic problems to solve such as literacy and health care for its younger population.

Another substantial contrast is that in Kerala ethnicity is related to caste and religion, whereas in Burkina Faso, with its more than sixty ethnic groups, language and other cultural criteria are important. Other contrasts to Burkina Faso are the considerable societal changes that Kerala experienced in the last century. These changes are the result of the struggles of the oppressed class of politically conscious landless agricultural labours in social movements and trade unions, led by upper class and upper caste ruling Communists. The Pulayas were also strongly involved in these change processes. On the one hand, the collective actions, together with the urgency of the ageing problem, was favourable with regard to the creation of a kind of welfare state in Kerala in the sense of "the formal institution of social protection as a social responsibility" (Spicker 2000: 145). Moreover, a strong tradition of religious charity and welfare already existed there. These factors favoured housing, "pensions" and health care for the elderly Pulayas, and it thus enabled the use of citizenship on a larger scale than in the case of Burkina Faso.

On the other hand along with increased class consciousness, as already mentioned in the introductory chapter on Kerala, a rupture of relationships of kinship, caste and locality took place. As far as kinship relations are concerned we also referred to this in the preceding section in the elaboration on qualitative changes of filial and conjugal relationships in that single sons have become more important as support-givers for elderly parents and bonds between spouses have become stronger. The caste system has been transformed in that more geographical and upwards social mobility of the lower castes has taken place, but there has also been some downward social mobility of higher caste households, for example of the Nayars. Locality was also affected in that through public welfare measures differences between rural areas and towns were neutralized.

Finally, the kinship systems, including household composition and mode of marriage, differ in the two societies. Even if we assume that the Pulayas have a patrilineal, and not a matrilineal kinship system,[1] it does not have the character and significance of patrilineality in Burkina Faso. There it corresponds to rather strict principles of seniority

---

[1] The rule of inheritance of houses in the male line, for example, can be taken as an indication that descent is also rather patrilineal.

and authority of lineage elders, particularly in the rural context. This also applies more or less to elderly females, and it implies that younger male kin such as sons or nephews do not have the decision-making power over elderly women as in Kerala.

Family units are also different in that in Burkina Faso, consistent with a patrilineal lineage system, they mostly consist of agnatic groups of brothers, their wives, their children and possibly other patrilineal kin. Extended family households in Kerala, however, generally consist of parents, a married child, mostly male, the spouse and their children today, whereas previously they also consisted of married brothers or married sisters and their children.

In Burkina Faso, polygamous marriage is widespread, not only as an important value, but also in practice. For example, at least one third of the informants of the lower income and of the middle-income classes both in the rural and urban locality practice this kind of marriage. This means security or insecurity for women, depending on the circumstances, but for men it always means security. In Kerala today marriage is monogamous and its importance has increased, whereas earlier polyandry and polygyny existed with a stronger significance of the natal family. Furthermore, dowries, although legally forbidden since the beginning of the 1960s, are an "invention of tradition" in Kerala since the last century, adapted from higher castes in other parts of India. This kind of marriage transaction threatens the security in old age of poor working class Pulayas with daughters. Instead of making savings possible for old age, a concept that is locally used and appreciated but due to poverty seldom practiced, savings have to be made for dowries in addition to a house, both of which are of equivalent value in town. The tiled house is an important new hereditary asset and can be considered as a guarantee of security in old age. Dowries, on the other hand, are a drain on the old age security of parents, and particularly of widows with daughters. Apart from a possible gain of higher social status and rights of provision as a housewife for the daughter in the new household, meaning an increase of symbolic capital for the younger generation of the daughter and her husband, dowries are delivered without any certain return of economic or practical aid for the givers, her poor parents and other kin. Dowries and being a housewife seem to reinforce each other among the poor working class and result in disempowering rather than empowering women in marriage. We thus can say that marriage among the Pulayas has become more gendered than before, with negative consequences for women. These processes particularly threaten the conditions of poor elderly widows and probably make their old age more insecure in the future.

Beside these differences we can also discern similarities in both societies such as for example the strong emphasis on familial solidarity with regard to security in old age. But as the four case studies have illustrated, this solidarity is limited. In Burkina Faso generalized reciprocity is still valid as an ideal, but in practice it is mostly limited to relationships between parents and children. Due to socioeconomic developments, the implicit generational contract has narrowed. Whereas the obligation to care for the elderly generation also included the children of siblings as well as the children of co-wives, today only one's own children have a duty to care for elderly parents. Cases, where the "extended family", represented by the children of a co-wive, looks for a destitute widow, can still be found in villages like Kuila, but they are becoming rare. In Kerala, the exclusive economic care of a son for his parents among the Pulayas is a relatively new phenomenon; earlier, landlords also provided care for the elderly. This is not acknowledged by the ahistorical discourse of filial piety by Indian governmental institutions and many social science scholars. In Kerala, as in Burkina Faso, the continuous preparation for old age through good care for the children determines to a large extent the later commitment of the children towards the parents in old age. The duty of parents includes providing the children with a good education and marriage, a house and savings, all of which is restricted for the poor, however.

Besides intergenerational support by children, intragenerational support between spouses is important for social security in old age. The fundamental character of the conjugal relationship is similar in both regions. Marriage is considered as a lifelong bond during which the spouses can make their income and their relationships available to each other. The husband has the authority and functions outside the home, the wife functions inside. Woman's responsibility for the care of the elderly and the sick seems to be universal (cf. Albert and Cattell 1994). In practice, the security of elderly women is also dependent on the fulfilment of her husband's obligations towards her.

In all the four research localities, the widows live under precarious conditions, also due to the worsening of the lifelong limited access to resources in old age which reinforces their poverty. The more or less improved status they achieve in old age, depending on the societal context, cannot prevent this. Moreover, these women mostly do not possess their own homes or savings (cf. also Cattell 2002).

However, family support is to some extent a myth due to the fact that kin relationships are dependent on economic and symbolic resources which are claimed by different kin members. This makes even these intimate relationships ambivalent and insecure. For the elderly it is important to dispose of economic resources to have bargaining power. For their children these resources are important to be able to care for the parents and also for their own children and themselves. Thereby, the interests of parents and children may diverge due to different educational levels and consumer needs of the elder and younger generation.

With regard to security relationships other than with children, balanced reciprocity instead of generalized reciprocity is important in that equivalent values are exchanged within a certain span of time. This also applies to non-kin relationships: no exchange and no social security without a minimum of economic resources. A further aggravating factor is that with longevity the period of dependence also increases and the social security system becomes more burdened.

The term "extended neighbourhood" by de Jong (in this volume) covers the manifold social security relationships of poor elderly in urban and rural Kerala which comprise and exceed the extended family. In Burkina Faso this also applies to the middle-income class. What differs between the two groups is the "structural redundancy" (Elwert 1980) of the support relationships. In rural Burkina Faso the extended family and the extended neighbourhood are identical because all villagers are related by kinship or marriage.

Lastly, gender differences in old age in Kerala and Burkina Faso can be summarized as follows. In both countries old age is gendered in that women experience more insecurity in old age. Concerning the political-economic dimension of gender, poor elderly women in Burkina Faso, especially in town, seem to still have the possibility of running a small business into old age, whereas the elderly women in Kerala have less access to low-earning jobs and there is a stronger tendency to become housewives. The economic condition of elderly women in Burkina Faso even enables them in certain cases to support their children, instead of, as usual, the other way around. Moreover, due to the stronger cultural value of seniority in Burkina Faso, younger male kin have no decision-making power over these women as in Kerala, unless they are completely infirm.

Through their agency, women in Kerala and Burkina Faso try hard to adapt to the conditions of old age, to make both ends meet through their own efforts, with the possible help of the spouse and children, as well as of their neighbourhood. They remain active with care tasks as long as they can in their households, or they try to remain at least friendly in their interactions with kin and neighbours. Women protect their husbands against the threat of a possible bad reputation, and particularly in urban Burkina Faso they support children who actually have the obligation to protect them. Their daughters also support them as much as they can. Thus, whereas support giving by children is not strongly gendered, support receiving is.

Although structures and values in Kerala and Burkina Faso are differently gendered and the way poor people are doing gender also differs, in both societies the poorest of the poor elderly women live in insecurity. Due to the differently gendered postcolonial developments in both societies, particularly with regard to education and health, however, the degree of the insecurity of these women as well as its character varies.

Community Development:
A New Perspective on Social Security in Old Age

The four case studies provide a new perspective on social security in old age. With regard to community work with elderly and related social policies we believe that the following issues should be taken into consideration:

- Principally, an approach is important which looks at both normative and actual support relationships, whether it be for an elderly or a younger person, a female or a male, and in the context of her or his life-course.
- The elderly should not be considered as an isolated and homogeneous group. Their heterogeneity should be acknowledged, and they should be looked at in relation to the younger generations. Thereby the specific character of generational relationships has to be grasped with regard to gender and age, in the sphere of kinship and citizenship.
- Security in old age is negotiated in a conflictive field because gender and age hierarchies are changing as a result of societal transformations, material resources are scarce due to economic developments and interests and needs among household members are generally different. Reciprocity is thus continuously renegotiated according to age, gender and individual means.
- Poverty, and thus insecurity, in old age cannot be explained by a small network of kinship relations, but rather by the fact that being poor affects a person's ability to participate in exchange relationships with kin (and other persons) and thus his or her kinship (and general local) network shrinks.
- The term "extended neighbourhood", coined by de Jong, visualizes that the caring extended family is a myth in that it points to the diversity of the security relationships, not only within the family, but also beyond it.
- Lack of resources cannot be compensated by the implicit intergenerational contract or by filial piety. The younger generation becomes further impoverished if they fulfil the obligation to care for

their parents. At the same time the elderly also suffer from further impoverishment if they remain responsible for the care of unemployed children and grandchildren. In these cases external financial and social support is necessary.

- A first step is to acknowledge and to make the public aware what elderly people actually accomplish; through their daily efforts and involvement they contribute to their households as well as to the community and the state. Ideas and initiatives can be generated by a debate on these issues.
- In order to advance issues of social security, it is important to create occasions for continuous dialogues between scholars and practitioners in which both parties can learn from the experiences and reflections of the other and thus integrate new issues and perspectives in their respective work. A favourable basis for such dialogues are North-South research partnerships.

Vieillir dans l'insécurité
Sécurité sociale et genre en Inde
et au Burkina Faso
Etudes de cas

Préface

Il y a vingt ans, quand des collègues me demandaient sur quoi je travaillais et que je leur répondais que je faisais des recherches sur la sécurité sociale dans un pays en voie de développement, leur réaction était souvent un mélange d'incrédulité et de commisération. Qui aurait l'idée d'étudier un sujet si clairement lié au monde moderne, occidental, en particulier à l'État-providence de l'Europe occidentale ? Il appartenait aux sociologues du Nord d'étudier ce champ, mais certainement pas aux anthropologues faisant des études dans les pays en voie de développement. Depuis l'ouvrage pionnier de James Midgley écrit en 1984 « Social Security, Inequality, and the Third World » (Sécurité sociale, inégalité et le Tiers Monde), dans lequel il a mis le doigt sur le manque d'études empiriques concernant les pays en voie de développement, de nombreux ouvrages sont parus, traitant de la sécurité sociale et contribuant à la compréhension théorique de ce domaine. Sous différents labels, la sécurité sociale constitue un thème majeur dans la sociologie de développement, les études de développement et l'anthropologie sociale. En outre, les communautés de donateurs internationales et bilatérales ont inscrit ce thème sur leur agenda. La sécurité sociale est donc un sujet de recherche admis, mais qui demeure néanmoins peu traité.

Deux séries de raisons me paraissent appropriées pour expliquer pourquoi les sciences sociales ne s'ouvrent pas sans réserve à ce sujet tel qu'il se présente dans les pays pauvres, spécialement les pays avec un État faible. L'une des raisons en est que la sécurité sociale reste généralement associée aux politiques de l'État ; et comme on ne peut pas s'attendre à grand-chose de la part de l'État dans les pays pauvres, cela ne vaut pas la peine de s'y attarder. C'était le cliché qui prévalait, et il a la vie longue auprès de certains chercheurs. Manifestement, il s'agit là d'un point de vue distordu. Nulle part dans le monde, la sécurité sociale ne se confine aux prestations de l'État. Même dans les systèmes d'assistance sociale les plus étendus des pays nantis, les politiques officielles ne représentent qu'une partie de l'ensemble. Dans l'histoire spécifique de l'industrialisation occidentale, la lutte politique fut menée pour la création de cercles de solidarité suffisamment vastes pour parer aux principaux risques inhérents à la production indus-trielle : perte de revenu pour cause de maladie, d'infirmité, de licen-ciement, de vieillesse. Au sommet de l'assistance sociale, l'accent a été presqu'entièrement mis sur l'État et ses politiques. Mais toute femme s'étant occupé des enfants ou d'un parent âgé au foyer sait que l'aide publique peut tout au plus alléger la tâche. De plus, la sécurité sociale serait beaucoup moins efficace sans l'énorme engagement bénévole.

La deuxième raison pour laquelle les chercheurs en sciences socia-les et les politiciens ont mis du temps à commencer à réfléchir sur la sécurité sociale dans les pays pauvres est que la sécurité sociale a été pour ainsi dire entièrement associée au revenu. Ceci convient peut-être pour les pays où l'absence de salaire est la cause la plus importante de la pauvreté. Dans les pays pauvres, le manque de salaire est évidem-ment aussi un problème majeur. Cependant, cristalliser l'attention exclusivement sur l'argent rétrécit considérablement notre com-préhension de la sécurité sociale ; pour une compréhension approfon-die, nous devons tenir compte du travail, dans ses deux formes, à sa-voir la production et les soins, et de la disponibilité des ressources. Heureusement, les décideurs ont réalisé que le domaine de la sécurité sociale requiert une approche plus inclusive. De nos jours, des rap-ports du Bureau International du Travail, de la Banque Mondiale et des principales agences de bailleurs de fonds reconnaissent certes ce fait, mais il leur semble encore difficile de tirer les conclusions qui s'imposent.

Parallèlement, les chercheurs en sciences sociales se sont rendu compte que la sécurité sociale ne s'arrêtent pas à la politique gouver-nementale. Bon nombre d'entre eux ont abordé le sujet en partant d'une perspective des études sur la pauvreté ou les moyens de subsis-tance (*livelihood*). Ces dernières en particulier ont révélé l'importance des relations sociales, débattues actuellement sous la notion en vogue de capital social, et l'importance de l'éducation et de la santé, en par-ticulier la santé reproductive. Ces études ont également apporté d'importantes lumières sur les profils à risque spécifiques aux pauvres, profils qui diffèrent de ceux des nantis. Tandis que ces points sont tous d'une importance cruciale pour une vraie compréhension de la sécurité sociale, les études sur la pauvreté et les moyens de subsistance partagent un point faible : elles favorisent une approche centrée sur les personnes adultes et aptes et peut-être les enfants, mais elles ne traitent pas de façon approfondie la situation des malades, des faibles, des personnes âgées et des infirmes. La supposition sous-jacente est que les pauvres peuvent en principe travailler et gagner leur vie si l'accès au crédit, au marché, à l'éducation et à la santé s'améliore. Alors que ceux qui sont inaptes à travailler ou dont la capacité de travail est réduite, ne sont pas a priori complètement exclus des études sur les moyens de subsistance ou la pauvreté, mais ils ne reçoivent généralement qu'une attention plutôt marginale. Les catégories des personnes les moins visibles dans les processus de production demeurent aussi relativement invisibles dans les études sur la pauvreté et les moyens de subsistance. Mais à moins que nous ne les prenions aussi en compte, nous passerons à côté des aspects de la vie sociale qui dépassent largement le cadre de ces catégories : comprendre la sécurité sociale est crucial pour comprendre la vie sociale en général.

La recherche dont le présent volume est l'aboutissement englobe une vaste perspective sur la sécurité sociale. Afin d'étudier la sécurité sociale de manière fructueuse, il s'avère nécessaire non seulement de se pencher sur les institutions conçues spécifiquement pour la sécurité sociale, mais aussi de considérer tout l'éventail des possibilités permettant de venir en aide aux nécessiteux. Une telle approche inclusive comprend la sécurité sociale fournie par l'État, le marché, les organisations bénévoles, la parenté et les communautés. Les sociétés ont des structures normatives définissant ce qui est considéré comme comportement ordinaire et ce qui constitue le besoin, et quelles sont les motivations pour une demande légitime de soutien. Ces structures normatives définissent aussi les cercles de solidarité et les différenciations sociales internes. Cependant, le droit officiel peut avoir des notions différentes quant au besoin et à l'obligation de soutien que les systèmes légaux coutumiers ou la loi religieuse. Dans la pratique, les prestations de sécurité sociale se négocient au sein de ces différents

cadres normatifs ; les gens se créent des mélanges se référant aux différents ensembles de règles et de régulations, et en s'inspirant de différents modèles de sécurité sociale, basés sur la religion, la loi coutumière et la législation gouvernementale.

Bien que le nombre de monographies traitant de ce sujet va croissant, on compte relativement peu de travaux comparatifs semblables à
ceux présentés dans ce livre. Le présent projet de recherche est important pour diverses raisons. Tout d'abord, c'est une tentative de
concevoir la recherche en collaboration étroite avec des personnes
issues des régions étudiées, au lieu de louer des assistants de recherche
pour faire le travail empirique et laisser le cadre théorique aux chercheurs du Nord. Deuxièmement, il faut bien du courage pour essayer
de faire des comparaisons entre des pays aussi différents l'un de
l'autre comme le sont l'Inde, le Kerala plus précisément, et le Burkina
Faso. Les anthropologues, pour autant qu'ils s'embarquent dans des
comparaisons, ont tendance à les faire à l'intérieur des frontières
régionales relativement réduites, et beaucoup milite en faveur de telles
comparaisons restreintes. Mais une comparaison qui traverse les frontières régionales habituelles a ses avantages, spécialement si dès le
départ elle est intégrée au projet de recherche. Elle permet aux chercheurs de questionner des aspects qui ne surgiraient pas si l'on s'était
cantonné dans un seul pays ou une seule région, et de questionner
aussi certaines choses habituellement considérées comme allant de
soi.

Bien que ce volume ne se focalise pas sur la migration, observer
l'urbanisation et mettre en comparaison les situations urbaine et rurale
permettrait d'inclure dans l'analyse les cercles de solidarité à distance,
qui se modifient et se différencient à l'intérieur.

Alors que l'Europe occidentale, et les États-Unis dans une moindre
mesure, ont répondu à l'urbanisation et aux nouvelles méthodes de
production par des systèmes étatiques de sécurité sociale, les pays
pauvres n'ont pas développé un solide système étatique de sécurité
sociale. Ils ne disposent pas d'une base de ressources et refusent souvent d'allouer à la sécurité sociale les maigres moyens dont ils disposent. Dans les pays où cela s'est fait, les fonds destinés à la sécurité

sociale ont notoirement donné lieu à des pratiques de corruption. D'autre part, contrastant avec l'Europe occidentale, les institutions publiques jouent en général un rôle primordial dans la sécurité sociale, pas dans leur capacité officielle, mais sur la base de l'ordre parallèle et non officiel auquel elles participent. Par conséquent, l'application des programmes d'austérité du type de l'ajustement structurel n'entraîne pas seulement la menace de perdre son emploi ; ces programmes ont des implications beaucoup plus grandes sur la sécurité sociale. C'est à cause de cette double menace que ces politiques engendrent angoisse, insécurité et déception aussi profondes.

La présente recherche se révèle particulièrement fructueuse du fait qu'elle remet en question l'idée selon laquelle la famille est nécessairement une base fiable pour la sécurité sociale dans les pays en voie de développement. En observant de près la situation des personnes âgées pauvres, cette recherche a mis en lumière le fait que la famille n'offre pas toujours le cercle de solidarité comme le présument les politiciens. Bien que les cercles de solidarité basés sur la parenté sont, dans beaucoup de cas, virtuellement les seules formes de sécurité sociale disponibles, ils sont très fragiles et offrent en somme peu de sécurité. Ceci devient évident car, dans ce volume, les chercheurs mettent l'accent sur le segment de la population probablement le plus vulnérable au sein de la société : les personnes âgées démunies. La grande majorité des femmes et des hommes âgés les plus pauvres n'ont pas de réseau de parenté solide qui pourrait les prendre en charge. En effet, n'avoir pas de famille proche, notamment n'avoir pas d'enfants, semble être un facteur majeur qui fait basculer les personnes âgées dans la pauvreté. Comme le présent ouvrage le montre, cette situation est exacerbée par le fait que vivre dans la pauvreté veut aussi dire que l'on ne peut pas prendre part à l'échange nécessaire pour entretenir de façon significative des relations de parenté. Résultat : les pauvres ont un réseau de soutien restreint, bien qu'il pourrait y avoir un large groupe de parenté qui pourrait potentiellement être mobilisé pour le soutien. À cause des ravages du sida et du taux de migration très élevé, compter sur la famille comme principale source de sécurité sociale s'avère être une stratégie résolument problématique. Les contributions du présent volume offrent une base empirique pour voir combien précaires sont les réseaux de parenté pour la sécurité sociale. Cette recherche est par conséquent majeure à la fois pour ceux qui ont un intérêt théorique pour la sécurité sociale, et pour les politiciens et les agences de développement œuvrant pour la mise en place de réseaux de sécurité sociale.

Keebet von Benda-Beckmann
Halle, octobre 2004

Introduction : une perspective étendue sur la sécurité et l'insécurité sociales

Willemijn de Jong

Le thème, le projet, les études de cas

Le vieil âge et l'insécurité

« Vieillir dans l'insécurité » – dire que les pauvres des pays du Sud comme l'Inde et le Burkina Faso vivent dans l'insécurité sociale semble être une lapalissade. En revanche, moins bien connus sont l'aspect actuel de leurs réseaux de soutien en constante mutation et l'échelle de leur sécurité sociale. Lorsqu'on discute des questions concernant la « sécurité sociale » parmi les académiciens, ce sont les perceptions des mesures publiques et souvent gouvernementales qui dominent l'esprit. Si l'on aborde les questions relatives aux « réseaux de sécurité informels », l'idée que les besoins sont couverts par « la famille » vient en avant. Au Sud, l'image persistante selon laquelle la « famille » est considérée comme l'institution par excellence qui procure entière protection et réseau de sécurité à ses membres – comme le fait « l'État » au Nord, malgré les réductions – jette le voile sur les pratiques actuelles de l'aide et l'entraide sociales dans le vieil âge.

En tant que chercheurs originaires du Nord, nous avions également tendance à adopter cette perception. Mais tout au long du processus de recherche, nous avons du modifier notre perspective en la matière. Au début, en investiguant à la fois les couches à revenus moyens et les couches à bas revenus, nous nous sommes essentiellement concentrées sur la sécurité sociale. À la fin, et en nous focalisant essentiellement sur les couches à bas revenus pour le présent ouvrage, nous avons au fur et à mesure constaté que la sécurité sociale dans la vieillesse est une affaire délicate pour la population défavorisée et la conséquence d'une lutte perpétuelle contre l'insécurité au sein des structures marquées par les inégalités sociales. Une fois le vieil âge atteint, une partie de la population démunie n'a pas de sécurité sociale. Elle n'est pas

« en mesure de satisfaire certains besoins de base », tels que « s'organiser pour se nourrir convenablement, se vêtir confortablement,
échapper à la morbidité et à la mortalité évitables » (Drèze et Sen
1991 : 7, 8).

Cet ouvrage a pour objectif de mettre en évidence les spécificités
des réseaux d'aide et d'entraide sociales ou des arrangements de sécurité sociale des personnes âgées, en matière de sécurité et d'insécurité
en milieux rural et urbain en Inde et au Burkina Faso. Ces connaissances pourront servir pour la planification des actions destinées au
développement communautaire, surtout à l'heure où les inquiétudes
vont croissantes quant à la prise en charge de personnes âgées dont le
nombre ne cesse d'augmenter. La différenciation ou la non-différen-
ciation selon le genre de leurs réseaux de sécurité revêt alors un intérêt
particulier (*gendering, degendering*).[1]

Une approche étendue récemment développée relative à la sécurité
sociale constitue notre point de départ, elle ouvre de nouveaux hori-
zons sur la façon de percevoir la pauvreté. Nous l'avons mise en rapport avec des approches selon le genre dans le champ des nouvelles
études sur la parenté et sur la citoyenneté. Les personnes dont il est
question dans les quatre études de cas appartiennent principalement à
la catégorie de petits paysans et de journaliers qui assument la survie
avec des revenus irréguliers. De brèves comparaisons avec les conditions de vie de groupes issus de la classe moyenne seront faites dans le
dessein de mieux dépeindre la situation des pauvres.

Sécurité sociale locale et genre en Inde et au Burkina Faso

Le présent ouvrage est l'aboutissement d'un projet de recherche intitulé « Sécurité sociale et genre en Inde et au Burkina Faso » (de juillet
2000 à décembre 2003) conduit dans le cadre du programme de
« Partenariat de recherche avec les pays en voie de développement »
du Fonds National Suisse et de la Coopération Suisse au Développe-

---

[1] *Gendering* : p. ex. un domaine social commence à être marqué par la différenciation selon le genre ; *degendering* est le phénomène contraire : la différenciation
selon le genre commence à se perdre.

ment. Il se décline en quatre sous-projets. Le choix de nos partenaires de l'Inde et du Burkina Faso ainsi que de leurs pays s'est fait suite aux expériences de recherche antérieures et aux contacts des partenaires du Nord qui sont à l'origine du projet. Il revêt un caractère interdisciplinaire car les partenaires du Sud sont des sociologues tandis que celles du Nord sont des anthropologues sociales.

Un article de Keebet von Benda-Beckmann (1991) portant sur les femmes immigrées indonésiennes et leurs modèles de « sécurité sociale » changeants aux Pays-Bas nous a donné l'idée de mener un projet sur ce sujet. Nous nous sommes senties interpellées par l'approche qu'elle avait développée en collaboration avec Franz von Benda-Beckmann dans de nombreuses publications. Ces auteurs ont établi la sécurité sociale comme un champ d'étude « inclusif ». Leur approche a eu un impact aux Pays-Bas et bien au-delà. Pour les recherches en Afrique, les travaux de Robert Vuarin (2000) sur la « protection sociale » au Mali ont également été importants. Au sujet du lien entre la sécurité sociale ou les « circuits de soutien » d'une part et la parenté et le genre d'autre part, les publications de Rajni Palriwada et Carla Risseeuw (1996) et celles de Carla Risseeuw et Kamala Ganesh (1998) nous ont servi de modèles. Tous ces chercheurs nous ont personnellement conseillées.

En Inde, l'État du Kerala constitue le foyer de notre recherche parce qu'il fournit un contraste absolu et stimulant par rapport au Burkina Faso. Le Kerala en Inde du Sud-ouest et le Burkina Faso en Afrique de l'Ouest sont aux antipodes en matière de développement postcolonial. Nous avons présumé que ces différences auraient une influence sur la sécurité sociale. Au Kerala, les mouvements de réforme sociale et d'autres facteurs ont précipité le déclin de l'agriculture et créé l'assistance sociale qui a conduit à des améliorations en matière d'éducation et de santé, comme il ressort des indicateurs de qualité de vie comparables aux pays développés. La modernité du Burkina Faso se résume, quant à elle, en une économie essentiellement basée sur l'agriculture de subsistance, avec peu d'assistance publique et beaucoup d'aide étrangère au développement. En revanche, la différence entre ces deux pays est moins prononcée en matière de revenu par habitant (voir appendice). Comme nous nous attendions à ce que les disparités entre le milieu rural et le milieu urbain du Kerala et du Burkina Faso aient des incidences sur la sécurité sociale, nous avons mené des études comparatives dans ces deux contextes.

L'objectif de notre projet était d'ouvrir une brèche à de nouvelles perspectives sur les conditions locales de sécurité sociale au Kerala et au Burkina Faso, avec une attention particulière sur le genre. Perspectives qui pourront servir de base aux nouveaux efforts en matière de développement. Nos interrogations principales de recherche étaient : Jusqu'à quel point les réseaux de sécurité sociale existants fournissent-ils du soutien ? Quel type de pratiques les gens utilisent-elles vis-à-vis de la famille, la parenté, la communauté et l'État afin d'éviter la baisse de leur niveau de vie ? Quelles sont leurs idées en la matière ? Et quels sont les effets du marché, des structures gouvernementales et des processus historiques ?

Durant la première année, nous avons examiné la situation générale des conditions de sécurité sociale dans les quatre régions. Nous nous sommes ensuite concentrées sur le vieil âge, thème familier à deux des partenaires de recherche qui avaient déjà eu l'opportunité de le traiter. La question de la prise en charge dans le vieil âge a depuis peu accusé un regain d'intérêt auprès des chercheurs et des politiciens grâce à la prise de conscience et à cause des appréhensions quant à l'augmentation de la population âgée engendrée par la hausse de l'espérance de vie ; pas uniquement au Nord, mais aussi au Sud (p. ex. Irudaya Rajan et al. 1999, Makoni et Stroeken 2002). Nous avons accordé une attention soutenue aux limites du soutien familial vu que la littérature et nos propres données nous ont fourni des indications sur le fait que les personnes âgées sont placées dans une situation d'insécurité sociale à la fois par l'inconsistance de l'aide publique et, plus sérieusement encore, par le soutien familial qui s'avère être une ressource délicate et incertaine. Cet intérêt pour la parenté fait également sens car, dans les pays du Sud, la sécurité sociale basée sur l'État se cantonne principalement à une minorité de fonctionnaires.

Nous avons mené des recherches sur le terrain d'une durée de trois mois chacune en 2000, 2001 et 2002, et chaque année nous avons approfondi nos connaissances en la matière. Environ trente entretiens semi-structurés à composantes narratives ont été menés lors de chaque phase de recherche sur le terrain. La plupart étaient des entretiens individuels avec des personnes âgées et leurs enfants, issus des catégories à bas revenus et à revenus moyens, portant sur leurs efforts de sécurité sociale. Certains entretiens contenaient des perspectives biographiques, d'autres ont été faits avec des représentants d'organisations (p. ex. organisations de castes, maisons de retraite, organisations de charité et d'assistance sociale). Par convenance empirique, nous avons défini le fait d'« être âgé » par avoir 55 ans et plus. Des données exploratives ont aussi été obtenues des entretiens de *focus group*. L'observation participante a été incorporée comme méthode complémentaire, elle a permis d'inclure des informations provenant de nombreuses conversations plus ou moins informelles. En outre, dans les sous-projets indiens, un échantillonnage par quotas avec des hommes et des femmes d'éducation et d'occupation moyennes et appartenant à la génération d'âge moyen a été réalisé au terme de la recherche sur le terrain. L'échantillonnage comprenait 80 questionnaires en milieu rural et 120 en milieu urbain. Ainsi, certaines questions clé, telles les ressources financières, les relations de soutien et le logement ont pu être vérifiées.

En ce qui concerne la collecte et l'analyse des données empiriques, nous avons en principe suivi les principes méthodologiques de la « grounded theory », théorie ancrée, développée par Glaser, Strauss et Corbin (1994, 1998 [1967]). Compte tenu des disciplines de recherche différentes des partenaires du projet, cette procédure s'est avérée tout à fait applicable. Nous avons commencé par des hypothèses relatives aux questions de recherche mentionnées plus haut. En collectionnant et en analysant les données, nous avons d'une part différencié nos hypothèses, et d'autre part généré de nouvelles. De façon correspondante, nous avons conduit les premières étapes d'évaluation durant la recherche sur le terrain. Ce processus a nécessité énormément de temps, mais grâce à cette « méthode comparative constante » (Strauss et Corbin 1994 : 273), nous étions en mesure d'acquérir rapidement une compréhension plus approfondie de l'objet de recherche.

Durant la période de recherche d'environ cinq ans, l'équipe de recherche a travaillé en très étroite collaboration durant les phases de recherche sur le terrain, lors des trois ateliers à Zurich après la phase d'évaluation des données, et par courrier électronique pour la mise au point de divers articles et celle de la présente publication. André Leliveld et Juliette Koning – participants d'un cercle de recherche sur la sécurité sociale dirigé par Keebet et Franz von Benda-Beckmann aux Pays-Bas dans les années 1990 – nous ont servi de conseillers lors de deux ateliers à Zurich. Peter van Eeuwijk, chercheur suisse spécialisé dans le domaine de la santé et du vieil âge, nous a accompagnées lors du troisième atelier.

Nous avons clôturé le volet officiel de notre projet par une conférence internationale intitulée « Débats Sud-Nord : Relations de sécurité sociale et genre » qui s'est tenue en décembre 2003 au Burkina Faso. Cette rencontre nous a permis d'avoir des échanges avec une cinquantaine de chercheurs et de praticiens – en majorité burkinabé, mais aussi en provenance d'Inde et d'Europe – sur la sécurité sociale et les résultats de notre recherche. Keebet von Benda-Beckmann et Robert Vuarin ont apporté les contributions principales.[2] Les communications présentées par l'équipe de recherche ont été révisées et sont publiées sous forme d'études de cas dans le présent ouvrage.

Les limites du soutien familial dans le vieil âge

Comme nous l'avons déjà mentionné, les discours publics et académiques dominants dans les pays du Sud suggèrent généralement que les arrangements de sécurité sociale pour le vieil âge peuvent plus ou moins être assimilés à la « famille », en mettant l'accent sur le soutien du « fils ». Au cas où la famille n'est pas en mesure de satisfaire cette attente normative, particulièrement demandée par l'État, une aide publique devrait au moins être accordée aux soutiens de famille afin

---

[2] Un site internet contenant les résultats de la conférence et les interventions présentées est disponible jusqu'à la fin de l'année 2005 (www.northsouth.ch).

qu'ils puissent remplir leur devoir (p. ex. Nations Unies 1994). Bien que nous pensions également que la famille et les relations de parenté jouent un rôle majeur, nous avons été contraintes de remettre en cause ces suppositions après l'analyse des données émanant de notre première année de recherche. Dès lors, les limites du soutien familial et l'insécurité sociale du vieil âge sont devenues notre priorité de recherche.

Afin d'obtenir des réponses claires et d'ôter nos doutes sur le mythe et/ou la norme de la « famille » comme institution dispensatrice de sécurité sociale par excellence et sur l'image du « fils » comme l'ultime soutien pour les parents âgés, nous avons fait face, dans les études de cas, aux questions suivantes:

– Jusqu'à quel point les personnes issues de groupes sociaux démunis sont-elles en mesure de mobiliser du soutien des membres de leur famille et de leur parenté dans le vieil âge, selon les idées et les pratiques prévalentes ? Et quelles alternatives s'offrent à elles ?
– Jusqu'à quel point la sécurité sociale dans le vieil âge des personnes issues de groupes sociaux démunis est-elle différenciée selon le genre ? Et quelles en sont les conséquences ?

Les questions portant sur la nourriture, le logement et les soins dans la vie quotidienne occupent une place prépondérante dans ces études de cas. Néanmoins, la santé est également évoquée comme problème. De ce fait, nous nous sommes concentrées sur les réseaux de sécurité sociale et la parenté, et avons également jeté un regard sur la citoyenneté.

Dans les quatre sous-projets, nous avons commencé par les mêmes questions de recherche et utilisé les mêmes procédures méthodologiques qualitatives et les mêmes catalogues de questions. Mais dans les études de cas présentés ici, nous avons en partie mis l'accent différemment, au gré des découvertes pertinentes selon les différents lieux. En outre, vu que le présent ouvrage est le résultat d'une recherche Nord-Sud, nous n'avons pas cherché à niveler mais avons plutôt délibérément laissé le champ libre à la diversités des expériences de recherche des chercheurs, en matière de formation, de durée de la recherche sur le terrain, de présentation des découvertes et de culture académique (cf. de Jong 2002). Dans deux courts chapitres précédant les études de cas en Inde et au Burkina Faso, nous mettons en exergue des aspects cruciaux sur les plans social, économique, politique et historique concernant ces deux pays. Les informations sur le contexte structurel et historique sont censées fournir des éléments permettant de mieux comprendre les insécurités sociales auxquelles sont confrontées les personnes âgées avec lesquelles nous avons travaillé. Dans le dernier chapitre, nous avons tiré des conclusions sur les éléments de comparaison les plus importants obtenus de nos études de cas.

Le contexte théorique

Le concept de sécurité sociale locale

De nombreuses études portant sur la sécurité sociale partent d'une perspective institutionnelle et américano-européenne, se focalisant sur l'État et d'autres organismes publics comme agences principales procurant assistance dans des situations spécifiques de besoin et de détresse. Cette approche est profondément marquée par des organisations internationales telles que le Bureau International du Travail (BIT) qui est à l'origine de la standardisation de la sécurité sociale publique dans les pays développés et dans les pays en voie de développement depuis les années 1940. Dans une récente publication du BIT, la sécurité sociale est définie comme « bénéfices que la société accorde aux individus et aux ménages – à travers des mesures publiques et collectives – afin de leur garantir un niveau de vie minimum et de les préserver de la détérioration des conditions de vie, due à de nombreux risques et besoins de base » (van Ginneken 2003 : 11, traduction libre). La Banque Mondiale se concentre elle aussi sur les « interventions publiques » (Banque Mondiale 2001 : 9). Avec ces approches institutionnelles, le large éventail de soutien procuré par la famille et d'autres relations plus ou moins institutionnalisées dans le Sud et dans le Nord demeure dans l'ombre, et l'infime offre de soutien public est davantage mise en avant.

Dans les années 1980, Franz et Keebet von Benda-Beckmann, spécialisés dans l'anthropologie de la loi, se sont attelés à développer une approche « inclusive » de la sécurité sociale basée sur leur recherche auprès de différents groupes d'Indonésiens.[3] Le terme « inclusif » se réfère à l'envergure de leur étude qui ne porte pas uniquement sur les institutions ou organisations de soutien public, mais aussi sur les individus et groupes d'individus auxquels s'adresse ce soutien. Des chercheurs de disciplines diverses qui ont mené des recherches sur la sécurité sociale en Asie et en Afrique ont suivi leur approche.[4] La façon dont les auteurs et leurs collègues ont établi la sécurité sociale comme champ d'étude est particulièrement montré en exemple dans les volumes « Between Kinship and the State : Social Security and Law in Developing Countries » (1988) et « Coping with Insecurity : An Underall Perspective in Social Security in the Third World » (2000 [1994]).

Dans l'essai « Coping with Insecurity », qui reflète le plus fidèlement le programme de leur travail sur la sécurité sociale, les auteurs exposent leur modèle dynamique de la sécurité sociale, basé sur une nouvelle perspective sur l'organisation sociale. Leur notion de la sécurité sociale, utilisée dans un sens plus vaste, bien que le terme ait émergé en rapport avec la sécurité sociale étatique, est évidemment épistémologiquement motivée : ils considèrent en effet la notion d'insécurité comme le pivot de l'organisation sociale, plutôt que les notions de conflit ou de rupture (F. et K. von Benda-Beckmann 2000 [1994]).

En suivant l'approche de Franz et Keebet von Benda-Beckmann, nous considérons la sécurité sociale comme partie intégrante de la vie économique et sociale et comme une clé permettant de comprendre l'organisation sociale et le changement social. La sécurité sociale est prise en compte sous le double aspect du social et de l'économique,

---

[3] Cf. F. von Benda-Beckmann 1988, K. von Benda-Beckmann 1988, K. von Benda-Beckmann 1991, K. von Benda-Beckmann et F. Leatemia-Tomatala 1992, F. et K. Benda-Beckmann 1998, K. von Benda-Beckmann 2004, et F. von Benda-Beckmann et R. Kirsch 1999 concernant l'Afrique.
[4] Cf. p. ex. Vel 1994, Leliveld 1994, de Bruijn et van Dijk 1995, Hirtz 1995, Biezeveld 2002, Nooteboom 2003, et Koning et Hüsken 2005.

tandis que les approches institutionnelles tendent à n'en voir que l'aspect économique. La conversion des ressources économiques en besoins de sécurité sociale est cruciale, à tous les niveaux de pauvreté et d'aisance.

En ce qui concerne la dimension empirique de la sécurité sociale, nous adoptons la définition suivante : « Empiriquement, la sécurité sociale se réfère au phénomène social par lequel le domaine abstrait de la sécurité sociale est rempli : les efforts des individus, groupes d'individus et des organisations à venir à bout des insécurités inhérentes à leur existence, notamment en matière de nourriture et d'eau, de logement, de soins et de santé physique et mentale, de formation et de revenu dans la mesure où les aléas ne sont pas considérés comme une pure responsabilité individuelle, tout comme les conséquences voulues ou non de ces efforts » (ibid. : 14, traduction libre).

Cette approche se concentre sur les pratiques sociales des acteurs individuels et collectifs en matière de sécurité sociale. Celles-ci sont aussi liées aux idées culturelles générales et aux notions individuelles de sécurité sociale, tout comme aux droits et obligations institutionnels, de même qu'aux relations sociales actuelles des personnes qui donnent et celles qui reçoivent la sécurité sociale. De plus, les conséquences des pratiques sont tout aussi intéressantes. Ce qui est moins mis en exergue dans leur modèle sont les contextes structurel et historique des discours et des pratiques de sécurité sociale, ainsi que la différenciation selon le genre bien qu'ils aient, dans leurs publications, fait allusion à cet aspect, en particulier en rapport avec l'État.

Lorsque la sécurité sociale est réalisée, on peut en déduire que les relations sociales liées renferment une qualité de sécurité due au « mécanismes de sécurité » qui permettent aux ressources naturelles, économiques et sociales d'être converties en prestations de sécurité sociale actuelles. Les auteurs soulignent que des ressources, à elles seules, ne produisent pas de sécurité sociale. Avec des déclarations telles que « On ne peut pas manger une rizière » et « L'argent ne fait pas la cuisine », un informateur d'Indonésie leur a ouvert les yeux sur l'importance des « chaînes de conversion » (ibid. : 22, traduction libre).

Le sociologue français Robert Vuarin (2000, 2004) se concentre aussi sur la constitution et l'utilisation des réseaux de soutien qu'il qualifie de « protection sociale », et il se penche en outre sur la reconstruction de ces réseaux sous les conditions actuelles de la mondialisation. Dans son modèle de « système de protection », il distingue dans un premier temps quatre pôles de structuration et de légitimation qui se combinent différemment dans chaque configuration sociale. À savoir : l'État avec sa sécurité sociale formalisée et l'assistance sociale, la religion avec sa charité institutionnalisée, le marché avec ses assurances institutionnalisées et la société civile sous laquelle il classe la parenté et autres relations personnelles ainsi que les organisations bénévoles, c'est-à-dire les associations et les mutuelles. En outre, au niveau des interactions individuelles, il conceptualise une « relation élémentaire de protection ». Cette relation doit se négocier dans la pratique. En ce qui concerne les systèmes de soutien dans les zones urbaines du Mali en Afrique de l'Ouest, il s'intéresse particulièrement à la capacité de la société civile de fournir sociabilité et protection, à savoir des réseaux de soutien réciproque parmi les parents et les amis, les relations entre patrons et clients et les organisations bénévoles. Il décèle beaucoup de potentiel de relations de protection sociale dans les associations et surtout les mutuelles avec une adhésion basée sur l'égalité puisque les hiérarchies de pouvoir existantes dans d'autres types de relations peuvent être évitées à cause de la dépersonnalisation de la redistribution et l'institutionnalisation des objectifs altruistes. Pour finir, il plaide pour une institutionnalisation de la protection sociale qui empêche les hiérarchies et les inégalités, que ce soit sous forme d'aménagement formel du gouvernement ou d'aménagement civil formel (Vuarin 2004 : 10).

Les efforts de sécurité sociale locaux sont plutôt des réponses aux insécurités et non aux risques. Le terme de « risque » est étroitement lié aux assurances. Ulrich Beck, qui a introduit le terme de « Risikogesellschaft », société de risques, remarque par exemple : « Les risques concernant la modernisation constituent un *big business*. Ce sont les besoins créés par des économistes mais qui ne peuvent être satisfaits. La faim peut être assouvie, des besoins couverts. Les risques inhérents à la civilisation sont un gouffre sans fond qui ne peuvent être couverts, ils s'auto-reproduisent » (Beck 1986 : 30, traduction libre). De ce point de vue, les risques sont créés et, par des processus subséquents, des sécurités sont produites. En même temps, le pouvoir est exercé et des profits engrangés. Dans cet ordre d'idée, le vieil âge peut être considéré comme un risque dans les discours publics actuels, aussi bien dans les pays du Nord que dans ceux du Sud. Mais lorsque les démunis, personnes au cœur de nos études de cas, évoquent le vieil âge, c'est principalement par rapport à l'insécurité sociale menaçante et à leurs vœux de sécurité sociale.

Les termes clés utilisés dans nos études de cas sont formulés comme suit. Par la notion « sécurité sociale locale », l'approche fonctionnelle poursuivie est soulignée. Dans notre conception, la notion inclut les discours et pratiques des gens d'une localité spécifique ainsi que les conditions de sécurité sociale dans cette localité en rapport avec le contexte du marché régional et les influences économiques et culturelles, ainsi que l'État. Nous désignons par « arrangement de sécurité sociale » l'ensemble des efforts pour se procurer la sécurité sociale ou le mélange de sécurité sociale d'un individu, d'un groupe d'individus ou d'une organisation. Nous concevons les arrangements de sécurité sociale de certains groupes sociaux comme composé d'un réseau de relations sociales pouvant être mobilisées pour recevoir du soutien. Toutefois, les arrangements de sécurité sociale des personnes âgées défavorisées sont composés de liens sociaux qu'ils peuvent mobiliser dans des situations de détresse, que ce soit des relations avec certains membres de la famille, certains membres de la communauté locale ou certaines organisations. Les différents arrangements de sécurité sociale des différents groupes sociaux constituent le « système de sécurité sociale » d'une société. À l'instar de Franz et Keebet von Benda-Beckmann, nous essayons, en adaptant cette perspective, de surmonter les dichotomies usuelles telles que la sécurité sociale traditionnelle et moderne, la sécurité sociale formelle et informelle ou encore la sécurité sociale publique et privée.

Emplois de la parenté et de la citoyenneté

Les relations de parenté ou assimilables à la parenté avec des voisins et des amis sont primordiales pour la sécurité sociale au sein des sociétés ne disposant pas de prestations publiques suffisantes. C'est la raison pour laquelle, en plus des recherches sur la sécurité sociale, nous avons basé notre recherche sur les études portant sur la parenté. Nous faisons surtout référence aux anthropologues Sylvia Yanagisako et Jane Collier (1987) qui ont développé une très influente « analyse unifiée sur le genre et la parenté ». Par ce modèle analytique, qui présuppose que les constructions de parenté et de genre sont étroitement liées, avec pour objectif de surpasser les dichotomies analytiques comme le sexe et le genre, la nature, la culture et la production, le privé et le public (cf. de Jong 2001). Leur publication a initié « les nouvelles études sur la parenté », une renaissance des études sur les problèmes relatifs à la parenté et à la famille qui furent autrefois au cœur des préoccupations des anthropologues. Elles basent leur modèles sur les positions de David Schneider (1972), célèbre pour ses études sur les significations culturelles de la parenté et de la famille, et de Pierre Bourdieu (1977), qui a énormément contribué à la promotion des études orientées vers la prise en compte intégrée des systèmes et des acteurs.

L'approche analytique de Yanagisako et de Collier relie l'environnement social des acteurs, leurs idées, leurs perceptions et leurs actions aux structures sociétales de l'inégalité et aux développements historiques. Nous prétendons ici, en accord avec leur approche, que la sécurité sociale, comme d'autres champs sociaux étudiés, est structurée par des inégalités sociales qui influent sur les individus, en particulier en matière de genre et de classe. En même temps, nous devons prendre en considération le fait que les individus reproduisent et transforment les structures à travers leurs actions. Un point important de cette approche, contrairement à l'approche des études sur les femmes, est le fait qu'aucune supposition n'est faite a priori selon laquelle les hommes et les femmes pensent et agissent différemment. C'est pourquoi elles aussi prennent en compte un « système d'inégalité non différencié selon le genre » (Yanagisako et Collier 1987 : 40), comme dans les sociétés de chasseurs et de cueilleurs. Toutefois, si l'analyse indique que des valeurs culturelles et des processus sociaux font la discrimination entre hommes et femmes, ceci s'explique par le caractère différencié selon le genre de leurs champs d'action. Curieusement, les auteurs se heurtent également aux insécurités et ambivalences dans les systèmes de parenté et de genre liés aux processus historiques lorsqu'ils déclarent : « Nous pouvons constater comment des aspects d'idées et de pratiques qui, dans nos modèles systématiques semblent se renforcer et se reproduire, se minent et se déstabilisent en même temps » (ibid. : 47, traduction libre).

Carla Risseeuw, Rajni Palriwala, Kamala Ganesh et d'autres scientifiques ont appliqué l'approche combinée de la parenté et du genre de Yanagisako et Collier dans les études portant sur « les réseaux de soutien changeants » dans divers pays d'Asie du Sud et d'Afrique subsaharienne.[5] Elles se sont concentrées sur les relations de parenté changeantes sous la colonisation, sur les systèmes de législation et de formation changeants et la famille, sur les conditions économiques changeantes et la parenté, tout comme sur la négociation de la sécurité et de l'insécurité au sein des sociétés elles aussi changeantes. Les scientifiques indiens Rajni Palriwala et Kamala Ganesh ont mené une étude sur les relations familiales changeantes et le système d'assistance publique au Pays-Bas (cf. Palriwala 2000). Les auteurs critiquent les constructions statiques de la famille, très souvent politiques et idéologiques, et soulignent les transformations des relations familiales et de parenté et le caractère négocié des réseaux de soutien. Elles intègrent également la citoyenneté dans leur analyse et l'associent principalement aux systèmes légaux d'un État colonial et post-colonial. Nous avons adopté leur classification des systèmes de sécurité sur trois niveaux : le niveau domestique, le niveau de la communauté et le niveau de l'État.

L'une des suggestions majeures faites par Risseeuw et Palriwala (1996) pour nos études de cas touche l'insécurité et l'ambivalence. Elles affirment : « Le mariage, la famille et la parenté sont des domai-

---

[5] Cf. Palriwala et Risseeuw 1996, et Risseeuw et Ganesh 1998.

nes sociaux caractérisés par la dualité. Ils portent en eux des éléments de contrôle – voire d'oppression – en limitant les possibilités des individus à réaliser leur propre bien-être et leurs intérêts, ou ceux des personnes envers qui ils ont une responsabilité particulière. Les intérêts des membres socialement et économiquement les plus influents d'un réseau aussi bien que les intérêts de groupe peuvent créer et créent des formes d'oppression auxquelles les plus dépendants et les plus vulnérables ne peuvent se soustraire facilement, s'ils y parviennent. À présent, ces structures demeurent les principales arènes sociales procurant de l'aide dans les régions dont il est question ici » (ibid. : 39, traduction libre).

Dans cet ordre d'idée, les catégories de parenté et de genre, la catégorie d'âge, ensemble avec d'autres catégories telles que la classe, la caste, la race, l'ethnicité et la nationalité sont toutes conçues de manière analytique comme des catégories socialement et structurellement construites dans les récentes approches des sciences sociales.[6] Rubinstein (1990) se réfère explicitement à l'approche de Yanagisako et Collier et soutient qu'une « analyse unifiée sur le genre et la parenté » devrait inclure la génération et l'âge. Cette perspective est également valable pour notre recherche. La littérature sur la phase de vie du vieil âge affirme que les femmes réalisent plus de pouvoir de décision au cours de leur vie mais que l'asymétrie entre les genres n'est que légèrement diminuée avec l'âge (cf. aussi Albert et Cattel 1994). Aussi peut-on en déduire que le principe structurant de l'âge est subordonné au genre et qu'il est important d'analyser le genre en tant que catégorie changeante sous l'angle du cours de la vie et de la génération. Dans les sociétés au sein desquelles le vieil âge, synonyme de respect, est un important principe structurant, le genre peut toutefois être subordonné.

Dans ce contexte, il s'avère également important de souligner que le vieil âge a une signification différente selon les sociétés. En particulier, « être âgé » est un concept relatif selon le contexte socio-culturel (cf. Sokolovsky 1993). C'est principalement lié à l'âge chronologique dans le discours étatique, p. ex. au Kerala, l'âge officiel de la

---

[6] Cf. p. ex. Rubinstein 1990, Sokolovsky 1990, et Cohen 1994.

retraite est de 55 ans ; et dans le discours académique, en Inde par exemple, il équivaut à 60 ans et plus, et être « très âgé » correspond à 70 ans et plus (cf. Irudaya Rajan et al. 1999).

Quoi qu'il en soit, les personnes âgées elles-mêmes n'emploient certes pas des critères chronologiques, mais elles se réfèrent plutôt aux rôles économiques et sociaux changeants, ce qui peut correspondre à un processus graduel, p. ex. au fait de devenir vieux dans le sens de n'être plus en mesure de gagner de l'argent. Souvent, la catégorie des personnes âgées est différenciée selon les personnes âgées en bonne santé et aptes d'une part, et les malades et infirmes d'autre part. Celles qui tendent à être négligées sont les personnes âgées infirmes et faibles (cf. aussi E. et L. Holmes 1995). Ces pratiques à l'égard des personnes âgées sont aussi liées aux dimensions d'insécurité ou d'ambivalence vis-à-vis de l'ordre social, de la parenté et de la famille. Le fait que les attitudes de négligence et d'ambivalence de la parenté à l'égard des personnes âgées dans les sociétés non-européennes peuvent passer inaperçues est lié au fait que les scientifiques reportent souvent des idéaux culturels de la piété filiale envers les personnes âgées, alors que les pratiques actuelles sont tout autre. Comme les enquêtés, ils tendent à construire des mythes d'un « âge d'or » ou d'« île des bienheureux », ce qui a déjà été critiqué en gérontologie (Nydegger 1983).

Dans nos études de cas, nous employons l'expression « être âgé » comme synonyme de « être en âge avancé » et « vieillesse » (cf. Makoni et Stroeken 2001 : 5) ; tandis que nous utilisons « vieil âge » pour nous référer à la phase ultime de la vie. Bien que vieil âge et être âgé sont souvent assimilés à la maladie et au déclin des forces physiques dans les sociétés occidentales, il ne nous semble pas justifié de remplacer ces termes par des euphémismes telles que troisième âge ou seniors, termes qui pourraient masquer les réalités sociales.

Les relations de parenté jouent aussi un rôle majeur pour les personnes âgées du Nord, comme le montrent les rares études disponibles sur ce sujet (p. ex. Cantor 1980). La recherche britannique faite par Janet Finch et Jennifer Mason (1993) sur la parenté et les responsabilités familiales, qui inclut également les personnes âgées, est intéressante parce que les auteurs examinent minutieusement la négociation des relations de soutien au sein des réseaux familiaux et de parenté. Elle nous a également fourni des clés importantes en matière de conceptualisation du « soutien social » ou de « l'aide » dans un sens plus large. En ce qui concerne les systèmes de soutien au Sud, nous avons élaboré une classification plus simple, à trois niveaux, à savoir « soutien matériel » (fournir argent, nourriture et logement), « soutien physique » ou « soins » dans un sens restreint (travaux domestiques et soins physiques des enfants, des personnes âgées et des malades), et « soutien émotionnel » (y compris la socialisation et les conseils).

De nombreuses publications relatives au problème de « soins » (soins familiaux et communautaires) ont paru ces dernières années, aussi bien en matière de citoyenneté que d'aide publique (p. ex. Waerness 1987, Fraser 2000, Ungerson 2000). Mais ceci ne peut être appliqué aux pays pauvres du Sud à cause des prestations d'aide publique très limitées dans ces régions par rapport aux pays du Nord.

Durant notre recherche, nous avons au fur et à mesure pris conscience du fait que les problématiques nationales et transnationales de la sécurité sociale peuvent être analysées favorablement à travers de nouvelles perspectives sur la citoyenneté. Les travaux de Nira Yuval-Davis sont particulièrement indiqués pour clarifier les problèmes relatifs à la citoyenneté et au genre. Dans la même veine que les débats récents sur la citoyenneté, elle l'envisage « comme concept à paliers multiples » qui s'applique à l'adhésion des gens à une variété de collectivités – locales, ethniques, nationales et transnationales » (Yuval-Davis 1997 : 68, traduction libre). Par conséquent, elle considère ces collectivités comme constructions idéologiques et matérielles dont les frontières, les structures et les normes sont le résultat de processus constants de luttes, de négociations et de développements sociaux. La citoyenneté comporte également les dimensions individuelle et collective. Les castes inférieures en Inde par exemple jouissent de droits collectifs grâce à la discrimination positive que l'État applique à leur encontre, par le biais des avantages qui leur sont concédés pour l'éducation et pour des postes de travail dans le secteur public.

En ce qui concerne les femmes, Yuval-Davis soutient que la citoyenneté de la femme doit non seulement être considérée en comparaison avec celle de l'homme, mais aussi en relation avec l'affiliation des femmes aux groupes dominants et subalternes, leur ethnicité, leur origine et leur résidence urbaine ou rurale, et en prenant en compte les problématiques globales et transnationales. Du point de vue individuel, des attributs tels que le genre, l'appartenance à une classe sociale, la religion, l'origine, la capacité et l'étape de vie déterminent la citoyenneté d'un individu, à telle enseigne que « la plupart des membres de la majorité des familles, le plus souvent les enfants, les malades, les personnes âgées et les femmes, n'ont guère le loisir de déterminer elles-mêmes leur vie ni au sein de la famille, encore moins à l'extérieur » (ibid. : 91, traduction libre). Afin de dépasser les limitations de la dichotomie analytique privée et publique, l'auteur distingue trois sphères : la sphère des relations familiales, p. ex. « les réseaux et foyers sociaux, économiques et politiques, organisés autour des relations de parenté ou d'amitié » (ibid. : 14, traduction libre), la sphère de la vie civile et celle de l'État.

Les questions relatives à la citoyenneté sont également traitées dans les études de cas ci-après, bien qu'elles n'en constituent pas le thème central. Elles sont plus importantes dans les études de cas en Inde que dans celles effectuées au Burkina Faso.

Une approche fonctionnelle du genre

Les théories, qu'elles soient plus ou moins explicites, influencent notre façon d'interpréter les données. C'est la raison pour laquelle nous indiquons la façon dont notre recherche a été théoriquement et empiriquement influencée par des études précédentes sur la sécurité sociale, la parenté, la citoyenneté et le genre. Le cadre ainsi posé, nous sommes à présent en mesure d'articuler plus clairement notre propre approche du genre. En fait, nous ne considérons pas les femmes et les hommes âgés comme de simples « victimes » de leurs conditions sociales, bien que nous soyons conscientes du fait que leur marge de manœuvre peut être étroite. C'est par une approche orientée vers l'acteur et le genre que nous nous sommes penchées sur le problème que pose la sécurité sociale dans le vieil âge, en nous concentrant sur l'instrumentalisation des relations sociales par les personnes âgées et leurs enfants, à la fois comme receveurs et donneurs de sécurité sociale.

Dans les interactions discursives et les pratiques des acteurs, nous distinguons des dimensions plus ou moins marquées de « faire du genre » (*doing gender*), p. ex. la production du genre dans les activités quotidiennes (West et Zimmermann 1987). Au sein de ces interactions plus ou moins différenciées selon le genre, certaines relations avec d'autres individus et groupes d'individus sont utilisées pour assurer la sécurité sociale du vieil âge.

En outre, les structures et les processus sociétaux peuvent également être perçus comme plus ou moins différenciés selon le genre, p. ex. ils sont institutionnellement et idéologiquement imprégnés selon le genre, ce qui engendre l'exclusion sociale. D'une part, le genre est un principe-clé structurant dans le partage du travail, de la propriété et d'autres ressources de valeur dans une société et a souvent pour conséquence que les femmes ont moins accès au revenu, à la terre et à d'autres biens. C'est la dimension politico-économique du genre. D'autre part, le genre est le principe-clé structurant dans « l'éventail des griefs » subis par les femmes dans différentes sociétés, à savoir la banalisation, le dénigrement, les représentations dépréciées des choses « féminines », la discrimination dans l'attitude, le harcèlement sexuel, la violence domestique et le déni de ses droits en tant que citoyenne à part entière. Ceci est lié à la dimension du genre marquée culturellement ou par les valeurs (Frazer 1997, Kabeer 2000). Par rapport à la sécurité sociale du vieil âge, ceci signifie que l'instrumentalisation des relations de parenté et de citoyenneté généralement différenciées selon le genre aboutit à des arrangements plus ou moins fiables, selon les structures économiques et culturelles et les processus, et leur différenciation selon le genre.

Le positionnement selon le genre devrait être considéré en rapport avec d'autres catégories sociales, en particulier l'ethnicité, la race, la classe et l'âge (cf. Moore 1994, Anthias 2002). À titre d'exemple, nous avons découvert que, en Inde comme au Burkina Faso, les positionnements selon le genre diffèrent de manière similaire selon l'occupation ou le niveau de revenu liés à la classe ; et la classe est elle-même en quelque sorte liée à l'ethnicité. Le genre est aussi lié à l'âge, mais de manière différente dans les deux contextes de recherche comme nous nous emploierons à le montrer.

Les fonctions de la sécurité sociale ou l'instrumentalisation des relations sociales ne doivent pas être confondues avec leurs causes, comme c'est le cas dans les approches fonctionnalistes. En accord avec la théorie de la pratique, nous prenons en compte les intérêts des acteurs individuels et nous posons la question de savoir pourquoi, pour qui, jusqu'à quel point et dans quelles circonstances certaines relations sociales fournissent la sécurité sociale (cf. Bourdieu 1977, 1990).

Poursuivre une telle approche fonctionnelle du genre contribue à une compréhension plus approfondie de la sécurité sociale (cf. de Jong 2005). Pour de telles investigations, l'accent est mis sur les actions des acteurs individuels ou collectifs plus ou moins différenciées selon le genre, et leurs relations visant à obtenir la sécurité sociale, à la fois dans la sphère privée que dans la sphère publique de la société civile et de l'État ; et non pas principalement sur les actions des acteurs collectifs dans la sphère publique, comme c'est le cas dans les approches institutionnelles. Cela implique aussi une prise de conscience des modernités spécifiques qui résultent des transformations, généralement différenciées selon le genre, sous l'effet d'impacts économiques et culturels mondiaux dans les différents contextes de la recherche.[7]

---

[7] Cf. p. ex. Stivens 1998a, 1998b en ce qui concerne la modernité et le genre en Asie.

Le Kerala, un modèle ?
Contexte des études de cas en Inde

Willemijn de Jong

Les études de cas en Inde concernent les ouvriers pauvres et, dans leur grande majorité, non qualifiés, de la caste des Pulaya au centre de l'État du Kerala. Sur des points pertinents, ils sont comparés aux employeurs de la classe moyenne appartenant à la caste des Nayar.[1] Nous avons focalisé notre attention sur eux car, sur le plan démographique, ces deux vastes groupes de population sont représentatifs des classes à revenus bas et à revenus moyens au Kerala. De surcroît, ils étaient professionnellement liés autrefois en ce sens que les Pulaya travaillaient comme esclaves agricoles pour les Nayar et ces deux castes sont relativement bien documentées dans la littérature.[2] Les idées développées dans ce chapitre sont forcément concises et devront être différenciées ailleurs.

À propos du système de castes, les gens sont classées dans des catégories de richesse et de statut, justifiées par des concepts de « pureté » et de « pollution ».[3] D'une manière générale, les riches symbolisaient les castes les plus élevées, détenaient le pouvoir et étaient rituellement « pures ». Les pauvres incarnaient les castes inférieures, sans pouvoir et « intouchables ». Le Kerala avait le système de castes le plus rigide et le plus élaboré de l'Inde. Les brahmanes, les Nayar et les chrétiens syriens représentent les castes supérieures les

---

[1] Nous sommes conscientes que les castes ne constituent pas des entités statiques ni homogènes et que la caste n'équivaut pas à la classe. Pour nos études de cas, les critères de classe sont plus importants que les critères de caste. Nous employons les noms des castes par convenance, mais nous faisons en fait allusion aux activités professionnelles des groupes d'ouvriers non qualifiés pour la plupart, respectivement aux cadres moyens.

[2] D'importantes publications sur les Pulaya sont Iyer 1981 (1909), Alexander 1968, Saradamoni 1980, et den Uyl 1996, 2000. Des publications majeures sur les Nayar ont été faites, entre autres, par Iyer 1981 (1912), Gough 1962, Fuller 1976, et Saradamoni 1999.

[3] Bien que le concept analytique des castes ait par nécessité été déconstruit (cf. Fuller 1997), empiriquement, il a conservé son importance (p. ex. Srivinas 1997, Osella et Osella 2000).

plus importantes et étaient les anciens propriétaires fonciers ; tandis que les Pulaya constituent la plus nombreuse des castes inférieures d'anciens esclaves. Entre les deux figurent les Izhava, les musulmans avec des occupations subalternes, et les catholiques latins.[4] Les Nayar, environ 15 % de la population du Kerala, sont aujourd'hui essentiellement des cadres moyens et supérieurs. Leur système de parenté est matrilinéaire, toutefois leurs règles d'héritage matrilinéaires se sont modifiées. En tant que caste dominante, les Nayar ont exercé une influence considérable sur le mode de vie et sur la société du Kerala. Les Pulaya, environ 8 % de la population, sont pour la plupart des journaliers non qualifiés qui travaillent dans l'agriculture et les services. Seule une partie de la génération des jeunes possède une formation. Il n'est pas tout à fait clair si cette caste est patrilinéaire ou matrilinéaire. Selon le gouvernement, les Pulaya appartiennent aux castes officielles (SC), p. ex. ils sont enregistrés et bénéficient de quotas dans l'éducation et le service public et obtiennent d'autres prestations de toutes sortes. Bien que leur niveau d'éducation se soit amélioré, il ne se traduit pas par des occupations plus élevées (Franke 1996).[5]

D'après le recensement réalisé en 1991, la population du Kerala compte environ trente millions d'habitants dont 57 % d'hindous, 24 % de musulmans et 19 % de chrétiens.[6] Les indicateurs sociaux du Kerala sont remarquables. En effet, par rapport à d'autres États de l'Inde et à d'autres pays du tiers-monde, le Kerala affiche un taux d'alphabétisation et une espérance de vie plus élevés, un âge de se marier plus retardé, un taux de natalité et de mortalité infantile plus bas, mais

---

[4] Contrairement à l'idée généralement répandue, le système des castes des États de l'Inde n'est pas composé uniquement que d'hindous. Les musulmans et les chrétiens y sont également inclus (cf. Fuller 1976 : 37). Des personnes d'origine tribale, p. ex. celles appartenant aux tribus officielles (*Scheduled Tribes ST)* et qui sont discriminées positivement par le gouvernement, ne sont qu'une petite minorité au Kerala, 4940 personnes selon le recensement de 1991.

[5] Avant l'indépendance, ils étaient appelés *harijan* mais de nos jours, les Pulaya s'identifient politiquement à d'autres castes inférieures qui ont lutté pour un meilleur statut social telles les *dalit* (cf. Webster 1999). D'après le recensement de 1991, le Kerala compte 241,750 personnes appartenant aux castes officielles (*Scheduled Castes SC*).

[6] Dans l'Inde entière, les hindous constituent de loin la majorité avec 82 %, pour 12 % de musulmans et 2 % de chrétiens.

aussi un meilleur accès à l'eau potable, à l'électricité, aux routes, à la scolarité et aux centres de santé (voir appendice). Comme conséquence de son développement, la modernité du Kerala est souvent qualifiée de « rurban » (urbano-rurale), car un énorme contraste ne se dénote pas entre les régions urbaines et les régions rurales.[7] Étant donné sa qualité de vie élevée, également en matière d'éducation et de l'état de santé des femmes, et malgré sa croissance économique modeste, le Kerala est devenu « un modèle » de développement « dont on peut s'inspirer ». Il reste maintenant à savoir si ce modèle est durable (Parayil 2000).

Le développement du Kerala est surtout attribué à l'action publique et à la politique gouvernementale et, outre l'histoire matrilinéaire, à une forte influence chrétienne, à son commerce mondial et à son économie coloniale.[8] Franke et Chasin (2000) soutiennent que cette dernière a engendré un prolétariat urbain moderne et ils constatent : « De manière plus abrupte que nulle part ailleurs en Inde, le Kerala a connu une rupture des liens traditionnels de parenté, de caste et de localité, créant un potentiel pour une prise de conscience accrue de la classe » (ibid. : 26, traduction libre).

En 1957, une année après la création de l'État du Kerala, les mouvements sociaux des paysans et des ouvriers ont été déterminants pour l'élection d'un gouvernement communiste. Depuis lors, des gouvernements communistes ont alterné avec ceux conduits par le « Congress Party » (parti du congrès). Sous la pression publique, des syndicats se sont créés et le gouvernement a initié des réformes sociales. La grande réforme agraire de 1969 a fixé le plafond de la dimension absolue des propriétés et a aboli le bail des rizières et celui des terrains à bâtir ; ces deux mesures ont conduit à une importante redistribution des terres. Avant ladite réforme, les pauvres devaient même payer aux propriétaires fonciers un loyer pour les terrains sur

---

[7] Le terme urbano-rural « rurban » est par exemple utilisé par Ramachandran 1997 et Kurien 2000.
[8] Des références importantes relatives à l'action publique et la politique gouvernementale sont données par Drèze et Sen 1991, Franke 1996, Kurien 2000, et pour les autres facteurs Jeffrey 1992, Gulati et al. 1996, Ramachandran 1997, et Franke et Chasin 2000.

lesquels leurs huttes étaient construites, ceci s'appliquait également aux Pulaya. Dans son étude de village détaillée portant sur les inégalités et la redistribution au Kerala central, l'anthropologue Franke (1996) conclut que malgré le fait que les Pulaya et d'autres indigents continuaient de manquer de ressources, « les luttes pour la réforme de la propriété foncière ont consolidé l'influence de ces groupes de castes inférieures et leur ont permis de progresser économiquement » (ibid. : 149, traduction libre).

En plus des réformes agraires, des mesures d'assistance sociale ont été instaurées. L'éducation a été largement promue, l'éducation des filles comprise. Écoles et lycées constituent « la plus grande industrie du Kerala » (Jeffrey 1992 : 150, traduction libre) pour laquelle le gouvernement, les organisations chrétiennes et les hindous étaient en compétition. L'école primaire publique est devenue gratuite. En matière de santé, les soins ont été développés, des centres de soins publics pour mère et enfant ouverts, des centres de planning familial se sont propagés.

Des organisations chrétiennes avaient déjà créé des centres médicaux, des orphelinats et des centres pour réfugiés dans le Kerala au dix-neuvième siècle et elles sont demeurées actives dans le domaine de l'éducation. Des organisations hindoues d'assistance sociale selon les castes, en l'occurrence la « Kerala Pulaya Mahha Sabha » (KPMS) et le « Nayar Service Society » (NSS) leur ont emboîté le pas au début du vingtième siècle. Ces organisations de la société civile ont développé des structures organisationnelles solides et mené à bien des activités d'assistance sociale au gré de leurs moyens (Jeffrey 1992, Kariyil 1995).

Des structures nationales de sécurité sociale, par exemple les mutuelles de prévision pour le personnel du secteur industriel de l'État ont été instaurés en Inde dans les années 1950. Les caisses de pension pour les fonctionnaires avaient déjà été créées à la fin du dix-neuvième siècle. Cependant, environ 90 % des personnes actives sont employées dans le secteur informel et touchent de bas revenus. Le programme national d'assistance sociale, « National Social Assistance Programme » (NSAP), est essentiellement conçu pour des personnes âgées sans fils adulte (Jain 1999). Dans le cadre du système de distribution publique, « Public Distribution System » (PDS), des produits de première nécessité tels le blé, le riz, le sucre, l'huile de palme et le pétrole sont proposés à prix réduits dans des magasins de ration aux détenteurs de cartes de ration. Si tant est qu'ils vivent en dessous du seuil de pauvreté, ce qui correspondait à un revenu annuel inférieur à 21'000 roupies (env. 420 US$)[9] en 2001 (cf. Kannan et Francis 2001).

Plus de trente caisses de sécurité sociale ont été élaborées au Kerala depuis 1960, les plus importantes étant la « Kerala Destitute and Widow Pension » (Caisse de pension pour les indigents et les veuves) et la « Agricultural Workers Pension » (Caisse de pension pour les ouvriers agricoles). Les statistiques indiquent que 25 % de la population âgée bénéficient de ces modèles (Irudaya Rajan et al. 1999 : 200). Franke constate que, en dépit du fait que les prestations sociales n'ont qu'un faible impact sur les inégalités sociales, elles n'en constituent pas moins une grande partie des revenus des ménages des personnes les plus démunies (Franke 1996 : 183).

En outre en 1972, le gouvernement a initié le programme de construction logement-type, « one *lakh*[10] housing scheme » ; l'un des plus vastes programmes de construction de logements pour les défavorisés en Inde. Il s'adressait en premier lieu aux personnes qui n'avaient pas pu bénéficier des réformes agraires. Bien que cet objectif n'ait été que partiellement atteint, loger la population est devenu une préoccupation constante de l'État (Jeffrey 1992, Franke 1996).

En matière de vieil âge, l'État du Kerala est d'autant plus intéressant qu'il dispose d'un grand nombre d'hospices pour personnes âgées, plus d'une centaine au total. La grande majorité de ces établissements sont gérés par des organisations chrétiennes et treize par l'État. La plupart des personnes âgées résidant dans ces hospices sont des chrétiens démunis et plus de 60 % d'entre elles n'ont pas de progéniture. Les indigents peuvent y résider gratuitement (Irudaya Rajan 2000).

---

[9] En 2002, 1 US$ valait presque 50 roupies, c'est-à-dire 48 roupies.
[10] Mesure de quantité, 1 *lakh* = 100,000.

Le modèle du Kerala connaît une crise, surtout depuis la récession des années 1990 et est depuis lors observé de près. Néanmoins, de profondes transformations sociales s'opèrent graduellement depuis les années 1970. Le secteur agricole est en déclin, le riz est importé et le secteur industriel est en stagnation. À l'heure actuelle, le secteur tertiaire affiche quant à lui le meilleur potentiel de croissance. L'embauche informelle est répandue. Entre 1987 et 1988, seuls 17 % des travailleurs avaient des emplois réguliers, près de 40 % travaillaient à leur compte et 43 % étaient des journaliers (Prakash 1999 : 35). Le taux de chômage, déjà élevé, est en hausse et l'est davantage dans des centres urbains à cause de la grande densité de la population. Résultat : la pauvreté urbaine est plus prononcée que la pauvreté rurale (Retnaraj 1999 : 158). En ce qui concerne le genre, le chômage touche davantage les femmes que les hommes, surtout dans les zones urbaines (Gulati et al. 1996 : 32). À cela s'ajoute les nombreux migrants de retour des pays du Golf. Avant ce phénomène, la migration avait énormément contribué à soulager la misère (Zachariah et al. 2002). Faute de moyens financiers et sous la pression des programmes d'ajustement structurel, les programmes d'assistance sociale et les prestations en matière d'éducation et de santé sont aujourd'hui menacés. Malgré tout, l'optimisme demeure de mise pour certains. Ils espèrent une croissance économique plus forte, induite par la nouvelle politique de décentralisation, sans pour autant perdre les acquis sociaux et les avancées démocratiques. Néanmoins, ces mêmes personnes observent avec anxiété les relations de pouvoir interne, tout comme la dépendance du Kerala à l'égard des processus nationaux et de la mondialisation.[11]

---

[11] Parmi les optimistes se trouvent Franke et Chasin 2000 et Véron 2000, tandis que Thomas Isaac 2000 montre, en coopération avec Franke, les résultats de la politique de décentralisation.

Au seuil de l'insécurité :
les personnes âgées pauvres au Kerala urbain

Willemijn de Jong

« Les personnes âgées peuvent être heureuses si elles parviennent à s'adapter à la société et à leur famille et si elles maintiennent l'harmonie. C'est un peu comme confectionner un collier de perles. Il faut faire preuve de patience et une fois le collier monté, il faut bien l'assembler sinon le fil se casse. » (Kanan, un ouvrier âgé, 2001)

Comme mentionné dans le chapitre précédent, dans l'État du Kerala – en contraste avec les autres États de l'Inde et le Burkina Faso – sous l'impulsion des mouvements de réforme sociale, un vaste éventail de mesures et de systèmes de sécurité sociale a été élaboré par le gouvernement et les organisations civiles au cours du vingtième siècle. Ces prestations publiques s'adressent également aux personnes âgées. Les questions que traitent cette étude de cas sont les suivantes : Jusqu'à quel point les pauvres vivant au Kerala urbain peuvent-ils mobiliser du soutien pour le vieil âge, pas seulement de leurs familles, mais également du gouvernement et d'autres organismes publics ? Et à quel point la sécurité sociale pour le vieil âge est-elle différenciée selon le genre ? D'après la littérature portant sur le développement et la politique sociale au Kerala, on peut présumer que les personnes âgées pauvres du Kerala urbain ne mobilisent pas seulement le soutien familial, en particulier celui du fils, mais aussi l'aide publique (p. ex. Irudaya Rajan 1999). De plus, la littérature dédiée au genre nous permet d'en déduire que la sécurité sociale s'avère particulièrement problématique pour les veuves âgées (p. ex. Gulati et al. 1996, Gulati 1998).

Ce chapitre entend illustrer comment, pour des raisons économiques et sociales, l'arrangement de sécurité sociale pour les pauvres âgés, issus de la classe ouvrière en milieu urbain du Kerala, est bien plus complexe que ne suggèrent l'imagerie locale et nationale sur le soutien au vieil âge. De ce fait, l'on découvrira qu'à cause des limites à la fois de l'aide et l'entraide familiale et du soutien public, les personnes âgées de la classe ouvrière sont sur le point de basculer dans l'insécurité sociale du fait que la plupart d'entre elles vivent dans une sécurité sociale fragile, les veuves les plus pauvres et d'autres femmes sans parenté proche éprouvent une insécurité sociale critique.

La recherche sur la sécurité sociale des populations pauvres en Inde est encore peu développée (cf. Cohen 1998). Le propos se focalise ici sur les hindous pauvres qui, pour certains aspects importants, sont comparés aux musulmans de la classe à bas revenus et aux hindous de la classe moyenne issus de la caste des Nayar. Nous avons également pris en compte les musulmans dans cette étude de cas parce qu'ils représentent une grande partie de la population dans la région où s'est déroulée l'étude.[1]

Le site de la recherche

Le travail sur le terrain en vue de la présente étude de cas a été mené dans la périphérie industrielle de Kochi appelée Kalamassery.[2] Avec environ un million d'habitants, Kochi est la plus grande et la plus importante ville commerciale de l'État du Kerala. La municipalité de Kalamassery s'est considérablement développée en termes d'habitants et d'industries depuis les années 1960. En 1961, elle comptait environ 17'000 habitants.[3] D'après le recensement 2001, la population s'élève à 63'106 habitants, dont 31'196 femmes et 31'910 hommes ; répartis en 14'023 foyers, dont 812 (environ 6 %) appartiennent aux castes officielles (« scheduled castes » SC). Avec d'autres défavorisés, ils

---

[1] Un sondage dans les bidonvilles de la région étudiée indique 54,35 % d'hindous, 29,28 % de musulmans et 15,92 % de chrétiens (Rajagiri 1996 : 3).

[2] Près de 100 entretiens individuels qualitatifs ont été réalisés à Thiruvananthapuram en 2000 et à Kochi en 2001 et 2002 (cf. de Jong 2003). En outre, un échantillonnage par quotas avec 120 questionnaires quantitatifs (40 ouvriers hindous, 40 ouvriers musulmans, 40 hindous de la classe moyenne) a été réalisé à Kochi en 2002. Des données supplémentaires ont été obtenues par l'observation participante, quelques entretiens avec des *focus groups* ainsi que de nombreuses conversations informelles. Les résultats ici présentés sont analysés sous l'angle de l'ensemble des données ethnographiques. Pour notre recherche à Kochi, nous avons reçu une aide inestimable du « Rajagiri College of Social Science », l'institut des sciences sociales et des organisations liées au développement communautaire CASP et RCDS ; mais aussi de deux assistants de recherche qui ont également fait office de traducteurs vu que nous ne parlions pas la langue dans ce cas.

[3] Source : Municipalité de Kalamassery le 16 août 2001.

vivent dans treize « colonies », lotissements. Les défis majeurs auxquels est confronté Kalamassery sont le problème des personnes sans
terre, l'insuffisance de l'éducation d'une grande partie de la population et le manque de débouchés professionnels.[4]

Les principales industries produisent de l'acier, des produits chimi-
ques, du caoutchouc et des dérivés électroniques. En 1981, on comptait soixante unités industrielles employant en tout plus de 7000 ouvriers. La pollution de l'air et de l'eau pose problème (Kuruvilla
1989). Cependant, le développement des industries de manufacture
stagne depuis les années 1990 (Mathew 1999). En fait, durant ces dernières années, nombre d'usines ont interrompu leur production.

Comme précisé dans le chapitre précédent, les personnes sur lesquelles la présente étude est centrée sont issues de la caste des Pulaya.[5] Ils vivent dans un lotissement appelé « slum pocket » (poche de
taudis ; cf. Rajagiri 1996), répartis dans cent-vingt foyers pulaya. Les
autres quatre-vingts foyers appartiennent en majorité aux « communities » (communautés) des Izhava, des musulmans et des catholiques
latins. La plupart des Pulaya étaient des squatters qui ont occupé leurs
quartiers à Kalamassery dans les années 1960. Mais petit à petit,
beaucoup d'entre eux ont réussi à faire enregistrer officiellement leur
petit lopin de terre.

Hommes et femmes, les Pulaya du lotissement sont des mains-
d'œuvre non qualifiées qui avaient d'abord travaillé dans le secteur
agricole et travaillent aujourd'hui surtout soit dans la construction et
les services de nettoyage, le jardinage et les travaux domestiques.
Seule une minorité, en général des personnes de la jeune génération,
occupent des postes permanents dans les usines en tant qu'ouvriers
qualifiés. La plupart des Pulaya âgés enquêtés étaient illettrés ou
n'avaient fréquenté l'école que quelques années. Les femmes âgées
étaient toutes illettrées. En revanche, les femmes plus jeunes avaient

---

[4] Source : « Kalamassery at a Glance : 10th Five Year Plan 2002-2007. Decentralisation Plan Report. Kalamassery Municipality » (Kalamassery en un coup d'œil :
10ème plan quinquennal 2002-2007. Rapport du plan de décentralisation. Municipalité de Kalamassery).
[5] En fait, ce groupe se désigne par le nom de « Pulayar » pour se distinguer des
« Pulayan ».

été à l'école pendant une période entre six et dix ans. Nous présumons que la situation des Pulaya peut être considérée comme représentative des personnes des classes à bas revenus dans les villes indiennes, qui sont aussi des ouvriers non qualifiés.

La sécurité fragile des personnes âgées pauvres de la classe ouvrière

Soutien public : logement et services de santé

Partant du fait que la littérature disponible relative au développement du Kerala souligne le rôle important de l'aide publique, nous tenons à savoir à quel point les Pulaya font usage de l'aide publique de l'État et de celle des organisations bénévoles en matière de sécurité sociale dans le vieil âge. Nombreux sont les Pulaya qui associent l'État au Kerala et non à l'Inde et le mettent en relation avec les prestations gouvernementales telles les « rations cards » (cartes ration), allocations pour retraite et logement. En outre, ils sont absolument conscients du fait qu'en tant que membres d'une caste officiellement reconnue, ils ont droit à des allocations particulières.

Dans une certaine mesure, les personnes âgées profitent des « rations shops » (magasins de ration) qui font partie du « National Public Distribution System » (PDS*)*, le système de distribution publique nationale. Ils achètent des produits tels que le pétrole ou du riz qui coûtait alors 10 roupies (env. 0.20 US$),[6] au lieu de 12 qui était le prix normal (env. 0.25 US$) en 2002. Mais beaucoup n'y achètent pas du riz car ils trouvent qu'il est de qualité inférieure. Des études montrent qu'il y a très peu de demande de blé et de variétés de riz de qualité inférieure, y compris parmi les plus défavorisés (p. ex. Mohandas 1999).[7]

---

[6] En 2002, un dollar américain correspondait à environ 50 roupies, c'est-à-dire 48.
[7] A l'instar des autres auteurs, Mohandas (1999 : 90) montre que le PDS est important pour les démunis du Kerala, mais il met ses lecteurs en garde : « Au Kerala, la demande de céréales complètes est quasi inexistante et il y a même moins de variétés de riz. Si elles étaient distribuées, cela réduirait davantage la consommation de

Deux conditions sont requises pour avoir droit à l'aide sociale, des soi-disantes « pensions » : ne pas avoir de fils adulte et avoir un revenu très bas. En plus, le chemin qui mène à l'octroi d'une telle assistance est semé de nombreux obstacles administratifs et nécessite que l'on ait des relations haut placées.[8] Les données figurant dans l'échantillonnage par quotas indiquent que 25 % des ménages ont accès à la « Kerala Destitute and Widow Pension Scheme » et à la « Kerala Agricultural Workers Pension Scheme »,[9] caisse de pension pour veuves et survivants et caisse de pension pour travailleurs agricoles. Ces sommes sont considérées modiques, respectivement 100 roupies et 125 roupies par mois (env. 2 à 2.5 US$), payées de surcroît à un rythme irrégulier. En moyenne, ces pensions correspondent à un revenu journalier de 150 roupies (env. 3 US$, cf. Irudaya Rajan 2001 : 615), l'équivalent de dix à quinze kilos de riz. La vieille veuve Vallothi (exemple 4) décrit ainsi sa pension : « Cela ne suffit même pas pour m'acheter de l'huile de noix de coco pour les cheveux. »

La politique gouvernementale en matière de logement semble avoir le plus profité aux Pulaya. Beaucoup d'entre eux possèdent un lopin de terre de trois à dix *cents*.[10] De nombreux chefs de famille ont obtenu leurs terrains du gouvernement lors des réformes agraires dans les années 1960. Les hommes de la jeune génération ont reçu en général trois *cents* du terrain de leurs pères afin de pouvoir construire à proximité de la maison familiale. Les Pulaya ne possèdent pas tous des titres fonciers. Certains n'ont pas encore réussi à faire enregistrer leurs terrains et continuent de squatter. En plus beaucoup avaient reçu du gouvernement un crédit hypothécaire (jusqu'à 35'000 roupies, env. 700 US$), sans obligation de remboursement ou avec l'obligation de n'en rembourser qu'une partie.

Comme mentionné dans le chapitre précédent, la politique de logement du Kerala inclut également des hospices pour personnes âgées.

---

céréales dans cet état, qui occupe l'avant-dernier rang en la matière (…) » (traduction libre).
[8] Cette constatation est également faite par I. S. Gulati et L. Gulati (1998).
[9] Pensions pour veuves n = 11 et pensions pour travailleurs agricoles n = 6, d'un échantillon total du sondage représentatif de 40 foyers pulaya.
[10] 1 *cent* correspond à 40.5 mètres carrés.

Pour en bénéficier, il faut avoir 55 ans et plus, être en bonne santé et n'avoir aucun soutien financier de ses enfants. Si une personne âgée devient grabataire, elle est transférée dans un centre de gériatrie chrétien. L'objet principal est d'offrir un foyer aux personnes âgées sans enfants ou ayant été abandonnés par eux. Les Pulaya n'y auraient recours que lorsqu'ils n'ont pas d'enfants et donc pas de soutien. Cependant, aucun d'entre eux n'en a encore eu l'expérience.

Pour les soins de santé, une organisation locale appelée « Rajagiri Community Developpment Scheme » (RCDS)[11] est à leur disposition. La tradition d'aide sociale chrétienne à Kalamassery remonte à quelques décennies, et bien plus longtemps encore dans le Kerala (Kariyil 1995). Ce programme implique qu'un médecin et une infirmière visitent le lotissement une fois par semaine et les gens peuvent elles-mêmes se rendre dans les locaux de l'organisation pour des check-ups. La plupart des gens dépensent entre 25 et 100 roupies (env. 0.50 à 2 US$) par mois pour des médicaments. Les consultations et les médicaments sont gratuits pour les personnes âgées. Les Pulaya utilisent beaucoup ses services.

En outre, les Pulaya peuvent mobiliser toutes sortes d'aide d'une organisation de caste locale appelée « Kerala Pulayar Maha Sabha » (KPMS). Un petit bâtiment abritant une antenne de ladite organisation se trouve dans le lotissement, antenne fondée dans les années 1960. Elle s'appuie sur la tradition d'activités d'aide sociale de son organisation faîtière au Kerala depuis le début du vingtième siècle, à l'instar d'autres organisations de caste (Jeffrey 1992). Dans ce district situé à l'est de Kochi (Kannayannur Taluk), on compte pas moins de trente-cinq antennes, ce qui prouve à quel point les Pulaya sont organisés. Le KPMS local porte assistance en matière de logement, d'hospitalisation, de mariage, de décès et de conflits familiaux. Elle requiert une cotisation de deux roupies par mois à chaque foyer. Cette organisation

---

[11] Le RCDS et le CASP, qui parmi d'autres institutions offrent un soutien aux enfants pauvres en matière d'éducation, sont rattachés au Ragajiri College of Social Sciences. Cette institution fut fondé en 1955 par les Carmelites of Mary Immaculate (CMI), une société chrétienne autochtone, et elle fut déplacée à Kalamassery en 1967. Le collège fait à présent partie d'un bien plus important complexe d'institutions de formation prestigieuses et d'organisations-satellites de service social.

de caste intervient en effet auprès du gouvernement pour effectuer les démarches d'enregistrement des naissances, mariages, décès, tout comme les admissions à l'hôpital et les demandes d'allocations pour logement. Elle se charge également des formalités et des cérémonies lors des crémations. En cas de décès dans la communauté, une taxe est prélevée dans chaque foyer pour couvrir les frais. De plus, l'organisation offre des divertissements à l'occasion des fêtes annuelles et organise des pèlerinages, ce qui donne aussi lieu à la collecte. Bien qu'ils estiment qu'une telle organisation ne peut remplacer la famille, les Pulaya jugent toutefois ses activités utiles. Pour ce qui a trait au vieil âge, les allocations pour le logement et l'hospitalisation qu'elle fournit sont très importantes.

Somme toute, bien qu'il existe de nombreuses formules de soutien public au Kerala, elles semblent avoir beaucoup moins d'impact sur les personnes âgées défavorisées du lotissement. En tant que citoyens, les Pulaya sont fortement impliqués dans les différentes activités de l'organisation de caste locale qui est bien intégrée dans le lotissement et dans la société du Kerala. Cette organisation d'aide sociale hindoue est un médiateur essentiel entre les Pulaya et l'État, en particulier en matière de logement et d'hospitalisation. Dans le domaine de la santé, les organisations d'aide sociale chrétiennes jouent un rôle supplémentaire. Néanmoins, ces organisations religieuses laissent la population défavorisée dans l'insécurité pour ce qui est de leurs besoins à long terme en matière de nourriture, d'argent et de soins. Une autre problématique est le fait que des collectivités fortement basées sur les castes renforcent les clivages entre les communautés. Elles contredisent ainsi les principes démocratiques et séculaires de l'État indien.

Imagerie nationale en matière de soutien : « la famille » et « le fils »

Outre l'importance de l'aide publique soulignée dans la littérature portant sur le développement au Kerala, un grand cas est fait de l'aide et l'entraide familiale dans les études en sciences sociales ainsi que dans les documents officiels concernant le Kerala et l'Inde.[12] Etant donné que la problématique de l'entraide familiale et de ses limites se situe au cœur de notre recherche, il serait indiqué d'observer de plus près l'imagerie qui se dissimule derrière ces discours nationaux. Pour ce faire, nous nous limiterons à quelques exemples.

En 1999, sous l'impulsion des résolutions de l'ONU et d'autres forums sur le vieil âge, « Ministry of Social Justice and Empowerment », le Ministère de la Justice Sociale et de la Responsabilisation, a publié un document intitulé « National Policy on Elderly Persons », document présentant la politique nationale en faveur des personnes âgées. Il sous-entend qu'« en Inde, les liens familiaux sont très forts et qu'une écrasante majorité des personnes âgées vivent avec leurs fils ou sont soutenus par eux » (Governement of India 1999 : 3). Le droit des parents âgés d'être soutenus par leurs enfants est en outre légalement établi. Étant donné que les familles vivant en ville ont de plus en plus du mal à assister financièrement à la fois les enfants et les personnes âgées, une série de stratégies d'action pour le soutien aux personnes âgées ont été proposées par des organisations gouvernementales et non gouvernementales, portant sur l'aide financière, la santé, la nourriture, le logement, l'éducation, l'aide sociale, tout comme la protection de la vie et de la propriété. En encourageant le partage des responsabilités entre fils et filles à l'égard des parents âgés, l'État vise à faire en sorte que les normes de soins ne soient plus différenciées selon le genre, bien que la condition dont dérive le droit à l'aide sociale demeure toujours le fait de n'avoir pas de fils adulte. La teneur générale du document se laisse résumer dans l'assertion : « La famille est l'institution sociale par excellence en Inde et la sécurité sociale informelle la plus vitale pour le vieil âge. La plupart des personnes âgées vivent avec un ou plusieurs de leurs enfants, surtout lorsque vivre seul devient impossible. C'est de loin le mode de vie favori et surtout le plus satisfaisant sur le plan émotionnel. Il est primordial que le système d'aide et d'entraide familiale continue d'être opérationnel

---

[12] Cf. p. ex. Chowdhury 1992, Gokhale et al. 1999, Rajagiri 1999, Shah 1998, 1999 pour le discours académique, et le Governement of India 1998, 1999 pour le discours national sur le soutien aux personnes âgées et la famille.

et que la capacité des familles d'assumer leurs responsabilités soit renforcée par des services d'aide sociales » (ibid. : 19, traduction libre).

Beaucoup d'études indiennes portant sur le vieil âge se déclinent dans la même veine. Très souvent, un âge d'or du soutien aux personnes âgées dans les familles élargies, bien que révolu, est présenté explicitement ou implicitement sans spécifications temporelle ni spatiale. En même temps, plusieurs scientifiques déplorent le fait que, de nos jours, les familles nucléaires ne soient plus en mesure de s'occuper convenablement des personnes âgées et que le statut de ces dernières régresse (p. ex. Irudaya Rajan et al. 1999). Lawrence Cohen (1998 : 103) a appelé de façon percutante ce discours le « récit de l'engouffrement dans la mauvaise famille ». En guise de commentaire critique, il affirme que la diversité des familles, dans le passé comme dans le présent, s'est ainsi estomper.

L'un des critiques les plus remarqués du concept de la famille en Inde est le sociologue indien A. M. Shah. Depuis les années 1960, il n'a cessé de plaider pour une analyse différenciée et mise en contexte des catégories familiales et de parenté. Il a par exemple montré que la famille élargie a été différemment conceptualisée dans les sciences sociales en Inde. Prise comme un ménage ou une unité de co-résidence, comme il le propose, c'était un ancien idéal sanscrit assez répandu mais pratiqué principalement par les castes et les classes supérieures. Le foyer moyen se composait de la famille nucléaire (Shah 1989). En ce qui concerne la recherche sur le vieil âge, Shah met en garde contre le discours populaire sur la désintégration de la famille élargie et de la glorification du passé. Ce genre de foyer n'était jamais exempt de tensions ni de conflits. Il montre qu'aujourd'hui davantage de personnes âgées vivent dans des foyers de famille élargie qu'il y a cinquante ans. Mais il ajoute que ceci ne signifie pas pour autant qu'elles sont toutes bien prises en charge. Néanmoins, il finit par plaider pour la vision de la sécurité sociale du vieil âge au sein de la famille, en l'occurrence le foyer élargi, qui devrait être ajustée aux exigences du monde moderne (Shah 1999).

Comme nous l'avons mentionné dans l'introduction du présent ouvrage, dans le domaine des études sur la parenté, les chercheurs indiens prennent une autre position du fait qu'ils incluent le genre dans leurs considérations.[13] Ils insistent sur le fait que les liens naturels entre la tradition, la famille et les femmes ont été, dans une large mesure, créés par les interventions de l'État dans le cadre de la réforme des lois portant sur les particuliers, et cela surtout depuis l'indépendance de l'Inde.[14] En outre, ils conceptualisent la famille explicitement comme une entité sociale changeante, ambivalente, et marquée par le genre. Une perspective similaire est appliquée dans la présente étude en ceci que les conditions changeantes de don et de réception de soutien dans les relations basées sur la parenté sont prises en considération.

Nous résumons ceci en disant qu'en Inde, les idées relatives au soutien fourni aux personnes âgées sont ancrées dans un contexte globalisé au sein duquel les organisations internationales sont d'importants acteurs.[15] Le discours dominant sur le soutien dans le vieil âge tenu par l'état-nation et les académiciens souligne avec insistance, pour ne pas dire exclusivement, le rôle de la famille et la considère en général comme une catégorie fixe naturelle et ahistorique, sans spécifier ses différentes variétés selon la classe, la caste et le lieu. Au lieu de traiter du soutien de la famille, mieux vaudrait plutôt se demander quelles relations de parenté, différenciées selon le genre et la génération, sont significatives et utiles à la sécurité sociale pour certains groupes sociaux à un certain moment et dans un certain lieu, et pourquoi il en est ainsi.

---

[13] Cf. p. ex. Palriwala 1994, Dube 1997, 1998, Ganesh 1998, et aussi Agarwal 1991.
[14] Cf. p. ex. aussi Collier, Rosaldo et Yanagisako 1982, et Bourdieu 1996 en matière de la création de la famille par l'État.
[15] Une partie du débat sur le vieil âge et la famille par les Nations Unies est par exemple publiée dans « Ageing and the Family » (1994). Cf. Stivens 1998b pour un rapport plus récent traitant des impacts globaux sur la construction de la « famille asiatique ».

Soutien de la parenté : besoins quotidiens de nourriture,
d'argent et de soins

Chez les Pulaya, « la famille » implique en premier lieu « tous ceux
qui vivent en harmonie sous un toit » et coopèrent ensemble. Cette
notion de la famille basée sur le foyer comprend les parents et leurs
enfants célibataires, c'est-à-dire la famille nucléaire. Pour les parents
âgés, c'est un foyer avec un fils marié, sa femme et ses enfants, c'est-
à-dire un « foyer de famille élargie » (cf. Dube 1997, Shah 1998) ou
un foyer de famille étendue, comme nous le désignons aussi.[16] Les
premières personnes de qui la personne âgée attend l'aide financière et
des soins dans le vieil âge sont les membres de la famille résidant sous
le même toit qu'elle.

Le rôle du père est de « guider la famille dans la bonne direction ».
La mère doit « prendre soin de la famille ». S'occuper des enfants est
une responsabilité qui incombe exclusivement aux femmes, davantage
que chez les musulmans et les Nayar selon l'échantillonnage par quotas. Si les hommes sont des ouvriers non qualifiés, les femmes sont
également censées contribuer au revenu du foyer. En revanche, s'ils
sont des ouvriers qualifiés ayant un emploi régulier, en général les
femmes se cantonneront dans le rôle de femme au foyer. Les hommes
sont supposés s'occuper des affaires d'argent en dehors du foyer et les
femmes à l'intérieur.

Fournir les meilleurs soins aux enfants et investir dans leur éducation et leur mariage est considéré comme la règle de base pour s'assurer la sécurité sociale dans le vieil âge. Entretenir des enfants autres
que ses enfants biologiques n'est pas apprécié. Les enfants ne devraient pas se marier trop tard ; les fils devraient se marier au plus tard

---

[16] En anthropologie, « la famille élargie » désigne en général une famille fondée sur
les connections entre frères et sœurs, tandis qu'une « famille étendue » est fondée
sur les connections entre parents et enfants. Un foyer est une unité de cohabitation et
de consommation et, dans certains contextes, de production (cf. Keesing et Strathern
1998). Étant donné que la littérature indienne utilise le terme de famille élargie également dans le cas d'une unité comprenant trois générations fondées sur les connections parents-enfants, nous emploierons les termes famille élargie et famille étendue
comme synonymes. En Inde, dans les contextes locaux et nationaux, le mot « famille » signifie en général « foyer » ou « ménage » en termes anthropologiques.

à trente ans. Ainsi, ils seront établis d'ici le temps que leurs parents atteignent le vieil âge et seront donc en mesure de les soutenir. Un vieil homme s'exprime dans ce sens en affirmant : « Mes enfants constituent ma véritable épargne. » Conformément à l'imagerie nationale, l'idée locale dominante sur la sécurité dans le vieil âge est que le « fils » qui, de manière métonymique est souvent la « famille » ou « les enfants », apporte le soutien à ses parents âgés. De préférence, le fils cadet devrait fournir le soutien financier tandis que sa femme prend soin des besoins physiques. En contrepartie, le fils assurant le soutien est habilité à hériter de la maison. Une aide financière et une aide physique supplémentaires sont attendues de la fille « en cas de besoin » et « selon ses moyens », bien qu'elle « s'en ira » vivre chez son mari une fois mariée.

Selon le point de vue des femmes, le soutien des enfants n'est pas certain en fin de compte. Une épouse âgée signale que les enfants s'occupent plus de leurs parents tant que le père est encore vivant. Elle associe cela à l'autorité et au respect dont il jouit. Ceci insinue que les veuves vivent plus dans l'insécurité sociale. Une vieille veuve le confirme en disant : « Dieu est le seul être qui prend soin de vous. S'il estime que vous méritez que l'on s'occupe de vous, alors vos enfants prendront soin de vous. »

Fait intéressant, l'imagerie sur la sécurité actuelle assurée par les enfants est souvent contrastée avec l'âge d'or révolu, époque où les propriétaires fonciers fournissaient la sécurité matérielle et les enfants la sécurité sociale par les soins et le respect. Dans ce contexte, les « propriétaires fonciers » et les « enfants » sont souvent mentionnés comme des fournisseurs de soutien complémentaires, image aujourd'hui similaire au « fils » et à la « belle-fille ». On fit remarquer : « Jadis, le propriétaire foncier fournissait la nourriture et s'occupait de vous dans le vieil âge. Les enfants et la parenté prenaient également soin de vous. » En ce qui concerne les parents, ceci était étayé par la croyance selon laquelle ils étaient considérés comme des divinités qui pourraient jeter un mauvais sort sur leur descendance. Une femme âgée d'ajouter : « La faim n'existait pas d'antan, les gens dormaient sur un lit de riz. Nous étions entièrement dévoués à nos parents et

convaincus qu'ils étaient l'incarnation des dieux. Alors nous les ado-
rions et les respections, nous écoutions et suivions leurs conseils. »
Ces déclarations indiquent que la norme de la responsabilité financière
du « fils » vis-à-vis des parents n'est apparu dans la société que dans
les années 1960.

Jusqu'à quel point les enfants peuvent-ils réellement être considérés comme « une épargne » aujourd'hui ? Le rôle de fournisseur principal de soutien matériel aux parents est généralement assigné au fils
cadet. En plus les autres fils et les filles aident financièrement et physiquement, tout comme les épouses dont nous parlerons plus en détail
plus loin. L'échantillonnage par quotas le confirme également.[17] De
nos jours, les foyers pulaya ne comptent plus beaucoup d'enfants, tout
au plus deux ou trois.[18] Par contre le nombre d'enfants est beaucoup
plus élevé parmi les personnes de soixante-dix ans et plus. Ce petit
nombre d'enfants amplifie l'insécurité sociale des personnes âgées
pauvres, surtout lorsque l'accès à l'emploi est compromis.

Le soutien financier limité des parents, fourni par seulement un fils,
saute aux yeux si l'on se penche sur le revenu d'un ménage de la
génération intermédiaire. L'homme gagne entre 2000 et 3000 roupies
(env. 40 à 60 US$). Et la femme entre 500 et 2000 roupies (env. 10 à
40 US$) par mois. Les chiffres des entretiens qualitatifs sur les salai-
res moyens des ouvriers non qualifiés, qui travaillent irrégulièrement,
sont plus bas : 1500 roupies pour les hommes et 1000 pour les femmes
(env. 30 et 20 US$ respectivement).[19] Dans plus de la moitié des cas
deux personnes, le mari et la femme le plus souvent, contribuaient au

---

[17] Le fils est la personne la plus importante qui fournit une aide financière à la mère
(n = 23 sur 40), vient ensuite le mari (n = 13). La deuxième personne la plus importante est de nouveau le fils (n = 14), vient ensuite la fille (n = 10), suivi du frère (n =
9), et après le mari (n = 3) et le beau-fils (n = 3).
[18] L'anthropologue den Uyl (1996 : 180) qui a travaillé avec de nombreux Pulaya
dans un village de l'État du Kerala a découvert que de nombreux couples ont recours
à la stérilisation à laquelle les incitent des campagnes gouvernementales.
[19] En 2001, un manœuvre gagnait entre 175 et 200 roupies la journée, et une femme
entre 100 et 125 roupies. Pour être en mesure de dépenser un dollar par jour, un
ménage doit disposer d'un revenu mensuel d'au moins 1500 roupies. Dans
l'échantillonnage par quotas, nous avons distingué trois catégories de revenus de
ménage annuels : moins de 24'000 roupies, entre 24'000 et 60'000 roupies et plus de
60'000 roupies.

revenu du ménage. Presque 20 % des personnes interrogées vivent dans des ménages avec un revenu annuel en dessous du seuil de pauvreté de 21'000 roupies (env. 420 US$). Ce sont les mêmes à déclarer qu'elles ne consomment que deux repas par jour et ne parviennent pas à soutenir suffisamment les parents. 70 % des enquêtés disent vivre avec un revenu annuel très modeste. Les revenus de ces ménages suffiraient pour s'occuper des parents âgées, si « la pression économique sur la génération intermédiaire » n'est pas trop forte (cf. United Nations 1994), c'est-à-dire qu'il n'y ait pas de dépenses supplémentaires pour les personnes âgées (p. ex. hospitalisation), pour les enfants (p. ex. éducation, mariage), et pour la génération intermédiaire elle-même (p. ex. maison, hospitalisation). Pour les 10 % des ménages disposant d'un revenu relativement élevé, on peut escompter qu'il y aura normalement une personne possédant un emploi régulier.[20] Ces foyers sont le plus à même de soutenir financièrement les parents âgés. En outre, un peu plus de 20 % des ménages ont de l'épargne, le plus souvent à la banque ou quelques-uns sous forme d'assurance. En revanche, presque 70 % des foyers sont endettés.

Une étude antérieure de « bidonvilles » de Kalamassary complète l'image des conditions socio-économiques de la population (Rajagiri 1996) ; l'image est légèrement atténuée par l'échantillonnage par quotas. De la population-cible composée de 6728 personnes (ou 1426 « familles ») 38 % étaient dépendantes (moins de 18 ans et plus de 65 ans), 28 % étaient employées, 19 % faisaient un travail non qualifié et seuls 10 % avaient un travail qualifié. De plus, 1 % étaient dans l'agriculture, 2 % se débrouillaient en affaires et 3 % étaient des petits employés. Des personnes disposant d'un revenu, seuls 13 % gagnent un revenu annuel supérieur à 25'000 roupies (env. 500 US$), probablement les ouvriers qualifiés et les petits employés. Les ouvriers non qualifiés et les autres doivent gagner dans les 2000 roupies (env. 40

---

[20] Bien que les Pulaya aspirent à des emplois permanents, la situation du marché du travail est telle que seule une minorité en dispose. Comme déjà mentionné dans le chapitre précédent, 43 % des ouvriers du Kerala sont des travailleurs occasionnels et seuls 17 % ont un travail régulier (Prakash 1999 : 35). Le paiement du solde quotidien étant exonéré d'impôts, les employeurs ont peu d'incitations à embaucher des travailleurs permanents.

US\$) par mois. Ceci correspond aux résultats que nous avons obtenus lors des entretiens qualitatifs. Si l'homme et la femme sont tous deux des travailleurs occasionnels non qualifiés, ils disposent d'un revenu annuel entre 30'000 et 40'000 roupies (env. 600 et 800 US\$). Les hommes pulaya qui avaient un emploi régulier gagnaient deux fois plus, idem pour les musulmans de la classe à bas revenus. Les Nayar de la classe moyenne ayant une formation élevée gagnaient en moyenne huit fois plus en tant qu'employés.

Bien que le travail non qualifié fait par les Pulaya n'est pas fortement différencié selon le genre et que la productivité des femmes ne diffère pas beaucoup de celle des hommes, les femmes ne perçoivent que les deux tiers des salaires des hommes. Dans les ménages de la génération intermédiaire, dans plus de la moitié des cas, la femme contribue au revenu du foyer ce qui semble moins que parmi la génération aînée. D'autre part, c'est plus que parmi les Nayar et beaucoup plus que parmi les musulmans.

L'aide dans le sens plus étroit de soutien physique pour les personnes âgées est principalement fournie par la « belle-fille », mais en cas de besoin, fils, filles et mari y prêtent main forte.[21] La relation entre belle-mère et belle-fille est structurellement tendue en Inde à cause de leurs intérêts conflictuels par rapport aux ressources du fils. On imagine que les tensions se sont accrues du fait que la conjugalité a gagné en importance (Palriwala 1994, Dube 1998).

Les soins physiques sont assujettis à la proximité et donc aux règles de vie convenues. D'après l'échantillonnage par quotas, un tiers des ménages à famille élargie comportait des enfants et des personnes âgées, tandis que deux tiers étaient des familles nucléaires sans personnes âgées. Certaines personnes âgées de notre échantillon cependant vivent au sein des foyers à famille nucléaire ou ce qui restait desdites familles si le fils cadet n'était pas encore marié. Dans ces cas, il n'y avait pas d'aide directe de la part de la belle-fille pour le ménage, mais la femme âgée elle-même s'en occupait, aidée par sa fille ou son

---

[21] La première personne à apporter un soutien physique à la mère est la belle-fille (n = 31 sur 40) ou le mari (n = 6), et en deuxième lieu le fils (n = 20 sur 40) et la fille (n = 8).

fils. Par exemple, le fils célibataire de la veuve Kali (exemple 3) nettoie et prépare les repas quand sa mère est souffrante et ne peut s'en
occuper. Dans tous ces cas, les fils mariés et les belles-filles vivaient
dans l'entourage. Seule une femme âgée vivait seule dans un foyer car
elle avait été abandonnée par son mari et n'a pas d'enfant. Les musulmans âgés vivent, presque sans exception, avec un ou deux fils
mariés, tandis que les Nayar âgés ne vivent avec l'un de leurs fils ou
leur fille que si leur conjoint ou conjointe était malade ou décédé(e).
En matière de soutien, c'est un avantage pour les Pulaya que leurs
enfants émigrent rarement, peut-être parce que cela coûte beaucoup
d'argent. Ceci contraste énormément avec les enfants des catégories
plus aisées de la population du Kerala (cf. Zachariah et al. 2002).
L'exemple suivant illustre les rapports de soutien intergénérationnel.

**Exemple 1 : Kunjappan, sa femme et sa belle-mère –
soutien de la part des enfants**
Kunjappan (62), né en 1940, est déjà « vieux » selon les critères locaux. C'est un
grand-père mais il est encore capable de gagner de l'argent. Ces quarante-cinq dernières années, il a fait toutes sortes de petits boulots dans le couvent catholique
proche dirigé par des sœurs. Avec son poste de travail non qualifié mais permanent,
il touche 100 roupies (env. 2 US$) par jour. Il vit légèrement au-dessus du seuil de
pauvreté mais, selon lui, pas confortablement. Son revenu est utilisé pour les besoins
quotidiens du ménage et pour le soutien de sa belle-mère. Il n'a pas d'économies
pour des extras de la vie quotidienne ni pour le vieil âge, mais en revanche il n'a pas
de dettes non plus. Les sœurs du couvent l'ont aidé à payer la scolarité de ses enfants. Il leur avait également emprunté de l'argent pour construire sa maison titrée et
elles l'ont assisté pour mettre de l'argent de côté pour sa part dans la dot de sa fille.
Il estime que les membres de sa « communauté » le respectent mais que susciter du
respect des castes plus élevées est une autre paire de manches.
    Il a grandi et est allé deux ans à l'école à Eloor, une localité proche, où il a appris
à lire mais pas à écrire. À cette époque, les classes étaient encore séparées selon les
castes. Avant de se marier en 1966 à l'âge de 26 ans, il a travaillé comme ouvrier
agricole pendant sept ans. Son père est tombé sérieusement malade au milieu des
années 1960, il avait la tuberculose. Kunjappan prit soin de lui à l'hôpital et à la
maison et lui acheta des médicaments. Après la mort de son père, son frère aîné prit
sa mère en charge et hérita de la maison paternelle à la mort de cette dernière. Suite
à un conflit avec son frère, Kunjappan quitta la maison paternelle et renonça à sa
part d'héritage, puis alla s'installer à Kalamassery. Il y occupa quatre *cents* de ter-

rain à l'abandon appartenant au gouvernement et y construit une petite maison de chaume.

Ses enfants, une fille âgée de 36 et un garçon de 26 ans, ont fréquenté l'école pendant dix ans. Les deux sont mariés et, fait exceptionnel, ont tous deux des emplois fixes. Sa fille vient juste de se marier et vit, comme la coutume l'exige, au lieu de résidence de son mari, non loin de là. Son fils, ouvrier qualifié dans une usine, vit avec sa femme chrétienne et son fils de deux ans, ensemble avec Kunjappan dans un ménage de famille élargie. Le fils assure les dépenses quotidiennes supplémentaires du ménage. La belle-fille s'occupe des travaux domestiques. Contrairement à sa femme, Kunjappan s'est déjà accommodé de sa belle-fille : « Elle s'occupe de moi comme ma propre fille. »

Depuis deux ans, la femme de Kunjappan vit temporairement dans son lieu d'origine avec sa mère, alitée à cause d'une « maladie cérébrale », vu que ses belles-filles la négligent. À présent, la femme de Kunjappan s'acquitte de l'aide qu'elle avait reçue de sa mère lorsque ses propres enfants étaient encore en bas âge et qu'elle devait alors aller gagner de l'argent.

Pour l'avenir, Kunjappan est confiant : « Je me suis bien occupé de mes enfants pendant leur enfance et leur adolescence. Je les ai nourris, je les ai envoyé à l'école, je leur ai donné de l'amour et tout le reste. Alors je pense que mes enfants continueront de prendre soin de moi. Et en cas de besoin, ma fille viendra aussi apporter un soutien financier et affectif. » En contrepartie du soutien qu'il reçoit, il a décidé que son fils héritera de la maison et du terrain, il devra toutefois versé l'équivalent de la moitié du terrain (deux *cents*) à sa sœur. Ceci ne se fera qu'après la mort de Kunjappan et de sa femme, assure-t-il. Ainsi, il conserve un pouvoir de négociation dans ses relations avec ses enfants.

Le vieil âge de Kunjappan est plutôt bien assuré grâce à sa contribution aux relations d'échanges passées et actuelles, dans le sens d'une réciprocité généralisée avec son fils. Il ne peut vivre dans la sécurité sociale sans le soutien financier de son fils pour les dépenses extraordinaires comme la dot, ni sans l'aide physique de sa belle-fille qu'il considère comme sa propre fille. Pour une aide additionnelle, financière et physique, il peut également compter sur l'échange à long terme avec sa fille. C'est la raison pour laquelle une partie de l'héritage est aussi cédée à cette dernière.

Les relations entre les belles-mères et les belles-filles sont tendues dans cette famille. La belle-mère de Kunjappan ne peut pas compter sur l'aide physique de ses belles-filles comme l'exigerait la norme officielle. La femme de Kunjappan apporte un soutien physique considérable à sa mère en sa qualité de fille, soutien légitimé par l'aide que lui avait apportée sa mère en s'occupant de ses enfants, une réciprocité généralisée en somme. Lorsque les personnes âgées, les femmes en particulier, deviennent infirmes ou sont alitées, l'aide physique de la part d'une belle-fille n'est pas garantie (cf. aussi Shah 1999). Ceci pourrait également avoir une influence négative dans la relation entre la mère et le fils ou vice versa ; par exemple, il n'était pas tout à fait clair si le fils de la belle-mère de Kunjappan continue de donner de l'argent pour sa mère. Au moins Kunjappan le faisait à titre de beau-fils. Théoriquement, les personnes âgées peuvent faire appel au soutien des enfants à travers la médiation de l'organisation locale de la caste. Elles sont également soutenues par la loi en la matière.

La sécurité sociale de la femme de Kunjappan est garantie par son mari, son fils et sa fille. Cependant, il n'est pas tout à fait certain qu'elle recevra plus tard des soins physiques de la part de sa belle-fille. Cela dépendra de la manière dont elles auront négocié leurs responsabilités mutuelles dans leur actuelle situation relationnelle si délicate.

On peut présumer que Kunjappan continuera à jouir d'une sécurité sociale pour autant que la situation économique de son fils et de sa belle-fille ne se détériore pas et qu'il continue lui-même à « maintenir l'harmonie » (cf. citation initiale). En ce qui concerne sa femme, rien n'est moins sûr.

En contraste avec le soutien des « enfants », le soutien intergénérationnel est secondaire dans l'imagerie nationale et locale. Cependant, le mariage est associé à la sécurité chez les Pulaya. Ceci correspond à l'importance que revêtent les liens conjugaux en Inde et au Kerala aujourd'hui (cf. Palriwala 1994, Busby 2000). Les hommes insistent sur « une compagne à vie », ce qui implique l'amour et l'entraide ; certains qualifient cette relation de sacrée. Malgré cela, des époux en viennent à quitter leurs conjointes pour « manque de sincérité de cœur » comme le formule une femme abandonnée. Pour les femmes, le mariage est important à la fois pour échapper à la solitude et pour avoir la sécurité financière. Les épouses protègent leurs maris. Une femme âgée fit remarquer qu'une femme doit être forte de caractère.

Son mari n'était plus mentalement sain, mais elle se gardait bien de le dévoiler en public de peur de ternir sa réputation. Le veuvage est toutefois lié à l'insécurité croissante. Une veuve âgée déclare : « Aussi longtemps que votre mari est vivant, vous n'avez pas à vous inquiéter car vous avez un revenu additionnel et vous n'êtes pas seule. » Une autre veuve âgée regrette le décès de son époux malgré le fait qu'il était un ivrogne qui la battait de surcroît. Il était néanmoins un soutien, dit-elle, il lui remettait la moitié de son revenu pour les dépenses du ménage. Une troisième veuve lâcha avec amertume : « Le mariage ? C'est du passé ! Cela ne signifie plus rien pour moi dans mon vieil âge. »

Les époux tirent réciproquement profit de leurs revenus si l'un ou l'autre continue de travailler pendant le vieil âge. Cependant, les femmes en profitent plus que les hommes car ces derniers gagnent plus. Les femmes âgées bénéficient également de bonnes relations que leurs époux avaient établi tout au long de leur vie. Les hommes âgés tirent profit des enfants, particulièrement des fils, que leurs femmes avaient mis au monde et élevés, et de l'aide physique qu'elles sont en mesure d'apporter parce qu'elles sont en général plus jeunes et vivront probablement plus longtemps. On peut présumer que la relation conjugale est elle aussi importante pour la sécurité sociale dans le vieil âge. Mais tout compte fait, les femmes peuvent moins compter sur le mariage que les hommes pour garantir leur sécurité sociale car le plus souvent, elles survivent à leurs maris et tombent alors sous la dépendance des enfants.

Dans le vieil âge, on n'attend pas du soutien de la « parenté », c'est-à-dire des frères et sœurs, des autres membres de sa propre famille ou de la belle-famille car « ils sont pauvres eux aussi ». Toutefois, on attend d'eux qu'ils participent aux cérémonies rituelles et rendent visite en cas de maladie. Dans ce cadre des cérémonies, la parenté peut également être désignée par le terme de « famille », qui est cependant alors pris dans un sens plus large. En dernier recours, les frères donnent souvent un coup de main tant financier que physique, comme le confirme l'échantillonnage par quotas sur l'aide financière de la part du frère d'une femme (cf. note n°17). Ceci s'applique aussi aux sœurs des époux, surtout si elles sont encore célibataires et vivent dans le voisinage. Dans l'expérience, ce genre d'entraide donnait en général lieu à des actes de réciprocité dans un laps de temps déterminé.

En résumé, les conditions économiques des enfants qui doivent fournir du soutien aux parents âgés sont largement insuffisantes. Dans la plupart des foyers, il serait très difficile pour un fils d'être le seul à soutenir ses parents, quand bien même sa femme contribue elle aussi au revenu du ménage. Ainsi, les personnes âgées doivent elles-mêmes cultiver les relations avec les autres fils et filles, et parfois avec d'autres membres de la parenté afin de pouvoir survivre. Ce genre d'arrangement permet en général d'obtenir de bonnes conditions pour le soutien physique aux parents âgés, de même que le fait que la génération intermédiaire compte plus de femmes au foyer que la génération aînée. L'aide financière offerte par les enfants n'est pas aussi fortement différenciée selon le genre comme le discours existant voudrait le faire croire. En revanche, recevoir du soutien dans le vieil âge est différencié selon le genre, c'est-à-dire que la sécurité sociale des femmes, en particulier des veuves, est plus exposée au risque que celle des hommes. Ceci peut être lié aux relations ambivalentes entre belle-mère et belle-fille et par conséquent entre mère et fils.

Soutien des voisins et des employeurs :
besoins non quotidiens en nourriture et en argent

À la surprise générale, et ceci ne figure pas dans l'imagerie locale ni nationale, les voisins sont aussi d'importants donneurs d'aide matérielle et physique pour de nombreux Pulaya. Ils complètent le soutien fourni par la parenté. À un certain point, ils ressemblent aux relations de parenté et certains voisins sont considérés comme des « parents ». Quand les temps sont durs, des voisines donnent la nourriture quotidienne et un peu d'argent, tandis que les voisins contribuent aux besoins non quotidiens avec des sommes d'argent plus importantes. En outre, les employeurs, couramment appelés « patrons », fournissent un soutien matériel non quotidien sous forme de nourriture, de vêtements lors des fêtes annuelles, d'argent ou de bijoux en or pour une dot ainsi que des contributions financières pour la maison. La croyance générale veut aussi que les anciens grands propriétaires fonciers – à qui on a tendance d'attribuer des traits de parenté idéaux – étaient de meilleurs donneurs de soutien que les employeurs actuels. Les hommes en particulier considèrent les voisins, les amis et les employeurs comme d'importants donneurs de soutien dans le vieil âge. Les données de l'échantillonnage par quotas confirment l'importance du soutien des voisins et des employeurs chez les Pulaya,[22] tout comme l'illustre l'exemple suivant.

Exemple 2 : Kumaran – soutien du voisinage étendu
Kumaran, âgé de 75 ans, est né en 1927. Il avait deux enfants, un fils et une fille. Malheureusement, il y a douze ans, le fils est décédé à l'âge de trente-trois ans, laissant une femme, une fille et un fils. Kumaran vit dans un foyer de famille élargie avec sa femme, sa belle-fille et son petit-fils. Il travaillait comme ouvrier agricole et reçoit une « pension de travailleur agricole » de 125 roupies (env. 2.5 US$) par mois, dont le montant lui est transféré par semestre. Sa femme et sa belle-fille sont des domestiques qui gagnent jusqu'à 1000 roupies chacune (env. 20 US$) par mois. Le petit-fils, âgé de 21 ans, a reçu une formation et travaille comme mécanicien dans un garage pour un salaire de 750 roupies (env. 15 US$).

Le décès de son fils, causé par une insuffisance cardiaque, a semé la crise dans la vie de Kumaran. Sa femme, sa belle-fille et sa proche parenté l'ont assisté. De plus, les voisins l'ont soutenu. « Ce sont des personnes dignes de confiance », déclare-t-il. Il estime que l'homme et la femme gèrent les crises différemment : « La femme résout facilement les problèmes domestiques car elle est plus proche des enfants. Mais les hommes devraient être soutenus par leurs femmes car ils peuvent aussi aider à trouver des solutions aux problèmes. Les hommes sont beaucoup plus habitués aux personnes à l'extérieur du foyer. »

Une année plus tard, Kumaran tombe gravement malade et doit se faire opérer au cœur. Les frais du traitement étaient estimés à 5000 roupies (env. 100 US$). Mais comme il n'avait pas d'argent, il s'est rendu dans un hôpital public où un membre de sa parenté exerçait comme médecin. Ainsi, il a pu se faire soigner sans les moindre frais. En outre, il a reçu des médicaments gratuits de l'organisation chrétienne locale d'assistance sociale (RCDS).

---

[22] Les voisins sont cités en premier parmi les personnes qui, en dehors de tout lien de parenté, apportent du soutien à une mère (n = 35 sur 40), à côté des employeurs (n = 4 pour la plus importante personne non apparentée, et n = 17 pour la personne non apparentée seconde en importance).

Au sujet du rôle des personnes locales n'ayant pas de lien de parenté avec lui, Kumaran fait remarquer : « Si des parents n'habitent pas tout près, alors les voisins apportent du soutien. Ils peuvent également aider lors des cérémonies ou en cas de maladie. En situation d'indigence, les voisins offrent nourriture et argent. Les patrons donnent plutôt un soutien financier. » Il précise : « Je peux compter sur mes enfants à tout moment. En revanche, je peux compter sur mes parents et voisins en cas de besoin. »

Kumaran a tissé un réseau social bien dense. Il vit à Kalamassery depuis plus de cinquante ans. Il a travaillé comme gardien (de 1989 à 2000) dans la maison d'un homme qui travaillait à l'étranger et qui avait laissé sa femme et ses enfants au Kerala. Son employeur lui donnait vêtements et argent et lui rendait visite lorsqu'il était malade.

Pendant ses moments de loisirs, il cultivait ses relations sociales avec ses voisins et continue de le faire. « Mes voisins d'à côté sont comme des parents pour moi. » En outre, Kumaran était un membre fervent du Parti communiste. Il a particulièrement apprécié la politique agraire du gouvernement communiste des années 1960.

L'exemple de Kumaran illustre à quel point le soutien des enfants est délicat : son unique fils est décédé. Son petit-fils remplace son fils, mais plus sur le plan moral que sur le plan matériel. À cause de sa maladie, Kumaran ne peut plus assurer lui-même son vieil âge par un revenu, mais il peut compter sur le soutien financier de sa femme. En plus, les voisins viennent en aide en cas de besoin comme il le souligne : « En cas de pauvreté, les voisins offrent nourriture et argent. » Son réseau de relations avec des voisins qui se comportent envers lui comme des parents est dense et vaste. Les relations à objectif politique en font aussi partie, une affaire d'hommes. Pour les veuves, le soutien des voisins est important pour la simple survie, comme le montre l'exemple qui suit.

Exemple 3 : Kali – soutien du voisinage immédiat

Kali (âgée de 75 ans) est née en 1926 et a neuf enfants, dont quatre fils et cinq filles. Elle s'était mariée à seize ans et a travaillé toute sa vie durant dans le bâtiment et a coupé des herbes jusqu'à il y a deux ans. Son mari est décédé il y a quinze ans. Kali vit dans une maison en tuiles avec son avant-dernier fils âgé de 36 ans, le dernier à ne s'être pas encore marié.

Comme ouvrier non qualifié, le fils est journalier et gagne environ 1500 roupies (environ 30 US$) par mois. Il s'occupe de sa mère en lui donnant de l'argent et en faisant la cuisine et les travaux domestiques lorsqu'elle est souffrante. Il dépense son argent en premier lieu pour ses propres besoins, il en donne ensuite à sa mère, tantôt 50 roupies, tantôt 100 (env. 1 à 2 US$). Kali reçoit aussi de l'argent et des vêtements d'une de ses filles, les enfants de cette dernière l'assistent aussi. L'employeur de sa fille l'a également aidée pour la dot et a aidé sa fille à mettre l'argent de côté pour les bijoux. De son vivant, la sœur de Kali lui apportait également une aide matérielle.

Kali n'a pas pu constituer la moindre épargne pour son vieil âge. Elle n'a pas de biens. La maison est toujours au nom de son mari. Elle a toujours gagné juste de quoi subvenir à ses besoins quotidiens. Néanmoins, elle estime qu'une personne âgée devrait être aussi indépendante que possible. Elle espère ne pas devenir si vieille et diminuée au point de ne plus pouvoir faire les travaux domestiques. Sinon, elle s'attend à ce que son fils qui vit avec elle et ses filles lui viennent en aide le moment venu. Elle espère que son fils épousera bientôt « une fille bien ». Ainsi aura-t-elle, à son tour, une belle-fille pour prendre soin d'elle.

Elle propose que les personnes âgées reçoivent de l'argent et des médicaments pour améliorer leur situation. « En tant que personne âgée, il est important d'avoir de l'argent pour être respectée. »

En cas de besoin, elle peut s'adresser à plusieurs voisins pour obtenir de la nourriture ou de l'argent. « Mes voisins d'en face et ceux de derrière me donnent à manger quand j'ai faim et me donnent de l'argent lors qu'il m'en faut. Nous leur donnons aussi à manger quand ils n'en ont pas assez. »

Kali est soutenue financièrement et physiquement par son fils qui est toujours célibataire, donc sans autres obligations pour l'instant et financièrement par l'une de ses filles. Ses sept autres enfants ne sont pas disposés ou ne sont pas en mesure de lui venir en aide. Kali dépend beaucoup de l'aide additionnelle de ses voisins, surtout pour la nourriture. Comparé à celui de Kumaran, le réseau de voisins de Kali est plutôt centré sur les relations d'échange pour ses besoins de base au quotidien. Il faut tenir compte du fait que l'entraide entre voisins ne fonctionne que sur la base de la réciprocité équilibrée, comme dans les relations avec la « parenté ».[23] Ceci implique que les biens et services doivent être remboursés dans un laps de temps raisonnable. Or seuls les individus disposant d'un minimum de ressources économiques peuvent prendre part à ce mode de relations. Kali y participe car les jours où sont fils travaille et lui remet un peu d'argent, elle peut

---

[23] Cf. Sahlins (2004 [1965]) pour les termes réciprocité généralisée, équilibrée et négative.

s'acheter de la nourriture qu'elle partage alors avec les autres. Les deux exemples mettent aussi en lumière l'importance du soutien des employeurs.

Les contributions des personnes âgées : argent, soin et logement

Finalement, les personnes âgées elles-mêmes contribuent à leur sécurité sociale dans le vieil âge. Cette réalité ne figure cependant pas dans l'imagerie nationale et locale. Que pensent les personnes âgées du vieil âge et comment contribuent-elles à leur propre sécurité sociale ? Être âgé, pour l'homme comme pour la femme, est associé à un changement de leurs rôles économiques et sociaux. Ce qui marque le plus, c'est la capacité perdue de gagner de l'argent, beaucoup plus que le fait d'avoir atteint l'âge de la retraite qui est de cinquante-cinq ans pour les personnes de la classe moyenne. En outre, vieillir signifie devenir grands-parents et s'occuper des petits-enfants, tâche qui incombe surtout aux femmes âgées. On s'attend aussi à ce qu'elles fassent les travaux domestiques aussi longtemps qu'elles le peuvent. Les insécurités relatives au vieil âge les plus souvent exprimées concernent le manque d'argent et de soutien de la part des enfants. À l'instar de Kali (exemple 3), de nombreux Pulaya ont connu peu de sécurité sociale tout au long de leur existence. C'est la raison pour laquelle ils n'ont souvent pas une notion particulière de l'insécurité et n'éprouvent pas une grande envie d'en parler.

L'opinion répandue est qu'une personne âgée doit travailler et être indépendante aussi longtemps que ses capacités et son état de santé le lui permettent. L'auto-soutien paraît donc très important. De plus, une personne âgée doit se comporter bien, c'est-à-dire être serviable, sociable et pas querelleuse. Le respect est réputé être lié au fait d'avoir des moyens financiers et un bon comportement. C'est pour cette raison que les Pulaya âgés cherchent à gagner de l'argent le plus longtemps possible et s'évertuent à être aimables. Cependant, de nombreuses personnes âgées n'ont plus ni la force physique ni la santé pour faire les durs travaux dont elles étaient autrefois capables.

Certains hommes et femmes, se sentant encore suffisamment solides physiquement et ayant des employeurs indulgents, continuent de travailler jusqu'à l'âge de quatre-vingt ans et au-delà, pour des revenus très bas. Kunjappan (exemple 1) et un de ses collègues travaillent tous deux au couvent et perçoivent une paie journalière qui représente environ la moitié de ce que les hommes gagnent en moyenne. Quant à Vallothi (exemple 4), du haut de ses quatre-vingts ans, elle ne touche que 500 roupies (env. 10 US$) par mois comme balayeuse dans un temple. Il n'est pas possible de couvrir tous les besoins quotidiens avec un tel salaire, sans parler des besoins additionnels.

Chez les Pulaya, outre le fait de devoir subvenir aux besoins de ses propres enfants, construire une maison fait partie de la prévoyance pour le vieil âge comme l'indique l'exemple de Kunjappan. Une maison et un terrain de trois *cents*, d'une valeur marchande de 100'000 roupies (env. 2000 US$), constituent la ressource matérielle majeure que la plupart des Pulaya ont réussi à acquérir tout au long de leur existence grâce aux subventions publiques, comme nous l'avons vu plus haut. Ce sont des maisons en briques disposant d'une cuisine et de trois pièces minuscules, sans accès direct à l'eau et pour certaines, sans latrine. Elles ont de l'électricité subventionnée et sont sobrement meublées. Dans la majorité des cas le terrain et la maison sont au nom de l'homme. Les données de l'échantillonnage par quotas le confirment.[24] Mais à cause de la corruption et de la situation politique, tous ne sont pas légalement propriétaires de leurs maisons, bien qu'ils possèdent le titre foncier pour le terrain. Beaucoup ont certes commencé la construction de leur maison avec les subventions publiques, mais ils ont dû s'endetter davantage pour l'achever. Une épouse a par exemple dû mettre ses bijoux en gage pour garantir un prêt.

---

[24] Elles indiquent que, dans presque 75 % des cas (n = 28 sur 40), la maison appartient à l'homme. Tandis que ce pourcentage est beaucoup plus bas chez les Nayar et chez les musulmans (n = 22 et n = 20 respectivement sur 40). Les cas où les femmes sont propriétaires ou co-propriétaires sont moins fréquents chez les Pulaya (n = 12), plus fréquents chez les Nayar (n = 18) et, fait surprenant, les plus fréquents chez les musulmans (n = 20).

En général, vu que les femmes ne possèdent pas de maison, elles ont par conséquent peu de pouvoir de négociation à opposer à l'autorité de leurs époux ou de leurs fils, représentants officiels du foyer.[25] Seules quelques femmes possèdent des terrains dans leurs lieux d'origine en tant que natives de là-bas, mais jamais en tant qu'épouses dans leurs propres foyers.[26]

Dans la classe ouvrière, être propriétaire d'une maison est une énorme ressource et représente une position de force dans les relations d'autorité entre les parents âgés et les enfants, en particulier entre pères et fils. C'est plutôt un phénomène nouveau vu que ces personnes âgées sont la première génération à habiter dans des maisons en briques et non pas dans des huttes en chaume.

Pour finir, l'épargne a été évoquée comme ressource importante pour la prévoyance du vieil âge, mais seuls les travailleurs qualifiés ayant des emplois réguliers parviennent à épargner environ 250'000 roupies (env. 5000 US\$). Les Nayar âgés ont de l'épargne à la banque d'au moins le même montant, ainsi qu'une autre forme d'héritage, à côté d'une maison d'une valeur d'environ 1'500'000 (env. 30'000 US\$). Les journaliers ne sont pas en mesure de se constituer une épargne pour leurs vieux jours. La dot de leurs filles, qui s'élève à environ 100'000 roupies (env. 2000 US\$) par fille, le prix d'une maison, en est le principal obstacle. Ces montants n'étaient pas si élevés à l'époque où les personnes âgées se mariaient et n'existaient même pas du temps de leurs parents.[27] Dans leur grande majorité, les personnes âgées vivent au jour le jour et se complaisent à dire que leurs enfants constituent leur épargne.

---

[25] Dans la majorité des cas, la maison était toujours enregistrée au nom du mari, bien que celui-ci soit décédé depuis longtemps. On ne procède à un nouvel enregistrement qu'après la mort de la femme afin d'éviter des frais inutiles.

[26] D'après les données de l'échantillonnage par quotas, dans 6 cas sur 40, la femme était propriétaire d'une maison. Dans 4 cas, la mère est mentionnée comme propriétaire, ce qui signifie probablement que la maison est toujours enregistrée au nom du père défunt.

[27] La dot doit avoir fait son apparition chez les Pulaya dans les années 1960. Kunjappan (exemple 1) dit avoir reçu quelque chose pour sa femme, bien qu'il n'avait rien demandé. Dans les années 1930, à l'époque où ses parents se mariaient, les dots n'étaient pas apportées.

Afin de pouvoir vivre au moins dans une sécurité fragile, il est important qu'une personne soit encore capable de participer aux relations d'échange par un minimum de biens et de services, ou qu'elle ait suffisamment investi dans ses échanges avec son conjoint/sa conjointe et ses enfants, de sorte que les besoins de base tels la nourriture, l'habillement et le gît soit garantis. Les contributions à la sécurité sociale dans le vieil âge sont elles aussi différenciées selon le genre. Certes, les femmes âgées ne gagnent pas autant d'argent que les hommes et n'ont pas en général de biens comme une maison, mais elles s'occupent des enfants et des travaux domestiques aussi longtemps qu'elles le peuvent. Fait intéressant, les femmes âgées sont à la fois donneuses et receveuses de soutien.

L'insécurité critique des femmes âgées les plus démunies

À côté de la majorité des Pulaya âgés vivant dans une sécurité sociale fragile, se trouve une minorité de femmes qui vivent dans une insécurité sociale critique. Elles sont négligées à tel point que leurs besoins de base en matière de nourriture ne sont pas satisfaits. Il s'agit de femmes sans maris ni enfants. Ne recevant pas assez de soutien de leur parenté, elles ne peuvent pas participer au réseau de relations de réciprocité dans leur voisinage. Elles comptent parmi les Pulaya les plus démunis, à l'instar de Vallothi, la veuve âgée de l'exemple suivant.

Exemple 4 : Vallothi – en attendant la nourriture
Vallothi (âgée d'environ 85 ans) est née vers 1916 et a été veuve pendant la majeure partie de sa vie. Elle a eu cinq enfants : deux filles et trois fils dont l'un est décédé très jeune. Elle a perdu son mari quand elle était âgée d'une trentaine d'années et que ses enfants étaient encore en bas âge. Elle a pris soin de son fils cadet qui était handicapé et célibataire jusqu'à sa mort en 2002.
Vallothi n'a jamais été à l'école. Elle a d'abord travaillé comme ouvrière agricole, ensuite comme balayeuse dans un temple. Cela fait deux ans qu'elle a cessé de gagner de l'argent. Dans son dernier emploi de balayeuse, elle gagnait 500 roupies (env. 10 US$) par mois et recevait des vêtements. Au moment de prendre la retraite, parce que ses forces l'abandonnaient de plus en plus, elle reçut la modique somme de 2000 roupies (env. 40 US$). Elle la remit à son fils aîné qui lui fournit un à deux

repas par jour. Vallothi dit avoir faim le matin. Les gens disent que sa belle-fille la néglige et ne lui donne à manger que contrainte et forcée par son mari. Le fils de Vallothi ne peut cependant pas se permettre de grandes dépenses car il est lui-même déjà âgé d'environ soixante ans et ne travaille pas régulièrement. Il a heureusement trois fils.

Le gouvernement verse une pension de veuvage de 500 roupies (env. 10 US$) par an. « Cela ne suffit même pas pour m'acheter de l'huile de noix de coco pour les cheveux », fait-elle remarquer. Une fois par semaine, elle reçoit des médicaments gratuits de l'organisation de charité chrétienne (RCDS).

À l'époque où elle a dû élever seule ses enfants et qu'elle vivait encore dans son lieu d'origine, son employeur chrétien lui offrait régulièrement nourriture et argent et a aussi contribué à la dot des ses filles.

Avec un petit lit pliant pour tout meuble elle vit dans sa minuscule maison en briques, entourée d'un lopin de terre de trois *cents*. La maison, à son nom, venait d'être construite grâce à un « prêt » , mais elle paraît inachevée. Son petit-fils aîné a réaménagé le « prêt » (non remboursable) à la mairie par l'entremise de l'organisation de caste locale (KPMS). En contrepartie, il héritera de la maison après la mort de sa mère. Vallothi ne peut pas prendre toute seule des décisions concernant la maison. Son fils aîné et deux de ses petits-fils sont ses voisins immédiats. Ses filles vivent aussi non loin de là.

D'après Vallothi, les personnes âgées du lotissement sont en général satisfaites. Et malgré le fait qu'elle n'a pas assez à manger, elle semble en bonne condition mentale, physique et sociale. Elle souhaiterait seulement pouvoir prendre un petit-déjeuner tous les matins. Afin de se consoler, elle continue de fréquenter quotidiennement le temple.

Les Pulaya, dans leur grande majorité, continuent de penser que les personnes âgées de leur localité sont heureuses, bien qu'il y ait des cas d'insécurité et de négligence et, comme circonstances concomitantes, d'exclusion sociale. Néanmoins, dans les cas présents, il ne s'agit ni de négligence ni d'exclusion totales. Il se peut que les personnes âgées de la classe inférieure ne manifestent pas de mécontentement à cause du fait qu'elles ne sont que partiellement négligées ou exclues et qu'elles doivent « gérer l'image » (cf. Sokolovsky 1993) des insécurités sociales dans le vieil âge. Vallothi a eu trois fils et deux filles. Deux de ses fils sont déjà morts. Son unique fils vivant a un revenu irrégulier et sa femme et lui sont aussi en quelque sorte dans le besoin car ils sont déjà vieux. Dans cette situation délicate, en partie due à la longévité de Vallothi, sa relation avec sa belle-fille est ambivalente au point que cette dernière ne semble disposée à la soutenir. Ses propres filles pourraient lui apporter une aide additionnelle, mais lui fournir les repas quotidiens n'incombe pas à leur responsabilité. C'est ainsi que Vallothi doit vivre avec une ration quotidienne insuffisante et l'unique capital dont elle dispose pour les relations d'échange, qui semble insuffisante elle aussi, est sa gentillesse. Le dernier exemple relate la vie de Devu, une femme abandonnée et sans enfants.

Exemple 5 : Devu – mendiante pour se nourrir
Devu (âgée de 60 ans) est née en 1941. Elle a travaillé comme manœuvre dès l'âge de huit ans. Dû au fait que son père vint à tomber gravement malade, sa mère et elle ont dû couper et vendre de l'herbe pour faire bouillir la marmite. Plus tard, elle a travaillé dans le bâtiment. Comme elle n'a pas de frère, elle était aussi contrainte de participer aux frais du mariage d'une de ses deux sœurs.

Son mari a également travaillé dans le bâtiment. Juste à la mort de sa mère il y a huit ans, ce dernier l'a quittée. D'où sa remarque sur le mariage : « Le mariage représente la sécurité, cependant, certains hommes quittent leurs femmes car ils n'ont pas le cœur sincère. Une femme âgée doit être préparée à l'idée que son mari peut se désintéresser d'elle et la quitter pour épouser une femme plus jeune qu'elle. Elle doit alors avoir un toit où dormir et de quoi s'acheter à manger. » Devu n'a ni l'un ni l'autre. Elle ajouta que les hommes ne connaissent pas de telles crises car ils peuvent toujours se remarier. Elle a vécu cet abandon comme une crise majeure dans sa vie.

Elle est retournée s'installer dans son lieu d'origine, Kalamassery, où elle possédait un lopin de terre. Elle avait acheté à la municipalité un terrain de trois *cents* pour sa mère qui s'y était installée, suivie de la sœur de Devu et son neveu. Devu s'est construit une chambre sans fenêtre, juxtaposée à la maison de sa mère et y vit à présent. Depuis la mort de sa mère, Devu est toujours propriétaire d'un *cent* de la cour. Elle fait sa toilette et regarde la télévision chez son cousin.

Devu a continué à gagner de l'argent jusqu'à l'âge de 55 ans, époque où ses problèmes de santé ont commencé. En effet, ses bras se sont mis à enfler. Depuis lors elle va demander à manger à sa nièce ou à ses cousins. À défaut, elle va mendier hors du lotissement pour ne pas être reconnue. La fille de sa sœur cadette est sa parente la plus proche. Devu a contribué au financement de son mariage et elle lui léguera son coin de la cour (un *cent*) à sa mort. Des femmes musulmanes aident Devu à faire sa lessive, travail que sa maladie l'empêche de faire.

« Ma vie entière est une immense crise », résume Devu. Petite fille, elle a dû soutenir sa mère et une fois mariée, ce fut le tour du mari. Et à présent, la voilà livrée à elle-même. Le pire, à ses yeux, c'est de n'avoir pas d'enfant. Elle avait voulu en adopter mais son mari n'était pas d'accord. Son vœu le plus cher est que les personnes âgées obtiennent un soutien extérieur, surtout un peu d'argent et des médicaments.

Elle est l'une des rares enquêtés qui souhaite être placée dans un hospice pour personnes âgées car elle n'a personne pour s'occuper d'elle. Pour ce faire, elle a besoin de l'accord des enfants de son cousin. Ces derniers refuseront probablement car cela nuirait à leur réputation, s'imagine-t-elle. Elle continue donc à vivre de la sorte. Elle se dit que si elle venait à tomber gravement malade, elle se traînerait jusqu'à la rue et supplierait les passants de la transporter à l'hôpital public. « C'est certain qu'alors je mourrai. C'est ainsi que je finirai ma vie. »

Devu est l'une des informateurs peu nombreux qui estiment que les personnes âgées vivant dans le lotissement sont malheureuses. Son histoire illustre de manière criante l'insécurité critique des femmes démunies sans « famille ». Elle ne peut compter que sur des relations de parenté distantes et incertaines. Elle n'a pas droit au soutien public par le biais de la « pension pour veuves et survivants » car elle n'est pas officiellement divorcée. Elle pourrait être admise dans un hospice pour personnes âgées mais ses proches parents masculins n'y consentiraient pas parce qu'ils craignent pour leur réputation.

Les exemples de Vallothi et de Devu mettent en lumière des cas d'insécurité critique dans laquelle ni la parenté ni les voisins ne fournissent le soutien nécessaire lorsqu'il s'agit des besoins quotidiens les plus élémentaires, c'est-à-dire la nourriture. Leurs récits ne sont pas des discours de plainte dont se sert une personne âgée pour se garantir l'entraide familiale (cf. Rosenberg 1990, Cattell 1997). Bien qu'elles disposent toutes deux d'un bout de terrain, Vallothi a même une maison, ceci ne leur confère pas suffisamment de pouvoir de négociation pour leur sécurité sociale quotidienne. L'imagerie structurée par le genre et les relations de pouvoir contribuent au fait que les hommes âgés reçoivent en général plus d'aide de leurs enfants et de leurs épouses, et que les femmes âgées sans maris sont assujetties aux décisions des hommes plus jeunes de leur famille.

Ces cas ne sont pas isolés. Dans ses recherches sur les veuves au Kerala et dans six autres États en Inde, Chen (1998) a découvert : « Peu de veuves (si tant est qu'il y en ait) vivant seules sont entretenues, c'est-à-dire qu'elles reçoivent régulièrement à manger des autres foyers. Qui plus est, si une veuve vit dans un foyer sous l'autorité de son fils – fait encore plus marqué si elle est sous l'autorité de tierces personnes – elle est sujette à la négligence, à moins qu'elle n'apporte une contribution significative au foyer : par exemple les travaux domestiques, du terrain ou d'autres biens, un revenu ou une pension » (Chen 1998 : 39, traduction libre).

Parenté et insécurité

L'imagerie de l'aide et l'entraide familiale doit être remise en cause. Dans la majorité de nos cas relatifs au groupe de la classe ouvrière, nous avons découvert que les personnes âgée ne sont pas suffisamment soutenues par leurs familles, encore moins par un seul fils. L'imagerie nationale et locale dissimulent largement l'insécurité dans les relations intergénérationnelles. La famille peut s'avérer être un foyer d'insécurité sociale pour les personnes âgées, d'une part parce qu'elles manquent de ressources financières, d'autre part à cause des relations familiales ambivalentes. La sécurité sociale du vieil âge doit constamment se négocier par les actions des personnes âgées dans leurs relations d'échange avec les donneurs de soutien. Les investissements antérieurs et futurs dans l'échange généralisé avec le conjoint ou la conjointe et avec les enfants sont de la plus haute importance, comme l'a souligné l'une des personnes âgées (cf. citation initiale).

L'ambivalence des relations de parenté constitue un sujet intéressant dans les nouvelles études sur la parenté. Jusqu'à présent, ce thème a été très peu traité de manière théorique et empirique.[28] En nous référant à ladite littérature, nous employons le terme d'ambivalence dans le sens d'attitude conflictuelle et de pratiques inhérentes aux relations de parenté, attitude engendrée par des intérêts divergents pas seulement économiquement motivés, mais aussi symboliquement, par exemple lorsqu'il est question de prestige. Tel est par exemple le cas si, dans un foyer de famille étendue vivant près du seuil de pau-

---

[28] Cf. Risseeuw et Palriwala 1996, Ganesh 1998, Faubion 2000, Böck et Rao 2000, et Peletz 2001. Dans la littérature sur le vieil âge, il y a un certain débat sur les conflits intergénérationnels, mais principalement sous l'angle d'une approche fonctionaliste, p. ex. Foner 1984.

vreté voire même en dessous, la belle-fille est femme au foyer, prestige oblige. Le matériel ethnographique présenté ici consolide
l'argument selon lequel les relations de parenté n'apportent pas que
sécurité et soutien, mais qu'elles peuvent également engendrer négligence et insécurité sociale. La négligence est aussi signalée dans une
récente étude empirique sur l'exploitation des personnes âgées dans la
capitale du Kerala (Merlin 1999).[29] Le problème de l'ambivalence
peut conduire à la rupture ou simplement à la distanciation dans les
relations de soutien, surtout en ce qui concerne les femmes âgées.[30]

Conclusion

Jusqu'à quel point les personnes âgées pauvres du Kerala urbain peu-
vent-elles mobiliser du soutien de la part des organismes publics ou de
leurs familles ? Jusqu'à quel point le soutien pour le vieil âge est-il
différencié selon le genre ? Telles étaient les questions posées dans le
présent chapitre. Le soutien public en matière de besoins quotidiens
est moins sûrement garanti que présumé. Les prestations publiques
dans le domaine de la construction des maisons représentent une aide
des plus importantes. Ici, l'organisation de caste locale (KPMS) joue
un rôle important de médiation entre les travailleurs et l'État en matière de subventions pour la construction des maisons. Rajagari, l'organisation chrétienne non gouvernementale, apporte un soutien de
base en matière de santé. Les relations de citoyenneté avec ces associations chrétiennes et hindoues ont une importance considérable pour
les personnes âgées. Les échanges avec l'État sont généralement indi-
rects.

Cependant, ce qui rend la sécurité du vieil âge plus précaire est le
fait que même le modèle de « famille », qu'elle soit étendue ou élargie, ne joue pas le rôle protecteur comme le présument ou le réclament
souvent le gouvernement et les sociologues indiens. Ce discours sur

---

[29] Cf. aussi Rosenblatt et Antoni 2002.
[30] Ces observations concernant l'ambivalence des relations de parenté résultant d'un
processus plus long d'évaluation des données et d'une analyse approfondie
d'exemples mis en contexte doivent être développés ailleurs.

l'aide et l'entraide familiale devra être reformulé. Les relations conjugales et les relations avec les enfants ne produisent la sécurité sociale que sous certaines conditions économiques et sociales. L'arrangement de sécurité sociale des Pulaya est fortement diversifié. Les maris jouent un rôle important en ce qui concerne le soutien financier et parfois de soutien physique. Les filles apportent l'aide additionnelle, financière et physique. Le soutien financier est moins centré sur un seul fils, contrairement aux idées reçues. Les frères et la famille par alliance peuvent également jouer un rôle subsidiaire.

Pour bénéficier de la sécurité dans le vieil âge, les personnes âgées doivent mobiliser suffisamment de moyens dans leur réseau de parenté pour leurs besoins quotidiens et non quotidiens. Cela implique également que ces relations de parenté ne soient pas teintées d'ambivalences, c'est-à-dire d'attitudes et de pratiques négatives aboutissant à une forme de négligence. Cela suppose aussi des relations de réciprocité intactes (réciprocité généralisée avec les membres du foyer, réciprocité équilibrée avec les autres parents) avec des contributions apportées par les personnes âgées, telles les travaux domestiques et la garde des enfants.

De manière inattendue, les relations avec les voisins jouent un rôle complémentaire important pour satisfaire les besoins quotidiens. Elles ne peuvent toutefois se maintenir que si les provisions reçues, l'argent et la nourriture, sont remboursées dans un laps de temps raisonnable (réciprocité équilibrée). En outre, les relations avec les employeurs offrent du soutien pour les besoins non quotidiens tels l'acquisition de maisons et la constitution de dots en contrepartie du surplus de travail déjà investi.

Vu l'importance d'un réseau de soutien local élargi dans la classe ouvrière pauvre, je suggère d'innover le terme « voisinage étendu » qui comprend toutes sortes de relations de parenté et de citoyenneté mises en œuvre dans la localité en matière de sécurité sociale pour le vieil âge. Hormis les personnes âgées vivant dans une sécurité sociale fragile, p. ex. celles dont la satisfaction des besoins quotidiens peut changer à tout moment pour cause de problèmes financiers ou de tensions familiales, il existe des personnes âgées qui connaissent une insécurité critique. Leurs besoins quotidiens en nourriture ne sont pas satisfaits. Il s'agit de veuves et d'autres femmes ne disposant ni de capital économique ni de capital social.

L'étude de cas a révélé trois modes de vie quotidienne dans le vieil âge : 1) le soutien des membres du foyer est suffisant dans des cas où le revenu du ménage est suffisant et l'ambivalence familiale neutralisée, 2) le soutien des membres du foyer est complété par le soutien des voisins et d'autres personnes locales dans des cas où le revenu du foyer est temporairement suffisant et l'ambivalence familiale prononcée, et 3) le soutien des membres du foyer est insuffisant et ne peut être complété par la parenté plus éloignée, des voisins ou d'autres personnes locales (employeurs actuels ou anciens) dans des cas où le revenu du foyer est insuffisant et l'ambivalence familiale prononcée.

Le soutien des enfants à l'égard des personnes âgées n'est pas fortement différencié selon le genre. Les filles contribuent aussi en donnant de l'argent et les fils apportent une aide physique lorsque cela s'avère nécessaire. Néanmoins, les soins qu'offrent les femmes âgées sont beaucoup plus élaborés que ceux fournis par les hommes, par exemple les faits de s'occuper des petits-enfants et prendre soin de parents malades. Par ce mécanisme, les personnes âgées sont à la fois donneuses et receveuses d'aide. Le soutien des voisins est différencié selon le genre en ceci que les fils et d'autres hommes ont tendance à offrir un soutien financier tandis que les femmes apportent nourriture et soins physiques.

Recevoir du soutien est fortement différencié selon le genre. Les femmes âgées sont désavantagées en la matière et disposent d'un pouvoir de négociation moindre car elles ont moins accès aux ressources (peu d'éducation, revenus bas, pas de maison) et elles ont moins d'autorité que les hommes, même lorsqu'elles sont beaucoup plus âgées. Les femmes âgées les plus démunies et sans enfants souffrent tout particulièrement d'insécurité. Autant les femmes s'adaptent mieux que les hommes à la phase de la vieillesse, autant elles s'accommodent moins bien de leurs belles-filles. La dépendance de la mère à la prise de décision du fils est plus marquée que celle du père, surtout si la mère ne peut plus compter sur son mari pour lui prêter main forte. Dans pareil cas, elle devra s'accommoder des éventuels intérêts divergents entre son fils et sa femme, ses enfants et elle-même. Eu égard à l'espérance de vie croissante des femmes, ceci peut devenir un problème considérable avec le temps.

Ces personnes âgées de la classe ouvrière ne reçoivent de sécurité sociale ni de l' « État » ni de la « famille ». Les musulmans à bas revenus et ayant un travail régulier semblent eux pouvoir compter plus exclusivement sur les membres de leurs familles. Les Nayar de la classe moyenne quant à eux peuvent avoir recours à une pension de l'État, à leurs propres biens, au soutien physique des domestiques, des infirmières à domicile et des membres de leurs familles. La sécurité sociale des ouvriers Pulaya non qualifiés est plus ou moins successivement basée sur un réseau complexe, tel un patchwork de relations de parenté spécifiques et changeantes (en tant que conjoint, conjointe, mère, père) et de citoyenneté (en tant que voisin, travailleur, membre d'une association, d'une municipalité, d'un État et d'un état-nation). Tout cela exige des efforts constants des personnes âgées pour maintenir leur réseau flexible au sein des structures existantes. Un tel arrangement de sécurité sociale peut être qualifié de « réseau de voisinage étendu » qui, en fin de compte, semble être plus important pour la sécurité des personnes âgées démunies que la famille étendue ou élargie. En ce qui concerne les personnes âgées pauvres de la classe ouvrière, nous suggérons alors que l'accent soit mis sur le maintien des relations de soutien de ce réseau de voisinage étendu, plutôt que sur la famille étendue ou tout autre famille, imaginée en bien ou en mal.

L'étude de cas ci-après sur le Kerala rural vient confirmer les résultats les plus importants de la présente étude de cas. Curieusement, nous avons constaté moins de différences que présumées en matière de sécurité sociale des personnes âgées démunies entre ces deux terrains de recherche qui contrastent pourtant sous certains aspects.

Sécurité sociale limitée
des personnes âgées pauvres au Kerala rural

Seema Bhagyanath

En 2001, les Nations Unies avait prédit qu'une personne âgée sur sept serait indienne.[1] L'Inde passera d'une « société mûre » à une « société vieillissante ».[2] Le profil démographique changeant pose un défi quant à la prise en charge des personnes âgées. En Inde, se pencher sur la sécurité sociale de la population âgée de l'État du Kerala s'avère intéressant pour deux raisons. D'abord parce que le Kerala a déjà fait la transition démographique d'une « société mûre » à une « société vieillissante », avec une population de 8,77 % et qui est estimée à 11,74 % en 2011 (Irudaya Rajan et al. 1999 : 45). Deuxièmement parce que l'État du Kerala est connu pour ses nombreuses prestations de sécurité sociale pour les personnes âgées, comme indiqué dans les chapitres précédents.

Réalisée dans le Kerala rural, la présente étude de cas se cristallise sur les relations de sécurité sociale des personnes âgées de la classe ouvrière, appartenant à la caste des Pulaya. Pour des aspects pertinents, elles sont comparées aux employés de la classe moyenne, membres de la caste des Nayar. Tout au long de ce chapitre, nous examinerons les questions suivantes : Tout d'abord, de quelle nature sont les insécurités sociales vécues par les personnes âgées ? En second lieu, quelles ressources économiques et quelles relations sociales leur sont accessibles pour obtenir le soutien dont elles dépendent pour leur survie ? Pour finir, à quel point le vieil âge est-il différencié selon le genre ? Le résultat principal de cette étude corrobore avec celle menée au Kerala urbain : au Kerala rural, les personnes âgées de la

---

[1] D'après l'Organisation centrale de la statistique (2000 : 1), la population âgée de l'Inde, qui était de 56,7 millions de personnes en 1991, atteindra 137 million en 2021, selon les estimations.
[2] Une société avec une population âgée de 4,7 à 7 % est appelée « société mûre », tandis qu'une société dont le taux des personnes âgées est supérieur à 7 % est qualifiée de « société vieillissante ».

classe ouvrière dépendent elles aussi d'un réseau de soutien diversifié pour leur sécurité sociale.

Le terrain de recherche

Situé dans le district d'Ernakulam dans le Kerala central, Kadamakuddy est le nom du village où nous avons mené l'étude de terrain entre 2001 et 2002, pendant une durée totale de six mois.[3] Cette localité a été choisie pour sa forte concentration de Pulaya (Rajagiri 1991). Le village compte 14'668 habitants.[4] Les chrétiens syriens et les catholiques latins représentent la grande majorité de la population, il n'y a pas de famille musulmane. Diverses castes hindoues y vivent, à savoir les Izhava, les Kudumbi, les Pulaya, les Kanaka et une minorité de Nayar. D'après les experts locaux, en 1995, Kadamakuddy comptait environ 278 foyers pulaya. Notre travail de terrain, avec à peu près 120 foyers, s'est déroulé sur l'une des îles.

Jusqu'en 2001, on ne pouvait atteindre l'île qu'en bateau. Ces dernières années, le gouvernement a entamé la construction d'une bretelle faisant partie d'une nouvelle autoroute nationale et censée relier l'île au continent. En 2002, la bretelle était quasiment achevée. Cependant, les routes du village sont restées d'étroits sentiers en terre battue, de sorte qu'on s'y déplace surtout à pied. Certains villageois possèdent des bicyclettes et quelques-uns des mobylettes. Les femmes vont toujours à pied. Se rendre à des endroits comme l'hôpital peut prendre jusqu'à une heure de temps. Les insulaires pensent qu'une fois que l'île sera réellement reliée au continent, son développement connaîtra un essor fulgurant.

Jusqu'à présent, les recettes fiscales du village sont les plus réduites du Kerala vu que sa topographie inaccessible n'était guère favora-

---

[3] Cette étude de cas est basée sur les données qualitatives collectées auprès de 52 personnes, c'est-à-dire 40 entretiens individuels et 12 avec des experts en matière de castes, de la communauté et des questions concernant les personnes âgées. En outre, pour avoir une idée plus claire de la population étudiée, un échantillonnage par quotas couvrant 80 foyers a parallèlement été fait, c'est-à-dire 40 foyers pulaya et 40 foyers nayar. La plupart des personnes interrogées étaient hindoues, communauté religieuse la plus répandue au Kerala.
[4] Source : Département de l'Économie et des Statistiques 1995.

ble à l'installation d'entreprises. En matière de fonds de développement, le village dépend des subventions gouvernementales. L'agriculture, qui constituait autrefois la principale source d'emploi, est aujour-
d'hui en déclin parce qu'elle n'est plus rentable.[5] D'autres débouchés
d'emploi sont offerts par l'élevage des crevettes, de poisson, la production d'argile, le travail manuel tel la construction et le bêchage des
tranchées pour l'évacuation des eaux, et aussi l'enseignement. Beaucoup d'habitants vivant sur l'île travaillent dans le continent, en
l'occurrence des fonctionnaires, des enseignants, des vendeurs, des
mécaniciens et des manœuvres. Dans le village, la commercialisation
a été récemment stimulée suite à l'acquisition de terrain par une entre-
prise privée désirant construire des maisonnettes servant d'habitations
aux ouvriers.

L'abondance des déchets émis par une industrie chimique dans une
grande partie de l'île pose problème aux villageois. La pollution qui
en découle nuit à la pêche et cause des problèmes respiratoires aux
habitants. Afin d'esquisser une image des conditions de vie des Pulaya
âgés, nous présenterons des faits socio-économiques généraux sur ce
groupe social au sein du village.

Milieu socio-économique des Pulaya

Tous les Pulaya âgés, hommes et femmes confondus, ont travaillé
comme ouvriers agricoles. Pour compléter cette occupation saison-
nière et gagner leur vie, ils ont également vaqué à d'autres activités
manuelles telles le traitement de la pellicule des noix de coco pour en
faire des fibres, transporter des briques, du sable et de la terre sur la
tête pour la construction, creuser des tranchées. Jadis, les emplois
agricoles étaient mal payés, le plus souvent en nature. Pour avoir
cultivé et moissonné 100 kilos de riz, un ouvrier en recevait 10 et le
propriétaire 90. Les rémunérations étaient tout aussi modiques pour
d'autres travaux manuels. Ainsi, les ouvriers n'étaient pas à même

---

[5] Après la réforme agraire, les dimensions des propriétés agricoles ont beaucoup
diminué. En plus, les coûts relatifs à la préparation des terres à cultiver sont élevés et
la production des petites propriétés agricoles n'est pas suffisante pour être rentable.

d'épargner de l'argent. Dans leur grande majorité, les Pulaya âgés ne travaillent plus pour des raisons de santé, mais aussi parce que l'agriculture a perdu de son importance dans le village. Certains travaillent comme domestiques dans des foyers aisés, les hommes faisant de petits travaux comme désherber la propriété, fendre du bois pour faire la cuisine,[6] tandis que les femmes font les travaux domestiques. Une prestation d'assistance sociale ou une « pension » de 110 roupies (env. 2 US$)[7] par mois est l'unique revenu fixe que les Pulaya âgés du village peuvent espérer recevoir. Toutes les personnes âgées ayant participé aux entretiens qualitatifs reçoivent une telle assistance sociale. En revanche, le sondage représentatif a montré que la moitié des personnes interrogées ne touchent pas une telle pension.[8]

La situation économique des Nayar de la classe moyenne est tout autre. Seuls les hommes exercent une activité professionnelle tandis que les épouses sont femmes au foyer. Ils sont enseignants, fonctionnaires ou employés dans le secteur privé. Ainsi peuvent-ils épargner pour leurs vieux jours. Les anciens fonctionnaires ont le privilège de recevoir une pension moyenne de 5000 roupies (env. 100 US$). Dans l'un des cas, un Nayar âgé perçoit une pension de 12'000 roupies (env. 240 US$) par mois.

Comme les Pulaya âgés n'ont quasiment pas de revenu, il s'avère important d'examiner si leurs enfants en ont. La génération des personnes d'âge moyen travaille surtout comme ouvriers semi-qualifiés. La plupart sont en contrat à durée déterminée et touchent une paie journalière. Ils sont mieux payés que ceux qui sont employés à la journée. Mais comme ils ne sont pas sous contrat permanent, leurs conditions de travail ne sont pas sûres.[9] D'après l'échantillonnage par quotas, les hommes gagnent un modeste salaire mensuel entre 2000 et

---

[6] Les foyers aisés préfèrent parfois utiliser le feu de bois qui, selon eux, confère plus de goût aux repas. Le chauffage de l'eau et la cuisson du riz requérant une grande consommation de fuel, le feu de bois lui est préféré.
Le bois à brûler, provenant surtout des branches de cocotiers tombantes, est aisément disponible.
[7] Les roupies sont converties en dollars dans tous les cas.
[8] N = 21 sur 40.
[9] Comme journalier, un homme gagne 150 roupies (env. 3 US$) par jour et une femme 120 roupies (env. 2.5 US$) pour le même genre de travail.

3000 roupies (env. 40 à 60 US$) et les femmes en général entre 500 et
2000 roupies (env. 10 à 40 US$). De nombreuses jeunes mariées, étant
femmes au foyer, ne perçoivent pas de salaire.

En tenant compte des revenus du ménage, auquel peuvent contribuer plus d'une personne, ils se situent presque tous au-dessus du seuil
de pauvreté, c'est-à-dire au-dessus d'un revenu annuel de 21'000 roupies (env. 420 US$). Etant donné que les revenus ne sont pas recensés
et qu'ils vivent visiblement dans des conditions de pauvreté, ils
bénéficient néanmoins des avantages de la carte de ration, « ration
card ». Comme mentionné dans les chapitres précédents, une telle
carte leur permet de se procurer du riz et d'autres denrées de première
nécessité à des tarifs subventionnés. Ces conditions contrastent avec
l'étude menée au Kerala urbain où une grande majorité des foyers
vivent au-dessous du seuil de pauvreté. En outre, la vie au village est
moins chère qu'en ville. Les taxes foncières, les impôts sur la propriété et les prix des denrées telles le poisson et les légumes sont plus
réduits.

Les Pulaya sont fiers d'avoir été à l'école. Toutes les personnes
âgées ont reçu deux ans d'éducation officielle dans le village insulaire,
certaines un peu plus. Beaucoup d'entre elles avaient dû interrompre
l'école au bout de quelques années pour des raisons familiales. Ils
avaient dû soit commencer à travailler, soit garder un petit frère ou
une petite sœur pendant que les parents étaient au travail. La génération des personnes d'âge moyen, sans distinction du genre, a fréquenté
l'école pendant presque dix ans et la jeune génération totalise au
moins dix années d'école. À l'instar de l'étude d'un village faite par
Franke (1996) au Kerala central, l'éducation scolaire ne garantit cependant pas un emploi permanent aux Pulaya. À titre d'exemple, un
homme qui a fait des études de physique, fait exceptionnel, travaille
pourtant dans la construction pour une paie journalière de 225 roupies
(env. 4.5 US$).

Presque toutes les personnes âgées de la classe ouvrière possèdent
une maison. Ceci est le résultat de la réforme agraire introduite dans
les années 1970 au Kerala. Toute personne ayant travaillé comme ou-

vrier agricole avait eu droit à dix *cents*[10] de terre dans un endroit spécifique. Or au moment du partage effectif, les gens ne reçurent que six *cents*. Ils réussirent à se construire une maison sur ce terrain grâce à un prêt. En général, la maison est au nom de l'époux, mais elle revient à la femme en cas de décès de ce dernier. D'après l'échantillonnage par quotas, dans 75 % des cas, la maison appartient à l'homme contre 25 % à la femme.

La maison est une structure en ciment composée de trois pièces, avec un toit en tuiles. De nombreuses maisons ont l'électricité. Certaines sont recouvertes de grandes feuilles de plastique à défaut de vraies fenêtres. De nombreuses habitations sont construites dans les bas-fonds au bord de l'eau, ce qui signifie qu'en saison des pluies, elles risquent à tout moment d'être inondées. Elles n'ont pas non plus d'eau courant pour la plupart. Pour se laver, les Pulaya se servent de l'eau de la rivière, et pour boire et cuisiner, ils vont chercher de l'eau potable dans les fontaines publiques. Lorsqu'il y a pénurie d'eau en été, la municipalité du village organise des citernes d'eau sur des bateaux. La corvée d'eau incombe uniquement aux femmes.

De cette brève description, nous pouvons déduire la contribution qu'apportent les Pulaya âgés à leur propre sécurité sociale : ils possèdent une maison pour s'abriter et une modique pension. Il leur arrive même d'avoir de petits boulots irréguliers, ce qui leur assure un modeste revenu supplémentaire. Mais cela ne suffit pas pour couvrir tous les besoins essentiels, en d'autres termes, ils dépendent généralement de leur progéniture. La question est de savoir à quel point et de quelle manière.

La crainte de l'insécurité sociale dans le vieil âge : pas d'argent, pas de nourriture, pas de soins médicaux

Les Pulaya âgés se représentent le vieil âge comme une phase de déclin, une période de la vie où ils ne sont plus en mesure de se déplacer aisément et de travailler normalement, où leur état de santé se détériore. D'une façon générale, ils lient le concept de sécurité sociale

---

[10] 1 *cent* correspond à 40.5 mètres carrés.

dans le vieil âge au fait d'avoir quelqu'un qui les soutienne, c'est-à-dire qui prenne soin de leurs besoins. Cette responsabilité pressentie s'adresse aux enfants, en particulier aux fils et, à défaut, aux filles. Étant donné que les personnes âgées n'ont guère de revenu, manquer d'argent pour satisfaire les besoins élémentaires tel que celui de se nourrir constitue une grande source d'inquiétude pour elles. L'une des femmes âgées a néanmoins dit qu'obtenir à manger n'était pas si difficile pour elle puisque l'on cuisine de toute façon dans le foyer où elle vit avec son fils marié. Se procurer les médicaments dont elles ont besoin constitue leur deuxième grand souci. Rien ne dit qu'elles seront encore en mesure de s'acheter des médicaments si elles dépendent entièrement de leurs enfants.

Les questions relatives à la santé angoissent les personnes âgées, en particulier l'idée de devenir grabataire. Elles craignent d'être considérées comme des fardeaux et d'être alors négligées. Nombreuses sont celles qui expriment le désir de rendre l'âme avant d'atteindre pareil stade car cela reviendrait à dépendre des autres pour tous leurs besoins fonctionnels. Elles souhaitent tout, sauf devenir encombrantes pour leur enfants.

L'état de santé des personnes âgées influe sur leur qualité de vie car dans certains cas, cela se traduit par une mobilité réduite qui, à son tour, affecte négativement les relations sociales. Dans notre échantillon, deux femmes âgées dont la vue avait baissé ne pouvaient plus quitter la maison. Un homme âgé atteint de tension n'osait pas sortir seul de peur de s'évanouir en cas de malaise. Un autre, convalescent, ne sortait pas non plus. Les seules possibilités d'avoir des échanges dans tous ces cas étaient avec les membres de la famille et les personnes qui venaient leur rendre visite. Ceci confirme la découverte de l'étude menée par Willigen, Chadha et Kedia (1996) selon laquelle les personnes âgées ayant une santé déficiente ont un réseau de relations réduit. Le manque de relations sociales peut donner le sentiment de solitude et d'exclusion. Quelques Pulaya âgés se plaignent du fait que de nos jours, la vie trépidente ne permet pas tellement aux jeunes d'avoir du temps à consacrer à la génération aînée.

En rapport avec la sécurité sociale dans le vieil âge, un autre facteur fondamental aux yeux des personnes âgées est le fait d'avoir rempli toutes leurs responsabilités. La plus importante d'entre elles étant le fait de réussir à marier leurs enfants. Trouver une conjointe adéquate ou un conjoint adéquat à leurs enfants s'avère crucial car leur sécurité sociale dans le vieil âge dépendra en premier lieu d'une bonne entente avec la belle-fille ou le beau-fils. Le mariage est aussi lié à la question de la dot. Offrir une dot est inéluctable pour être à même de donner une fille en mariage. En milieu rural, la dot d'une jeune fille pulaya varie entre 24'000 et 41'000 roupies (env. 480 et 832 US$).[11] Ce montant est beaucoup moins élevé qu'en milieu urbain où la dot avoisine les 100'000 roupies (env. 2000 US$). De nombreux Pulaya âgés sont parvenus à constituer la dot de leurs filles en hypothéquant leurs maisons et en contractant des dettes auprès des tiers. Rembourser des dettes n'est possible que si l'on dispose toujours d'un revenu de travail. Marier leurs filles durant leur vie active est donc vital pour eux.

Relations et ressources de soutien dans le vieil âge

Nous nous penchons maintenant sur la question relative aux ressources économiques et aux relations sociales dont disposent les Pulaya en matière de soutien dans le vieil âge. Cet aspect peut être traité en termes de soutien familial, de soutien communautaire et de soutien public.

Soutien familial

Patricia Uberoi (1993) signale qu'en Inde, la définition de la famille change selon le contexte dans lequel elle est utilisée. Dans le contexte d'un foyer composé de deux générations, on parle de la famille en termes de parents et enfants ; dans le contexte d'un foyer composé de

---

[11] Plus précisément, les dots se composent de 5000 roupies et 5 *pavan* d'or à 15'000 roupies et 7 *pavan* d'or, 1 *pavan* d'or représentant huit grammes d'or d'une valeur de 3800 roupies en 2002.

trois générations, la famille implique les parents, les enfants et les petits-enfants. Dans le contexte des cérémonies, la famille inclut frères et sœurs, tantes, oncles et cousins, cousines. Comme unité familiale, nous examinons ici les relations des personnes âgées avec leurs enfants, leurs conjoints et la parenté au-delà du foyer.

De nombreux écrits de scientifiques donnent à penser qu'autrefois, le système de famille élargie offrait aux personnes âgées la sécurité, l'amour et l'affection dont elles avaient besoin, et que son démantèlement leur pose problème de nos jours (p. ex. Bose 1988, Mahanty 1989, World Bank 1994). Dans la société indienne, la norme selon laquelle les personnes âgées doivent être prises en charge au sein de la famille est culturellement transmise par des écrits hindous et socialement relayée. La notion préconisant que les enfants ont une énorme dette envers leurs parents pour les avoir mis au monde, nourris et éduqués pendant leur enfance et leur adolescence est unanimement reconnue. Ainsi la relation parents-enfants est-elle perçue en Inde comme une relation à vie. Dans son étude portant sur les personnes âgées menée dans le village indien du nord de Rayapur, Vatuck (1980) affirme : « Le vieil âge est perçu comme une phase de dépendance légitime du soutien d'une famille étendue (d'un fils adulte plus exactement) » (ibid. : 127, traduction libre).

Dans le cas des Pulaya, les personnes âgées s'attendent à ce que leur progéniture prenne soin d'elles le moment venu. Elles estiment que si elles ont un fils, ce dernier doit s'occuper d'elles. En l'absence d'un fils, c'est à la fille que revient ce rôle. Il est généralement admis qu'une fois qu'une fille se marie, elle intègre son domicile conjugal et sa disposition à soutenir ses parents dépendra surtout du bon vouloir de son époux. Un homme âgé déclare : « Si tu t'occupes de tes enfants et satisfais leurs besoins dans leur jeunesse, ils s'occuperont à leur tour de toi dans le vieil âge. » Un jeune homme d'ajouter : « Tout enfant se doit de prendre soin de ses parents. Les abandonner ou les négliger serait un péché. » Ces paroles font écho à l'opinion largement répandue parmi la génération d'âge moyen qui pense qu'il appartient aux enfants d'épauler leurs parents. Les enfants vivant loin de leurs parents ressentent un sentiment de culpabilité. L'un des jeunes hommes qui avait déménagé continue de s'occuper de sa mère veuve, malgré la grande distance qui les sépare. Il paie les taxes de sa maison et lui rend régulièrement visite afin de s'assurer que tout va bien. Son frère cadet vit avec leur mère. Cet exemple prouve que les fils cadets ne sont pas les seuls à soutenir financièrement leurs parents âgés.

La grande majorité des Pulaya interrogés vivent dans des foyers de trois générations comprenant un fils ou une fille, sa conjointe ou son conjoint et leurs enfants. D'après l'échantillonnage par quotas, toutes les personnes âgées vivent entourées de leur famille, aucune ne vit seule. La proportion des familles étendues est elle aussi beaucoup plus grande qu'en milieu urbain. En ce qui concerne le soutien aux femmes âgées, la belle-fille est la personne responsable en premier lieu des soins physiques à apporter à sa belle-mère. L'aide de l'époux, de la fille, du fils ou de la parenté est également importante. En matière d'aide financière, les femmes âgées dépendent principalement de leur fils et, dans une certaine mesure, de leurs époux. Dans certaines circonstances, les filles et les frères prêtent aussi main forte.[12] La belle-fille, respectivement le fils assurent les soins physiques et le soutien financier. Cependant, la parenté vivant sous le même toit ou dans d'autres foyers procure aussi des soins physiques et une aide financière dans certains cas.

L'exemple suivant met en lumière la situation de Tilotamma, une femme âgée mariée qui souligne l'importance de la relation avec son fils par rapport à la sécurité sociale dans le vieil âge. Son fils s'occupe de ses besoins quotidiens et lui achète des médicaments. Mais en fait, c'est le soutien de son époux et de sa belle-fille qui assurent la sécurité sociale de Tilotamma.

---

[12] La personne qui procure en premier lieu des soins physiques à la femme âgée : la belle-fille n = 30, l'époux n = 5, la fille n = 5 ; en deuxième lieu : le fils n = 20, l'époux n = 9, la belle-fille n = 7, le gendre n = 3.
La personne qui donne en premier lieu l'aide financière à la mère : le fils n = 30, l'époux n = 8, la fille n = 1, le gendre n = 1 ; en deuxième lieu : la fille n = 12, le frère n = 10, le fils n = 8, le gendre n = 6, l'époux n = 4.

Exemple 1 : Tilotamma – soutenue par son fils et sa belle-fille

Tilotamma (âgée de 61 ans) est née en 1940 dans un village appelé Puttampally. Après la mort de son père survenue lorsqu'elle était enfant, sa famille s'est installée à Kadamakuddy, lieu d'origine de sa mère. Elle a fréquenté l'école jusqu'à la troisième classe et s'est ensuite mise à travailler, principalement comme ouvrière agricole. Elle a également traité les noix de coco pour en faire des fibres. Tilotamma s'est mariée à l'âge de seize ans. Son mari était également un ouvrier agricole. Il a été contremaître dans un champ situé dans le village mitoyen. Elle y a souvent travaillé elle aussi. Ils ont réussi à construire une maison qui est au nom de son mari. Ils ont cessé de travailler tous les deux à cause de leur état de santé. Son époux souffre d'asthme et elle de tension artérielle. En tant que journaliers, ils ne sont pas parvenus à se constituer une épargne. Ils reçoivent néanmoins la pension pour ouvriers agricoles, qui représente un petit revenu pour le vieil âge. Ils ont un fils unique âgé de trente-trois ans qui vit avec eux, entouré de sa femme et ses deux enfants. Pour Tilotamma, le soutien de son fils maçon est primordial : elle prie le ciel qu'il continue à s'occuper d'elle jusqu'à la fin de ses jours. Sa belle-fille s'occupe aussi d'elle, bien que leur relation connaisse parfois des conflits. Mais Tilotamma sait pertinemment qu'elle peut compter sur elle en cas de besoin, comme lorsqu'elle était tombée malade. Tilotamma participe aux tâches ménagères et garde ses petits-enfants quand il le faut.

Lorsqu'elle avait été gravement malade et alitée pendant des semaines à cause de la pression artérielle, son mari et sa belle-fille avaient pris soin d'elle. Elle est sous traitement homéopathique. Les médicaments homéopathiques n'étant pas distribués gratuitement par l'assistance publique, c'est son fils qui prend en charge son traitement. Fervente croyante, Tilotamma est persuadée que les prières la protègent de tout malheur.

Les perceptions relatives à la vieillesse ne correspondent pas toujours à ce qui est pratiqué, et ce qui est pratiqué est moins marqué selon le genre qu'il n'y paraît à première vue. Nous avons rencontré deux cas où la fille et le beau-fils assurent le soutien. Dans ces deux cas, la fille et son mari vivent avec les parents de la fille et le beau-fils apporte le soutien financier à ses beaux-parents âgés. Dans l'un des cas, le beau-fils avait déjà perdu ses parents et dans l'autre, la mère veuve vit avec le frère cadet. On constate alors que le fait d'être mariées n'empêche pas pour autant les filles de s'occuper de leurs parents âgés, comme on le présume. Une Pulaya âgée qui a deux filles nous a confié qu'elle est à la recherche de deux gendres appropriés pour elles. Pour l'une d'elle, elle désire un gendre qui viendrait vivre dans sa maison à elle après le mariage, afin de s'assurer que sa fille et son gendre l'assisteront lorsqu'elle sera très âgée et dépendante. Le soutien des enfants ne va pas de soi, comme l'illustre l'exemple suivant.

Exemple 2 : Vallom – dans une insécurité sociale imprévue
Vallom (âgé de 75 ans) est né en 1927. Il a sillonné tout le Kerala et a travaillé dans différents endroits comme ouvrier agricole et manœuvre. Depuis son mariage à l'âge de vingt-quatre ans, il a vécu et a travaillé à Kadamakuddy. Il a une fille mariée âgée de quarante ans et un fils marié âgé de trente-deux ans. Vallom et sa femme ont construit une maison en 1985, du temps où ils travaillaient encore. Ils ont pu économiser sur les frais de construction en la construisant eux-mêmes, mais ils ont dû prendre un crédit pour pouvoir s'acheter les matériaux de construction. La maison est à son nom.

Cela fait plus de huit ans qu'il a cessé de travailler. Il souffre de pression artérielle et de vertige, du coup, il ne sort même plus de la maison. Il vit reclus à présent, assis sur la véranda à longueur de journée à regarder les gens passer. Son fils, qui travaillait dans la construction, et sa belle-fille vivent avec eux et prennent soin d'eux. En 2001, son fils fut victime d'un accident qui lui a causé des fractures multiples à une jambe, qui a dû être plâtrée pendant plus d'un an. En 2002, sa jambe n'était toujours pas guérie. Comme il doit régulièrement se rendre à l'hôpital pour les contrôles, il a aménagé chez ses beaux-parents qui habitent plus près de l'hôpital de la ville.

Afin de pouvoir payer les soins médicaux de son fils, Vallom a hypothéqué sa maison pour 5000 roupies. Il ignore comment ils vont pouvoir rembourser cette somme car ni lui ni sa femme ne travaillent régulièrement. Sa femme travaille occasionnellement comme domestique dans une résidence voisine et reçoit un maigre revenu. Il leur reste encore une dette de 1000 roupies contractée lorsque Vallom était lui-même tombé malade. Ils reçoivent chacun une petite pension mensuelle de 110 roupies (env. 4.5 US$), somme qui les empêche de crever de faim certes, mais elle ne leur permet pas de rembourser leurs dettes. Cela fait des mois qu'ils n'ont pu rien donner et ils sont tourmentés à l'idée de devoir évacuer leur maison. Leur fille, mère de deux enfants, vit à proximité mais elle n'est pas non plus en mesure de leur porter secours car elle ne gagne pas d'argent et son mari, qui se remet d'une crise cardiaque, est actuellement au chômage.

Vallom et sa femme se retrouvent brusquement dans l'insécurité sociale. Leurs enfants ne sont pas à même de les soutenir, malgré leur bonne volonté. Vallom pense que si sa femme et lui avaient eu davantage d'enfants, l'un d'eux au moins aurait pu les aider aujourd'hui.

De nos jours, l'espérance de vie des personnes âgées a augmenté. En 1961 au Kerala, l'espérance de vie était de 46,2 ans pour les hommes et de 50 ans pour les femmes. En 1991, elle atteignait 60,5 pour les hommes et 62,1 pour les femmes. Dans le même temps, le taux de natalité a baissé. Il est passé de 4,1 enfants en 1971 à 1,8 en 1991 (Irudaya Rajan et al. 1999). Résultat : le nombre de personnes susceptibles de procurer la sécurité sociale aux personnes âgées dans la famille s'est réduit de manière drastique, tandis que la durée du soutien augmentait. Le fait que les parents vivent avec les enfants ne doit pas laisser croire qu'ils sont bien pris en charge. Les contraintes économiques qui pèsent sur la famille peuvent créer un soutien insuffisant à l'égard des personnes âgées. Le Ministère des affaires sociales (1987 : 10) a noté une grande tendance des familles à investir davantage dans la formation des enfants. Cette tendance a un impact sur la distribution du revenu au sein de la famille en faveur de la jeune génération.

L'échantillonnage par quotas a dévoilé le nombre élevé des Pulaya qui ont à la fois des enfants et des parents à charge. Bien qu'aucun des Pulaya n'ait fait allusion à la négligence, certains ont laissé entendre qu'ils ne reçoivent pas toujours les médicaments dont ils ont besoin par manque d'argent. Dans certains cas, la dépendance financière des personnes âgées de leurs enfants peut conduire à une forme d'exclusion sociale. Une chrétienne âgée rencontrée au « Day Care Centre » (DCC) situé de l'autre côté du village nous a raconté qu'elle vivait avec son fils et sa belle-fille. Tant qu'elle gagnait de l'argent, tout allait bien. Mais sitôt qu'elle cessa de travailler il y a deux ans, la situation s'envenima. Elle reçoit à manger mais nul ne lui adresse la parole. Elle se sent seule et a le sentiment d'être devenue un fardeau pour la famille.

De nombreux chercheurs ont constaté le fait que si les parents âgés vivant avec leurs enfants disposent de ressources financières, ils ont alors un meilleur statut au sein de la famille grâce à leur pouvoir de négociation (Reddy et Rani 1989, Vatuk 1990). Des études faites dans un village du sud de l'Inde par Marulisiddiah (1966) et par Reddy et Rani (1989) ont mis le doigt sur le ressentiment des enfants à l'égard de la dépendance économique de leurs parents âgés. Suite à une re-

cherche sur les personnes âgées issues de la classe inférieure au nord
de l'Inde, Mahajan (1992) a découvert que la dépendance économique
est la cause majeure des abus.

Bien que les Pulaya disent attendre du soutien de leurs enfants, ils
essayent en même temps d'offrir une aide en retour chaque fois qu'ils
le peuvent car ils ne veulent pas être considérés comme un fardeau. La
maison et le terrain sont laissés à l'enfant qui s'occupe d'eux. La
femme âgée participe aux travaux ménagers. Quelquefois, l'homme
âgé fait de petites courses, de menues réparations dans la maison. Leur
pension est ajoutée au revenu du foyer. Un jour, nous avons été
témoin d'une scène où une femme âgée venait de toucher sa pension :
sur le champ, sa belle-fille et elle sont allées acheter du riz avec cet
argent dans le magasin subventionné.

Dans la classe moyenne, les enfants vivent généralement en ville
ou à l'étranger, vu le peu d'opportunités d'embauche au Kerala. Malgré le fait que les personnes âgées préféreraient vivre leurs vieux jours
entourés de leurs enfants, elles vivent seules, parfois avec l'aide d'un
domestique. La distance géographique n'implique pas forcément une
distance affective, car les enfants maintiennent le contact avec leurs
parents à travers des visites régulières, des appels téléphoniques et en
leur envoyant de l'argent. En occident, ce mode d'interaction est appelé « intimité à distance » (Treas 1975).

Des études ont montré qu'avoir une épouse en vie influe positivement sur le bien-être dans le vieil âge.[13] Parmi les Pulaya âgés, l'opinion répandue est que dans une relation conjugale, on peut compter
l'un sur l'autre dans les moments difficiles, on a de la compagnie, on
ne connaît donc pas la solitude. Le soutien de sa femme est important
pour le Pulaya âgé. Dans son rôle d'épouse, la femme âgée s'occupe
de presque toutes les tâches pour le bien-être de son conjoint. Elle lui
fait la lessive, lui chauffe l'eau pour le bain et satisfait ses autres besoins. En revanche, pour les femmes âgées, l'importance de l'époux,
en particulier en matière d'aide financière, est incertaine. Celles qui
travaillent de temps à autre et gagnent de l'argent, tout en recevant
une pension, ne dépendent donc pas entièrement de l'époux ni des

---

[13] Cf. p. ex. Raj et Prasad (1971), et Gurudoss et Lakshminarayanan (1989).

enfants pour leur sécurité sociale. L'une des femmes âgées déclare :
« Si tu as une bonne relation avec ton époux, alors tu as de quoi te
réjouir de partager ta vie avec lui.» Et elle ajoute qu'avant, son mari
avait l'habitude de boire et de gaspiller tout son argent. Maintenant
qu'il a cessé de s'enivrer, elle estime qu'ils vivent ensemble une bien
meilleure relation. Dans un autre exemple, une femme âgée s'offus-
que : « Mon mari passe à présent ses vieux jours à ne rien faire. Au
moins avant, il gagnait quelque chose et pouvait ainsi contribuer aux
frais du foyer.» La situation de Leela illustre comment le soutien de
l'époux dépend de la qualité de la relation conjugale.

Exemple 3 : Leela et son vieil âge dans l'insécurité sociale
Leela (âgée de 58 ans) est née en 1943. Elle est mariée et a quatre filles et un garçon.
Sa fille aînée a trente-trois ans et son fils cadet en a dix-neuf. Leela a eu une enfance
difficile. Étant l'aînée de douze enfants, elle a dû quitter l'école au bout de deux
années de scolarité pour aller travailler et compléter le revenu de ses parents. Son
mariage n'a pas arrangé les choses. Au début, son mari dépensait tout son argent en
alcool et en tabac. Il lui arrivait même de la battre lorsqu'elle s'avisait à lui demander de l'argent. Il s'est amélioré avec l'âge, il lui arrive même de contribuer au revenu du foyer. Ils ont construit une maison et il a consenti à la laisser au nom de
Leela. Sa vie entière, elle a travaillé comme ouvrière agricole et manœuvre. Et elle
travaille encore. Comme les places de travail se font rares dans l'agriculture, elle
travaille sur les chantiers. Tous ses enfants ont reçu une éducation formelle et deux
de ses filles sont mariées. Les deux autres restent à marier. Elle estime que c'est une
énorme responsabilité surtout parce que tout repose quasiment sur elle seule. Le
mariage de sa deuxième fille fut une lourde charge financière, il leur a coûté environ
100'000 roupies (env. 2000 US$). Ils ont dû hypothéquer leur maison à 30'000 rou-
pies (env. 600 US$). Son frère cadet et le grand frère de son mari ont donné une
contribution financière. Ils ont également utiliser une partie de l'argent du fonds de
prévision de la fille qui s'est mariée. Leela déclare qu'elle ne songe pas à marier une
autre fille avant qu'elle n'ait payé l'hypothèque.
    Le fils est un étudiant brillant ; son école avait été sponsorisée par une ONG ap-
pelée CASP. Il suivait une formation professionnelle pour devenir électricien, mais à
cause des difficultés financières, il a dû l'interrompre et travaille à présent dans une
boulangerie. Cette situation culpabilise Leela, mais elle n'avait pas le choix. Aujourd'hui, son mari reçoit une pension de vieillesse. Il fait lui aussi de petits boulots
pour gagner un peu d'argent, mais sa contribution au revenu du foyer n'est pas fiable. De nombreuses questions tracassent Leela quant à son vieil âge : Réussira-t-elle
à marier ses deux autres filles ? Pourra-t-elle rembourser son hypothèque ? Son fils

pourra-t-il achever sa formation d'électricien et obtenir un meilleur emploi ? Elle se demande quelle tournure prendront les choses lorsqu'elle sera plus âgée et ne pourra plus travailler. Toutefois, elle espère que son fils aura trouvé une situation d'ici là et qu'il prendra soin de sa sécurité sociale.

Leela se plaint que son mari ne contribue pas assez au revenu du foyer car il continue de dépenser de l'argent dans l'alcool. Sa sécurité sociale à elle dépend uniquement de ses enfants, principalement de son fils.

Chez les personnes âgées de la classe moyenne, à l'instar de la classe ouvrière, la femme prend soin de tous les besoins de l'homme âgé. Toutefois, contrairement aux Pulaya âgées, les femmes âgées de la classe moyenne dépendent beaucoup plus de leurs maris. Elles sont généralement femmes au foyer et comptent entièrement sur leurs maris pour leurs dépenses quotidiennes. La plupart du temps, la femme possède des biens surtout immobiliers comme un terrain, une maison, mais aussi des bijoux. Ces biens pourraient être vendus en cas de difficultés financières. Tandis que la majorité des hommes de la classe moyenne ont fait des études, les femmes ont peu de formation et sont très peu confrontées au monde extérieur ; elles dépendent donc de leurs maris même pour les conseils. La compagnie et le soutien affectif sont importants pour l'homme et pour la femme.

Dans les moments difficiles, les Pulaya âgés se tournent aussi vers leur « parenté », par exemple vers leurs frères et sœurs mariés ou leurs beaux-frères. Ceci est fréquent en cas de maladie grave ou pour le mariage de leurs filles. L'aide reçue de la parenté doit être rendue. Un homme âgé l'a clairement dit : « Il faut être proche de sa parenté et avoir des liens affectifs forts pour s'attendre à recevoir de l'aide. » Dans l'exemple de Thangamma, célibataire, on constate que les liens d'échange et d'affection entre la parenté éloignée comme les neveux peuvent, dans certaines circonstances, engendrer une relation de soutien fiable.

Exemple 4 : La célibataire Thangamma et ses « enfants créés »
Thangamma (âgée de 63 ans) est née en 1939. Elle avait deux sœurs aînées, un frère aîné et un frère cadet. À présent seuls ses deux frères et elle sont encore en vie. Elle

a fréquenté l'école pendant huit ans et a cessé d'y aller car elle était en échec scolaire. Les responsabilités familiales l'ont empêchée de se marier. Sa sœur aînée qui avait eu deux fils est devenue veuve très jeune. Au début, Thangamma ne travaillait pas ; elle devait garder ses deux neveux lorsque sa sœur se rendait au travail. Lorsqu'elle commença à gagner de l'argent elle préféra aider sa sœur à élever ses enfants, au lieu de se marier. Elle ne regrette pas l'avoir fait car à présent, ses neveux se comportent envers elle comme ses propres fils. Sa sœur et elle avaient construit une maison ensemble. La maison était au nom de sa sœur et à la mort de cette dernière, c'est le plus jeune de ses neveux qui l'a héritée. Ceci n'a posé aucun problème à Thangamma car son neveu a toujours reconnu ses sacrifices. Elle continue donc à vivre avec lui et son épouse. Toute sa vie durant, elle a travaillé comme ouvrière agricole. Ce dur labeur lui a abîmé le dos ; de plus, elle s'était fracturé un bras au travail et elle en a gardé des séquelles. Aujourd'hui, elle ne peut plus soulever des objets lourds. Sa vue a également faibli. À cause de ces infirmités, elle ne travaille plus depuis sept ans. Son neveu, manœuvre, et sa femme la soutiennent en grande partie. Son frère aîné qui vit à proximité l'aide également. Son frère cadet, un instituteur, l'aide de temps à autre. Elle touche une pension agricole depuis 1999. Elle s'en réjouit car cet argent lui permet de s'acheter ses médicaments homéopathiques et de contribuer un peu au revenu du foyer. Son état de santé ne lui permet pas d'aider dans les travaux de ménage. D'après elle, la meilleure façon pour les personnes âgées de contribuer à leur sécurité sociale est de se contenter de ce qu'elles reçoivent et d'éviter d'être une nuisance.

Thangamma ne regrette pas de n'avoir pas eu ses propres enfants. Elle affirme que ses neveux la traitent avec respect, en particulier celui avec qui elle vit. Même sa femme prend soin d'elle. C'est aussi une bonne chose que son frère et sa famille vivent tout près ; elle s'y rend quand elle a besoin de compagnie et d'une oreille attentive. Il est donc évident que principalement les enfants – et dans certains cas les enfants des frères et sœurs – jouent un rôle majeur dans le réseau de soutien des personnes âgées en matière d'aide physique.

Soutien de la communauté

En cas de besoin, les personnes âgées sollicitent du soutien au sein de la communauté villageoise. Ceci est fréquent pour l'aide matérielle comme la nourriture ou les médicaments qu'elles n'obtiennent pas de leur parenté. Dans la communauté, les personnes âgées ont accès aux voisins, amis, employeurs et aussi aux organisations locales qui peuvent jouer un rôle de soutien.

Chez les Pulaya, c'est souvent une relation de donnant-donnant qui caractérise les échanges avec les voisins qui procurent de la nourriture et de l'argent, et occasionnellement de la compagnie. Dans le village Kadamakuddy, la réforme agraire a accordé des terres aux Pulaya dans un quartier spécifique appelé Korampadam où ils se sont installés. Beaucoup d'entre eux vivent dans le village depuis de nombreuses années et se connaissent bien entre eux. Leur familiarité et la proximité favorisent les relations de soutien mutuel. Une femme âgée affirme : « Si nous sommes en bons termes avec nos voisins, nous avons en quelque sorte de la sécurité sociale car en cas d'urgence, les voisins seraient les premières personnes à qui nous ferions appel. » Elle raconta ensuite ce qui s'était passé lorsque son mari avait eu une attaque paralytique. Aucun de ses enfants n'était présent, ce sont les voisins qui le mirent dans le bateau pour le conduire à l'hôpital. Les amis sont particulièrement importants pour les hommes âgés. Ils passent leur temps ensemble à échanger leurs pensées et leurs sentiments. Ayant grandi ensemble et vécu dans le village pendant quasiment leur vie entière, ils ont tissé des liens solides. La sociabilité quotidienne est un besoin pour les hommes. L'exemple de Bava montre comment, après les enfants, les amis peuvent être source de soutien.

Exemple 5 : Le veuf Bava – soutenu par ses enfants et ses amis
Bava (âgé de 87 ans) est né en 1914. Il a été ouvrier agricole. Il n'a cessé de travailler qu'il y a une dizaine d'années, à cause de la cataracte et suite à un accident qui l'a blessé au bras et au genou. Il a trois filles et trois garçons. Sa fille aînée a environ cinquante ans et le fils cadet en a vingt-huit. Il a perdu sa femme il y a une douzaine d'années. Bava possède un toit car il s'était construit une maison à l'époque où il travaillait encore. Le gouvernement lui verse une pension d'ouvrier agricole de 110 roupies (env. 2 US$) par mois. Il utilise cette modique somme pour contribuer au revenu du foyer, en gardant pour lui une infime partie pour s'offrir du thé et du tabac. Son fils cadet, son épouse et ses enfants vivent avec lui et le soutiennent mais en période de difficultés, tous ses enfants lui prêtent main forte. Lorsqu'il eut son accident par exemple, ses enfants ont épuisé leurs ressources pour payer son traitement qui coûta 2000 roupies (env. 40 US$). Ils ont également porté plainte afin que

Bava obtienne une compensation, mais les procédures judiciaires sont lentes et une prise de décision peut prendre cinq ans.

Son fils est ouvrier agricole et sa belle-fille employée de maison. Bien qu'ils parviennent à vivre au jour le jour, ils ne peuvent pas satisfaire bon nombre de leurs besoins. Bava devrait se faire opérer de la cataracte mais l'opération s'avère trop chère pour eux. La maison est en ruines et peut s'écrouler à tout moment. Quand la pluie se déferle, il n'arrive pas à dormir de peur que le toit ne s'effondre. Bava a quatre amis, ils sont tous allés à l'école ensemble. Ses amis et lui avaient l'habitude de se rencontrer à l'échoppe de thé pour bavarder et lire les journaux ensemble. Ces derniers temps, son état de santé ayant réduit sa mobilité, ses amis se rendent chez lui pour faire la causerie. Souvent, ils viennent même le chercher pour le conduire à l'échoppe de thé. Bava estime que ses enfants et ses amis sont ses plus grands soutiens. Le soutien de ses amis est d'autant plus important que Bava se retrouve seul pendant la journée car son fils et sa belle-fille sont au travail et ses petits-enfants à l'école. Son état de santé devient alors un handicap vu qu'il ne peut plus sortir tout seul. À cause de son vieil âge et de son piètre état de santé, Bava craint que quelque chose ne lui arrive lorsqu'il est seul à la maison, mais si ses amis sont là, ils peuvent immédiatement le secourir. Mais il se réjouit aussi de leurs visites pour la compagnie que cela lui procure.

En revanche, les femmes perdent contact avec leurs amies dès qu'elles partent s'installer au domicile de leurs maris après le mariage. En outre, elles sont si accaparées par leur nouvelle famille qu'elles n'ont guère le temps de socialiser. C'est la raison pour laquelle elles reçoivent plus de soutien des voisins que des amies.

Jadis, les employeurs jouaient un rôle significatif en matière de soutien aux Pulaya âgés. En cas de besoin, les propriétaires agricoles pour qui ils travaillaient leur donnaient du riz et de l'argent. Ils leur offraient des vêtements lors des fêtes et apportaient une contribution financière lorsqu'ils mariaient leurs filles. Aujourd'hui, les employeurs sont eux-mêmes âgés et ne sont plus en mesure de se montrer aussi généreux. Beaucoup d'entres eux ont transféré leurs propriétés à leurs enfants qui estiment que les Pulaya ont suffisamment été indemnisés avec la réforme agraire et qu'ils ne leur doivent plus rien. De nos jours, l'ouvrier agricole et son employeur ont une relation contractuelle et les échanges sont impersonnels et dépourvus de soutien réel.

Grâce à leurs relations de longue date dans le village, les personnes âgées peuvent faire des achats à crédit dans les magasins du village pour des denrées de première nécessité telles les légumes et le poisson. Une nouvelle tendance a récemment fait son apparition : les gens achètent à crédit et remboursent par paiements échelonnés. Les vêtements sont généralement achetés de cette manière. Les Pulaya âgés font usage des opportunités de crédit à la banque et à la coopérative du village. Ces crédits sont en général accordés contre une hypothèque sur la maison ou le terrain, voire sur les deux.

Les organisations religieuses et de caste locales offrent aussi un peu d'assistance aux personnes âgées, principalement en matière de soins médicaux ; et dans certaines circonstances, elles donnent de l'argent et des graines. Bien qu'étant hindous dans leur grande majorité, certains croient aussi en Jésus et Marie. Ceux qui prient à la manière des catholiques romains reçoivent de l'église des avantages tels des graines. De temps à autres, la secte hindoue « Satya Saibaba Trust » et l'organisation de la caste des Izahvas, le « Sree Narayana Dharma Paripalana Trust » (SNDP) organisent des camps de santé dans la région rurale et les personnes âgées peuvent en bénéficier. Une femme âgée dont les deux yeux étaient atteints de cataracte s'était rendue à un camp organisé par le SNDP consacré au thème de la vue en compagnie de son fils. Elle s'était fait opérer et peut à présent voir à l'aide de lunettes à verre épais. Ainsi, dans certains cas, les activités bénévoles des groupes religieux profitent aux personnes âgées.

Une branche locale de la « Kerala Pulaya Maha Sabha » (KPMS), organisation de la caste des Pulaya, est aussi présente à Kadamakuddy. Tous les Pulaya en sont membres. Cette organisation assiste généralement lors des funérailles et contribue à hauteur de 1000 roupies (env. 20 US$) pour les frais de cérémonie. Autrefois, elle gérait un fonds pour les frais médicaux. Une enquêtée avait reçu du fonds 100 roupies (env. 2 US$) lorsqu'elle était tombée malade. Faute d'argent, ce fonds a été dissout. Le KPMS a également un programme qui donne une bourse aux meilleurs élèves. Contrairement aux fonds, l'organisation ne manque pas de bras. En cas de besoin, toute sorte d'assistance physique peut être mobilisée, par exemple pour les cérémonies de mariage ou de funérailles.

Toutefois, les personnes âgées ne comptent pas tellement sur l'antenne du KPMS de Kadamakuddy. Une des raisons en avait été que la direction laissait quelque peu à désirer et il n'y avait guère de transparence en matière d'utilisation des fonds. Du coup, les gens avaient eu le sentiment que les fonds étaient détournés. En 2002, il eut un changement au sein de la direction du KPMS. C'est à présent un retraité du service public, une personne hautement respectée, qui en est le président. Il souhaite faire du KPMS une organisation rentable à nouveau car elle est censée œuvrer pour le bien-être de toute la « communauté » pulaya.

Kadamakuddy est un village unique en son genre car il possède un centre journalier pour personnes âgées (Day Care Centre DCC). Ce centre est situé à Kothad, dans la partie du village où vivent essentiellement des chrétiens. En 1997, le DCC a été créé en tant que projet conjoint de l'organisation populaire du « Kothad Grama Vikasana Samiti » et le « Rajagiri College of Social Sciences » (Institut des sciences sociales) et la « Community Aid and Sponsorship Programme » (CASP ; programme d'aide et de soutien à la communauté) comme principaux bailleurs de fonds.[14] Les autorités locales ont mis à disposition le terrain du bâtiment. Les gens ont contribué avec des dons et du travail bénévole. Le DCC opère sur la base de dons individuels et de subventions des autorités locales. Les personnes âgées s'y rencontrent deux fois par semaine. Les réunions commencent par des prières. Ils lisent ensuite de nouveaux articles intéressants et s'adonnent à des jeux divers. Ils reçoivent aussi le déjeuner. Le DCC a également un centre de soins ouvert pour tous les villageois une après-midi par semaine. Les consultations et les médicaments de base sont gratuits. La majorité des Pulaya âgés de notre échantillon n'étaient cependant pas intéressés à se rendre au DCC. Le concept de personnes âgées se rencontrant pour chanter et faire des jeux leur paraît étrange, de plus le centre se trouve à une bonne distance de marche pour eux.

---

[14] En collaboration étroite avec l'organisation des gens à Kothad, par exemple sur la base d'un modèle de développement participant, le CASP, l'organisation de développement de la communauté Rajagiri, a dirigé divers projets, en matière d'éducation et d'assainissement, depuis 1992 (cf. Antoni 1996).

Il s'avère donc que la communauté du village Kadamakuddy soutient les personnes âgées dans leurs besoins de base. Les voisins et
amis procurent de l'aide matériel et de la compagnie. Les organisations de castes et les groupes religieux offrent essentiellement une aide
dans le domaine de la santé. Cependant, cette aide est épisodique et ne
peut être assurée sur une longue durée.

Pour les personnes âgées de la classe moyenne, le soutien des voisins est crucial, en particulier lorsqu'elles vivent seules, sans enfants.
En dehors de cela, elles n'ont guère besoin du soutien de la communauté. Un dernier point que nous souhaitons mentionner en matière de
soutien de la communauté est le fait que les personnes âgées de la
classe moyenne sont de plus en plus conscientes qu'elles peuvent former des groupes pour venir en aide aux personnes âgées en détresse.
On trouve de tels groupes d'organisation dans un village mitoyen de
Kadamakuddy. Quelques personnes âgées de la classe moyenne ont
formé une organisation appelée « Sauhridum » ayant pour objectif
d'aider les villageois âgés et démunis de leur village.[15]

Soutien de l'État

Le Kerala a instauré divers programmes d'assistance et de sécurité
sociale. Il s'avère donc pertinent d'examiner le soutien qu'obtiennent
les Pulaya âgés de l'État. Dans le village, les habitants associent la
citoyenneté en premier lieu au fait d'être Malayalee, citoyen du Kerala. À cause de leur sens de responsabilité politique, les Pulaya prennent le vote très au sérieux et ils estiment qu'ils assument leur devoir
en votant en tant que caste. En même temps, ils estiment que la
corruption est largement répandue au sein du gouvernement et que
tout membre du gouvernement essaye d'augmenter ses propres revenus, sans se soucier outre mesure du peuple. Les inquiétudes se font
jour quant à la stratégie des partis d'opposition à destituer le parti au

---

[15] Au niveau national, un mouvement des citoyens âgés cherche à agir comme
groupe de pression afin d'obtenir certains avantages du gouvernement, mais il n'en
est qu'à ses balbutiements.

pouvoir et prendre eux-mêmes le pouvoir. C'est l'homme ordinaire qui souffrirait durant ce processus.

Comme nous l'avons mentionné dans le chapitre d'introduction sur le Kerala, il existe trois principaux programmes d'assistance sociale qui offrent directement des pensions aux personnes âgées démunies. À savoir: le « Kerala Agricultural Workers Pension Scheme », le « Kerala Destitute and Widow Pension Scheme » et le « Special Pension Scheme for the Physically Handicapped and Mentally Retarded » (cf. Irudaya Rajan 1999).[16] Le « Kerala Agricultural Workers Pension » est un bon exemple qui montre que le rôle actif des gens à exiger une aide publique, également dans le vieil âge, a porté ses fruits. Les ouvriers agricoles du Kerala ont été à l'avant-garde des mouvements syndicaux depuis 1920. Leur demande de sécurité sociale remonte à 1960 (Gulati 1990). Après des années d'agitation, la pension pour les ouvriers agricoles est entrée en vigueur en 1980. D'après les statistiques, on estime à 345'000 le nombre de personnes ayant bénéficié de ladite pension en 1993, dont 58 % de femmes (Irudaya Rajan et al. 1999).

Comme déjà mentionné, de nombreux Pulaya âgés reçoivent une « pension » mensuelle de 110 roupies (env. 2 US$). Elle est versée tous les trois mois sous forme d'ordre de paiement. Au Kerala, les programmes de pension de vieillesse occupent une place importante dans les provisions de sécurité sociale du gouvernement. On a estimé sa couverture à environ 60 % des personnes âgées démunies au Kerala pour l'année 1991 (Kanan et Francis 2001 : 423).

D'après les registres de la municipalité de Kadamakuddy,[17] 351 personnes âgées touchaient la pension pour ouvriers agricoles, 90 la pension pour infirmes et handicapés, 84 femmes âgées la pension pour veuves et 61 personnes une pension vieillesse.[18] Le « Public Distribu-

---

[16] Caisse de pension pour ouvriers agricoles ; Caisse de pension pour veuves et orphelins ; Caisse de pension spéciale pour les handicapés physiques et mentaux.
[17] Données non publiées de la municipalité de Kadamakuddy, notées en septembre 2002.
[18] C'est un programme de pension introduit par le gouvernement central sous le « National Social Assistance Scheme » (programme d'assistance social national) en 1995.

tion System » (PDS ; système de distribution publique) constitue un autre important programme de sécurité sociale au Kerala. Il touche 92 % de la population (Kanan et Francis 2001 : 432). La disponibilité de la nourriture à travers le PDS a été le facteur majeur pour en fournir aux pauvres et aux personnes âgées.

Néanmoins, si une évaluation devait se faire pour savoir si les programmes de sécurité sociale disponibles pour les personnes âgées au Kerala sont adéquats, on serait amené à se poser des questions en ce qui concerne leur suffisance matérielle. Jusqu'à quel point les pensions couvrent-elles l'alimentation de base et les autres besoins ? Ce modèle de sécurité sociale gouvernementale part du principe que le soutien aux personnes âgées est en premier lieu la responsabilité de la famille, principalement des enfants. La pension vise simplement à alléger le fardeau de la famille afin de rendre les personnes âgées plus acceptables.[19] Une Pulaya âgée s'exprime ainsi à ce sujet : « Autrefois, il y avait aussi des demandes mais le gouvernement se montrait indifférent aux besoins [des personnes âgées] et ne daignait pas leur accorder le moindre soutien. »

Les Pulaya âgés qui ont pris part à notre étude sont reconnaissants pour la pension qu'ils reçoivent car elle constitue une source de revenu pour eux dans le vieil âge. Il faut ajouter que les obstacles bureaucratiques rencontrés pour remplir les formulaires entravent l'accès à la pension pour les personnes âgées. Dans un cas, une femme âgée s'était vue refuser la pension pour motif que son fils avait un revenu. Heureusement pour elle, une fonctionnaire pour qui elle avait fait des travaux jadis au bureau du village l'a aidée à bien remplir les formulaires à la deuxième fois et à obtenir ladite pension.

Vu que la plupart des Pulaya sont alphabétisés, ils lisent les journaux, écoutent la radio et débattent de la politique. Ils sont donc conscients du fait que le Kerala a des problèmes financiers. Ils souhaitent que le gouvernement augmente le montant de la pension mais ils savent que ce n'est pas possible.

---

[19] Cf. Gulati 1990, Gulati et Gulati 1995. Dans une étude menée par P. K. B. Nair, 97 % des personnes qui reçoivent une pension d'ouvriers agricoles ont déclaré que ce revenu leur a permis d'être mieux acceptées (Nair 1987, cité par Gulati 1990).

Ils aimeraient en outre que le système de santé soit amélioré. L'aide médicale la plus proche est le « Primary Health Centre » (PHC ; le centre de santé primaire gouvernemental) situé dans le village voisin, accessible uniquement en bateau. L'inconvénient est qu'il n'est ouvert que quelques heures pendant la journée, la plupart des médicaments requis ne sont pas disponibles et les instruments pour faire des analyses font défaut. De plus il n'a pas de lits. Pour toute maladie nécessitant une hospitalisation, les patients doivent se rendre à l'hôpital public situé en ville. L'éloignement de l'hôpital pose problème à la fois aux personnes âgées et aux personnes qui s'occupent d'elles.

Vieil âge et genre

Au Kerala, l'espérance de vie à la naissance et à l'âge de soixante ans indiquent que les femmes vivent plus longtemps que les hommes (CSO 2000 : 35). En moyenne, les hommes épousent des femmes plus jeunes qu'eux, de sorte que, les trois quart du temps, l'homme âgé dispose d'une épouse en mesure de prendre soin de lui dans le vieil âge. D'autre part, les femmes, dans leur grande majorité, sont veuves le vieil âge atteint, privées ainsi de la compagnie et du soutien d'un mari.

L'impact du vieil âge sur les femmes diffère aussi de celui des hommes car elles ont un autre statut et un autre rôle dans la société indienne. Les spécificités liées au genre, établies tôt dans la vie, ont leur impact dans le quotidien du vieil âge. Elles dissuadent les femmes à s'engager socialement en dehors de la sphère privée du foyer et de toute autre interaction liée. Une attitude généralement admise veut que les femmes doivent être protégées et des restrictions leur sont ainsi imposées, dans leur propre intérêt (Bali 1997). Les femmes âgées consultées dans notre étude avaient elles aussi intériorisé cette attitude et ne sortaient pas seules, sauf pour se rendre au travail. Cette attitude a un impact sur le réseau de soutien des femmes âgées car elle le restreint à la famille, le voisinage proche et l'employeur.

De surcroît, les femmes âgées ne jouissent d'aucune autorité au sein de la famille. C'est en général l'homme qui prend les décisions.

L'une des femmes âgées, Thangamma (exemple 4) souhaiterait se rendre au DCC, mais son neveu qui la soutient l'en empêche car cette idée ne lui plaît pas. À Kadamakkudy, les hommes âgés mènent généralement une vie d'oisiveté tandis que les femmes âgées sont censées contribuer aux travaux domestiques. La majorité des Pulaya âgées continuent de cuisiner, de faire la lessive, de nettoyer et de balayer, et aussi d'aller quelquefois chercher de l'eau et du bois.

Chadha, Aggrawal et Mangla (1990) ont montré que le réseau de relations sociales des personnes âgées dont les conjoints sont encore en vie est beaucoup plus vaste. Nous avons pu le constater dans notre étude car ceci s'applique particulièrement aux femmes âgées de notre échantillon : elles ne se rendaient à des cérémonies que lorsqu'elles étaient accompagnées de leurs époux ou de leurs enfants. Pour ces femmes, le veuvage n'était pas seulement la perte d'un compagnon, mais également la réduction de leurs possibilités d'interaction sociale.

Au Kerala, il existe une énorme différence entre la situation des veuves du milieu urbain et celles du milieu rural. En milieu urbain, les veuves les plus démunies vivent dans une insécurité sociale critique, leur ration quotidienne de base n'est par exemple pas garantie (voir de Jong dans ce volume). D'autres études ont indiqué que le veuvage entraîne la négligence (Marulisiddiah 1966, Sahayam 1988). Or, notre étude ne confirme pas ce phénomène. Cela pourrait s'expliquer par le fait que toutes les femmes de la classe ouvrière disposent d'un revenu. Comme elles avaient travaillé, elles avaient pu contribuer à la construction des maisons dans lesquelles elles vivent à présent. Dans le vieil âge, elles reçoivent une pension qui leur permet de contribuer aux dépenses du foyer. Dans certains cas, en particulier lorsqu'elles sont veuves, la maison et le terrain sont à leurs noms. Celles qui le peuvent encore participent également aux travaux domestiques. Toutes ces contributions font en sorte que les femmes âgées ne sont pas marginalisées au sein de leurs familles. Pour étayer ce point, nous souhaiterions mentionner les exemples de Tara et de Kunni (exemples 6 et 7). Toutes les deux sont devenues veuves très jeunes et elles ont géré leurs vies et celle de leurs enfants en puisant dans leurs propres ressources et avec le soutien de la parenté. A présent qu'elles ont atteint le vieil âge, leurs enfants les soutiennent.

Exemple 6 : La veuve Tara et sa crainte d'être devenue un fardeau
Tara (âgée de 83 ans) est née en 1918. C'est l'une des femmes les plus âgées de notre échantillon. Elle est allée à l'école jusqu'à la quatrième classe et a travaillé toute sa vie comme ouvrière agricole et manœuvre. À cause de sa vue et de sa santé défaillantes, elle n'a plus gagné de l'argent depuis une dizaine d'année. Elle s'était mariée à dix-sept ans mais son mari était décédé un an après. Elle était retournée vivre à Kadamakuddy, son village natal. Elle n'avait pas eu d'enfant avec son défunt mari. Elle s'est alors remariée à l'âge de vingt-sept ans et a eu cinq enfants de cette union, quatre garçons et une fille. Sa fille aînée est âgée de cinquante-quatre ans et son fils cadet a quarante-deux ans. Son second époux est mort après vingt ans de mariage. Une fois de plus, elle est retournée vivre chez ses parents à Kadamakuddy. Quelques années plus tard, elle s'est construit sa propre maison avec l'aide de sa sœur aînée et de sa sœur cadette. Le mari de sa sœur aînée qui est charpentier l'a aidée pour la construction de sa maison. Entre-temps, son fils aîné travaillait déjà et pouvait ainsi contribuer aux dépenses du foyer. La perte de deux de ses fils, l'un dans l'enfance et l'autre il y a cinq ans, et le veuvage prématuré de sa propre fille chagrinent beaucoup Tara. Aujourd'hui, elle vit avec son fils cadet, qui est journalier, et sa femme et leurs enfants. L'âge a eu raison de son dos voûté et elle se déplace avec difficulté. Elle souffre de tension artérielle qui lui donne des vertiges lorsqu'elle reste debout très longtemps. Elle avait la cataracte dans les yeux et s'était fait opérer dans un camp consacré à la vue en 1996. Pendant son hospitalisation qui a duré cinq jours, c'est sa belle-fille qui s'était occupée d'elle. Elle a retrouvé la vue qui est restée légèrement trouble, ce qui l'oblige à prendre des gouttes tous les jours. Ce médicament étant cher, elle est souvent contrainte de s'en passer car elle n'a pas les moyens de se l'acheter régulièrement. Elle reçoit une pension d'ouvrière agricole qu'elle ajoute au revenu du ménage. Son manque d'autonomie la gêne d'autant plus qu'elle dépend de son fils et de sa belle-fille pour beaucoup de choses. Malgré tout, elle fait du mieux qu'elle peut pour éviter d'être considérée comme un fardeau.

Bien que son fils et sa belle-fille prennent bien soin d'elle, la veuve Tara ne peut s'empêcher de se faire du souci quant à sa sécurité sociale, probablement à cause de la situation économique délicate de son fils. Ceci contraste avec l'exemple de la veuve Kunni qui suit.

Exemple 7 : La veuve Kunni et son vieil âge sécurisé
Kunni (âgée de 80 ans) est née en 1922. Elle a fréquenté l'école pendant quatre ans. Elle est entrée dans la vie active à l'âge de quatorze ans environ, en travaillant sur-

tout comme ouvrière agricole, et elle en est sortie il y a une dizaine d'années lorsqu'elle perdit la vue. Elle s'est mariée à l'âge de vingt-quatre ans. Elle a trois garçons et deux filles. Tous ses enfants ont une formation. Son mari est décédé en 1977 et elle avait la responsabilité de marier leur fille cadette. Son ancien employeur lui donna de l'argent, du riz et des noix de coco et elle obtint le reste avec l'aide de ses fils et de son frère. Elle possède sa propre maison que son mari et elle avaient réussi à construire juste avant sa mort. Elle y vit avec son fils cadet, sa femme et ses enfants. Ce dernier travaille comme tailleur de pierres et gagne entre 225 et 250 roupies (env. 4.5 et 5 US$) par jour. Son fils aîné travaille sur un chantier naval. Comme c'est une entreprise d'État, elle reçoit des réductions pour des traitements hospitaliers. Il y a quelques années, elle avait été hospitalisée pendant un moment parce qu'elle souffrait de pression artérielle. Son deuxième fils avait payé le traitement. Et une fois rentrée à la maison, sa belle-fille s'était occupée d'elle et lui avait fait prendre ses médicaments à temps, en veillant particulièrement à son régime alimentaire sans sel et sans gras. À présent, elle prend aussi des médicaments ayurvédiques. Elle est complètement aveugle et dépend entièrement de sa belle-fille dont elle ne tarie pas d'éloges. Etant donné qu'elle ne peut pas sortir toute seule, elle passe le plus clair de son temps à l'intérieur à écouter la radio offerte par son deuxième fils. Vu que ses filles vivent en ville, elle ne s'attend pas à une aide de leur part.

Le exemples de Tara et de Kunni montrent que, bien qu'elles soient veuves et âgées, leurs familles ne les négligent pas pour autant. Tout simplement parce qu'elles ont un pouvoir de négociation qui se base sur des contributions antérieures et actuelles. Néanmoins, à certains égards, leurs besoins ne sont pas entièrement satisfaits : Tara ne reçoit pas toujours ses médicaments et Kunni n'a pas de compagnie. Une autre spécificité du genre liée au vieil âge est la question des soins. Les femmes sont considérées comme les principales personnes qui procurent des soins dans la famille. On s'attend à ce qu'elles satisfassent à la fois les besoins de leurs enfants, de leurs époux et des parents âgés. Il a été prouvé que lorsque la femme travaille à l'extérieur, son rôle de donneuse de soins est négativement affectée (Panda 1998, Kumar 2000). Si les femmes se cantonnent au rôle de donneuses de soins, ceci aura pour conséquence qu'elles ne disposeront pas, la vieillesse venue, de moyens financiers qu'elles pourraient utiliser comme pouvoir de négociation pour se procurer du soutien. Sans ressources financières, les femmes courent le risque d'être négligées dans le vieil âge.

Conclusion

Les facteurs cruciaux pour la sécurité sociale des Pulaya âgés sont liés à la question de savoir qui les soutiendra dans leur vieil âge, qui sera en mesure de leur offrir les repas quotidiens et les médicaments dont ils ont besoin, et s'ils seront encore suffisamment en bonne santé pour rester autonomes et vaquer à leurs activités quotidiennes sans dépendre de quelqu'un. Ils appréhendent l'idée de devenir un fardeau. Pour les Pulaya âgés de la classe ouvrière, le soutien des enfants est vital. Le fait que leurs enfants n'ont pas émigré pour des raisons professionnelles constitue un avantage pour eux. Ils espèrent que leurs enfants seront en mesure de satisfaire la plupart de leurs besoins matériels, à savoir la nourriture et les médicaments, mais aussi tout autre soutien physique. Cependant, il est important de souligner que soutenir les parents âgés ne dépend pas uniquement des liens d'affection, mais est assujetti aux contraintes financières telles des revenus bas, le chômage, l'inflation, la formation des enfants et d'autres facteurs compétitifs.

Les personnes âgées s'évertuent à bien gérer leurs relations avec leurs enfants. On constate surtout qu'elles estiment elles-mêmes que la génération âgée est beaucoup moins autoritaire aujourd'hui qu'elle ne l'était autrefois. Elles prennent garde de ne pas contrarier la génération plus jeune car elles redoutent la situation fâcheuse et les conflits que cela entraînerait dans la famille. Il s'opère un changement dans les relations de pouvoir entre les générations, les parents âgés se soumettent à l'autorité de leurs enfants.

À certains égards, le soutien dans le vieil âge est différencié selon le genre. Par exemple dans un foyer de famille étendue, le soutien est différencié selon le genre car donner des soins physiques est considéré comme une tâche incombant exclusivement à la femme ; tandis que l'homme est pris pour l'unique fournisseur du soutien financier. Même si la femme travaille à l'extérieur et contribue ainsi au revenu du foyer, procurer des soins, dans un sens étroit, est entièrement à sa charge. Dans la pratique, pour la majorité des Pulaya âgés, le fils est plus important pour le soutien financier et la belle-fille pour le soutien physique. On note toutefois des exemples de filles vivant avec leurs parents et leur apportant du soutien physique. Dans ces cas de figure, c'est le beau-fils qui apporte le soutien financier à ses beaux-parents. Les hommes âgés reçoivent le soutien affectif et physique de la part de leurs épouses ; les femmes âgées en revanche peuvent beaucoup moins compter sur un tel soutien de la part de leurs époux.

Au sein de la vaste parenté, les personnes âgées échangent un soutien financier avec des frères sur la base de la réciprocité. Dans certaines circonstances, les filles peuvent contribuer financièrement. Les personnes âgées comptent également sur l'aide des personnes en dehors de la parenté telles les voisins, les amis et les anciens employeurs. Cependant, ce type d'aide est irrégulier et à court terme.

Aussi longtemps qu'une femme âgée possède un bien ou dispose encore de sa force de travail comme ressource lui servant de pouvoir de négociation, elle n'est pas négligée. Comparés aux femmes, les hommes sont en meilleure posture car ils ont un meilleur accès au travail et gagnent plus que les femmes pour le même type de travail. Cela leur confère une indépendance économique.

Mais si l'homme ne travaille plus et ne reçoit plus qu'une pension, il n'y a plus de différence en matière de revenu car le montant de la pension est le même pour les hommes comme pour les femmes. En outre, la perception culturelle fait que l'homme a plus d'autorité et de pouvoir de décision dans le foyer que la femme pour qui la vie sociale et l'accès au monde extérieur sont limités. Il en résulte que, quand elles se trouvent dans le besoin, les femmes ne peuvent s'adresser qu'à leur entourage immédiat. Ceci représente un autre désavantage par rapport aux hommes.

La présente étude de cas illustre également que les enfants, bien qu'étant l'élément central de la sécurité sociale dans le vieil, n'en sont pas les uniques agents. Les Pulaya âgés pratiquent ce que Willemijn de Jong (dans ce volume) appelle un « arrangement patchwork » de sécurité sociale ; ils ne s'appuient pas sur aucun modèle de famille, par exemple sur la famille étendue, mais plutôt sur le « voisinage étendu ». Les enfants ne parviennent à fournir aide et soutien à leurs parents âgés qu'en combinaison avec de nombreux autres facteurs.

Les enfants, les subventions d'assistance sociale de l'État du Kerala, le rôle des organisations d'assistance sociale, le soutien donné par d'anciens employeurs, le rôle de la parenté élargie, des voisins et des amis constituent une charpente qui, assemblée, révèle l'éventail du réseau de sécurité sociale des personnes âgées de la classe ouvrière. En nous appuyant sur cette recherche, nous dirions que les personnes âgées de Kadamakuddy ont une sécurité sociale limitée, qui repose sur un fil. Bien qu'aucune d'entre elles ne souffre de faim, comme cela arrive en ville, la moindre rupture d'un des éléments constituant leur réseau peut faire voler en éclats leur sécurité sociale.

Le Burkina Faso : pays favori des donateurs ? Contexte des études de cas

Claudia Roth

Le Burkina Faso figure parmi les pays les plus démunis de la planète (voir appendice). La structure de l'économie burkinabé n'a guère évolué depuis l'indépendance du pays en 1960 (Lachaud 1994) : en incluant les citadins, environ 90 % de la population totale du pays, estimée actuellement à treize millions d'habitants, vivent toujours de l'agriculture de subsistance. Au nord, les paysans produisent des cultures vivrières dans des conditions des plus pénibles à cause des pluies irrégulières et de l'aridité du plateau, comme dans le village Kuila (étude de cas rural). Tandis qu'au sud-ouest arrosé et fertile, la région de Bobo-Dioulasso (étude de cas urbain), une agriculture de rente pour les marchés national et international est praticable. Le coton représente le plus important produit d'exportation du Burkina Faso, viennent ensuite le bétail et l'or. L'industrie, avec ses 15'000 employés, est restée au stade embryonnaire et se limite à une petite fabrication de produits de consommation (Lejeal 2002). Les femmes sont beaucoup plus frappées par la pauvreté que les hommes et les différences entre la ville et la campagne sont énormes (Kinda 1998, Nioumou et al. 1997).[1]

Pour la France, puissance coloniale, l'ancienne Haute-Volta constituait un réservoir de main-d'œuvre, ce qui explique le fait que l'essentiel de ses efforts de développement n'était pas destiné à ce pays aride et au sous-sol pauvre en richesses minières. Après l'abolition du travail forcé[2] en 1946, la migration vers la Côte d'Ivoire et le

---

[1] Paupérisation persistante résultant de la crise pétrolière (des années 1970), crise de l'endettement (des années 1980), programmes d'ajustement structurel (des années 1990), dévaluation du franc CFA en 1994, ainsi que de la tendance généralisée de la mondialisation de l'économie, avec pour conséquences que l'Afrique, en tant que continent, ne participe au marché mondial qu'à hauteur de 2 % symboliques (Rogerson 1997). Environ 46,4 % des Burkinabé vivent en dessous du seuil de pauvreté de 82'672 FCFA (env. 130 €) par an (cf. Nioumou et al. 1997, Somda/Sawadogo 2001).
[2] Travaux publics, travaux de plantation, construction de chemin de fer et de routes en Côte-d'Ivoire et au Ghana.

Ghana n'a guère ralenti. Jusqu'à l'éclatement de la guerre civile en
Côte d'Ivoire en 2000, on estime que deux à trois millions de Burkinabé y résidaient (Hagberg 2001 : 17-18). En outre, la migration rurale à l'intérieur du pays, du nord aride vers le sud-ouest fertile et de
la campagne à la ville, est très accentuée.

Sur le plan politique, le Burkina Faso possède une tradition
d'institutions civiles puissantes et bien organisées, en particulier syn-
dicales et estudiantines, très engagées dans la lutte politique. Ces organisations, composées surtout d'une petite élite intellectuelle, font
peser leur poids dans tout événement politique. Le charismatique
président Thomas Sankara – qui dirigea le pays de 1983 jusqu'à son
assassinat en 1987 – incarnait avec son programme révolutionnaire
d'auto-détermination et d'anti-corruption une Afrique nouvelle :
« radical sur le plan politique et bon sur le plan moral » (ibid. : 19,
traduction libre). Depuis 1990 et parallèlement aux programmes
d'ajustement structurel, un processus de démocratisation fut enclen-
ché, toutefois, les pauvres en sont exclus, ne maîtrisant ni l'écriture ni
le français, langue officielle (ibid. : 18-21).[3]

Plus de soixante ethnies qui parlent presqu'autant de langues cohabitent au Burkina Faso. Les Moose, originaires du nord, région de la
capitale Ouagadougou, constituent le groupe majoritaire de la population totale (avec env. 40 %). Avant l'ère coloniale, une grande partie
de l'actuel Burkina Faso était sous l'autorité des différents royaumes
moose (ibid. : 15). Par leur organisation fortement hiérarchisée, les
Moose se distinguent des petites sociétés de l'ouest et du sud-ouest du
pays (autour de Bobo-Dioulasso) qui reposent quant à elles sur une
organisation essentiellement décentralisée. Ces différentes formes de
hiérarchisation se manifestent dans les rapports entre hommes et
femmes.

En 1995, 25 % de la population vivaient dans des villes de plus de
5000 habitants (IRD 2000 : 2). Sur l'ensemble du territoire, seule une
infime partie de la population bénéficie du système de sécurité sociale

---

[3] Contrairement à la situation qui prévaut dans l'État de Kerala en Inde, où les pauvres peuvent prendre part aux processus politiques du fait de leur accès à l'éducation
de base (voir «Le Kerala, un modèle ? » dans ce volume).

de l'État. En 1996, le secteur formel a empoyé 3,5 % de la population (Kinda 1998) ; à Bobo-Dioulasso par exemple, cela représente 25 % des habitants (IRD 2000 : 29). La retraite est assurée par la Caisse Nationale de Sécurité Sociale (CNSS) et la Caisse Autonome de Retraite des Fonctionnaires (CARFO). Les assurés perçoivent par trimestre 20 % de leur revenu moyen des cinq dernières années d'activité. En clair, même le niveau de vie des personnes ayant autrefois exercé dans le secteur formel baisse considérablement à l'âge de la retraite si elles n'ont pas pris des précautions à temps.

Pour tous les autres citoyens reste l'offre d'assurance étatique provenant des activités de l'Action Sociale. A Bobo-Dioulasso, en 2000, à peine 0,5 % du budget municipal était alloué au social.[4] Le personnel de l'Action Sociale conseille, informe, sensibilise et soutient les femmes, les filles-mères, les enfants de la rue, les orphelins, les handicapés, les personnes âgées, mais aussi les associations – pour autant qu'il y parvienne sans moyens financiers. À la campagne – à Kuila par exemple – l'Action Sociale est tout simplement inexistante. Les populations doivent s'adresser à la Direction Provinciale de l'Action Sociale basée à Ziniaré, la commune la plus proche.

Les donateurs internationaux actifs au Burkina Faso sont pléthore. À côté des grandes institutions de l'ONU, la Banque Mondiale, le FMI et l'UE, interviennent également de nombreux États et environ 150 ONG (Hagberg 2001 : 21). Le Burkina Faso : pays favori des donateurs ? À Bobo-Dioulasso seulement quelques ONG et associations religieuses lancent ponctuellement des actions sociales, sans pour autant cibler précisément les personnes âgées. Et l'exemple du village Kuila illustre bien le fait que les aides au développement suscitent des attentes, mais en fin de compte, ne bénéficient pas durablement aux plus pauvres et à plus forte raison aux personnes âgées.

Une dizaine d'associations locales et nationales se consacrent aux besoins des personnes âgées (Besana 2001 : 27). Le problème est qu'elles ont été créées, pour la plupart, par des fonctionnaires. Elles

---

[4] 0,5 % du budget en 2000 : 8'800'000 FCFA (env.13'400 €). Entretien, en 2000, avec Drahman Ouattara, Directeur de l'Administration et des Finances de la Mairie de Bobo-Dioulasso.

ont donc tendance à privilégier les intérêts particuliers des retraités de cette catégorie (cf. aussi Ministère de l'Action Sociale 2001 : 18). Un soutien spécifique de l'État et de la société à l'endroit des personnes âgées fait donc défaut.[5] Résultat : au Burkina Faso, la parenté demeure le pivot de la sécurité sociale pour la vieillesse, à la campagne comme en ville. Les deux études de cas burkinabé mettent en lumière dans quelle mesure et sous quelles conditions la famille étendue survient effectivement aux besoins des femmes et des hommes âgés.

---

[5] Cf. aussi l'inventaire dans Besana (2001).

Dépendance menaçante :
limites de la sécurité sociale, vieil âge et genre en milieu urbain burkinabé

Claudia Roth

À Bobo-Dioulasso, l'opinion selon laquelle la « famille étendue » s'occupe de la sécurité sociale de ses membres est largement répandue. Le mythe de la « solidarité africaine » (Vidal 1994) dissimule le fait que de nombreux femmes et hommes vieillissent dans une insécurité quotidienne et que la plupart d'entre eux courent le risque de sombrer dans la grande misère une fois le vieil âge atteint. Dans une situation de grande misère, l'acquisition de la nourriture quotidienne est incertaine ; dépendant des autres, on se trouve dans l'incapacité de réaliser ces « actes qui forcent l'admiration sociale » (Hagberg 2001 : 59). Ainsi se trouve-t-on socialement marginalisé et abandonné.

Nous l'avons déjà souligné, le Burkina Faso n'est pas un État social. Dans un tel contexte, la parenté et d'autres relations de sécurité sociale jouent effectivement un rôle primordial. La recherche menée à Bobo-Dioulasso a toutefois révélé le fait que la quantité des relations sociales entretenues par un individu est directement proportionnelle au montant de ses ressources matérielles. La solidarité repose sur des relations réciproques, et la réciprocité est conditionnée par les moyens dont on dispose. En même temps que diminuent les ressources d'une personne, son réseau relationnel se restreint, au sein de la parenté et en dehors – et sa sécurité sociale s'en trouve encore réduite. Il en va de même pour les femmes et hommes âgés. Ceux qui appartiennent à la couche des pauvres n'ont pas la possibilité d'épargner pendant la vie active en prévision du vieil âge. Se pose alors la question : comment les femmes et les hommes parviennent-ils, tout au long de leur vie, à nouer des relations qui amèneront certaines personnes à leur être redevables et à les soutenir dans le vieil âge ?

À Bobo-Dioulasso, la sécurité sociale locale s'appuie sur un réseau très diversifié de relations de sécurité sociale qui comprend la parenté, les voisins, les amis, les collègues, les patrons, les coreligionnaires et les membres des associations de toutes sortes. La sécurité sociale est le résultat de la « redondance structurelle », terme utilisé par El-wert (1980) pour désigner les superpositions des différentes relations de sécurité : « Dans certains cas, les mêmes personnes sont liées par différentes relations, dans d'autres, un individu peut escompter la même prestation de plusieurs personnes, en raison des différentes relations dans lesquelles il se trouve impliqué » (ibid. : 689, traduction libre).

Nous tenterons en premier lieu de déceler les limites de l'arrange-ment de sécurité sociale des femmes et des hommes de la couche des pauvres, ce qui conduira à s'interroger sur ce qui fonde la sécurité sociale dans le vieil âge. D'après les résultats de notre recherche, vit dans la sécurité celui ou celle qui, même dans le vieil âge, arrive à conserver son indépendance – la possession d'un revenu personnel, des enfants adultes qui se sentent redevables envers leurs parents âgés, ainsi que le mariage, en constituent les éléments-clé. Le vieillissement est un processus tout au long duquel les femmes et les hommes s'évertuent sans cesse, en tant qu'acteurs, à retourner la situation présente à leur avantage. Nous expliquerons vers la fin les différentes stratégies dont disposent les femmes et les hommes âgés de la couche des pauvres pour échapper à la dépendance qui les menace.

Le terrain de recherche

Avec environ 400'000 habitants, Bobo-Dioulasso est la deuxième grande ville du Burkina Faso. La ville a toujours été multi-ethnique. Environ vingt-cinq ethnies y cohabitent.[1] À cause de la sécheresse qui sévit au nord du pays, de nombreux Moose, comme diverses ethnies

---

[1] Au total, nous avons mené des entretiens avec des membres de 21 ethnies. Toute-fois les Dafing, les Zara, les Bobo (toutes trois des sociétés mandé ou imprégnées par la culture mandé), les Senoufo et les Moose constituent la majorité de mes in-terlocuteurs.

du sud-ouest, sont venus s'installer dans la ville, en quête d'un emploi.[2]

Grâce à sa position géographique avantageuse, Bobo-Dioulasso fut jadis un comptoir commercial et un centre de la religion islamique. À l'époque de la colonisation française, en tant que centre industriel, elle fut considérée comme « capitale économique » du pays – une ville prospère. Son déclin économique s'est amorcé dans les années 1960. C'est dans le secteur informel – dont l'agriculture – qu'environ 50 % des richesses locales sont produites et plus de 70 % de la population y travaille (IRD 2000 : 3-7). Les programmes d'ajustement structurel des années 1990 ont entraîné davantage de licenciements et de fermetures d'entreprises. Aujourd'hui, beaucoup de jeunes se trouvent au chômage.

Avec environ 10'000 habitants, Koko est l'un des plus petits quartiers de Bobo-Dioulasso et, loti par les Français en 1929, il est l'un des plus anciens. La vie politique et sociale du quartier a depuis toujours été marquée par deux lignages influents : les Dagaso et les Kassamba Djabi. Ces derniers sont aujourd'hui l'une des trois puissantes familles de marabouts de la ville et possèdent trois des cinq mosquées de Koko. Ils régissent la vie religieuse et la communauté des croyants dans le quartier. En outre, à côté des lignages Zara, des familles d'autres ethnies, les Bobo, Dioula, Dafing, Peul, Sénoufo, Moose, Gourounsi, etc. y habitent. Elles vivent à Koko depuis des générations et possèdent des concessions familiales dans lesquelles des parents immigrés entre 1940 et 1960 ont trouvé un toit.

La structure sociale de Koko est relativement stable, les concessions familiales n'ont quasiment pas changé de mains et sont, dans leur grande majorité, encore de nos jours des propriétés collectives habitées par les descendants des premiers occupants et des locataires. On se connaît depuis des générations. Sur le plan économique, Koko est un quartier plutôt modeste. Ceux dont la situation économique s'améliore vont pour la plupart s'installer ailleurs, dans d'autres quar-

---

[2] En 1990, 22 % des « chefs de ménage » étaient nés à Bobo, tous les autres étaient des migrants originaires des régions plus ou moins proches (Ministère de l'Equipement 1990 : 37-38).

tiers ou dans une autre ville. Restent les femmes et les hommes âgés
avec leurs enfants au chômage et leurs petits-enfants – en somme, une
population à très faible revenu ou sans revenu du tout. C'est ainsi que
deux dynamiques s'opposent à Koko. La vie sociale se caractérise par
des rapports de parenté, de voisinage, et d'appartenance aux communautés islamiques qui se renforcent mutuellement, engendrant ainsi
une solidarité rassurante : la « profondeur générationnelle » – notion
par laquelle Vuarin (2000 : 187) désigne la caractéristique particulière
des relations sociales des anciens quartiers – ralentit le processus de
marginalisation provoqué par la paupérisation. Par contre, les jeunes
travailleurs qui quittent le quartier accentuent par là même cette tendance.

Nous avons mené des entretiens avec plus de 5 % des femmes et
des hommes âgés du quartier, sur le thème de la sécurité sociale dans
le vieil âge.[3] Les douze femmes et hommes de la couche moyenne que
nous avons interviewés étaient autrefois soit des fonctionnaires bien
rémunérés qui disposent aujourd'hui d'une pension de retraite soit des
professionnels indépendants. En revanche, les deux tiers des vingt-
quatre femmes et hommes âgés de la couche des pauvres avec lesquels
nous avons parlé vivent dans la précarité ou sont socialement marginalisés. Ce qui signifie, entre autres, qu'ils n'ont pas de quoi se nourrir
tous les jours. Ils n'ont pas toujours vécu ainsi. Ils appartiennent aux
générations jeunes des années 1940, 1950 et 1960. Sur le plan politique, l'avenir était fort prometteur avec l'accession à l'indépendance
en 1960. L'économie prospérait et connaissait une forte croissance.
Elle offrait des emplois et des opportunités de gagner sa vie en ville –

---

[3] 36 personnes représentent environ 5 % : en 1996, selon un recensement, 9098
personnes vivaient à Koko, dont 669 femmes et hommes âgés de 55 ans et plus
(données de base cf. INSD/RGPH 1998). Entre 2000 et 2002, nous avons mené plus
d'une centaine d'entretiens qualitatifs, entre autres avec 52 personnes âgées (36
étaient de Koko) et 24 jeunes de la ville (12 étaient de Koko), et plusieurs entretiens
de *focus group* avec des jeunes et des personnes âgées. Les nombreux entretiens
avec les responsables du quartier et de la ville, les experts locaux de la génération
âgée de Koko, les conversations quotidiennes spontanées et l'observation participante nous ont permis de situer dans leur contexte les entretiens menés avec les
femmes et les hommes. Notre connaissance de Koko depuis une quinzaine d'année
nous a été d'une grande utilité pour ce travail (cf. Roth 1996).

les deux tiers des nos interlocuteurs avaient quitté les villages avoisi-
nants pour émigrer à Bobo-Dioulasso. Sur le plan social, c'était une
période de transition : la famille étendue qui, à Koko, vivait encore en
communauté collective dans les concessions, a commencé à se frac-
tionner en foyers individuels. La monétarisation et la modernisation
ont lentement transformé les structures des relations sociales (cf. Marie 1997). À cette époque, plus de la moitié des mariages étaient arrangés par les aînés des familles et environ la moitié des ménages était
polygame. Les femmes mettaient au monde jusqu'à douze enfants
dont à peine la moitié atteignait l'âge adulte. Les hommes étaient re-
passeurs, réparateurs de motos, maçons, muezzins, chauffeurs,
paysans ; les femmes étaient petites commerçantes, blanchisseuses,
fabricantes ou vendeuses de savon, fileuses, tresseuses et paysannes.
Ils étaient alors en mesure de nourrir et d'habiller leurs enfants, de les
envoyer à l'école pendant quelques années, de prendre part aux
cérémonies et d'entretenir des relations sociales. En somme, ils arri-
vaient à conserver leur rang social au sein de la communauté. En revanche, ils ne pouvaient ni épargner, ni acheter du terrain, ni construire une concession : leurs revenus étaient beaucoup trop modestes
pour cela. Ils étaient pauvres certes, mais ils ne vivaient pas dans la
précarité. Et ils espéraient qu'à l'heure de la vieillesse, leurs enfants
s'occuperaient d'eux. Or, c'est l'inverse qui s'est produit : aujour-
d'hui, de nombreux femmes et hommes se voient dans l'obligation de
prendre en charge leurs enfants chômeurs, tout comme leurs petits-
enfants, bien qu'ils ne sachent pas eux-mêmes de quoi demain sera
fait.

La sécurité sociale diversifiée et ses limites

Le modèle par excellence de la solidarité est la réciprocité généralisée,
ancrée dans l'ancien ordre sociétal. Cette norme influe sur le comportement, y compris en milieu urbain. En s'appuyant sur Polanyi et Sahlins, Elwert (1980 : 684) définit la réciprocité généralisée comme :
« un don qui n'est pas compensé directement, mais qui peut revenir à
chacun sous la même forme et dans des circonstances semblables ».

Contrairement à la réciprocité équilibrée[4], où les équivalents sont
échangés dans un espace de temps limité, l'attente du contre-don n'est
pas déterminée dans la réciprocité généralisée. Le devoir diffus de
rendre le don quand le donateur en a besoin demeure (Sahlins 2004
[1965] : 193-195). Ce principe se retrouve dans les propos de nombreuses personnes âgées, par exemple dans le discours de Ami T.
(exemple 2).

En milieu urbain comme à Bobo-Dioulasso, on observe par rapport
au continuum des différentes formes de réciprocité[5] suggéré par Sahlins, qu'une évolution de la réciprocité généralisée vers la réciprocité
équilibrée se profile. Il ne s'agit certes pas de simples échanges de
dons équivalents, mais les dons et contre-dons doivent à peu près
correspondre en ordre de grandeur. Et dans la pratique, l'intervalle de
temps admis est limité par la nécessité d'entretenir les relations sociales continues afin de ne pas perdre la sécurité sociale qu'elles contien-
nent. Ainsi constate-t-on par exemple lors des cérémonies – fondées
sur la réciprocité généralisée – que la nature et la valeur des dons de
chacun sont notées avec une précision croissante. De plus, les parents
pauvres sont de moins en moins invités et se voient mal servis par
rapport aux parents aisés.

Le don induit la circulation de la dette, les relations de protection
en dérivent, et ces dernières ne se limitent pas aux relations de parenté : « La relation de protection n'est en somme que l'activation de
cette créance » (Vuarin 2000 : 38). Chacun a intérêt à faire un don car
tout don sera tôt ou tard rendu. L'individu reconnaît ses propres dettes, c'est-à-dire les créances des autres, à cause du code d'honneur qui
en appelle à la solidarité, la générosité et le respect des créances mutuelles. « Le code d'honneur est donc, pour le solliciteur comme pour
le sollicité, la référence normative des procédures d'aide (entre un
supérieur et un inférieur) et d'entraide (entre égaux statutaires), que

---

[4] « Perfectly balanced reciprocity » serait l'échange simultané des équivalents (Sahlins 2004 [1965] : 194).
[5] Continuum entre la réciprocité généralisée – équilibrée – négative (cf. Sahlins 2004
[1965]).

son expression soit positive, l'accomplissement du devoir, ou négative, la honte, sanction du manquement à ce devoir » (ibid. : 149).[6]

Sur les plans familial et communautaire, les relations de sécurité
sociale sont nombreuses et vont, dans la terminologie de Vuarin
(ibid.), du « pôle civil » (parenté, voisins, amis, collègues, patrons,
communautés religieuses, associations) au « pôle économique » (entre
autres tontines, assurances privées), y compris le « pôle religieux »
(les aumônes). Les arrangements de sécurité sociale de la couche
moyenne et de la couche des pauvres sont également diversifiés.
Toutefois, c'est la quantité des différentes relations de sécurité qui les
distingue, elle est déterminée à son tour par les ressources disponibles.
Tandis que la couche moyenne peut accumuler simultanément son
capital économique et son capital social « grâce à une accélération de
la conversion », la couche des pauvres les perd simultanément (Vuarin
1994 : 269). Les femmes et les hommes se paupérisent alors. La redondance structurelle de leur arrangement de sécurité sociale diminue.
Plus loin, nous aborderons les conséquences de la stratification sociale
sur l'arrangement de sécurité sociale des personnes âgées pauvres. En
premier lieu, nous tenterons d'expliquer, indépendamment de l'âge, le
fonctionnement de la sécurité sociale diversifiée. Nous décrirons ensuite la situation des personnes âgées.

La parenté conditionnelle

La parenté est la base de la sécurité sociale. Celui qui ne peut pas
compter sur la parenté ne peut compter sur personne. La recherche
menée à Bobo-Dioulasso met ce fait en lumière. En revanche, l'idée
selon laquelle le réseau de parenté, modèle et incarnation de la solidarité africaine, prendrait systématiquement en charge les personnes
âgées, les pauvres et les malades, n'est pas conforme à la réalité (cf.
aussi Apt 1996). Il s'avère donc intéressant de se demander : qui, sur
la base de quelle relation, s'occupe de qui ? Il faut cependant différen-
cier les composantes de la notion de parenté. La parenté propre doit

---

[6] Pour une analyse plus détaillée du complexe de l'honneur, du devoir et de la honte
cf. Vuarin (2000).

être distinguée de la belle-famille, la famille paternelle de la famille maternelle, et compte tenu de la polygamie, les frères et sœurs de même père (*fadenya*) de ceux de même mère (*badenya*), tout comme la relation parents-enfants de la relation conjugale. Chacune de ces relations est caractérisée par des droits et devoirs spécifiques, par des normes et des valeurs différentes et procure ainsi, à différents degrés, une sécurité sociale.[7] Enfin, il faut savoir si la parenté est envisagée en tant que groupe ou à travers les différentes relations individuelles qui la constituent.

En cas de « problème » (*kunko*), la parenté est définie comme groupe. En enquêtant, on s'aperçoit que le terme « problème » constitue une allusion aux cérémonies, funérailles, mais aussi mariages et baptêmes. L'enterrement représente la cérémonie la plus importante : « Seuls les membres de la parenté peuvent enterrer un mort », ce qui signifie que la présence de la parenté est indispensable lors d'un enterrement. Lors des funérailles, la stratification sociale de la parenté joue un moindre rôle. Par contre, dans les cas des mariages et des baptêmes, les parents riches prennent moins part aux cérémonies de leurs parents pauvres et ces derniers sont moins invités aux cérémonies des riches. La tendance vers la réciprocité équilibrée, enclenchée par le processus de distanciation sociale, se note donc clairement.

À l'occasion d'un « problème personnel » (*i yere ta kunko*), on peut compter sur des relations spécifiques, individuellement tissées avec des membres de la famille et des personnes en dehors de la parenté. L'appartenance au gropue de parenté[8] est socialement déterminée par l'origine, c'est-à-dire la descendance, et liée à certaines relations et valeurs.

La parenté, envisagée comme collectivité, crée donc des conditions-cadres spécifiques. Mais la façon dont les relations de parenté se traduisent dans la pratique dépend des investissements, des engagements, du comportement et surtout de la situation matérielle de cha-

---

[7] Pour une analyse de la *badenya* comme élément central de l'arrangement de sécurité sociale d'un individu et pour la « badenyanisation » des relations afin de s'assurer une sécurité sociale cf. Roth (2003b).

[8] Dans une société patrilinéaire, l'appartenance à un lignage précis se détermine à travers la ligne paternelle.

cun. Il appartient aux individus de voir comment ils réalisent la réciprocité généralisée, pivot de la vie sociale et de leur propre sécurité sociale. La parenté ne perd pas son importance, elle demeure le point de référence, mais elle se vit de façon individuelle et non pas collective ou automatique.

Les relations avec les voisins s'apparentent aux relations de parenté. En milieu urbain, les voisins sont même plus importants que la parenté car ils accourent les premiers en cas de malheur (enterrement), comme beaucoup l'affirment. L'entraide revêt un rôle majeur en particulier lors des cérémonies. Celui qui prend part aux cérémonies est intégré dans le voisinage. Tout comme avec la parenté, on se garde de solliciter l'aide des voisins car on a honte. Dans le registre du voisinage, comme dans celui de la parenté, les relations individuelles sont essentielles.

L'intimité amicale est l'une des rares relations dénuées de tout sentiment de honte.[9] L'amie intime d'une femme et l'ami intime d'un homme sont aussi appelés *gundonyogonfokela*, personne avec qui l'on échange des secrets, à qui l'on peut s'adresser même dans une situation désespérée et auprès de qui l'on peut solliciter de l'aide. Les personnes les plus démunies de notre échantillon n'ont pas d'amis. « L'amitié ne s'entretient pas sans argent », lance une femme âgée.

Pour employer l'expression de Sahlins (2004 [1965] : 193-194) « l'extrême solidaire » de la réciprocité généralisée est lié à une grande proximité sociale. Les personnes âgées de la couche des pauvres sont liées à leurs enfants et à leurs conjoints par la grande proximité sociale, ce sont les deux seules relations familiales qui donnent droit à un soutien régulier dans le vieil âge.

Les conséquences de la stratification sociale dans le vieil âge

À plusieurs reprises, les femmes et les hommes âgés nous ont dit n'avoir pas de parents, du moins pas de parents fiables. « Quand tu es

---

[9] Vuarin (1993 : 309-310) analyse l'axe de l'intimité qui va des voisins (*siginyogon*) aux personnes de confiance (*lemineyasira*), aux personnes d'espoir (*jigi*), jusqu'à l'ami(e) (*teri*).

pauvre, tu ne peux pas compter sur la parenté », nous confia un homme âgé démuni du *focus group*. Néanmoins, ils se rendent aux funérailles de la parenté, à contrecœur car ils y sont traités sans respect : ils ne sont pas salués et sont à peine servis. La monétarisation a contribué à l'apparition d'une stratification sociale et à la transformation de la famille étendue[10]. Les entretiens menés avec les experts locaux[11] portant sur leur enfance et leur adolescence, nous permettent d'appréhender ce processus. À Koko, jusqu'aux années 1950, les membres d'une famille vivaient encore selon les normes classiques, sous l'égide de l'aîné qui gérait les revenus des fils : l'un était fonctionnaire, l'autre cultivateur. Tout le monde mangeait dans le même plat. Faire la différence était chose bannie. Dans les années 1960, la disparité des revenus a commencé à se manifester : ceux qui gagnaient plus étaient de moins en moins disposés à se priver de leurs avantages au profit de la famille étendue. Suite à cela, les foyers individuels se sont multipliés au sein des familles étendues. « On disait à ce sujet : pour te réaliser, il faut quitter la famille, sinon tu n'aboutiras à rien », relate un homme âgé de soixante-trois ans issu de la couche moyenne. En raison de la division de la famille étendue en foyers individuels, il n'est pas rare de trouver des individus disposant de revenus et de moyens d'existence fort disparates vivant dans l'espace restreint d'une concession sans pour autant qu'il y ait redistribution d'argent ou de biens.

La recherche à Koko a mis en lumière la dynamique suivante : plus les individus sont économiquement indépendants, plus ils ont ten-

---

[10] Dans les sociétés partilinéaires et patrilocales, la famille étendue est composée de frères et de leurs épouses, de fils mariés et de belles-filles, de fils et de filles célibataires et de petits-enfants ; et selon les circonstances d'un neveu, d'une nièce ou de la sœur aînée veuve qui est revenue vivre dans la concession familiale. Lorsque la situation économique et les conditions d'hébergement le permettent, ils vivent patrilocalement ensemble dans la concession familiale, mais ils sont le plus souvent répartis en plus petites unités dans la ville, sans pour autant se transformer en famille nucléaire de type occidental (cf. Le Bris et al. 1987, Vuarin 2000 : 74-75).

[11] Par expert local, nous entendons les personnes qui – par leurs activités en tant que griot, marabout, activiste dans des organisations de femmes ou dans le quartier, par leurs intérêts et leur engagement social – s'occupent de manière réflexive des conditions socio-historiques de Koko. Nous avons eu de nombreux entretiens avec cinq femmes et hommes des deux couches sociales.

dance à s'extraire du cycle de la réciprocité généralisée en définissant plus étroitement les conditions de l'aide. De subtils codes de distanciation sont utilisés. Une personne sollicitée s'exclamera : « Ah, si tu étais venu hier, j'aurais pu t'aider ! » et la personne solliciteuse de comprendre, non sans honte, qu'elle n'obtiendra rien par là.[12] De plus, ceux qui veulent restreindre le cycle de la réciprocité généralisée affichent les valeurs de la modernité, orientées vers le « sujet autonome », comme le succès individuel, ou la logique prospective du souci de l'avenir des enfants (cf. Marie 1997b). Stahl (2001 : 200) constate elle aussi que les membres aisés d'une famille sortent le plus souvent du système de réciprocité généralisée (de la « solidarité traditionnelle »). À l'opposé se trouvent les personnes qui, en raison de leur situation économique, ont de plus en plus du mal à se maintenir dans le cycle de la réciprocité généralisée. Leurs relations sociales s'amenuisent jusqu'à disparaître. Des moyens financiers croissants permettent donc de sortir volontairement du cycle de la réciprocité généralisée, tandis que les moyens financiers décroissants conduisent à en être exclu.

Dans la couche des pauvres âgés, on différenciera ceux qui sont pauvres, ceux qui vivent dans la précarité et ceux qui se retrouvent socialement marginalisés (cf. Roth 2003a). Les personnes âgées pauvres disposent encore d'un capital économique, social ou symbolique – par exemple la connaissance du Coran ou des plantes curatives indigènes – et peuvent ainsi entretenir des relations sociales. Les personnes en situation de précarité par contre se demandent tous les jours ce qu'elles vont bien pouvoir manger, et leurs cotisations aux cérémonies sont aléatoires, leur réseau relationnel est restreint. Beaucoup d'entre elles disent « n'avoir pas de parents » et se considèrent elles-mêmes démunies. Leur pauvreté est définie selon Hagberg (2001 : 59, traduction libre) « par une performance sociale inférieure ; la personne pauvre est sans parenté et vit dans la solitude. En plus de son incapacité à travailler, elle est perçue comme un individu incapable de réaliser des actes qui forcent l'admiration sociale. » Les personnes âgées socialement marginalisées, troisième segment de la couche des pau-

---

[12] Voir aussi une déclaration analogue dans Hagberg (2001 : 57).

vres, se trouvent d'ores et déjà hors du système de réciprocité du fait qu'elles vivent de la mendicité.

Sur le plan individuel, la vieillesse est une phase d'appauvrissement (baisse de vitalité, baisse du revenu), de risque de ruptures sociales telles que le veuvage, le chômage ou le décès des enfants, ou encore de traumatismes personnels (maladie chronique par exemple). Toute crise économique intervenant au niveau global de la société, accroît la pauvreté et réduit en même temps l'autonomie financière des ménages et des individus. Cette situation oblige les personnes âgées à choisir entre la satisfaction de leurs besoins essentiels et l'entretien de leurs relations sociales. Celui qui se voit contraint de sacrifier ses relations sociales pour répondre à ses besoins immédiats fragilise ainsi son appartenance sociale et se prive de son droit au soutien collectif, accélérant ainsi lui-même le processus d'appauvrissement et d'isolement social (Vuarin 2000 : 191). Le nombre des personnes marginalisées ou vivant dans la précarité semble s'accroître considérablement dans le vieil âge. Deux tiers de nos vingt-quatre interlocuteurs vivent dans la précarité ou sont socialement marginalisés.[13]

Nouvelles solidarités I : les associations

La ville de Bobo-Dioulasso compte environ 400 associations de toutes sortes (cf. IRD 2000 : 62). À Koko, les associations ethniques sont actuellement très importantes pour les personnes âgées. Tout aussi importantes sont les rencontres informelles des croyants dans la mosquée, les réunions des hommes âgés autour du thé et les visites mutuelles des femmes âgées. Toutes ces formes de sociabilité font partie intégrante de la vie du quartier. Les associations ethniques – dont les adhérents sont surtout des immigrés d'un même village – servent en premier lieu à garantir le bon déroulement de l'événement social primordial pour la famille, l'enterrement, et cela même en situation de pauvreté. En cas de décès, tous les adhérents cotisent une somme fixe.

---

[13] Exemples du texte : « pauvres » – exemples 2 et 6 ; « précaires » – exemples 3 et 4 et 5 ; « socialement marginalisé » – exemple 1.

Les jeunes hommes se rencontrent quotidiennement autour du thé, les hommes âgés continuent cette pratique. En témoignent les deux cercles d'hommes jeunes et âgés avec lesquels nous avons mené des entretiens de *focus group*. Le dernier groupe se compose d'hommes ayant vieilli ensemble. Même ceux qui se sont installés dans un autre quartier pour une raison quelconque viennent à Koko pour cette rencontre quotidienne. Ils commentent l'actualité, rendent ensemble visite aux malades, participent aux cérémonies et se transmettent des relations utiles. Obtenir de l'aide en cas de maladie est possible, comme nous l'assurera un membre lors d'un entretien individuel, mais évoquer les problèmes de nourriture est tabou.

Les années 1970 et 1980 ont vu éclore de nombreuses associations de femmes à Koko, et au début des années 1990, nous avons connu une myriade de tontines. On n'en trouve plus trace aujourd'hui. Pour quelle raison ? L'experte locale consultée répond : « Par lassitude. Aujourd'hui, les femmes n'ont plus d'argent, c'est pour ça qu'elles ne participent plus. Tu as 200 francs[14] (env. 0.3 €) le matin et tu dois acheter la bouillie de mil aux enfants. Même sans association, tu peux te rendre aux baptêmes et aux funérailles. Les femmes cotisent, chacune donne par exemple 50 francs (env. 0.07 €), ce qu'elle peut. (…) Il ne reste plus que les tontines faites dans les cours. Autrefois, elles étaient organisées dans le quartier, ce n'est plus le cas aujourd'hui car beaucoup de femmes ont disparu dès qu'elles ont reçu leur part. Ce n'est pas possible dans une cour. » Faute de moyens, les pauvres femmes âgées ne prennent pas part aux tontines.

Nouvelles solidarités II : la charité

Koko est un quartier musulman influencé depuis ses origines par le lignage de la famille de marabouts Kassamba Djabi. Contrairement à l'État, les institutions islamiques offrent une certaine sécurité sociale aux personnes en détresse (cf. de Bruijn/van Dijck 1994). La mendicité n'est pas liée à un réseau personnalisé entretenu quotidiennement par la sociabilité et le don d'argent. Elle implique plutôt des croyants

---

[14] 1 € = 655.95 FCFA (francs CFA).

anonymes qui font l'aumône sans rien attendre en retour, le don charitable portant déjà en lui la bénédiction de Dieu. Il s'agit de relations de sécurité sociale unilatérales et anonymes (Vuarin 2000 : 150). Toutefois, la notion de réciprocité est exprimée dans les déclarations de nombre de femmes et d'hommes qui y voient l'effet assuré de la foi : la foi comme don et un bienfaiteur envoyé par Dieu comme contre-don.

Les personnes interrogées ne donnent guère le *zakat* – un prélèvement annuel sur la fortune accumulée – aux nécessiteux. En revanche, le *zakat-el-fitr* – une mesure de céréales fixée par membre de la famille – est offert pendant le ramadan par les personnes de la couche moyenne et par quelques personnes de la couche des pauvres à des démunis qu'ils connaissent, ce sont pour la plupart des parents ou des voisins âgés. Cela varie d'un à deux sacs de mil, selon la taille de la famille.

De nombreuses personnes font des sacrifices (*saraka*) afin de s'assurer la bonne marche d'un projet ou de conjurer un cauchemar. Pour ce faire, l'on se rend dans la rue à l'aube et remet à un pauvre l'offrande prescrite par le marabout, il s'agit par exemple de petites galettes de mil ou du riz, et l'on reçoit des bénédictions en guise de remerciement. « À l'aurore, entre cinq heures et six heures trente lorsque le soleil se lève, les pauvres peuvent se promener dans les rues. C'est le moment où les gens cherchent des pauvres pour faire leurs sacrifices », explique un expert local. Toutefois ces dons n'assurent pas la subsistance quotidienne.

Lors des cérémonies, des sacrifices (*saraka*) sont également distribués : une partie du repas et une certaine somme d'argent sont réservées aux pauvres. De nombreuses personnes âgées y trouvent de quoi se nourrir. Bien que huit hommes et femmes de la couche des pauvres soient tributaires de ce type d'offrandes, ils estiment qu'elles ne valent pas la peine d'être mentionnées. Un homme âgé qui entretient son arrière-petit-fils déclare : « Le dédain à l'endroit des pauvres est également visible lors des cérémonies, par la manière dont ils sont traités. La distribution des sacrifices commence par les personnes les plus respectées. Le plateau est alors quasiment vide lorsqu'il arrive au niveau des pauvres, il contient peut-être encore 25 ou 10 francs. Tu vois les autres pauvres qui sont traités comme toi, tu vois qui est assis à côté de qui : ceux qui en ont et ceux qui n'en ont pas ! »

À la mosquée, il est également possible d'exhorter les fidèles à faire l'aumône par l'intermédiaire de l'imam. Mais seules les personnes extérieures au quartier s'y hasardent, les pauvres du quartier ont honte, car la prière se déroule en public. Les pauvres de Koko se rendent alors dans d'autres quartiers ou à la grande mosquée de la ville. De nombreux mendiants, femmes et hommes, parcourent alors la ville et attendent devant les mosquées.

Au sein de la communauté religieuse musulmane coexistent les relations réciproques et unilatérales. Les fidèles se rendent mutuellement visite en cas de maladie. À l'occasion des cérémonies, ils dispensent des contributions (réciproques et personnalisées), et ils font l'aumône aux pauvres (de façon unilatérale et anonyme).

Exemple 1 : L'aumône contre la grâce divine
Salimata K., âgée d'environ cinquante-cinq ans, s'est installée comme jeune épouse avec son mari au quartier Koko de Bobo-Dioulasso en provenance du village. Elle était deuxième coépouse d'un foyer de trois coépouses. Elle a eu deux filles et un fils. Aujourd'hui, elle assume la charge de sa fille aînée handicapée – enfant, elle a été atteinte d'une méningite qui lui fit perdre la vue et la faculté de parler, mais elle entend et suit attentivement notre conversation. Salimata K. s'occupe aussi de son petit-fils de sept ans que sa deuxième fille, mariée à Ouagadougou, lui a confié après la mort de son mari. Son fils cadet, en formation de menuisier, vit à Ouagadougou dans la famille de son premier mari. Ce dernier est décédé il y a dix-sept ans. Salimata K. s'installa alors dans une petite pièce située dans une grande concession où elle continue de vivre avec sa fille infirme et son petit-fils, pour un loyer mensuel de 1200 FCFA (env. 2 €). Elle n'a ni eau ni électricité. En saison des pluies, elle recueille l'eau dans un tonneau et en saison sèche elle doit en acheter.

Son premier mari était un marabout. Durant leur mariage, Salimata K. cultivait un champ à l'orée de Bobo-Dioulasso en saison des pluies et était fileuse de coton en saison sèche. Aujourd'hui, elle en est réduite à mendier. Elle se rend à toutes les cérémonies susceptibles d'offrir des sacrifices (*saraka*) sous formes de mil, de noix de cola ou d'argent. En outre, tous les jeudis, les vendredis et les lundis, accompagnée de sa fille, elle va mendier dans la rue, « non, nous n'allons pas à la grande mosquée car les hommes âgés qui y occupent déjà le terrain ne veulent pas que les femmes âgées se joignent à eux ». Dans la rue, Salimata K. reçoit l'aumône et à

l'aube des *saraka* comme des habits, un tissu, des galettes de mil, un paquet de sucre
– selon l'offrande prescrite par un marabout.

Salimata K. s'est remariée il y a onze ans. Son mari est mendiant comme elle. Il
vit chez sa deuxième jeune coépouse et y prend ses repas. « Il passe de temps à autre
et me remet 150 ou 200 francs (env. 0.3 €). »

Salimata K. est livrée à elle-même. Lorsqu'on lui demande qui la lave et lui
donne à manger, lui fait la lessive quand elle est malade, elle rétorque : « C'est moi-
même qui le fais ! Je n'ai personne pour m'aider. Tout s'entasse jusqu'à ce que je
recouvre la santé. » Lorsqu'elle est souffrante, elle s'achète à la pharmacie de la rue
un comprimé d'amphétamine à 25 FCFA (env. 0.04 €), médicament surnommé « la
vieille femme qui joue au football » (*musokorobabalantonke*).

Si elles ne sont pas entièrement rompues, ses relations avec sa parenté sont pour
le moins distantes. « C'est difficile d'entretenir des relations de parenté lorsqu'on a
rien. Tu ne peux pas te rendre chez eux et ils ne viennent pas te voir. Ce que je
reçois suffit à peine à nourrir ma fille, mon petit-fils et moi, avec quoi pourrais-je
entretenir des relations de parenté ? Il ne me reste rien ! En plus, le fait que je men-
die pour me nourrir entrave mes fréquentations familiales. Qui plus est, tous mes
parents vivant ici à Bobo-Dioulasso sont aussi des mendiants. Ils vivaient tous du
fruit des champs à l'orée de la ville et voilà que ces champs n'existent plus. Et nous
voilà tous plongés dans des difficultés. »

La base de la sécurité dans le vieil âge :
un revenu, des enfants, le mariage

Aussi variées que soient les définitions des relations de protection
selon la société, Vuarin (2000 : 38-40) estime qu'elles manifestent
toutes une constante universelle : le droit au soutien est lié au « devoir
d'autonomie ». Cela signifie en premier lieu qu'une personne doit
travailler – elle participe au partage du travail social et assume ainsi
des responsabilités. De ce fait, elle n'est pas tenue pour responsable
du malheur qui lui arrive.[15] Ce devoir d'autonomie se confronte à la
vieillesse qui est une phase de dépendance. Du point de vue des membres de la société, la pauvreté et la vieillesse ont une caractéristique
commune : la diminution des forces.

Un expert local de la couche moyenne définit ainsi la notion de la
pauvreté : « En dioula, pauvreté (*fantanya*) veut dire sans force (*fan-*

---

[15] Le vol constitue l'autre façon de s'aider soi-même et de rester autonome (ibid.).

gatan). *Fangatan* est une personne sans force. (…) *Se t'a ye* – la capacité [de faire quelque chose] – lui manque, il est incapable. *Se t'a ye* se dit de celui qui vit dans la pauvreté. La pauvreté n'est donc pas un manque matériel, mais plutôt l'incapacité de faire ce qui est nécessaire pour vivre décemment. Celui qui est en bonne santé ne passe pas pour pauvre vu qu'il dispose de forces pour faire quelque chose. N'est pas non plus considéré comme pauvre celui qui peut compter sur le soutien des enfants ou de tierces personnes. Est pauvre celui qui non seulement ne possède rien, mais ne peut y remédier ni compter sur des personnes qui lui sont redevables, en l'occurrence ses enfants. (…) Dépendantes et pauvres sont donc les personnes livrées à la merci de la bonne volonté d'autrui. Elles vivent dans l'insécurité. »

Suite à une étude qu'il a menée au Burkina Faso, Hagberg (2001) décrit lui aussi cette notion de la pauvreté et attire l'attention sur « le manque de pouvoir d'action » et le « manque de capacité de faire des actes socialement valorisés » qui en découlent. Les gens n'excluent pas les explications structurelles de la pauvreté, écrit-il. « Mais la pauvreté est toujours considérée comme une expérience profondément personnelle se résumant à l'incapacité d'améliorer la situation » (ibid. : 44, traduction libre). Les personnes âgées considèrent aussi la vieillesse comme une expérience hautement personnelle – comme « le résultat d'une vie vécue ». En font partie le « bon comportement » (*kewuali nyuman*), des enfants qui ont réussi et se sentent redevables envers eux, le mariage et un bon réseau relationnel.

Le travail dans le vieil âge

Toutes les personnes âgées s'évertuent à gagner de l'argent tant qu'il leur en reste encore des forces (cf. aussi Schoumaker 2000 : 387). Les femmes âgées de la couche des pauvres sont le plus souvent actives dans le petit commerce et vendent du charbon, de la bouillie de mil, des condiments ou du *lemburuji,* une boisson au gingembre et au citron. Ou alors elles travaillent comme blanchisseuses, tresseuses, ou fileuses de coton. Les hommes sont maçons, muezzins, mécaniciens, fabricants de filets. Parmi les efforts déployés pour se constituer un revenu, nous prenons aussi en compte les visites des cérémonies, les promenades matinales et la mendicité (cf. exemple 1). Les revenus dont disposent les personnes âgées peuvent être aussi diversifiés que celui d'Ami T. (exemple 2).

Exemple 2 : Le revenu du vieil âge diversifié
Ami T. (âgée de 60 ans) est retournée vivre il y a plus de vingt ans dans la concession de son père, lieu de son enfance. Pendant son premier mariage (son défunt mari était un fonctionnaire), elle était une commerçante en gros qui réussissait dans le négoce de bovins, de motos et de cigarettes entre Bobo-Dioulasso, Ouagadougou, Lomé et Abidjan. Elle a cinq enfants. Un de ses fils marié, son épouse et leurs deux enfants, ainsi qu'une de ses filles, mère de deux enfants, vivent avec elle et mangent dans son plat. « Je porte mes enfants sur le dos », dit Ami T., « je me lève à quatre heures du matin afin de pouvoir les nourrir tous, alors que c'est moi qui devrais être nourrie ! Ma sécurité sociale n'est pas assurée. J'ai tout investi dans les études de mes enfants en me disant qu'une fois qu'ils auront réussi, ils s'occuperont de moi quand je serai vieille. Mais il n'en est rien, cela n'a pas marché. » À la mort de son premier mari il y a de cela vingt ans, Ami T. a dû abandonner son commerce et prendre soin de sa mère malade jusqu'à il y a dix ans. Aujourd'hui, sa fille et elle font un petit commerce de bouillie de mil. La recette du matin de 500 FCFA (env. 0.8 €) lui revient et celle du soir appartient à sa fille qui peut ainsi satisfaire ses propres petits besoins. Et quand cela ne suffit pas, sa mère lui donne la somme manquante, dit-elle.

Ami T. s'est remariée pour « avoir le soutien d'un homme. Mais », commente-t-elle, « on ne peut pas dire que mon mari soit un soutien pour moi. Il paie l'électricité, c'est tout ! » Il mange à midi chez Ami T. et vit le reste du temps dans une autre concession avec ses deux premières épouses, neuf de ses dix-sept enfants et trois de ses sept petits-enfants. En somme, il se trouve dans la même situation qu'Ami T. : il nourrit ses enfants adultes ainsi que ses petits-enfants.

Comment Ami T. s'en sort-elle avec un foyer d'une dizaine de personnes à nourrir ? Son revenu est diversifié : il se compose d'une petite pension de veuvage trimestriel d'un montant de 19'655 FCFA (env. 30 €), de sa recette journalière de 500 FCFA (env. 0.8 €), du loyer de deux foyers dans la cour familiale, de la contribution régulière de son mari pour l'électricité. En outre, un bon ami de son fils chômeur la soutient. « Il m'aide beaucoup ! Quand il vient me saluer et tombe sur un problème, il le résout. Mes neveux aussi, les enfants de ma sœur aînée, me donnent souvent 5000 francs (env. 8 €) ou 2500 francs.» Son fils vivant à Lomé lui fait parvenir de l'aide de temps en temps. Ami T. explique : « Lorsque les gens viennent me solliciter, je leur viens en aide. Et si je n'ai rien, je me débrouille pour en trouver. Comme je suis toujours en train de donner, je connais des difficultés matérielles aujourd'hui.

J'ai honte quand je ne peux pas donner, ça a toujours été ainsi. Je partage tout ce que je possède. » Elle ajoute qu'elle le faisait aussi en prévision du vieil âge. « Comme jeune femme mariée, si tu aides d'autres enfants à réussir, et pas uniquement les tiens, tu en profiteras une fois la vieillesse venue. Mais si tu n'aides personne, il ne faudra pas t'étonner que personne ne t'assistera dans le vieil âge. Je vis relativement bien aujourd'hui parce que je me suis bien comportée auparavant : j'ai toujours porté assistance chaque fois que je le pouvais. Tu ne peux solliciter que les parents que tu avais aidés autrefois. J'ai aidé beaucoup parmi les nombreux enfants des sœurs et frères de ma mère – je peux me tourner vers eux aujourd'hui. »

Leurs seuls gains ne permettent pas aux personnes âgées de la couche des pauvres d'assurer leur minimum vital dans le vieil âge. Ceci est dû à la fois à la diminution des forces physiques et à la compétition des jeunes sur le marché du travail. Qui plus est, les dépenses ne baissent pas, elles augmentent plutôt lorsque les personnes âgées doivent prendre en charge leur progéniture, comme Ami T. (exemple 2). Pour les femmes âgées s'ajoute à cela la discrimination économique subie durant toute leur vie, qui a fait obstacle à leur accès aux ressources et le contrôle des ressources (revenu, biens, propriété) et à leur maîtrise. De ce fait, les femmes âgées sont plus exposées à la pauvreté que les hommes (cf. Cattell 2002, Lachaud 1997). Au cours de leur vie, les pauvres ne peuvent pas économiser en prévision du vieil âge, comme le font les membres de la couche moyenne qui peuvent déposer de l'argent à la banque ou investir dans un troupeau de bovins – la forme d'épargne traditionnelle –, construire des concessions, acheter des champs ou des vergers, ouvrir un commerce. Les revenus des membres de la couche moyenne sont diversifiés dans le vieil âge et se composent par exemple d'une pension, de loyers, de recettes agricoles et de l'épargne. Ils sont propriétaires de concessions. En général, les pauvres ne possèdent pas de concessions : la moitié d'entre eux vit dans la concession du père ou dans celle de la famille paternelle, un homme vit dans la concession du frère de sa mère. Trois d'entre eux sont des locataires et cinq sont « hébergés gratuitement », c'est-à-dire qu'à l'issue d'une longue co-habitation, un propriétaire généreux les a exonérés du loyer.[16] La règle de résidence patrilocale confère une certaine sécurité d'habitat dans les concessions familiales collectives. Pour bon nombre de personnes âgées pauvres, l'hébergement leur pose moins de problèmes que l'entretien du logis.

En élevant bien leurs enfants et en entretenant bien leur réseau de relations sociales, les femmes et les hommes de la couche des pauvres ont donc la possibilité de prévoir la sécurité sociale pour leur vieil âge de manière indirecte. Ils peuvent y parvenir par la socialisation orientée selon la valeur de la *mogoya*[17], de l'humanité, en se comportant en personne solidaire et généreuse, dévouée aux autres. Ami T. se considère ainsi (exemple 2).

Le contrat implicite entre les générations[18]

De nos jours, seuls les enfants – autrefois c'était les fils – ont le devoir d'entretenir leurs parents âgés (cf. aussi van der Geest 2001 : 20). Les beaux-fils doivent assumer des responsabilités lors des cérémonies. Jeunes et vieux sont unanimes sur la définition de ce contrat implicite fondé sur la « loi de la dette » (Marie 1997a : 68-80). La pratique du contrat entre les générations est toutefois contradictoire. Si l'on ne s'en tient qu'à l'entretien physique des parents âgés, le contrat entre les générations semble alors assumé, à peu près à cent pour-cent : au moins une fille ou un fils, mais généralement plusieurs enfants, vivent avec leurs parents dans une concession. Les trois-quarts vivent dans

---

[16] « Hébergés gratuitement », c'est la rubrique correspondante dans les statistiques du recensement. En 1996, ils représentaient 23 % des habitants de Koko (cf. INSD 1998).

[17] Pour une explication du concept *mogoya*, cf. Vuarin (2000 : 100-101). C'est un terme bambara/dioula : *mogo* = être humain, *ya* = suffixe exprimant l'abstraction. *Mogoya* signifie plus ou moins « politesse, relations sociales, bonté, serviabilité » (Bailleul 1996). Cf. aussi Marie (1997a : 70) concernant l'habitus marquée par « les principes de la solidarité, de la hiérarchie, de l'identité collective et de la répression corrélative des pulsions individualistes » (socialisation primaire des anciennes sociétés).

[18] En nous appuyons sur Cattell (1997 : 159), nous utilisons le terme « contrat implicite » pour les relations entre les générations, compris comme vision partagée, valeurs et habitudes partagées, et comportement exigé par rapport aux relations et à l'échange.

un foyer de trois générations. Les femmes et les hommes expriment à quel point la présence physique de leurs enfants est importante. Outre le respect social que la proximité des enfants suscite, les coups de main, les soins et les aides pratiques comme faire de petites réparations dans la maison en font aussi partie.

Pour ce qui est du soutien financier, le contrat entre les générations se manifeste sous une forme particulière chez les pauvres. Seule une femme sur vingt-quatre personnes bénéficie d'un soutien qui couvre ses besoins quotidiens. Quatre femmes et quatre hommes reçoivent certes un soutien d'un, voire de plusieurs enfants, mais il ne leur permet pas de survivre et ils doivent alors se battre tous les jours pour arriver à joindre les deux bouts. Et la moitié des personnes âgées de la couche des pauvres, comme de la couche moyenne vivent un « contrat entre les générations à l'envers » : elles doivent entretenir leurs enfants adultes et/ou leurs petits-enfants.[19]

Exemple 3 : Le fils comme dernier recours
Sibiri G. (âgé de 71 ans) est né en 1931 dans un village. À quinze ans, il a émigré à Bobo-Dioulasso chez une tante paternelle. Il s'est marié par la suite et a eu six fils avec sa femme. Deux sont encore en vie. L'un est malade et vit ailleurs, l'autre, âgé de 27 ans, est demeuré avec Sibiri dans la concession où ils sont hébergés gratuitement depuis des décennies, grâce à une relation « héritée » du père de Sibiri. La cour est à l'abandon et dégradée. Le fils de Sibiri G. raconte : « Mon père vie dans la crise. Cela me préoccupe beaucoup. J'ai beau me battre, je n'arrive pas à gagner le minimum vital. Il se lève tous les matins et se débrouille, je me lève tous les matins et je me débrouille... Je devrais être en mesure d'entretenir mon père. Seulement voilà, je dois m'occuper de tout à la fois : soutenir mon père, construire ma propre concession, fonder une famille comme je le souhaiterais, j'ai besoin d'un emploi – dire que je dois réaliser tout ça ! »

C'est en tant que cultivateur que Sibiri G. a entretenu sa famille. Sa femme vendait au marché de Bobo-Dioulasso le mil et le maïs qu'il produisait. « A l'époque », dit-il, « je ne pouvais pas songer à l'avenir, je n'avais pas la possibilité de mettre quelque chose de côté. Je devais trouver à manger tous les jours afin d'assurer la survie quotidienne de la famille, je ne pensais qu'à ça. »

La femme de Sibiri est décédée il y a plusieurs années. « C'est l'immense crise dans la vieillesse. Tu n'as pas de soutien. Il n'y a personne d'autre pour t'aider »,

---

[19] Contrat entre les générations : « assumé », exemple 6 ; « assumé, sans garantie de subsistance », exemples 3 et 4 ; « à l'envers », exemples 1 et 2 et 5.

dit-il. « Si ma femme était encore en vie, elle serait une source de sécurité pour moi. Quand on a une femme, rien ne peut arriver. Elle m'aiderait à faire face. Quand la femme a des enfants, ces derniers aident leur mère à s'occuper de leur père. Sans moyens, on ne trouve plus d'épouse. » La défunte femme de Sibiri G. avait de bonnes relations à Koko et était responsable du groupe de femmes à l'époque de Thomas Sankara (1983-1987). Il dit avoir vécu dans son ombre, c'est pourquoi aucune de ces relations n'a pu devenir sienne.

Son fils, un menuisier sans emploi, travaille dans un kiosque et touche 500 FCFA (env. 0.8 €) par jour. Tous les matins, il remet 250 FCFA à son père pour la nourriture. Il en faudrait pourtant 300 à Sibiri G. : trois fois par jour, il s'achète un plat de riz avec sauce qui lui coûte 100 FCFA (0.15 €). Affaibli et souffrant des poumons, Sibiri G. est le plus souvent assis sur une chaise devant la cour, les passants lui donnent l'aumône et de temps à autre, des jeunes sollicitent ses bénédictions, « parce qu'ils savent que c'est très bien pour leur avenir », dit-il. « Et lorsqu'une cérémonie se donne quelque part, je m'y rends. Même quand je ne me sens pas bien, je m'efforce d'y aller car j'espère pouvoir recevoir 100 ou 200 francs. » Son fils s'occupe de lui, il lui fait la lessive, nettoie sa chambre et le soigne lorsqu'il est malade. Sibiri G. peut compter sur son fils. Il n'a personne d'autre sinon. « En ville, je n'ai pas de parents, en tout cas pas le genre à entretenir des relations familiales. Et ceux du village, les enfants de mes frères, ils pensent certes à moi, mais ils n'ont pas les moyens. Ils ont eux-mêmes beaucoup trop de charges et ont du mal à survivre comme paysans. » Il ne peut pas solliciter les voisins. Et il dit ceci d'un ami, qui en fait n'en est pas un : « Il ne se dit pas : mon fils a réussi, je vais donc de temps en temps ramener un sac de riz à mon ami. Cela ne lui traverse même pas l'esprit. »

En ce qui concerne le contrat entre les générations, la recherche menée à Koko permet de poser les constatations suivantes :

Le contrat entre les générations est une relation de sécurité sociale élaborée et aménagée par les parties prenantes, comme d'autres relations de sécurité sociale. Le droit des parents à être soutenus dans la vieillesse est conditionné par la façon dont ils ont assumé leur devoir, c'est-à-dire aidé les enfants à grandir et à obtenir une situation à l'âge adulte. En milieu urbain, cela implique d'assurer la scolarisation, la formation, de leur trouver du travail. Y sont-ils ou non parvenus ? Les négociations s'effectuent dans le contexte urbain – la dette absolue est conditionnée et relative aujourd'hui (cf. Marie 1997b : 436). Si l'enfant estime que son père ou sa mère n'ont pas assez fait pour lui

dans son enfance et sa jeunesse, il leur refuse son soutien dans le vieil
âge.

Une fois âgées, les femmes peuvent compter sur le soutien de leurs
enfants car, en tant que mères, elles leur ont donné tout ce qu'elles
possédaient, sur les plans affectif, matériel, financier. Le mariage est
devenu une source d'insécurité pour les femmes (voir plus bas). Elles
misent donc tout sur leurs enfants. Il n'est pas rare que les mères
reçoivent plus que les pères, en cachette, afin de ne pas remettre en
cause l'autorité des pères dans une société à structure patrilinéaire.
D'autre part, ce sont aussi les femmes qui, plus que les pères, prennent
en charge leurs enfants adultes « qui n'ont pas réussi ». Les pères po-
lygames ne peuvent guère compter sur les enfants qu'ils avaient
négligés autrefois ou dont ils avaient maltraité la mère.[20]

Le manque de moyens n'explique pas à lui tout seul la difficulté
des jeunes à prendre soin de leurs parents âgés. Ils ont aussi leurs propres besoins et désirs, des perspectives de vie qui diffèrent de celles
des aînés. Ils s'évertuent à résister, sans rupture avec la parenté, à la
pression sociale qui exige d'eux qu'ils règlent les problèmes de toute
la famille avec leur salaire (cf. aussi Rosenmayr 2002). Il est fréquent
de voir les fils ayant un revenu aller s'installer dans un autre quartier,
voire dans une autre ville, et ils se justifient par leurs propres charges
familiales. Les filles mariées – qui ne sont en fait pas tenues de soutenir leurs parents âgés, contrairement aux fils – sont pourtant promptes
à le faire. À côté du soutien pratique, si elles habitent à proximité, et
des dons (tissus ou habits), elles donnent de plus en plus d'importantes
sommes d'argent (processus de *degendering* du don). Selon les dires
des femmes et des hommes, leurs dons sont plus réguliers et plus fiables que ceux des fils.

Puisque le mariage, nous l'avons dit, peut s'avérer être une source
d'insécurité sociale pour les femmes, elles poursuivent donc parallèlement deux stratégies de sécurité sociale : en tant que mères, elles
misent sur les enfants en prévision de la vieillesse, et en tant que filles
mariées, elles consolident leurs liens avec leur famille d'origine par

---

[20] Le même phénomène a été constaté par van der Geest (2001 : 29) dans une petite
ville du Ghana.

des dons, se garantissant ainsi une position sociale et la possibilité de pouvoir y retourner en cas de crise majeure dans leurs ménages.

Le contrat entre les générations à l'envers est un phénomène urbain : les personnes âgées ne peuvent pas céder un terrain à cultiver à leurs enfants comme cela se fait en milieu rural où les fils remplissent le contrat entre les générations, toutefois sans garantie de subsistance (cf. aussi Badini-Kinda dans ce volume). Le taux de chômage élevé en ville et le taux de mortalité lié au sida parmi les jeunes expliquent en partie cette inversion du contrat.

Demeure la question : pourquoi les personnes âgées sont-elles disposées à soutenir leurs enfants adultes ? La grande famille patrilocale culturellement ancrée dans le sud-ouest du Burkina Faso, où les fils mariés demeurent à vie dans la concession paternelle, explique en partie pourquoi les enfants adultes ne sont pas mis à la porte. D'une part, leur présence consolide l'autorité de l'aîné comme chef de la famille étendue, d'autre part les aînés, dans leur propre compréhension de leur rôle, se sentent responsables de la reproduction de la grande famille patrilocale, aussi longtemps qu'ils sont en vie (cf. Roth 1998). C'est la raison pour laquelle les personnes âgées se sentent contraintes de prendre en charge leurs enfants adultes. « Tu ne peux pas rejeter ton enfant ! » s'exclame Ami T. (exemple 2). Sa fille, vivant chez elle avec ses deux enfants, partage cet avis. D'après elle, il incombe aux parents de nourrir, d'élever et de trouver du travail à leurs enfants. Les enfants « qui n'ont pas réussi » oscillent alors entre la honte de n'être pas en mesure d'assumer leur devoir envers leurs parents et la notion qu'ils partagent avec leurs parents, à savoir que ces derniers doivent leur trouver du travail. Le cas le plus dur des contrats entre les générations à l'envers est celui d'un ménage où les grands-parents (le plus souvent des femmes) élèvent seuls leurs petits-enfants orphelins ou conçus hors mariage – les uns et les autres sont sans ressources et sans force (voir exemple 1).

Le mariage dans le vieil âge

À côté du contrat implicite entre les générations, le contrat de mariage représente la deuxième relation de sécurité sociale la plus importante dans le vieil âge. En principe, le mariage permet aux femmes et aux hommes d'être socialement reconnus comme une personne sérieuse et respectable. Facteur d'intégration sociale, le mariage est la base de toutes les autres stratégies de sécurité sociale des individus. Il est source de sécurité aussi longtemps que les ressources suffisent, que l'homme et la femme remplissent chacun leurs devoirs et coopèrent. Ils peuvent jouir ensemble de leurs revenus et participer indirectement à l'arrangement de sécurité sociale de l'autre. Au cas où une partie de l'arrangement de sécurité sociale de l'un viendrait à échouer, celui de l'autre resterait disponible et vice versa (cf. aussi Leliveld 1994 : 270). Un autre aspect sécurisant du mariage est le fait qu'il réunit quatre patrilignages et augmente ainsi le potentiel du capital social de la femme et de l'homme.

Le contrat de mariage est différencié selon le genre (*gendered*), il n'offre pas les mêmes sécurités sociales aux hommes et aux femmes à cause de leurs positions sociales différentes, des valeurs y associées, du partage du travail selon le genre et de la séparation des biens.[21] Pour un homme âgé, une épouse incarne la sécurité sociale à plusieurs niveaux. Tout d'abord, c'est elle qui lui fait la cuisine, la lessive, le ménage et lui prodigue des soins, souvent avec l'aide d'une belle-fille vivant dans la concession. Ensuite, étant donné qu'il est le chef de famille et une personne respectée, donc distante, c'est son épouse qui peut lui faciliter ou entraver le lien avec les enfants. Un homme déclare : « Si tu as fait souffrir une femme, elle dira à son enfant qui a réussi de ne pas s'occuper ni de toi ni de ses coépouses. » Enfin, c'est l'épouse qui vole au secours de son mari si ce dernier, suite à la vieillesse, à la maladie ou au chômage, n'est plus en mesure de subvenir

---

[21] Dans de nombreuses sociétés du sud-ouest du Burkina Faso, la femme en tant que mère occupe le premier rang, en tant qu'épouse le deuxième et l'homme occupe le premier rang en tant qu'époux et le deuxième en tant que père, selon un « hidden transcript », comme Koné (2002 : 22) désigne la critique de l'autorité patrilinéaire dans les coulisses au sein des sociétés mandé (cf. aussi Hoffman 2002).

aux besoins de la famille. Elle assume ce devoir tacitement. C'est un des secrets du mariage – un *furugundo* (cf. Roth 2003a). La moitié des femmes âgées de la couche des pauvres, mais aussi de la couche moyenne vivent ce secret du mariage et prennent en charge tous les frais du ménage. C'est ainsi que la sécurité qu'offre le mariage à l'homme peut s'avérer être une source d'insécurité pour sa femme. En outre, les mariages sont de plus en plus conflictuels. Les crises économiques se reflètent dans les crises conjugales. Une ancienne commerçante en gros nourrit sa famille aujourd'hui grâce à un petit magasin d'alimentation parce que son mari a fait faillite. Elle s'exprime : « Les hommes veulent s'adonner à de grandes activités et une fois que les affaires périclitent, ils ont du mal à recommencer à zéro. Ils préfèrent ne rien faire que d'entreprendre quelque chose de petit. Ils ont honte, contrairement aux femmes. Les jeunes hommes ne veulent pas non plus commencer au bas de l'échelle, tandis qu'une jeune femme peut commencer son commerce avec 1000 ou 5000 francs (env. 8 €). Aucun homme autrefois prospère n'est disposé à recommencer à zéro. Il préfère s'asseoir et croiser les bras. » La littérature regorge d'exemples illustrant cette tendance qu'ont les hommes à se décharger de leurs devoirs et responsabilités sur les femmes en période de crise économique. Ces dernières élargissent, intensifient et diversifient alors leurs activités afin de pouvoir nourrir toute la famille.[22]

Exemple 4 : Sécurité dans le mariage
Siriki C. (âgé de 65 ans) est né en 1937. Il a immigré à Bobo-Dioulasso à l'âge de 20 ans et s'est installé définitivement à Koko en 1965. Il vit dans la même concession depuis 1970 – actuellement avec sa troisième femme, leur fille de quatre ans, deux de leurs fils sont décédés en bas âge. L'une de ses deux filles adultes issues de son deuxième mariage habite aussi chez lui. Ils vivent à quatre dans deux pièces. Autrefois, Siriki C. payait 4000 FCFA (6 €) de loyer mensuel, mais depuis qu'il est tombé gravement malade il y a de nombreuses années, il est hébergé gratuitement. « Le propriétaire de la cour et sa sœur me traitent comme leur grand frère », dit-il. Sikiri C. définit avec précision qui il considère comme parent. « Une personne de même

---

[22] Voir entre autres Baerends (1998), Bop (1996), Endeley (1998), Lachenmann (1994, 1997), Risseeuw/Palriwala (1996).

mère et de même père n'est pas forcément ta famille. Un véritable parent est la personne qui te soutient. Le propriétaire de la concession et sa sœur étaient d'abord des
voisins pour moi, aujourd'hui, ils font partie de ma famille. » Ils l'assistent en cas de
détresse et lui donnent un peu d'argent ou des médicaments comme la Nivaquine
lorsque ses médicaments traditionnels ne semblent pas agir.

Siriki C. est devenu guérisseur comme le fut son père. Son revenu est bas et irrégulier. « Lorsque j'ai des clients, j'arrive à nourrir la famille. Je remets quotidiennement 150 francs (0.25 €) à ma femme. Avec cette somme, elle achète de la farine
de mil à 100 francs et des condiments pour la sauce à 50 francs. Il m'arrive de ne
pas avoir de l'argent, alors c'est ma femme qui nourrit la famille avec son petit
commerce d'arachides qu'elle vend devant la cour. Parfois, elle doit aussi acheter à
manger à sa propre parenté ou alors les enfants de sa famille viennent manger chez
nous. »

Sa fille adulte l'aide de temps à autre grâce à son travail de tresseuse, c'est en effet un soulagement qu'elle puisse s'occuper d'elle-même, estime Siriki C. Sa femme
et le propriétaire de la cour assurent donc sa subsistance dans le vieil âge. « Non, je
n'ai jamais répudié une femme », dit Siriki C. à propos de son troisième mariage,
« elles ont choisi de partir. Une femme apporte la sécurité dans un couple si elle est
bien intentionnée et vit en harmonie avec son mari. »

Les veuves et les veufs de la couche des pauvres connaissent le même
degré de précarité. Il ne leur reste plus que les enfants comme soutien
régulier possible. En général, ces derniers expérimentent la même
pauvreté (cf. exemples 3 et 5). Mais on dénombre en fait beaucoup
plus de veuves que de veufs.[23] L'espérance de vie[24] des femmes est
plus élevée que celle des hommes, et de plus la génération actuelle des
femmes âgées a cinq à dix ans de moins que leurs maris. Ajoutons à
cela que 25 % des femmes ayant participé aux entretiens vivent seules
car leurs maris sont allés s'installer chez une coépouse plus jeune. Il
en résulte qu'ils ne contribuent même plus aux dépenses du foyer,
comme dans le cas de Salimata K. (exemple 1). Schoumaker (2000 :
385) signale lui aussi que les hommes ont, dans le vieil âge, plus de
chances que les femmes de vivre en couple et d'être soutenus par une
épouse, en raison de la polygamie et du remariage fréquent.

---

[23] Au Mali dans l'année 1987 par exemple, 5 % des hommes et 46 % des femmes de
plus de 60 ans étaient veufs (Schoumaker 2000 : 386).
[24] Par rapport aux hommes, les femmes sont 20 % de plus à atteindre l'âge de 60 ans
et 60 % de plus à atteindre 80 ans et plus (Schoumaker : 385).

Exemple 5 : Le veuvage – source de déchéance sociale
Bintou S., 55 ans environ, troisième coépouse, est veuve depuis cinq ans. Son défunt mari, qui travaillait dans la vente de mil en détail, lui a laissé à elle et aux enfants, pour tout héritage, la possibilité d'être gratuitement hébergés dans la cour de sa famille. Bintou a cinq enfants qui ont entre quinze et quarante ans. Deux de ses filles, son fils aîné au chômage depuis des années, sa femme, trois de ses petits-enfants ainsi que sa mère âgée mangent dans son plat aujourd'hui. « Ma mère vivait seule au milieu des champs, dans une vieille hutte », raconte Bintou, « elle entend et voit mal, elle a le dos courbé, elle ne peut plus faire la cuisine. C'est pourquoi je l'ai prise avec moi il y a deux ans. » À elle seule, Bintou S. a la charge de ce foyer de quatre générations : « Je souhaite que mes enfants trouvent du travail, même pas pour moi, je voudrais simplement qu'ils puissent s'occuper d'eux-mêmes. »

Bintou S. est née et a grandi à Bobo-Dioulasso. Elle a brièvement fréquenté l'école coranique. Elle s'est installée dans la cour de sa belle-famille comme jeune mariée. Toute sa vie, elle a confectionne et vendu des boules de savon. Aujourd'hui, elle fait le commerce de potasse et d'huile qu'elle achète à l'usine Citec. C'est avec son maigre revenu qu'elle fait bouillir la marmite. « Quand tu es malade, tu ne peux pas compter sur la parenté, car se faire soigner coûte cher. Tu dois t'en sortir toute seule », déclare Bintou S. Lorsqu'elle se trouve confrontée à une telle situation, elle prend un petit crédit qu'elle rembourse par la suite. « Par contre, il est possible de recevoir des soins. Lorsque je suis malade, c'est ma sœur cadette qui me soigne. »

« Le risque le plus grand dans la vie d'une femme, c'est de devenir veuve », souligne Bintou S., « tu n'as personne pour t'aider et tu dois t'en sortir toute seule. Cela vaut pour les jeunes femmes comme pour les femmes âgées. Tout le bien que ton mari t'a fait de son vivant, plus personne ne te le fera. »

Un facteur d'insécurité : le vieil âge et la maladie

Aucune des personnes âgées avec lesquelles nous avons eu des entretiens n'est grabataire. Cependant, un homme a perdu la vue il y a des années et nombreux sont ceux qui ressentent des fatigues et des douleurs de toutes sortes. Traditionnellement, on s'occupe bien des personnes âgées fragiles, dit-on, surtout parce qu'elles sont déjà près des ancêtres. La situation actuelle des jeunes ne leur permet pourtant pas d'acheter aux personnes âgées les médicaments dont elles ont besoin. Les maladies s'accumulent dans la vieillesse et les médicaments sont, comparés au niveau de vie, beaucoup trop chers pour qu'on puisse demander à des parents de les payer. Les traitements à l'hôpital, en clinique ou dans les dispensaires sont onéreux et doivent être réglés avant toute admission.[25] C'est pourquoi les personnes âgées appréhendent la maladie et craignent de devenir grabataires, ce qui est, à leurs yeux, la plus grande insécurité du vieil âge (cf. aussi Kinda 2003). Un expert local de la couche moyenne explique : « Tu verras rarement un malade qui, à la question : ça va ?, répondra : ça ne va pas aujourd'hui ! C'est ainsi à cause des relations sociales. Lorsque quelqu'un est malade, son entourage a le devoir de l'assister. Et le malade, à son tour, a le devoir de ne pas faire état de sa maladie afin de ne pas démoraliser les autres. C'est une obligation subtile. Si la maladie dure un, deux, trois voire six mois, elle devient dérangeante. Les enfants ne peuvent pas consacrer tout leur temps et encore moins prendre en charge tous les frais médicaux, comme le devoir l'exige. C'est pourquoi beaucoup de personnes âgées en viennent à souhaiter, au cas où elles tomberaient gravement malades, que la maladie soit courte et qu'elles meurent le plus vite possible, afin de ne pas faire souffrir leurs enfants. Plus la maladie est longue, plus les enfants risquent de se retirer. Ils ne le font pas par manque de compassion, mais parce qu'ils n'arrivent pas à faire face, le fardeau étant devenu trop lourd. »

D'après l'image qu'elles ont d'elles-mêmes, aînés autonomes et responsables de leur propre situation, les personnes âgées s'appliquent alors à ne déranger ni leurs enfants ni leur entourage. Elles dissimulent leurs maux. Il n'est pas rare qu'elles aillent elles-mêmes chercher des plantes locales. Une veuve[26] âgée de 62 ans ayant six enfants vivant très loin d'elle ou n'ayant presque pas de revenu déclare : « Tu sais que tu n'as pas les moyens et tu sais que tes enfants et tes petits-enfants en manquent aussi. Lorsque tu es malade, tu es obligée de le cacher, de faire tout pour qu'ils ne le sachent pas, parce que s'ils sont

---

[25] Depuis le 1er mars 2001, Bobo-Dioulasso possède une clinique spécialisée en gériatrie, un établissement créé sur l'initiative d'un infirmier psychiatrique français et financé par des capitaux français. En outre, on compte deux mutuelles de santé, une locale et une autre initiée par l'aide au développement française.
[26] L'assistant Blahima Konaté a mené en 2001 des entretiens à Koko avec un homme marié de 72 ans et une veuve de 62 ans (les deux appartenant à la couche des pauvres) portant sur le vieil âge et la maladie.

au courant, ils vont se gêner, étant donné qu'ils n'ont pas les moyens. »

Les soins physiques aux malades sont prodigués par les femmes – comme partout dans le monde (cf. Albert/Cattell 1994). Pour les personnes âgées, ce sont les belles-filles et les filles, voilà pourquoi la proximité physique des enfants est capitale. Les femmes âgées encore valides prennent aussi soin des malades.

Agency, vieil âge et genre

Lorsque l'on aborde le problème de la vieillesse, les personnes âgées de Koko interprètent la question posée comme une interrogation se rapportant à leur vécu, à ce qu'elles ont fait tout au long de leur vie en prévision du vieil âge, en quelque sorte à leur capital accumulé sous forme de réputation, de relations sociales et de ressources. Tout au long de ce processus qu'est le vieillissement, il est essentiel qu'une personne, jusqu'à l'âge le plus avancé, soit productive ou active et puisse conserver une certaine autonomie. Elle doit entretenir ses relations et continuer à participer à l'échange par les visites, les conseils, le règlement des conflits, les dons (cf. Finch/Mason 1993 : 173-174). Pour cela, les femmes et les hommes disposent de stratégies différentes.

En premier lieu, le vieillissement se manifeste comme un processus de *degendering*. Dans beaucoup de sociétés du sud-ouest du Burkina Faso organisées de manière décentralisée, la situation des femmes, la vieillesse venue, commence à ressembler à celle des hommes. Elles gagnent en influence, en pouvoir de décision, en autorité sur des femmes et hommes plus jeunes. Elles interviennent dans les affaires familiales ou les affaires du quartier et leurs avis compte (voir le cas d'Awa T., exemple 6). Par contre, les hommes, une fois la vieillesse venue, lorsqu'ils ne gagnent plus d'argent et sont plutôt entretenus par leurs enfants adultes ou dépendent de leurs épouses, deviennent de plus en plus faibles et effacés, comme le constate Koné (2002 : 23).[27]

---

[27] Les femmes, respectées dans leurs belles-familles en tant que mères et dans leurs familles d'origine en tant que sœurs aînées, peuvent jouer un rôle considérable en

Par ailleurs le vieil âge implique des situations différenciées selon le genre (*gendered*). Nous l'avons déjà évoqué, les femmes sont limitées dans leur pouvoir d'action (*agency*) par la discrimination économique subie toute leur vie. Par contre, elles disposent d'autres possibilités que les hommes pour entretenir leurs relations sociales. Ce fait est lié au partage du travail selon le genre, au rôle de mère et aux valeurs qui les orientent. En tant qu'épouses, les femmes possèdent des savoir-faire domestiques et thérapeutiques qui leur permettent de participer activement à l'échange réciproque, même à un âge avancé. Elles peuvent ainsi maintenir le droit à la sécurité sociale dans le vieil âge (cf. aussi Cattel 1997 : 172-173)

Comme le montre la recherche conduite à Bobo-Dioulasso, les femmes misent sur les enfants. Dans le meilleur des cas, les enfants s'occupent d'elles le moment venu ; et dans le pire des cas, elles prennent en charge leurs enfants adultes. En revanche, les hommes parient sur le mariage, leur unique possibilité d'avoir constamment accès à l'entretien et aux soins.[28] En outre, les femmes, dans leur rôle de mères, s'occupent aussi d'enfants qui ne sont pas les leurs, dans l'espoir que ces derniers leur rendront la pareille. En témoignent les trajectoires d'Ami T. et d'Awa T. (exemples 2 et 6).

Exemple 6 : Des enfants « gagnés »

Awa T. (âgée de 51 ans), est née en 1951. Elle a quinze « petits-enfants » et se considère comme une femme âgée. Elle n'a pas eu d'enfants mais a aidé son frère et sa sœur à élever les leurs. Bien qu'elle soit mariée dans un ménage polygame, elle n'est jamais allée rejoindre son époux au village. Elle vit, depuis sa naissance, dans la concession familiale de sa famille paternelle.

Enfant, elle a fréquenté l'école coranique et plus tard, elle a gagné sa vie grâce à un commerce de légumes. Lorsqu'elle est « tombée » au début des années 1990, elle a abandonné complètement ce commerce. C'était l'époque de la démocratisation, de nouveaux partis poussaient comme des champignons. Awa T., qui était déjà une

---

prenant de l'âge. En ce qui concerne l'ambiguïté de la position sociale des femmes dans diverses sociétés africaines cf. Baerends 1998, Udavardy/Cattell 1992 et dans les sociétés mandé cf. Hoffman 2002, Koné 2002.
[28] Håkansson/Le Vine (1997) ont constaté le même phénomène chez les Gusii au Kenya.

figure clé dans diverses associations, est entrée en politique. Aujourd'hui encore, elle entretient ces relations issues de ses anciennes activités politiques.

« Je n'ai pas d'enfants et cela aurait pu faire en sorte que je sois délaissée dans le vieil âge », raconte Awa T., « mais j'ai bien géré la situation, j'ai contribué à élever mes nièces et mes neveux, et c'est pourquoi ils s'occupent de moi à présent. » Au quotidien, un de ses neveux est particulièrement important pour elle. Il a pu devenir chauffeur par son entremise. Il soutient sa propre mère et Awa sans discrimination, il leur achète à manger, des médicaments et paie leurs frais médicaux. Awa peut aussi se tourner vers ses autres nièces et neveux quand elle a besoin d'argent. « Cela dépend toujours de la situation des enfants, c'est-à-dire s'ils ont du travail, de l'argent ou des problèmes personnels à régler. Quand ils ne peuvent pas m'aider, ils vont demander de l'argent auprès d'autres personnes. J'évite cela, car j'ai honte. » Quand Awa T. est malade, ce sont les femmes de ses neveux qui la soignent.

Pour Awa T., le vieil âge est la phase la plus difficile de la vie. « On ne sait pas comment les choses vont se terminer. Tout peut arriver. Mon neveu chauffeur peut très bien se dire : elle est devenue un fardeau pour moi. Sa femme peut aussi, un beau jour, le pousser à le dire car ils ont des enfants et ces derniers grandissent et auront des besoins plus importants. Ses moyens suffiront-ils à la longue pour nous tous ? Que ferai-je lorsqu'il cessera de me soutenir ? Voilà pourquoi le vieil âge est une période difficile, beaucoup de choses peuvent changer, tu ne maîtrises pas tous les paramètres, tu ne sais pas ce qui va bien pouvoir t'arriver. Aujourd'hui, je regrette un peu de n'avoir pas eu mes propres enfants. Je me demande combien de temps ce soutien va pouvoir durer. »

Conclusion

La dépendance et, avec elle, l'insécurité sociale dans la vieillesse menacent les femmes et les hommes qui n'ont ni leur propre revenu, ni biens, ni épargne, ni enfants qui les soutiennent. Leur arrangement de sécurité sociale perd en redondance structurelle, la parenté, les voisins, les amis se détournent d'eux. La sécurité sociale locale, en principe diversifiée et riche à plusieurs niveaux, exige que l'on dispose d'un minimum de ressources pour pouvoir entretenir les relations de réciprocité. Comme le constate Vuarin (2004 : 4), la « vertu redistributive » du système de sécurité est faible et des inégalités économiques sont ainsi reproduites au lieu d'être atténuées. Le processus de paupérisation des femmes et des hommes âgés de la couche des pauvres s'en trouve ainsi accéléré. Par là se trouve confirmée la thèse selon laquelle la « solidarité africaine » n'est plus qu'un mythe aujourd'hui.

La solidarité ne peut guère fonctionner dans les conditions socio-économiques actuelles. Les années de dépendance potentielles augmentent avec la croissance de l'espérance de vie et les conditions économiques ne cessent de se détériorer.

Comme toutes les collectivités, la parenté a commencé à se stratifier socialement dans les années 1950. De ce fait, même au sein de la famille étendue, la redistribution n'est plus de mise. On pourra ainsi déceler une différenciation interne au sein de la couche des personnes âgées pauvres. Les critères suivants nous sont apparus pertinents : un individu peut-il encore participer au cycle de réciprocité, et à quel degré ? D'après lui, dispose-t-il encore de parenté ? Dans les sociétés patrilocales, la « famille étendue » offre cependant une sécurité d'hébergement.

À côté de leur propre revenu, le contrat implicite entre les générations et le mariage constituent la pierre angulaire de la sécurité sociale des personnes âgées pauvres, car les enfants et les conjoints sont les seules personnes qui leur sont effectivement redevables dans la vieillesse. Conformément à la réciprocité généralisée, les enfants doivent s'occuper de leurs parents âgés – il s'agissait des fils autrefois et, de nos jours, les filles y participent de plus en plus avec des contributions matérielles (*degendering* du don). Toutefois, aujourd'hui plus que jamais, le contre-don attendu par les personnes âgées est incertain. Les enfants auront-ils la possibilité de les entretenir et seront-ils disposés à le faire ? Le contexte urbain transforme les conditions du contrat. La « dette » est devenue relative et se négocie entre les personnes concernées. En raison de l'espérance de vie et du contexte économique, la situation de la femme est liée à la survie de son conjoint, puis au revenu dont il dispose. Les veuves et les veufs âgés vivent dans la précarité, entre autres parce que les relations de sécurité du conjoint ou de la conjointe font défaut. Comme nous l'avons signalé, il n'en reste pas moins qu'il y a plus de veuves que de veufs. Les raisons en sont multiples. L'une des plus importantes est que les hommes peuvent plus facilement se remarier.

En raison du partage du travail selon le genre et de leur rôle de mère, les femmes comptent sur leurs enfants pour assurer leur sécurité sociale dans la vieillesse – dessein qui oriente leurs actions tout au long de leur vie. Les hommes cherchent cette sécurité dans le mariage, se servant ainsi de leurs épouses qui leur facilitent l'accès aux enfants. Ces deux relations de sécurité sociale sont ambivalentes pour les femmes car elles fondent une communauté de destin : si les enfants trouvent du travail, les mères reçoivent souvent plus que les pères ; s'ils n'en trouvent pas, les femmes prennent en charge à la fois leurs enfants adultes, leurs petits-enfants et leurs époux. La recherche à Koko révèle une forte concordance entre le contrat entre les générations à l'envers et le « contrat conjugal à l'envers ».

Vieillir dans la dignité et le respect implique que l'on soit autonome et actif, que l'on ait de l'influence et donne des conseils ; on doit également avoir acquis le droit d'être soutenu par des enfants redevables envers leurs parents – il n'y a pas de honte à solliciter de l'aide. Rien de tout cela n'est accessible aux femmes et aux hommes âgés vivant dans la précarité ou la marginalisation sociale. Dans le contexte économique du Burkina Faso, la pauvreté ne cesse de prendre de l'ampleur. Les enfants ne sont pas en mesure de compenser les effets d'une telle conjoncture. Le cas des personnes âgées pauvres de Koko est emblématique. Menacées de tomber dans la dépendance, de voir leurs relations se déliter faute de ressources, de se trouver socialement marginalisés, elles vivent dans un état de tension et de préoccupation constantes. Dans la vieillesse, la déchéance sociale n'est pas moins douloureuse que le manque de nourriture.

L'écart entre idées et pratiques : l'insécurité sociale des personnes âgées en milieu rural burkinabé

Fatoumata Badini-Kinda

« La parenté est obligation » dit-on chez les Moose,[1] ce qui signifie que l'individu a l'obligation de soutien et d'assistance vis-à-vis de ses parents. De nos jours les personnes pauvres des villages bénéficient-elles du soutien familial et communautaire dans leur vieil âge ? Quelles sont les logiques auxquelles obéissent ces formes d'assistance et de sécurité sociale et leurs limites ? Sous quelles conditions une personne âgée peut-elle attendre du soutien ? Les résultats de la recherche menée dans le village de Kuila révèlent un écart significatif entre idées et pratiques du soutien familial et communautaire pour les pauvres : dans les conceptions le réseau de relations familiales représente le principal réseau de soutien des personnes âgées à travers les relations conjugales, intergénérationnelles et dans la famille étendue. Toutefois dans la pratique, les possibilités de recours à travers les relations familiales et extrafamiliales sont très limitées et peu consistantes pour les personnes âgées pauvres, laissant la majorité dans la précarité et la misère. À Kuila, nombreuses sont celles qui vivent dans l'extrême pauvreté avec des jours sans repas.

Kuila, un village des « contrastes »

Situé à trente-cinq kilomètres de la capitale Ouagadougou, Kuila est un village moaga de 1357 habitants.[2] Si près de la capitale, Kuila de-

---

[1] Les Moose (au singulier Moaga) représentent l'ethnie majoritaire sur la soixantaine d'ethnies que compte le Burkina Faso.
[2] Cf. Institut National de la Statistique et de la Démographie, INSD 1998. De 2000 à 2002 nous avons pu réaliser au total plus d'une centaine d'entretiens (entretiens individuels, *focus groups*, entretiens avec des responsables institutionnels et locaux et des experts locaux) outre la collecte des données statistiques et l'observation participante. Nous avons parlé avec 44 personnes âgées et 22 jeunes de la couche moyenne et de celle des pauvres.

meure quand-même un village traditionnel, avec ses cases rondes en argile, ses greniers en paille mais surtout son organisation sociale qui demeure celle de la société traditionnelle moaga, fortement organisée et hiérarchisée. Ainsi Kuila compte à sa tête un chef de village et des chefs coutumiers et religieux aux côtés de la population du village. Les règles de vie sont celles de la société patrilinéaire fortement hiérarchisée et centralisée. Une des particularités de Kuila est que tous les membres du village sont des parents directs ou par alliance. Ainsi les voisins sont à la fois des parents.

Sur le plan religieux, Kuila serait un village chrétien à 80 % suivi par les musulmans 14,1 %, et le reste des animistes.[3] Cependant il y a lieu de parler de syncrétisme religieux car les rituels de l'animisme ne sont pas pour autant abandonnés par les convertis du village. Nombreux sont par exemple les individus qui portent deux prénoms (p. ex. Noaga Jean-Pierre, Guelbo Mahamoudou) dont le premier est un nom symbolique et de protection et le second, un nom de conversion. Les populations de Kuila demeurent attachées aux croyances ancestrales et pratiquent jusqu'à présent de nombreux rites traditionnels et coutumiers qui accompagnent les événements de la vie : naissance, mariage, funérailles, rites d'initiation et rites expiatoires et de protection comme le *basga*[4] dans le village.

À Kuila l'analphabétisme touche 66,5 % de la population.[5] Au niveau des activités socio-économiques menées, on a affaire à une agriculture d'autosubsistance peu productive et peu diversifiée. Les cultures de rente sont peu développées et celle maraîchère souffre des problèmes d'eau. L'élevage associé à l'agriculture se réduit dans la plupart des cas aux petits ruminants et à la volaille exception faite de quelques propriétaires de gros bétail. L'artisanat et le petit commerce sont pratiqués dans le village sans une renommée particulière. Le tra-

---

[3] Cf. Institut National de la Statistique et de la Démographie, INSD 1998. L'importance de la religion catholique à Kuila pourrait s'expliquer par le fait qu'il constitue un village mitoyen de Guilingou où l'église catholique se trouve implantée depuis le temps colonial.

[4] Le *basga* (en langue mooré) est une cérémonie coutumière qui intervient après les récoltes en guise de remerciement aux ancêtres et à la nature pour avoir accordé des pluies pour la saison agricole.

[5] Cf. Institut National de la Statistique et de la Démographie, INSD 1998.

vail salarié est quasi inexistant au village de même que les myriades de petits métiers très frappants dans les villes africaines.

Kuila fait partie des zones de fort peuplement et de pression démographique sur les terres cultivables : les bonnes terres font l'objet de convoitise et de disputes. Aussi le village n'échappe pas au phénomène de migration de ses fils. D'une manière générale, chez les Moose l'exode rural est une tradition et a souvent drainé les bras valides hors des villages en ne laissant que les femmes, les enfants et les personnes âgées. En effet la proportion des personnes âgées de 55 ans et plus s'élevait à 13,6 % de la population totale de Kuila. Ce qui est supérieur à la moyenne nationale de 8,88 %.[6] On pourrait attribuer cette surreprésentation de la population âgée au phénomène migratoire.

Si Kuila est un village où les forces sociales traditionnelles sont encore fortes, cela ne signifie pas que les populations ne sont pas confrontées à la modernité. En témoignent les enfants scolarisés ou bien des nouvelles valeurs comme l'individualisme qui s'infiltrent dans le village (cf. aussi Marie 1997). À Kuila on rencontre des jeunes plus fortunés que des anciens et des hommes du village plus riches que le chef.

À Kuila les riches et les individus de couche moyenne ont à manger pendant que les pauvres regardent. Certes sur le terrain il n'est pas toujours aisé de faire la distinction entre la couche moyenne et celle des pauvres. Nous nous sommes reportées à quelques indices visibles pour la classification. Appartiendraient à la couche moyenne les personnes disposant de moyens plus ou moins modernes de travail de la terre (charrue, bœuf, âne) et utilisation de techniques modernes de production (semis en ligne, engrais, fumure, semences sélectionnées). Les riches du village comptent en outre un troupeau de bétail. Les revenus agricoles dépendent de la pluviométrie mais sont énormément influencés par l'exploitation de ces moyens techniques de travail. Pour les experts locaux, la quantité de récoltes que l'on peut en tirer peut aller du simple au double, voire plus en fonction de ces possibilités. En nous référant à ces critères, seule une minorité relève de la couche

---

[6] Cf. Ministère de l'Action Sociale et de la Solidarité Nationale (2001 : 9-10).

moyenne à Kuila. Pour les enquêtés, la couche moyenne concerne ceux qui sont à l'abri des insécurités alimentaires, ceux qui ont des greniers pleins de récoltes avec des réserves des années antérieures, signe qu'ils arrivent à couvrir les besoins de leur famille en céréales pendant la période de soudure. La couche moyenne accède à des biens de consommation modernes : mobylettes, maisons en tôles, habillement moderne,[7] l'alimentation avec des produits comme le pain, le lait, les bouillons cube dans les sauces, les pâtes alimentaires, la boisson de fabrication industrielle. Au sein de cette couche on observe le recours au dispensaire ou à la maternité pour des soins. Chez les jeunes de couche moyenne notamment, une valeur est accordée à la monogamie et au libre choix du conjoint.

La couche des pauvres concerne ceux qui sont toujours réduits à assurer la production agricole avec des moyens rudimentaires tels que la houe *(daba)* et qui n'arrivent pas à obtenir des récoltes suffisantes pour toute l'année. Pendant les périodes de soudure, ils doivent acheter des céréales en petite quantité et au jour le jour pour la consommation familiale à des coûts relativement plus chers. Si l'élevage est pratiqué par cette catégorie de personnes il s'agit alors du petit élevage. Les individus en situation de précarité sont ceux qui, avec des récoltes insuffisantes et à défaut d'argent pour s'adresser au marché, sont dans l'obligation de solliciter l'aide d'autrui ou d'emprunter des céréales pour assurer la survie de la famille pendant la période de soudure. Sur les quarante-quatre personnes âgées (hommes et femmes) auprès desquelles des entretiens approfondis ont été réalisés, trente et une appartiennent à la couche des pauvres[8]. À titre illustratif sur les

---

[7] Le plus souvent, il s'agit d'habits de second usage appelés « au revoir l'Europe ».
[8] Une catégorisation des pauvres peut-être faite en trois groupes, 1. les pauvres, 2. ceux qui vivent dans la précarité et 3. ceux qui sont socialement marginalisés (cf. Roth 2003a) : sur les 44 enquêtés 31 sont pauvres.
a. sur les 31 pauvres, 28 (soit 90 %) ont un repas par jour, ils vivent dans une sécurité fragile.
b. sur les 31 pauvres, 11 (soit 35 %) connaissent des jours sans repas, ils vivent dans la précarité
c. sur les 31 pauvres, 4 (soit env. 13 %) ont recours aux institutions pour demander des vivres, ils vivent socialement marginalisés.
Par conséquent, sur les 31 pauvres, 15 (soit 48 %) vivent dans la précarité ou bien socialement marginalisés.

trente et un pauvres, vingt-huit soit plus de 90 % de cette catégorie sont réduites à un seul repas chaud par jour – généralement le soir. Une dizaine de la couche des pauvres exprime une situation de précarité : ils déclarent qu'il y a même des jours sans repas et où l'on se contente de grignoter. Les conditions de logement demeurent aussi précaires même si les intéressés sont des propriétaires. Les personnes âgées pauvres occupent des cases en argile plus ou moins délabrées, dorment à même le sol sur une natte ou sur de simples cartons ou chiffons. La maison en tôles caresse leurs rêves et elles souhaitent pouvoir y dormir avant de mourir. Les conditions d'habillement ne sont pas meilleures : haillons, habits de second usage ou torse nu à longueur de journée. Quant aux conditions de soins, elles semblent plus préoccupantes. La plupart n'ont pas accès aux soins modernes et quelques-uns refusent même ces soins. Les dons en argent aux personnes âgées sont des plus rares et concernent des sommes infimes : 100 FCFA (0.15 €).[9] Ces personnes âgées font-elles l'objet de soutien familial et communautaire ?

L'écart entre idées et pratiques de soutien familial

Pour les femmes et les hommes âgés de Kuila, la famille est d'abord un cadre de vie, d'appartenance et de référence. C'est en son sein que se définissent et s'organisent les rapports entre conjoints, entre parents et enfants, entre générations, que se prennent les décisions importantes concernant les membres, que s'exprime et se réalise la satisfaction de leurs besoins essentiels. De nos jours et dans le contexte rural burkinabé de Kuila, la conception de la famille comme garante de la sécurité sociale de ses membres demeure toujours forte. Pour les personnes âgées interrogées, intégrées au sein des cellules familiales, leurs relations de sécurité et de soutien s'organisent essentiellement à travers les relations de parenté. Pour ces enquêtés, être parent « c'est être sensible aux problèmes de l'autre et le secourir ». Ce qui signifie que si d'un côté on peut tout attendre de la parenté : aide, secours, assistance, de l'autre on a le devoir et l'obligation d'aider le parent dans le be-

---

[9] 1 € = 655.95 FCFA (francs CFA).

soin. De façon générale dans l'imagerie populaire, l'assistance aux membres de la famille est perçue comme une obligation incontournable (Eloundou-Enyegue 1992 : 8). « L'obligation d'aider le parent » dans son application introduit des règles de réciprocité, de « don contre don » qui indiquent que l'individu qui reçoit une aide contracte une dette sociale car il doit s'attendre un jour à rembourser cette dette d'une manière ou d'une autre. Pour matérialiser la réciprocité, nos enquêtés évoquent le proverbe moaga qui dit que « la parenté est un morceau de bois qui mérite de rester en contact avec l'autre pour garder le foyer de la parenté allumé », ce qui signifie que la parenté exige d'être entretenue et s'entretient grâce aux échanges réguliers qui s'opèrent.

La garantie d'un minimum de sécurité sociale repose sur la capacité de l'individu à se prendre en charge. Pouvoir compter sur soi-même d'abord est signe d'une relative autonomie et la base du soutien familial. « Lorsqu'on vous lave le dos il faut pouvoir vous laver le visage » dit un autre proverbe moaga. Dans la même optique, Vuarin (2000 : 39-40) parle de la valorisation de la prise en charge de soi et fait remarquer que « le soutien des autres ait comme première condition les efforts que tente la victime pour saisir la tête du lion : aide toi, les autres t'aideront ! »

À Kuila, on estime que la vieillesse se prépare tout au long de la vie active. Tout adulte doit être prévoyant et travailler sans relâche en songeant à ses vieux jours. Dans la pratique la préparation de la vieillesse est rendue difficile pour les pauvres en raison de l'étroitesse des ressources. Les revenus tirés du travail de la terre ne permettent pas de couvrir le minimum des besoins quotidiens des personnes âgées pauvres. Celles-ci évaluent leurs récoltes à dix ou quinze sacs de mil à peine pour nourrir toute l'année une famille d'une dizaine de personnes alors qu'il en faudrait le double pour honorer deux repas par jour. Malgré le poids de l'âge, vieux et vieilles, à l'exception des handicapés ou grabataires, gardent leurs champs et y travaillent avec l'aide des enfants pour le défrichage et le labour ; le champ du patriarche étant considéré comme le champ familial. L'élevage représente la principale source d'épargne, notamment pour les hommes mais se résume chez les pauvres aux poulets, pintades et dans le meilleur des cas à des ovins, caprins ou porcins. Chez les femmes l'épargne se fait à travers les ustensiles de cuisine, les bijoux, les pagnes traditionnels ; des objets d'ailleurs en perte de valeur aujourd'hui.

Historiquement, les travaux forcés du temps colonial ont pu influencer négativement la vie de ces personnes âgées interrogées. Certains d'entre elles ont eu à confectionner des routes, à travailler dans des plantations sans obtenir la moindre compensation aujourd'hui. Les migrations ont été développées depuis ce temps colonial et le Moaga, considéré comme un « gros travailleur », a beaucoup intéressé le colonisateur. Depuis lors le processus s'est poursuivi avec pour mobile la recherche du numéraire. Mais avec la crise économique galopante, la migration n'est plus synonyme de réussite et certains migrants âgés sont revenus bredouille au village suite aux exactions.[10]

En somme, la capacité de se prendre en charge des personnes âgées pauvres à Kuila est limitée en raison du poids du quotidien sur les ressources, de la faiblesse de l'épargne et des investissements. L'extrême pauvreté est synonyme d'imprévoyance car la vie se déroule au jour le jour et le présent pèse sur l'avenir. Pour la majorité des femmes et des hommes de Kuila, l'insécurité sociale est un fait caractéristique de leur quotidien. Pour ainsi dire ils souffrent de la faim toute leur vie et sont manifestement dans le besoin de soutien dans leur vieil âge. Le soutien familial passe par différents types de relations familiales telles que les relations conjugales, intergénérationnelles et celles au sein de la famille étendue. Par la suite, nous allons élaborer l'écart entre les idées et les pratiques de soutien familial à Kuila.

Les relations conjugales entre paradis et enfer

Les relations conjugales se veulent des relations sécurisantes dans le vieil âge à travers le respect social, le soutien mutuel et le partage du travail. Vis-à-vis de la société, le mariage garantit à l'homme et à la femme un statut social qui inspire le respect. À Kuila rares sont les personnes âgées qui ne se sont pas mariées. Les veufs se remarient

---

[10] Conséquences de la guerre en Côte d'Ivoire depuis l'année 2000.

systématiquement ou ont déjà d'autres épouses en raison de la polygamie. Les divorcés sont peu nombreux et le système de lévirat[11] replace les veuves quel que soit leur âge dans les circuits du mariage
(même si quelquefois il s'agit d'un mari symbolique ou la veuve a
pour époux désigné un enfant du lignage). Cette pratique encore en
cours de nos jours (sur les quarante-quatre enquêtés six veuves sont
dans le cas) permet aux veuves de rester dans la belle-famille et de ne
pas faire l'objet de pression sociale, de suspicion, d'accusations graves entraînant parfois marginalisation et exclusion sociale. Toujours
dans les conceptions le mariage répond à une nécessité sociale.
« Vieillir sans mariage c'est mourir sans funérailles », déclare un
vieux d'environ quatre-vingt ans, de couche moyenne. Plus qu'une
union entre deux individus, le mariage est celle entre deux familles,
entre deux lignées et forme un réseau supplémentaire de relations sociales à travers lequel se tissent aussi des relations d'assistance et de
soutien. « C'est toujours un système d'échange que nous trouvons à
l'origine des règles du mariage » (Zimmermann 1972 : 39).

Sous un autre angle le mariage induit des obligations sociales :
mari et femme se doivent secours et assistance. À travers les devoirs
conjugaux les charges et les responsabilités se trouvent partagées et le
fait que chacun joue sa partition est source de sécurité pour l'autre.
Pour la consommation familiale, le chef de famille est chargé de fournir les céréales et la femme les différents condiments. Au-delà du
soutien matériel, l'assistance morale et sociale est fortement ap-
préciée. Les conjoints doivent se soutenir mutuellement. Selon les
propos d'une vieille femme de couche moyenne : « Les vieux charo-
gnards se becquettent ... Avec l'âge nous causons de plus en plus ensemble ce qui n'était pas faisable dans le temps. Nous échangeons nos
idées. Ça aide à passer le temps et à combattre la solitude et l'idée de
la mort. Ça aide à vivre. » Si ces propos ne sont pas à généraliser,
nous avons tout de même là un signe d'élévation du statut de la
femme avec l'âge.

---

[11] Lévirat : obligation faite par la coutume au frère d'un défunt d'épouser la veuve
de celui-ci.

Dans la pratique, le mariage devient source d'insécurité lorsque se multiplient les conflits conjugaux ou avec la belle-famille. Le cas des veuves qui veulent se soustraire du lévirat au village est suffisamment évocateur des conflits avec la belle-famille. Une de nos enquêtées de 58 ans, de la couche des pauvres, raconte : « Je dois désormais me prendre en charge, élever pratiquement seule mes enfants, le dernier étant né en 1990. Mes problèmes n'intéressent plus tellement la famille de mon mari. Lorsqu'il y a un événement social dans ma propre famille personne n'est disponible. Tout cela parce que j'ai refusé de rester chez le frère de mon mari défunt. » Et lorsque les responsabilités familiales ne sont pas assumées comme l'exige la norme sociale, l'équilibre du foyer est menacé. Surtout si le chef de famille n'arrive pas à fournir la quantité de céréales nécessaire pour la consommation familiale, il est socialement perçu comme un vaurien (cf. exemple 6). Mais le plus souvent la femme évite de crier sur tous les toits cette défaillance du mari même si elle en souffre. Aussi chez les Moose, l'honneur de l'épouse consiste à couvrir l'incapacité de son mari et à prendre ses devoirs en main à sa place – tacitement. C'est un des secrets du mariage – un *furugundo*[12] (cf. Roth 2003a : 21). Chez les Moose la femme valorisée est la « femme muette » qui sait taire les difficultés du foyer et encaisser. En fait les femmes enquêtées disent toutes qu'il n'y a pas de foyer idéal, il faut surtout savoir y rester. C'est en cela que l'on peut considérer le fait que des hommes âgés comptent sur des jeunes épouses qui travaillent activement dans leurs champs comme une stratégie pour ne pas manquer de céréales (c'est le cas de ce couple où le mari a près de soixante-dix ans et l'épouse vingt-six). Les femmes se retournent vers leur famille d'origine pour solliciter une aide même si cela est socialement dévalorisant. D'un autre côté, la polygamie toujours pratiquée dans le milieu (16 cas sur 44)[13] est considérée comme source de sécurité aussi bien pour les hommes que pour les femmes. Aux hommes, elle leur procure des

---

[12] Un secret du mariage en dioula : *furugundo*, en mooré : *ya banguin zindi*.

[13] 7 cas de polygamie sur 13 au sein de la couche moyenne et 9 sur 31 chez les pauvres même si on a une forte proportion de catholiques où la religion prône la monogamie.

bras pour travailler dans les champs. Aux femmes, elle leur permet de diminuer la charge des corvées domestiques. En revanche la polygamie est de plus en plus source de conflits conjugaux et entre co-épouses, tensions qui se répercutent sur les enfants. À ce titre, la polygamie pose plus de problèmes qu'elle n'en résout. De façon générale, si le mariage procure la sécurité il a un coût social que mari et femme ont à payer. Le mari doit mériter son statut de chef de famille en assumant les charges familiales (nourriture surtout) et l'épouse doit entretenir la maisonnée, accepter de se soumettre et savoir sauver l'honneur de son mari.

Soutien dans le vieil âge : les relations intergénérationnelles

Les relations intergénérationnelles représentent le centre de gravité de la sécurité sociale des personnes âgées pauvres en raison du contrat entre les générations qui traduit cet accord plus ou moins tacite de prise en charge, entre aînés et cadets et principalement entre parents et enfants. D'après les conceptions, la progéniture constitue le premier soutien dans le viel âge. La richesse du pauvre est sa progéniture, dit-on au village. Chez les Moose le contrat entre les générations semble relever de l'ordre des choses. « Tu mets l'enfant au monde, tu t'occupes de lui jusqu'à ce que ses dents poussent dans l'espoir qu'il s'occupera de toi jusqu'à ce que tu perdes les tiennes», selon le proverbe. En d'autres termes, les parents s'occupent des enfants depuis leur naissance et en retour ces derniers doivent s'occuper des parents jusqu'à la mort. Une notion de solidarité intergénérationnelle, de réciprocité, de devoir mutuel et de dette existe entre parents et enfants. Ainsi, il revient aux jeunes de pourvoir aux besoins des personnes âgées qui en retour doivent leur prodiguer des conseils, des bénédictions pour leur réussite sociale et partager avec eux leur expérience, leur sagesse et les secrets de la vie.

Dans la pratique, à Kuila le contrat entre les générations est maintenu dans la majorité des cas (36 cas sur 44). Cependant, il affiche de sérieuses limites quant à la satisfaction des besoins élémentaires des personnes âgées pauvres. Ces personnes âgées des villages vivent en majorité dans une insécurité alimentaire prononcée comme expliqué plus haut à propos des conditions de vie des femmes et des hommes de la couche des pauvres à Kuila. Aussi bien dans la conception que dans la pratique, l'exemple de Jean Michel (exemple 1) révèle l'importance du contrat entre les générations.

Exemple 1 : La vie en sécurité de Jean Michel

Jean Michel est né vers 1940 à Kuila. À l'ouverture de l'école de Guilingou, un village voisin, ses parents l'y avaient inscrit, mais, au regard des conditions bien difficiles de fréquentation, Jean Michel a préféré fuir l'école pour se rendre chez ses oncles maternels à Zitenga non loin de Kuila. De Zitenga il a continué sur Ouagadougou avant d'entamer son aventure à l'extérieur du pays. Parti en Côte d'Ivoire en 1961 en quête d'une meilleure fortune, Jean Michel a d'abord travaillé dans une plantation de bananes pour un salaire de 4000 FCFA (6 €) par mois. Travail jugé peu rentable, il a ensuite essayé la maçonnerie qu'il abandonna pour la débrouillardise. Revenu pour une première fois au village en 1966, Jean Michel a regagné définitivement Kuila en 1973 et s'est marié en 1974, puis s'est remis au travail de la terre. Il confectionnait également des briques, s'adonnait au ramassage de vieilles chaussures pour les revendre à Ouagadougou. Mais petit à petit la vieillesse s'est installée. Jean Michel ne perçoit pas une autre assurance vieillesse que le soutien émanant de sa progéniture. « Ce sont ceux que tu as mis au monde qui vont d'abord s'occuper de toi. Quelqu'un d'autre du lignage peut t'aider mais ce sera toujours occasionnel. » Et Jean Michel dit : « Tout ce qu'on fait pour les enfants quand ils sont petits c'est pour que, une fois devenus grands, ils puissent à leur tour s'occuper de nous jusqu'à la fin de nos jours. » Père de six enfants, Jean Michel estime que ses quatre fils l'aident dans les travaux des champs. Le fils aîné et sa sœur par contre résident chez une tante à Ouagadougou où ils allaient à l'école. À défaut d'argent pour poursuivre la scolarité, le fils est au chômage depuis deux ans. La fille pour sa part a fait l'alphabétisation en langue mooré mais sans suite. « J'ai appris qu'elle vit présentement chez un copain gourounsi[14] à Ouaga que je ne connais pas. » Obtenir de l'argent pose problème, dit Jean Michel. Ni lui, ni sa femme, ni leurs enfants n'en possèdent. Parfois il leur est difficile de trouver ne serait-ce qu'une pièce de 100 FCFA (0.15 €). Un des fils garde le troupeau d'un des frères aînés de Jean Michel. Il lui aurait donné quelques chèvres en récompense. « Quand nous avons de sérieuses difficultés comme un problème de santé, je fais vendre une chèvre (7000 à 10'000 FCFA ou 10 à 15 €) pour résoudre le problème. » La cour de Jean Michel comprend des cases rondes, un hangar et des greniers en paille. Il n'y a pas de maison en tôles mais en dépit de tout cela, il ne se considère pas pauvre. « Le pauvre,

---

[14] Gourounsi : une des ethnies du Burkina Faso.

c'est celui qui n'a pas d'enfants et qui est obligé de compter sur les enfants d'autrui », fait-il remarquer.

Le récit de Jean Michel (exemple 1) montre que le contrat entre les générations peut fonctionner malgré de nombreuses limites. Le soutien des enfants à l'endroit des parents se veut le plus déterminant pour la sécurité dans le vieil âge. Seulement voilà : en la matière, même l'enfant le plus consciencieux ne peut donner à ses parents que ce qu'il a.

Handicapée, la personne âgée est encore plus dépendante de sa famille et de sa progéniture comme l'illustre l'histoire de Tinga (exemple 2). Aveugle de surcroît, Tinga a toujours besoin d'aide pour se déplacer ou pour obtenir la nourriture. Sa femme et ses enfants se sentent obligés de l'entretenir. « Il nous a mis au monde », dit le fils aîné.

Exemple 2 : (In)sécurité dans le vieil âge liée au handicap
Tinga est né à Kuila il a un peu plus de soixante-dix ans. Il a toujours connu le travail de la terre, l'élevage de petits ruminants et de volaille. Lorsqu'il était beaucoup plus jeune, il avait fait un séjour d'une année au Ghana dans les plantations de cacao mais depuis son retour, il n'a plus jamais quitté Kuila. Tinga se dit animiste et attache une grande importance aux cultes des ancêtres. A son avis, rien ne peut effacer totalement la tradition. Tinga fut polygame et avait deux femmes dont l'une est décédée. Il a également perdu beaucoup d'enfants, une dizaine, raconte-t-il. Aujourd'hui, outre son épouse, il lui reste trois fils et une fille. Ces fils lui ont donné six petits-enfants. Aucun membre de sa famille n'a eu la chance d'aller à l'école. Tinga est aveugle depuis près de vingt-cinq ans et, concrètement, il est à la charge de sa famille. « C'est ma femme et mes fils qui s'occupent de moi mais ils sont malheureusement très démunis. Je me contente du minimum qu'ils parviennent à faire pour moi. Je suis invalide et je ne peux plus cultiver. Ce sont eux qui s'occupent des champs pour nous procurer à manger et de tout le reste. Par moments je tresse des cordes que les enfants revendent au marché mais c'est pour tantôt 100 à 200 francs (0.3 €). Ils confectionnent eux-mêmes des briques en saison sèche et les revendent pour assurer les petits besoins de la famille. » Voisins et amis pensent de temps en temps à lui et lui rendent visite. Certains lui apportent de la noix de cola, du tabac ou de la bière de mil *(dolo)*. Pour ces derniers, Tinga est un des anciens du village et il mérite des honneurs. La mission distribue de temps en temps des vivres aux nécessiteux et aux handicapés et par le passé, Tinga en avait bénéficié mais c'était occasionnel. Aux dernières nouvelles, Tinga est décédé en mars 2004.

Donc 36 sur 44 hommes et femmes âgées à Kuila sont soutenus par leurs enfants ; parmi les pauvres, ce sont 29 sur 31. Comparée à la situation urbaine de Bobo-Dioulasso, on peut dire que le contrat intergénérationnel est pratiqué. Certains fils disent qu'ils aimeraient faire davantage et mieux soutenir les parents, mais ne peuvent le faire par manque d'argent. Leur contribution se limite aux travaux des champs. Dans 13[15] cas sur 44, belles-filles et petits-enfants habitent chez les personnes âgées, ce sont des cas de force majeure qui se rencontrent de plus en plus : décès ou départ à l'aventure d'un fils. Les belles-filles et petits-enfants travaillent dans le champ familial. « Le contrat entre les générations à l'envers » lié au chômage des jeunes – très frappant à Bobo-Dioulasso (cf. Roth dans ce volume) – est plus exceptionnel à Kuila : quatre cas sur quarante-quatre, dont trois relèvent de la couche moyenne. Cela s'explique par le fait qu'au village, la terre est gérée par les aînés comme autrefois et que le travail de la terre et l'organisation sociale moaga responsabilisent très tôt les jeunes en leur donnant un champ personnel à cultiver. Dans les faits, les familles regorgent de plus en plus des brebis galeuses qui soutiennent très peu ou pas du tout les parents âgés. Il s'agit des jeunes qui renient le travail de la terre, comme les quatre cas mentionnés de « contrat à l'envers ». Certains dépouillent les parents en leur volant chèvres, moutons et volaille pour les revendre au marché où ils passent ensuite tout leur temps à consommer bière de mil et brochettes. Ce qui est source de vives tensions entre parents et enfants. Au cours des entretiens de groupe, on nous a cité le cas de ce vieux à Kuila qui a poignardé son propre fils en 2001 alors que ce dernier tentait de lui voler une chèvre la nuit. Obsédés par les biens de consommation modernes, ces jeunes ne craignent plus les forces magiques des vieux et cherchent à obtenir de l'argent par tous les moyens.

Exemple 3 : « Le contrat à l'envers » selon le vieux Benoît

Pour le vieux Benoît né à Kuila en 1939, de couche moyenne et père de neuf enfants, le contrat à l'envers est aussi au village une réalité. Il parle de ses propres expériences. Un de ses fils est allé au collège à Ouagadougou et Benoît a eu à

---

[15] Sur ces 13 personnes, 9 comptent sur d'autres enfants qui les soutiennent.

dépenser 60'000 FCFA (env. 92 €) pour sa scolarité. Pendant toute l'année, l'intéressé a fait l'école buissonnière et à la fin, il n'a pas réussi. Actuellement, il est à Ouagadougou et ne lui rend même pas visite car il redoute sa colère.

De l'avis du vieux Benoît, ce que veulent les enfants aujourd'hui est différent de ce que souhaitent les vieux : « Ils n'acceptent pas le travail de la terre, ils fument la cigarette, consomment de l'alcool et jouent au baby-foot. Les jeunes d'aujourd'hui ne s'occupent plus des vieux mais plutôt de leur propre ventre. Ce n'est que quand ils ont un problème qu'ils se tournent vers toi. Aussi certains fils, une fois qu'ils ont pris femme, ne se préoccupent plus de leur père mais uniquement de leur femme. Mais il y a pire », dit-il, « quand les enfants souhaitent ta mort pour hériter et jouir de tous tes biens sans avoir trimé. » Selon le vieux Benoît « on met les enfants au monde aujourd'hui uniquement pour libérer ses entrailles ».

L'opinion du vieux Benoît (exemple 3) est partagée par beaucoup de vieux, hommes comme femmes. Si on regarde les chiffres de notre échantillon concernant Kuila, une vingtaine de personnes l'affirment. Il faut souligner qu'il s'agit encore d'un « discours de négligence » (Cattell 1997), et non d'un fait répandu au village.

Soutien différentiel par fils et filles : l'arbre a souvent caché la forêt

À Kuila, les générations cohabitent les unes avec les autres et on peut retrouver trois ou quatre générations dans une même concession.[16] La virilocalité fait en sorte que les fils mariés s'installent aux côtés du père contribuant ainsi à la perpétuation de la famille et au soutien pratique : travaux dans les champs, courses, assistance morale – ce qui rend plus visible le soutien des fils. Toutefois, la cohabitation ne garantit pas toujours la prise en charge des personnes âgées. L'atomisation des champs – chaque fils marié dispose de son propre champ dans le milieu – fait en sorte que certains fils travaillent de moins en moins au compte des parents âgés. Il arrive que les fils mangent sans partager leur repas avec les parents âgés. Dans ces cas, en plus du plat

---

[16] 11 cas sur 13 dans la couche moyenne et 19 cas sur 31 dans celle des pauvres. Traditionnellement cette cohabitation est un signe de richesses et de prestige. En effet, la richesse se mesurait aussi à travers le nombre de personnes que l'on a sous sa responsabilité et sa dépendance. On comprend aisément que moins de pauvres vivent dans un foyer comptant plusieurs générations.

familial, de petits plats améliorés (avec de la viande dans la sauce) sont consommés parallèlement par les jeunes sans qu'ils partagent avec les vieux. Certains vont manger de bonnes choses au marché pendant que les personnes âgées vont se coucher affamées (5 cas sur 31 chez les pauvres). Ces cas peuvent être considérés comme des cas manifestes de négligence à l'égard des personnes âgées.

Les filles pour leur part sont appelées à se marier en dehors du village et à ne revenir que de façon occasionnelle. Dans les conceptions, leur soutien est moins visible car le plus souvent occasionnel. Mais dans la pratique les personnes âgées reconnaissent de plus en plus l'importante contribution des filles à leur sécurité sociale. Certaines envoient des vivres, de l'argent et divers cadeaux. Lorsqu'elles reviennent au village, elles remplacent leurs mères dans les corvées domestiques. À Kuila, les filles soutiennent leurs parents avec l'appui de leur époux. Avec les mariages arrangés par les familles, la tradition impose aux gendres des devoirs et l'obligation d'entretenir les beaux-parents pendant leur vieil âge. C'est ce qui fait dire chez les Moose « que l'on met au monde une fille pour l'échanger contre un fils » en parlant du gendre.

Dans la pratique, des différences existent au niveau du soutien accordé par les enfants au père ou à la mère. En milieu traditionnel moaga, l'aide matérielle apportée par les enfants au père se veut généralement plus substantielle que celle réservée à la mère. Cela se confirme à travers les propos recueillis lors des entretiens. D'ores et déjà, les normes et les principes sociaux veulent que le soutien accordé par les enfants et surtout lorsqu'il est d'une certaine importance passe par le père. Cette pratique aurait tendance à rendre inférieur ou égal le soutien de la mère à celui du père. Dans les faits des aides ou cadeaux cachés existent de façon circonstancielle pour les mères. En plus, au-delà des capacités affectives des enfants, leurs capacités matérielles et financières peuvent influencer les rapports de soutien aux parents. Il arrive qu'un enfant qui gagne assez soutienne aussi sa marâtre, en plus de sa propre mère. Ceux qui ont plus de moyens peuvent donner plus à la marâtre que les propres enfants de l'intéressée.

En conclusion on peut dire que, selon le genre, le soutien des enfants a tendance à défavoriser les mères par rapport aux pères.

Faute d'enfants : la famille étendue, le voisinage, l'amitié

Au village, la notion de famille ou de parenté demeure très large et va au-delà des familles nucléaires pour englober les collatéraux et autres membres du lignage, voir de la belle-famille. Le soutien de la famille étendue se veut circonstanciel ou d'appoint et se fait le plus sentir lors des événements sociaux. Les rituels sont des occasions de rassemblements familiaux : mariage, baptême mais surtout funérailles où la famille des deux lignées sont toujours conviées et ne manquent pas d'exprimer leur solidarité à travers des échanges-dons. À des occasions comme les funérailles des règles de contribution symbolique existent. À titre d'exemple, chaque gendre doit fournir une chèvre ou un mouton, un coq, un canari de bière de mil (*dolo*) et des noix de cola pour les cérémonies coutumières des funérailles d'un beau-père. Ces cérémonies et sacrifices sont généralement gérés par les anciens du lignage. Au-delà des événements sociaux, le soutien de la famille étendue intervient dans le quotidien de certaines personnes âgées face à certaines circonstances. Au village, les personnes âgées qui n'ont pas eu d'enfant ou qui n'ont plus de progéniture sont à la charge de la famille étendue, à la différence de ce qui s'observe en ville.

Exemple 4 : La veuve Tennoaga – soutenue par la famille étendue
Tennoaga est née vers 1930 à Guieoghin Tinga, un village non loin de Kuila. Non scolarisée, son activité était l'agriculture en saison pluvieuse, la fabrication et la vente de bière de mil (*dolo*) et de beurre de karité en saison sèche. Mariée à l'âge de dix-sept ans, elle est veuve depuis une vingtaine d'années. Avec ses deux coépouses, elles sont restées dans la cour conjugale au sein du lignage (*buudu*). Seule la quatrième et plus jeune épouse de son mari s'est remariée avec un des fils préféré du vieux en raison du lévirat. Tennoaga a eu au total sept enfants mais toute sa progéniture a été rappelée à Dieu un à un. Les deux derniers à mourir étaient les aînés en 1995 et en 2001. Elle n'a plus que ses sept petits-enfants. Tennoaga se sent orpheline de ses enfants : « Si j'avais mes sept enfants, ma vie serait agréable et aurait un sens. Mais en leur absence je ne peux pas être heureuse. Quand on vieillit sans enfant, c'est un malheur. Qui va s'occuper de vous ? Qui va rester auprès de vous ? »

Ce sont en fait les fils et belles-filles du lignage *(buudu)* qui assurent le quotidien de Tennoaga. À la question de savoir qui s'occupe d'elle aujourd'hui, un long silence a suivi, puis un profond soupir, et après elle nous dit : « Dans la concession, les femmes me servent à manger et quand j'ai besoin de noix de cola ou de tabac les jeunes m'en achètent. C'est tout. » Et après un temps de silence elle conclut : « Oui – on s'occupe de moi ! »

Tennoaga continue à travailler. À chaque première pluie, elle sort comme tout le monde, utilise le peu de force qui lui reste pour travailler son petit lopin de terre avec une houe *(daba)* toute aussi usée par le temps. À la fin de la saison, elle ne tire pas grand chose comme récolte : quelques paniers de sorgho et de petit mil, des arachides et du haricot et surtout des feuilles comme réserves de condiments. Pour ses besoins d'argent Tennoaga se débrouille. Son fils aîné lui avait confié quelques chèvres de son vivant. De temps en temps elle fait vendre une chèvre pour satisfaire ses petits besoins. Les membres de sa famille d'origine lui rendent visite mais surtout au gré des cérémonies. Ils lui apportent des noix de cola, du tabac et quelque fois du mil ou un peu d'argent comme 100 ou 200 FCFA (0.3 €) mais sans plus. Du côté des voisins – ce sont en fait les frères de son mari défunt et leurs femmes et enfants – Tennoaga reçoit occasionnellement des mets ou plats traditionnels ou des vivres mais en petite quantité, par exemple deux kilos.

Les associations dans le village ne sont pas son affaire. « C'est l'affaire des plus jeunes et de ceux qui peuvent encore espérer quelque chose de ce monde », dit-elle. Elle se souvient par contre avoir bénéficié deux fois de suite d'une aide de la mission catholique, consistant en quelques plats de céréales.

Dans le quartier les autres membres du lignage lui font quelquefois des gestes mais elle se garde de les solliciter. Solliciter de l'aide de sa part serait interprété comme si on ne s'occupait pas d'elle au sein de la famille directe. Aussi dit-elle : « Si tu pars régulièrement solliciter les gens, on finit par t'accuser de certaines choses. Il suffit qu'un enfant tombe malade quelque part pour qu'on te soupçonne d'en être la cause ou d'être au courant. Mieux vaut rester tranquille dans ta case. »[17] Dans la vie sociale Tennoaga a tendance à s'isoler, ayant perdu tous ses enfants, elle a peur d'être traitée de sorcière : « J'évite les causeries de peur des paroles blessantes ou vexantes. Toujours cloîtrée, je passe mon temps entre ma case et l'ombre des hangars, des murs ou des karités. » Tennoaga vit pratiquement sans besoins ex-

---

[17] De façon implicite Tennoaga fait ici allusion aux accusations de sorcellerie à l'endroit des vieilles femmes toujours d'actualité à Kuila. Quatre cas d'accusation étaient en instance de traitement chez le chef en 2002. Les intéressées, souvent des vieilles femmes, sont considérées comme des « mangeuses d'âmes ». Victimes d'exclusion sociale, elles finissent par mourir toutes seules dans leur case si elles ne sont pas chassées du village. Les services de l'Action Sociale à Ziniaré nous ont notifié un ou deux cas à gérer en moyenne par trimestre et le Centre Delwendé de Tanghin à Ouagadougou accueillait sept femmes du Département de Ziniaré en 2001.

primés ou plutôt avec des besoins refoulés. Elle se contente de ce qu'on lui donne. Elle dit n'avoir plus ni faim, ni soif, ni sommeil. Son ventre et son cœur sont remplis de « pensées » et de « souffrances ». En mooré, elle a employé le terme *sountoogo*[18]. Elle compte sur le lignage de son mari pour bénéficier de funérailles qui l'aideront à rejoindre ses ancêtres et ses enfants dans l'au-delà.

Il faut dire que sur le Plateau central moaga, le phénomène de la sorcellerie est très redouté par les personnes âgées, notamment les pauvres. En effet, les accusations portent le plus souvent sur des personnes démunies, sans soutien et sans défense comme les vieilles femmes esseulées, sans enfant. Selon le proverbe moaga : « Personne n'osera accuser la mère du chef d'être sorcière. » Si le phénomène de la sorcellerie relève des croyances ancestrales, n'est-il pas dans les faits une conséquence de l'appauvrissement de l'individu ? Devant l'insuffisance des ressources, il constitue un moyen de se débarrasser de la charge, du poids social que constitue la personne incriminée. Par ce biais on légitime la non-assistance vis-à-vis d'elle.

Sous le poids de l'âge, Tennoaga (exemple 4) ne se suffit plus à elle-même. Elle est nourrie par la progéniture de ses coépouses. Seulement, le minimum des besoins de base est loin d'être couvert. Le soutien de la communauté villageoise, s'il n'est pas totalement inexistant, demeure exceptionnel et tout aussi limité. Tennoaga est surtout en marge, et hors du circuit de la solidarité du patron, de l'État, de la société civile et de l'aide internationale. Nous avons là un exemple de soutien familial à la personne âgée et, aussi minime soit-il, on se demande ce que serait devenue Tennoaga, perdue dans ce village, sans ce soutien familial ?

Le lévirat est traditionnellement un mécanisme de sécurité sociale pour les veuves mais de plus en plus de veuves et d'orphelins se trouvent spoliés par ce biais. Le soutien de la famille étendue peut aussi émaner de cousins, de neveux ou de la belle-famille résidant en ville comme le relate la veuve Pauline (exemple 5).

---

[18] *Sountoogo* : amertume, souffrances morales et psychologiques.

Exemple 5 : La veuve Pauline – soutenue par le mari de sa sœur

Pauline est née près de Kuila au village Oubriyaoghin, elle a plus de la cinquantaine. Veuve depuis 1991, son mari est mort en lui laissant dix enfants. Trois enfants sont mariés et se débrouillent de leur côté mais Pauline se soucie tant pour les sept autres qui logent chez elle, le dernier est de 1990. Pauline est avant tout agricultrice et comme pour tous les acteurs du domaine : « S'il ne pleut pas, c'est comme si on n'avait pas semé. Il n'y aura rien à récolter. Les temps de soudure sont des moments durs à passer. Lorsque les vivres finissent, c'est la grande misère qui commence en attendant les nouvelles récoltes. » En plus de l'agriculture, Pauline se livre à la fabrication de la bière de mil *(dolo)*, une activité organisée dans le village et assurée à tour de rôle par les productrices et qui peut rapporter 2000 à 2500 FCFA (env. 3 à 3,8 €) à chaque préparation réalisée tous les neuf jours.

Pauline exalte le soutien du mari de sa sœur résidant à Ouagadougou qui lui vient régulièrement en aide depuis le décès de son mari. « Chaque mois il me demande d'envoyer un enfant chercher quelque chose et lorsque l'enfant revient avec cinq ou six plats de vivres je ne peux que louer le Seigneur pour cela ; seulement en 2000, il est tombé malade et a subi une intervention chirurgicale et depuis ses propres charges se sont multipliées. »

Pour Pauline cela fait près de huit ans que son toit coule et que les moyens lui font défaut pour renouveler cette toiture. Pauline a inscrit ses deux derniers enfants à l'école mais ce n'est pas toujours facile d'assumer seule les dépenses. D'aucuns trouvent qu'une veuve ne doit pas envoyer ses enfants à l'école et que c'est un excès de zèle de sa part que d'inscrire ses enfants orphelins à l'école, comme les autres enfants. Elle le fait dans l'espoir qu'ils s'en sortiront un jour pour l'aider à oublier ces moments de souffrance. Quand les fêtes s'approchent c'est un autre cauchemar pour Pauline car ses enfants risquent de manquer de vêtements neufs ou de repas exceptionnels mais c'est la vie qui est ainsi faite, dit-elle. Et la parenté dans tout cela la soutient-elle ? Pour Pauline, « lorsque tu es riche tout le monde te reconnaît comme leur parent. Ils sont contents de te citer comme leur parent et de te compter parmi eux, même si tu es un parent très éloigné. Mais quand tu es pauvre comme nous autres et que tu n'as rien qui les intéresse tu es négligé. » Pauline trouve le réconfort à l'église. Elle est membre de l'association des femmes catholiques de Kuila et s'occupe du service d'ordre à l'église. De temps à autre, elle reçoit par ce biais quelques plats de vivres et des vêtements de la mission. Au dire de Pauline, lorsque l'État offre des vivres, c'est l'inégalité dans la distribution qui pose problème. Ces vivres sont le plus souvent détournés et ne parviennent pas aux plus démunis. Si elle devait mourir et renaître, dit Pauline, elle aurait voulu renaître homme car les hommes ont des droits et des pouvoirs que les femmes n'ont pas.

Au-delà des conceptions, dans la pratique le soutien de la famille étendue comporte de nombreuses limites pour les pauvres. Si la famille étendue est un soutien pour ceux qui n'ont pas d'enfants comme Tennoaga (exemple 4) ou ceux qui ont connu un drame comme Pauline (exemple 5), ce type de soutien est presque inexistant pour les pauvres. « Riche ou pauvre, la peine de chacun lui suffit », dit-on dans le milieu. D'ores et déjà, dans le milieu être dans l'obligation de demander ouvertement vous couvre de honte. À Kuila comme dans beaucoup d'autres régions en Afrique, les valeurs sociales comme la honte, la dignité, le code d'honneur amènent les agents sociaux à ne pas solliciter systématiquement le soutien familial (cf. Vuarin 2000 : 143-166). Cela est encore plus vrai des personnes âgées notamment les chefs de famille (exemple 6). De ce fait, si la famille étendue est très large, paradoxalement les possibilités de recours dans la pratique sont très orientées et limitées. En raison de la proximité physique, il est difficile de dire qu'on n'a pas de parents au village mais la personne âgée peut se retrouver sans soutien réel. D'un autre côté, l'exigence de la réciprocité dans les relations humaines et la loi de la dette conduisent à la marginalisation des plus démunis. Comme le dit Eloundou-Enyegue (1992 : 14) : « Les gens auraient tendance à diminuer l'aide qu'ils apportent à ceux qui ne peuvent rien leur donner en retour. Ceci conduit à terme à une marginalisation des plus pauvres et à un accroissement des inégalités. »[19] À Kuila un proverbe dit que « c'est le mil qui fait accourir les poussins ». Ainsi les pauvres profitent moins des relations de parenté.

Exemple 6 : De l'insécurité alimentaire au suicide
Michel était né vers 1950 à Kuila. Il déclare avoir eu une enfance difficile. En tant qu'aîné il a vu son père souffrir des famines. Il a dû commencer à travailler très jeune. Il lui arrivait d'aller aider certains à cultiver et en retour on lui donnait des vivres qu'il rapportait à la maison. Il a dû faire de multiples petits boulots pour réunir l'argent du transport et pouvoir quitter Kuila. Parti en 1968 pour la première fois en Côte d'Ivoire, Michel a d'abord été manœuvre dans la menuiserie, ensuite mécanicien et de nouveau manœuvre dans le transport du bois. Entre-temps, les choses allaient mieux pour lui et il pouvait s'occuper de ses parents au village en leur envoyant de l'argent. Suite au décès de sa mère en 1990, Michel a regagné le village et a retrouvé sa femme et son premier fils né en 1988.

---

[19] Cf. aussi Anspach (2000).

Les choses ont de nouveau recommencé à dégénérer. Depuis lors il n'a plus réussi à s'acheter un vélo. Entre-temps, il voulait repartir pour la Côte d'Ivoire mais n'avait plus de quoi payer le transport. Il a sollicité l'aide d'un ami résidant à Ouagadougou pour cela, mais comme le père de Michel ne voulait pas qu'il l'abandonne pour repartir, l'ami n'a pas voulu l'aider. Lui prêter de l'argent pour le transport serait cautionner son départ et se rendre complice. Alors l'ami l'a convaincu de rester. De temps en temps, il lui envoyait un peu d'argent au village. « Aujourd'hui, les choses sont difficiles pour moi », disait Michel, « je pratique l'agriculture mais sans la charrue et l'âne, je ne peux avoir grand-chose. En saison sèche, je me rends en brousse pour couper du bois pour le vendre. Je confectionne également des corbeilles ou des *seccos*[20] pour les vendre et entretenir la famille. » Et concernant le soutien, Michel dit : « Un parent, une connaissance, un ami peut te venir en aide mais tu ne peux pas tout bâtir sur cette aide. C'est occasionnel. Je n'ai pas de soutien régulier. » De quel soutien s'agit-il ? C'est surtout de la nourriture, des vivres mais rarement de l'argent. Chez Michel on se soigne à la médecine traditionnelle. On n'a pas les moyens pour aller au dispensaire. Pour ses deux enfants qui vont à l'école, chaque année il revendait les fournitures de l'année écoulée pour compléter et acheter celles exigées. « Si tu es un chef de famille sans ressources c'est difficile. Si j'étais une femme, je serais chez un mari. Les femmes dépendent de leur mari mais moi en tant qu'homme, la responsabilité de la famille m'incombe. » Néanmoins, Michel n'aurait pas voulu être une femme. Il préfère rester ce qu'il est. « Lors des fêtes, un voisin ou un parent qui a plus de moyens nous aide. Ils peuvent tuer un porc à Noël et nous envoyer un morceau de viande pour la famille. » En dépit de ces soutiens occasionnels Michel n'a pas pu s'empêcher de commettre l'irréparable. En 2001, il s'est pendu en laissant sa femme avec six enfants dont le dernier est un nouveau-né. Toujours sous le coup de la douleur et de la souffrance, sa femme reste muette sur ce drame.

En matière de soutien familial les femmes âgées semblent encore plus défavorisées à cause des règles de fonctionnement de la société patrilinéaire fortement hiérarchisée. Si de façon générale solliciter de l'aide est une honte, pour la femme la honte est double lorsqu'elle sollicite sa famille d'origine car cela dévoile l'incapacité de la lignée du mari. Aussi les femmes n'ont-elles recours à leur famille d'origine qu'en cas de force majeure car c'est socialement dévalorisant pour elles et pour la famille du mari.

---

[20] *Seccos :* paille tressée pour recouvrir les toits, faire des hangars ou des greniers.

Soudées par la parenté, les traditions communes et l'attachement au local, les relations de voisinage concourent à la proximité sociale à Kuila. Les voisins pallient surtout aux besoins immédiats : on va prendre le feu, demander un manquant de condiments ou carrément un service. Il s'agit là d'un soutien de proximité. En tant que relations de parenté au fond, elles se structurent selon la couche sociale et le genre. À titre d'exemple, lorsque le voisin va travailler dans le champ durant les travaux collectifs, le *sissoaga,* la voisine aide dans la préparation du repas et de la bière de mil *(dolo).* Les relations communautaires de voisinage et de parenté sont structurées en fonction du genre et obéissent aux règles de la réciprocité, ce au détriment des plus pauvres.

Les relations amicales ont également une importance dans la sécurité sociale des personnes âgées. Les gens de Kuila nouent des relations d'amitié quelquefois à l'extérieur du village et celles-ci peuvent être plus intenses que les relations parentales. Un bon ami fait parfois plus qu'un proche parent pour la sécurité de l'individu, même si cela ne se dit pas devant les parents. Cependant comme toutes les autres relations, les relations d'amitié connaissent aussi la loi de la réciprocité et de la dette. Dans le vieil âge certaines relations d'amitié souffrent des problèmes de distance. Les relations d'amitié sont aussi structurées selon le genre. En la matière, les vieilles femmes de Kuila déclarent qu'elles ont moins de réseaux d'amitié que les hommes. Leurs amies d'enfance sont le plus souvent dispersées dans des foyers conjugaux dans d'autres localités tandis que les hommes capitalisent leurs réseaux depuis l'enfance grâce à la virilocalité.

Le processus de distanciation ou de repli sur soi des parents nantis qui émerge à Kuila concourt à l'abandon des plus pauvres. Certaines personnes âgées pauvres disent : « Les nantis deviennent de plus en plus avares – attitude qui constituait jadis une tare au village. » En conclusion on peut dire : les personnes âgées pauvres qui sont le plus dans le besoin sont aussi celles qui bénéficient le moins du soutien familial.

Le soutien communautaire – défavorisant les pauvres

L'échelle de la communauté à Kuila maintient sa particularité qui est que tout le monde est pratiquement un parent – soit direct ou par alliance. C'est ainsi que des voisins, des membres de classe d'âge, des membres d'associations, des membres de communautés religieuses se trouvent être des parents. Aussi le soutien communautaire comporte-t-il une dimension individuelle et une dimension collective placée sous la responsabilité du chef de village chargé d'organiser des rites symboliques de protection contre la famine et les épidémies. Pour le chef de Kuila, sa notoriété dépend de sa capacité à assurer la sécurité collective. Les personnes âgées font largement confiance à ces rites et protections symboliques. En cas de sécheresse les responsables coutumiers se concertent autour du chef pour les rituels en la matière. Les chrétiens et les musulmans font également des prières pour demander la pluie.

Outre la protection symbolique, des travaux collectifs *(sissoaga)* existent à l'échelle du village. Il s'agit des séances de travaux collectifs dans les champs ou pour la réfection des toits de maison. Il reste que de plus en plus ces prestations de service demandent en retour un investissement relativement important en nourriture, bière de mil *(dolo),* noix de cola, tabac, voire en argent, ce que les plus démunis et les plus nécessiteux ne peuvent honorer et se trouvent du coup privés d'une telle aide.

Les cérémonies telles que les funérailles, la cérémonie de récolte *(basga)* ou bien les mariages réunissent tout le village et constituent des occasions de manifestations de la solidarité communautaire à travers des échanges de biens et services. Les sacrifices sont partagés entre les aînés et les parts sont le plus souvent redistribuées en fonction des statuts hiérarchiques (chefferie, richesse). C'est ainsi que lors des funérailles, les riches reçoivent un mouton ou une chèvre tandis que les pauvres doivent se contenter de poulets ou parfois d'un petit morceau de poulet.

Les œuvres de bienfaisance de l'église installées hors du village ne sont pas à négliger. Les missions catholique ou protestante offrent

occasionnellement des vêtements, des nattes et des vivres aux personnes âgées pauvres de Kuila lors des périodes de soudure ou de calamités. Le *zakat-el-fitr*[21] institué dans la religion musulmane permet
une redistribution de vivres en priorité aux personnes âgées nécessi-
teuses.[22]

Exemple 7 : Survivre grâce aux dons diversifiés

Boureima est né à Kuila en 1920 selon les écrits du colonisateur. Comme jeune
homme, il a eu à faire les travaux forcés à Bamako dans les chemins de fer, puis
s'est rendu à Kumasi au Ghana, cette fois à la recherche de l'argent. Il a fait plus de
dix ans au Ghana où il travaillait dans les plantations de cacao. Après le Ghana, ce
fut la Côte d'Ivoire pour des dizaines d'années. Boureima totalise plus de cinquante
ans de migration. En Côte d'Ivoire il travaillait dans les plantations de café avec sa
femme Bibata et ses enfants. Les récoltes étaient divisées en trois parts : un tiers lui
revenait et les deux tiers au propriétaire du champ.

Avec les exactions de ces dernières années à l'encontre des Burkinabé en Côte
d'Ivoire, Boureima a rejoint Kuila, son village natal, en 2001 avec son épouse
âgée de 56 ans et quatre de ses neuf enfants. Boureima n'est pas rentré les mains
vides. Ils avaient dans les 150'000 FCFA (env. 230 €) entre les mains et sa femme
100'000 FCFA mais, dit-il, tout est parti dans les dépenses d'installation et l'achat de
vivres. De retour, Boureima a d'abord occupé une case dans la cour familiale et avec
l'aide des enfants de ses frères aînés défunts et d'autres membres du lignage, ils ont
confectionné des briques et réussi à construire trois cases et une maison de dix tôles
pour loger sa famille. Boureima dit n'avoir pas eu de difficultés pour obtenir un
champ pour cultiver, mais contre toute attente, la saison a été particulièrement mauvaise en 2001. Son sort a été allégé grâce au soutien familial mais surtout grâce au
zakat-el-fitr et la distribution de vivres faite par les autorités de Ziniaré. « Ce qui
m'a aidé, c'est l'aumône, le *zakat-el-fitr* des musulmans. Les musulmans de Touma
m'ont envoyé du sorgho blanc et du petit mil, ceux de Goughin également et ceux de
Kuila. Ce que j'ai reçu par le *zakat-el-fitr* était deux fois plus que ce que nous avons
pu récolter. C'est ce qui nous a permis de tenir jusqu'à présent. À cela il faut ajouter
ce que le gouvernement donne aux nécessiteux : deux à trois plats de vivres de
temps en temps. Ma femme y va tous les dix jours pour faire la queue et ça nous
dépanne. Chez Antoinette[23], il suffit d'y aller et de se présenter avec son plat. Mais
moi en tant que chef de famille, j'ai honte d'aller m'aligner là-bas. »

---

[21] Le *zakat-el-fitr* est l'aumône offerte par le chef de famille pendant le jeûne musulman en fonction de ses ressources et de la taille de sa famille.
[22] Concernant la sécurité sociale procurée par l'Islam voir Roth (dans ce volume).
[23] Antoinette, la sœur du Président Blaise Compaoré du Burkina Faso qui a sa résidence à Ziniaré, reçoit de celui-ci des vivres pour les nécessiteux de la localité.

À ce sujet, sa femme Bibata dit : « N'ayant pas de grenier de mil à notre arrivée, nous avons passé tout le temps à acheter des vivres avec le peu d'argent que nous avions. Et quand c'est comme cela, si l'argent sort et qu'il n'est pas remplacé, il finit très vite. De temps en temps, je me rends dans ma famille (sa famille d'origine) et j'utilise l'argent que les uns et les autres me donnent pour acheter des vivres et rentrer. Un de mes frères travaille dans une banque à Ouagadougou et il me donne occasionnellement de l'argent. »

Boureima ne minimise pas l'aide des parents, le soutien du lignage *(buudu)* au village. « Au début de la saison, ce sont les parents qui nous ont donné des semences pour cultiver : sorgho, petit mil, haricot, arachide, tout... Par le passé, quand je revenais de la Côte d'Ivoire, je m'occupais d'eux et donnais des objets ou de l'argent aux uns et aux autres. Aujourd'hui, ils constatent que je n'ai rien ; ni poule, ni chèvre, ni mouton, ne parlons pas d'un âne ou d'un bœuf. Mes neveux (les enfants de ses frères) nous donnent de temps en temps de la nourriture, des vivres mais pas de l'argent. Au village ils sont incapables de t'aider à régler une dette de 10'000 à 15'000 FCFA (env. 15 à 23 €). Comment pourraient-ils t'aider à acquérir un âne et une charrue pour cultiver ? Eux-mêmes n'en possèdent pas. » Aujourd'hui, le rêve de Boureima c'est d'obtenir un âne et une charrue, moyens de travail avec lesquels sa femme et ses enfants pourront mieux cultiver la terre et l'entretenir jusqu'à la fin de ses jours mais il ne sait pas à qui s'adresser. Et sa femme Bibata note qu'en raison de leur situation presque exceptionnelle,[24] parents et voisins ne les abandonnent pas et leur témoignent leur solidarité. Même le chef du village les aide avec des vivres. Seulement, il s'avère très difficile d'assurer ainsi le quotidien de toute une famille.

L'histoire de Boureima et Bibata (exemple 7) illustre bien les difficultés des migrants qui rentrent. Quand la migration n'a pas permis d'épargner suffisamment et d'investir au village lorsqu'on revient pour ses vieux jours, il faut repartir à zéro, se créer un cadre de vie, un abri, un toit, un champ et se remettre dans les travaux champêtres. Leurs économies vite épuisées, le couple tient le coup grâce à l'aide familiale. Avant, Boureima avait aussi aidé certains parents – et c'est ce qui est à la base du soutien qu'il reçoit aujourd'hui (réciprocité généralisée). Nous avons là en plus du soutien familial un exemple de soutien de la communauté religieuse musulmane à travers le *zakat-el-fitr*. Non sans honte, le couple et particulièrement la femme se voit

---

[24] Situation exceptionnelle car ils sont revenus de la Côte d'Ivoire suite aux exactions.

contrainte de solliciter l'aide des autorités. La migration est de moins en moins synonyme d'ascension sociale.

Les organisations civiles et gouvernementales :
une goutte d'eau dans la mer

Sur le plan local, les organisations telles les associations de classe d'âge et les associations de culture sont des cadres de référence identitaire, de soutien, de secours et d'assistance. Ces associations sont créées dans l'esprit de s'épauler mutuellement. C'est ainsi que l'association des jeunes devrait se montrer utile aux personnes âgées : il leur incombe d'aider aux travaux des champs, à l'entretien de l'environnement, poser les toits de maisons, creuser les puits et les tombes. À côté, la classe des aînés et anciens représente le conseil des sages. Si certaines prestations s'imposent aux jeunes dans le village, par exemple creuser les tombes, d'autres se font de plus en plus rares – notamment pour les personnes âgées démunies. Les travaux des champs passent par les travaux collectifs (*sissoaga*) qui, comme déjà mentionné, nécessitent préalablement des moyens, ce qui prive les personnes âgées pauvres d'un tel soutien communautaire. Au sein de la génération des aînés, le soutien reste régi par les règles de la réciprocité ; ce qui implique que l'on doit disposer de ressources.

À Kuila, les associations à caractère moderne sont au stade de l'émergence. C'est le cas de l'association « Nimb gninga » créée en 2000 et dont le président fondateur est un ancien émigré du Gabon. L'association composée essentiellement de parents au village et de ressortissants résidant en ville fonctionne sur la base de cotisations et accorde des prêts d'argent ou de vivres aux membres. Mais le président fait remarquer : « Comme c'est entre nous, certains prennent de l'argent et ne remboursent pas et on ne peut rien dire, car c'est toi et ton parent. » Par le passé, l'expérience des groupements villageois avait été tentée mais sans succès. Sur la question des tontines, les personnes âgées de Kuila se disent trop démunies avec des revenus suffisamment aléatoires pour prendre les risques de la tontine. Une vieille femme dit à ce sujet : « Les expériences n'ont pas résisté à la pauvreté. » Le système de crédit demeure informel et fait appel à l'entourage. Sur le plan national et international, les efforts déployés par les associations ne touchent pas l'ensemble des villages et ne sont pas directement axés sur les personnes âgées. À Kuila les personnes âgées pauvres n'en font pas état. Les associations locales existantes connaissent une différenciation selon le genre en ce sens qu'elles sont beaucoup plus l'œuvre des hommes que des femmes. Les femmes âgées sont pratiquement absentes de ces associations.

En somme à Kuila le soutien des associations aux personnes âgées est moins diversifié et affiche les mêmes limites que le soutien familial. Le soutien aux personnes âgées émanant des organisations gouvernementales est le moins visible et le plus épisodique dans notre contexte. À Kuila, nombreuses sont les personnes âgées qui ne savent pas qui est l'État ou que fait l'État pour leur sécurité sociale. Dans le milieu, la contribution de l'État à leur endroit se résume à des opérations ponctuelles de dons ou de vente à prix social de vivres aux plus démunies lors des calamités, des catastrophes ou des sécheresses : par exemple moins de sept kilos de vivres par personne en période de soudure selon la directrice provinciale de l'Action Sociale.[25] En somme, on peut affirmer : les réseaux communautaires sont moins diversifiés que sous des conditions urbaines.

Conclusion

Au Burkina Faso, la question de la sécurité sociale des personnes âgées constitue un problème épineux longtemps resté sous silence. Le soutien familial à travers les relations conjugales, intergénérationnelles ou de la famille étendue représente, dans les idées, la principale source de sécurité sociale des personnes âgées au village. Ces différentes relations ont pour vocation de leur procurer secours, aide et assistance. La progéniture reste l'assurance vieillesse pour les personnes âgées pauvres.

---

[25] En 2002, un don international arriva à Kuila : 50 kilos de céréales pour 20 chefs de famille, ce qui fit du partage un grand problème.

Cependant, le caractère ambivalent du soutien familial et communautaire se montre dans de nombreuses limites. Le soutien ne satisfait pas les besoins élémentaires des intéressés. Cela est dû à la faiblesse générale des ressources surtout dans des villages du nord du pays comme Kuila. Le manque de ressources engendre l'écart entre imagerie et pratique du soutien aux personnes âgées. La parenté par exemple, source de soutien, se montre dans sa capacité d'exclusion, de délaissement et de marginalisation même si le proverbe moaga dit que « on ne saurait laver la parenté comme du linge », ce qui signifie ne pas s'en détacher. Ainsi les relations conjugales comprennent la protection et le soutien, mais aussi le contrôle et les conflits (Risseeuw/Palriwala 1996 : 16). Le soutien familial tel qu'il fonctionne est dans les faits limité pour les pauvres car ils sont incapables de suivre la « loi de la dette » (Marie 1997). Plus on est pauvre moins on peut honorer cette dette sociale et moins on peut profiter des relations familiales.

La migration des fils, eu égard à son caractère ambivalent, peut avoir pour conséquence la négligence des parents. D'une part les fils peuvent dans ce cas contourner leur devoir de s'occuper des parents. D'autre part ceux qui n'ont pas réussi ont du mal à retourner au village car ils ne seront plus respectés.

Les vieilles femmes sont aussi à Kuila les plus pauvres et les moins soutenues. Leurs possibilités de recours aux associations et aux organisations sont plus limitées que chez les hommes. Les plus à plaindre par-dessus tout sont celles qui sont accusées de sorcellerie et victimes d'exclusion sociale. Non contente de ne pas leur accorder une assistance, la société trouve ici un moyen « légitime » de se débarrasser de ces personnes âgées pauvres qui représentent une charge, un poids social.

Le soutien communautaire connaît la même ambiguïté que le soutien familial et est en train d'échapper aux pauvres. Le soutien communautaire habituel se fait de plus en plus « payant » en suivant de plus en plus une réciprocité balancée et le soutien communautaire moderne ne touche pas les plus démunis. Les œuvres de bienfaisance émanant des institutions religieuses, étatiques ou ONG, si elles sont présentes, restent entachées par leur propre nature, à savoir destinées aux nécessiteux. Alors pour en bénéficier il faut accepter d'« afficher publiquement sa pauvreté » et essuyer ainsi la honte sociale. Et pour ceux qui parviennent à le faire, ces œuvres de bienfaisance, en dépit de leur caractère occasionnel et épisodique, passent souvent sous le nez des pauvres. Destinées en principe aux nécessiteux, elles sont souvent détournées au profit des nantis qui ne sont pourtant pas dans le besoin.

Face aux nombreuses limites qu'impose la pratique du soutien familial et communautaire, où se situe la capacité d'agir *(agency)* des personnes âgées pauvres ? Au village, leur principal filet de sécurité passe par le contrat entre les générations. Le pouvoir économique à travers la possession, la gestion et le contrôle des terres notamment des hommes âgés maintient jusqu'aujourd'hui un pouvoir réel et symbolique sur les jeunes générations. De surcroît, les personnes âgées de Kuila peuvent encore compter sur des membres de la famille étendue. L'intégration des personnes âgées au sein des cellules familiales représente par ailleurs une force et une marge de manœuvre pour les intéressées. D'ores et déjà elle leur évite la rue et la mendicité comme c'est le cas en ville. Elle instaure également une opportunité d'implication à la vie familiale et sociale et des responsabilités sous certaines conditions toutefois : la personne âgée doit être sociable et au-dessus du soupçon de sorcellerie. La sorcellerie devient ici un énorme moyen de contrôle social qui demande aux personnes âgées d'être modestes et sans prétention. Les stratégies que développent les personnes âgées pauvres à ce niveau demeurent, entre autres, la bonne entente avec l'entourage et le bon caractère.

Conclusion
Vieillir dans l'insécurité – différences et similarités

Claudia Roth et Willemijn de Jong

La recherche menée conjointement et parallèlement dans les quatre localités en Inde et au Burkina Faso a affiné notre lecture des différences et des similarités en matière de sécurité sociale dans le vieil âge. Nous comparons ci-après les points les plus pertinents de notre recherche.

Burkina Faso : anciennes et nouvelles solidarités

Au Burkina Faso, il existe des liens étroits entre les milieux rural et urbain. Des enfants du village fréquentent l'école de la ville la plus proche ; des malades en provenance du village passent la nuit chez des parents lorsqu'ils doivent se rendre au dispensaire en ville, tandis que des citadins psychiquement ou physiquement atteints se souviennent des traitements médicaux traditionnels de leurs ancêtres au village. Des citadins assistent aux enterrements au village et les villageois en vont faire de même en ville. Des jeunes vont tenter leur chance en ville à la recherche d'emplois, des émigrés qui ont échoué retournent au village et repartent à zéro. Une fois le vieil âge atteint, les gens ont également tendance à retourner au village car le coût de la vie y est moindre. Si autrefois, en période de prospérité, les villageois étaient en mesure de soutenir leurs parents citadins en leur offrant du mil, cette aide est devenue symbolique aujourd'hui : ils font des « sacrifices » pour leur assurer le succès d'un projet. À l'inverse, le soutien matériel des citadins à l'endroit de leurs parents villageois s'est lui aussi réduit (cf. Potts 1997).

Chez les Moose au nord du pays, la migration des jeunes est beaucoup plus répandue que dans les ethnies du sud-ouest, notamment la région de Bobo-Dioulasso. Chez les Moose « faire l'aventure », c'est aussi devenir un homme. Dans les conditions actuelles, la migration des jeunes est devenue une affaire hasardeuse pour les personnes âgées. Les villages se vident de leurs bras, il n'est pas certain qu'un jeune homme qui va à l'aventure à l'étranger trouvera du travail et pourra envoyer de l'argent au village ou si, au contraire, il ne disparaîtra pas sans plus donner de ses nouvelles, parce que honteux de son échec. À Kuila comme à Bobo-Dioulasso, les personnes âgées ont fait part de leur expérience avec des jeunes qui ont émigré et ne donnent guère de leurs nouvelles – l'efficacité des « cercles de solidarité à distance » (voir préface) se trouve ainsi remise en question.

Malgré les liens étroits entre la ville et les villages environnants, la situation en milieu urbain et celle en milieu rural burkinabé se distinguent nettement. L'évolution de la société et la crise économique chronique se font sentir différemment en ville et au village. En matière de sécurité sociale pour le vieil âge, le fait qu'au village de Kuila les hommes âgés disposent encore de la terre, moyen de production primordial, constitue une différence capitale avec la situation qui prévaut en ville. Elle est déterminante pour le rapport entre les générations. En leur donnant accès à la terre, les hommes âgés accordent une base d'existence à leurs fils et disposent ainsi d'un potentiel de pouvoir, que les hommes âgés de la ville ont, quant eux, perdu. Ceci explique pourquoi, au village, le contrat implicite entre les générations est rempli à quatre-vingt-dix pour-cent, même si, par manque de ressources, les jeunes ne parviennent plus à assurer la subsistance de leurs parents âgés.

À Bobo-Dioulasso au contraire, les jeunes gagnent leur vie indépendamment des personnes âgées, ce qui leur fournit la possibilité de négocier la relation de pouvoir avec les aînés. La hiérarchie de l'âge ayant ainsi s'atténué, ils jouissent d'une relative autonomie que la situation économique difficile et le taux de chômage élevé qui en résulte limitent à nouveau : situation ambivalente pour les deux parties. De jeunes adultes, chômeurs et filles-mères y compris, qui en fait devraient se prendre en charge eux-mêmes, trouvent gît et couvert en raison du contrat entre les générations à l'envers : ils vivent donc comme « dépendants » dans la concession de leurs pères. Les femmes et les hommes âgés reprennent alors la position qui leur est bien familière et gèrent la « famille étendue », cependant sans la garantie de recevoir la contrepartie de ce qu'ils ont donné.

Une autre disparité substantielle entre la ville et le village concerne les nouvelles solidarités émergentes en ville, la « sociabilité 'secondaire' », conséquence du changement social. Elle inclut des relations volontairement créées, choisies et entretenues par les individus et construites au jour le jour au gré des rencontres et des situations individuelles, par exemple les associations ou les tontines (Vuarin 2000 : 187, cf. aussi Neubert 1990). Malgré ces associations qui sont en train de se créer à Kuila, la « sociabilité primaire », basée sur l'appartenance sociale héritée (lignage, clan, village) est déterminante pour les solidarités : d'une part les verticales, hiérarchiques, c'est-à-dire la hiérarchie de l'âge et du genre ; d'autre part les horizontales, égalitaires entre égaux statutaires, c'est-à-dire les groupes d'âge. En ville, l'arrangement de sécurité sociale des personnes âgées est en principe plus diversifié, mais en même temps dans le concret limité par la stratification sociale.

Au village comme en ville, le manque de ressources pose des limites aux relations de sécurité sociale au sein de la parenté et en dehors. La parenté ne va pas de soi, les individus doivent la créer et l'entretenir constamment. La crise crée un paradoxe : les ressources, à savoir les moyens de la solidarité tarissent alors même qu'ils sont plus que jamais nécessaires (cf. Marie 1997). Il en découle une multitude de tensions et conflits entre vieux et jeunes, hommes et femmes, belles-mères et belles-filles, frères et sœurs aînés et cadets – les intérêts divergents et les ressources de plus en plus insuffisantes aboutissent à des relations hautement ambivalentes et conflictuelles, étant donné que nul ne peut se soustraire : au village comme en ville, la sécurité sociale ne se procure pas en dehors des relations de parenté et de communauté.

À cause du sida, l'espérance de vie est de nouveau en baisse au Burkina Faso (voir appendice). En ville comme au village, les personnes âgées déplorent le fait d'avoir à enterrer leurs propres enfants. Elles se chargent alors, les femmes en particulier, de leurs petits-enfants orphelins. Le sida a un impact considérable sur la sécurité

sociale des personnes âgées tout comme sur celle des enfants (cf. aussi
Leliveld 2004). Le lévirat, une des anciennes formes de solidarité,
existe encore dans des villages comme Kuila, mais est il en voie de
disparition en ville, à cause du sida et de la pauvreté.

Historiquement, Bobo-Dioulasso est une ville multi-ethnique. Les
nombreuses ethnies qui la composent ne se distinguent pas par
l'appartenance à des couches sociales mais plutôt par leurs langues,
leurs coutumes et leur organisation sociale. Chez les Moose, les enfants adultes remettent leurs contributions de soutien à leurs pères
âgés et non à leurs mères – contrairement à ce qui ce fait dans bon
nombre de sociétés de la région du sud-ouest. Ceci est déterminé à la
fois par l'organisation sociale et le changement social. À Bobo-Dioulasso comme à Kuila, l'une comme l'autre sont différenciés selon le
genre (*gendered*). Dans le village de Kuila, les fils donnent plus aux
personnes âgées que les filles. Ils constituent donc leur sécurité sociale
comme le prévoit la société, et les pères reçoivent plus que les mères.
Par contre dans le quartier Koko, les filles sont souvent les donatrices
les plus fiables, comparées aux fils, et les mères reçoivent plus que les
pères. Nous interprétons ce phénomène d'une part comme caractéristique de la situation urbaine où, pour les femmes, la famille d'origine
est plus fiable que l'époux, et les femmes projettent leur sécurité sociale à travers leurs propres enfants, tandis que les hommes la voient
dans le mariage. D'autre part, nous le percevons comme expression
des sociétés organisées de façon plus ou moins hiérarchique, dans
lesquelles l'âge et le genre structurent différemment les comporte-
ments. Ceci se ressent dans le rapport entre homme et femme ainsi
que dans le pouvoir d'action (*agency*) des femmes.

Kerala : différentes qualités de relations de sécurité sociale

Une grande partie de la littérature indienne consacrée au vieil âge croit
constater une détérioration des conditions de soutien des personnes
âgées, souvent attribuée à la « modernisation » et à l'« urbanisation »
non différenciées. À quel point cela s'applique-t-il au cas du Kerala ?
À première vue, les différences en matière de sécurité sociale sont à

peine notoires parmi la classe ouvrière de la ville de Kalamassery et du village de Kadamakuddy. Dans les deux cas, les arrangements de sécurité sociale sont très diversifiés et peuvent être qualifiés d'« arrangement patchwork », pour lequel le « voisinage étendu » est important, par exemple dans les relations avec les habitants du lieu, en plus de celles entretenues avec la famille étendue. Spécialement en temps de crise, les Pulaya de la classe ouvrière s'attachent à obtenir la moindre ressource en mobilisant le soutien de la parenté, des voisins, des (anciens) employeurs, des organisations civiles et de l'État.

Ces similitudes s'expliquent tout d'abord par la modernité spécifique du Kerala, c'est-à-dire son caractère « rurban ». Les villes ont un aspect de campagne, à en juger par la disposition des habitations, seuls les grands centres urbains s'en distinguent (cf. aussi Kuruvilla 1989). D'autre part, la vie au village ne diffère guère de celle en ville grâce au développement dans les domaines de l'éducation et de la santé. En particulier l'éducation formelle des Pulaya est identique dans les deux études de cas. En général, les personnes âgées ont été à l'école pendant deux à trois ans, durée insuffisante pour être en mesure de lire et d'écrire le malayalam, tandis que la génération plus jeune a fréquenté l'école pendant une période allant jusqu'à dix ans.

En outre, l'agriculture était autrefois prédominante dans les deux contextes. Aujourd'hui, elle a perdu de son importance dans les deux localités, mais surtout à Kalamassery depuis le processus d'industrialisation entamé dans les années 1960. Mais à Kadamakuddy aussi, les emplois ont diminué dans le secteur agricole et sont remplacés par des embauches dans la construction et les services de nettoyage, en partie dans le village mais beaucoup plus à l'extérieur. Les personnes âgées des deux contextes ont donc continué de faire d'autres travaux manuels mal payés ; celles de Kalamassery dans une plus large mesure. Avec des revenus du ménage se situant légèrement en dessus du seuil de pauvreté, voire carrément en dessous, il n'est pas surprenant que les personnes âgées et leurs enfants mettent tout en œuvre pour parvenir à couvrir leurs besoins. Les arrangements de sécurité sociale diversifiés dans les deux cas sont largement conditionnés par la pauvreté.

Les ressemblances urbano-rurales s'éclairent aussi par la structure sociale du Kerala ou plutôt par notre focalisation sur la caste des Pulaya. Dans les deux études de cas, nous nous sommes concentrées sur les membres de la même classe sociale dans la même caste qui a un système de parenté, des structures familiales et de foyer similaires à travers le pays. À titre d'exemple, la majorité des Pulaya âgés vivent – aussi bien dans le contexte urbain que dans le contexte rural – avec un fils marié et ses enfants dans une famille élargie ou étendue. Dans les deux contextes, la composition de la famille étendue est plutôt stable car ces gens n'ont pas les moyens d'émigrer à l'étranger comme le font les personnes aisées du Kerala.

Néanmoins, en regardant de plus près, nous avons constaté des points intéressants qui contrastent dans une certaine mesure et qui nécessitent d'être élaborés et expliqués. En ce qui concerne le besoin quotidien d'argent, les foyers avec les membres âgés semblent être légèrement mieux lotis au village qu'en ville. Se nourrir ne pose donc pas problème à la campagne comme c'est le cas en ville parmi les personnes âgées les plus démunies. Par contre, très souvent, les médicaments font défaut. Au village, les personnes âgées gagnent moins régulièrement de l'argent en faisant de petits boulots car les opportunités y sont plus rares qu'en ville. En revanche, les prix des produits de première nécessité et les coûts liés au logement et aux taxes sont moins élevés au village. En même temps, les revenus du foyer y sont quelque peu plus élevés car presque tous se situent juste en dessus du seuil de pauvreté tandis que la ville compte plus de foyers en dessous du seuil de pauvreté. Par conséquent, moins de gens vivent dans des paillotes au village. Les revenus plus élevés qu'affiche le village pourraient s'expliquer par le fait que de nombreux hommes d'âge moyen du village travaillent sous contrat dans la ville voisine. Ce type de travail garantit un revenu pendant une durée déterminée et est donc mieux rémunéré que le travail occasionnel de journalier, qui demeure plus aléatoire.

De plus, les personnes âgées peuvent obtenir des aides publiques plus facilement au village qu'en ville, en particulier « les pensions pour ouvriers agricoles » et les « pensions pour veuves et orphelins »,

si elles n'ont pas de fils adulte. Au village, la familiarité de longue
date avec les employés municipaux constitue assurément un atout. Ces
relations facilitent aussi le renouvellement des enregistrements des
maisons à la suite du décès d'un mari et les rendent moins onéreuses
qu'en ville, de sorte que les veuves pulaya vivant au village sont davantage propriétaires et possèdent ainsi un pouvoir de négociation
plus accru.

Au village comme en ville, les soins médicaux de base sont fournis
par une organisation civile et une offre de soins médicaux de base est
aussi disponible au village. Les habitants du village ont difficilement
accès aux médicaments spécialisés vu qu'il n'y a pas de pharmacie et
se rendre à l'hôpital en cas d'urgence est aussi ardu. En 2002, le trajet
prenait une heure à cause de la situation isolée du village.

À côté des conditions économiques des foyers, la qualité des relations de soutien est légèrement différente au village par rapport à la
ville. Les enfants, les fils surtout, sont plus solidaires au village, tandis
qu'en ville le soutien apporté par les enfants est un peu moins fiable,
mais moins différencié selon le genre puisque les filles y participent
davantage. D'une manière générale, les relations de travail et de parenté ont connu des changements significatifs, voire des ruptures, tout
au long du siècle dernier. La classe des propriétaires fonciers et la
classe des sans-terre, à l'exemple des Pulaya étaient particulièrement
mêlées à ces transformations sociales. Les propriétaires fonciers ne
fournissent plus la sécurité sociale aux Pulaya comme ils avaient
coutume de le faire et les fils ont dû commencer à apporter une aide
économique à leurs parents âgés conformément à la norme largement
en vigueur en Inde. Un tel soutien s'avère davantage difficile plus le
foyer est démuni et plus ses différents membres exigent de manière
prononcée le capital économique mais aussi le capital symbolique (p.
ex. le prestige que confère le fait d'avoir, respectivement d'être une
femme au foyer). D'une manière générale, les Pulaya âgés vivant dans
des foyers étendus ont des besoins et des intérêts concurrençant ceux
de leurs enfants et petits-enfants, et les femmes des besoins concurrençant ceux des hommes. En milieu urbain, en plus des besoins de
consommation croissants (cf. Sooryamoorthy 1997), la génération

d'âge moyen semble être encline à, et aussi contrainte de, donner la priorité aux besoins de leurs enfants – et de prévoir ainsi leur vieil âge – et ce aux dépens de la satisfaction des besoins actuels de leurs parents âgés.

La relation conjugale a gagné importance et s'est davantage développée en une relation de soutien mutuel, sur les plans social et émotionnel, en particulier en ville. Aujourd'hui plus qu'autrefois, le décès d'un époux peut causer une insécurité sociale accrue à une femme, et c'est peut-être l'une des raisons pour laquelle les veuves vivant en ville connaissent plus d'insécurité sociale que celles vivant au village. L'importance croissante du mariage se réflète dans les montants des dots parfois quatre fois plus élevés en ville qu'au village. La pratique de la dot s'est introduite chez les Pulaya il y a seulement deux générations. En même temps, les femmes semblent plus mobiles en ville qu'au village.

Étant donné qu'il y a plus de pauvreté en ville (cf. aussi Retnaraj 1999), le recours aux relations de citoyenneté y est plus important qu'au village, en plus du recours aux relations de parenté. Par exemple, les voisins jouent un rôle plus important dans les échanges de nourritures et de modiques sommes d'argent. Des besoins non quotidiens en argent pour les dots et la construction des maisons peuvent plus facilement être soumis aux employeurs car les personnes âgées vivant en ville changent plus fréquemment de travail et travaillent plus longtemps. L'assistance sociale fournie par les organisations civiles et le gouvernement a également pris de l'ampleur, mais l'aide gouvernementale est moins accessible aux personnes âgées car leurs relations avec les fonctionnaires sont moins personnelles. Par conséquent, le rôle de médiateur de l'organisation de caste, intermédiaire entre la classe ouvrière et la municipalité, est particulièrement important.

Le Kerala et le Burkina Faso : fonctions différentes de la citoyenneté et de la parenté – insécurités similaires

Bien qu'étant toutes deux des sociétés en voie de développement, la modernité du Kerala se distingue de celle du Burkina Faso. Ceci saute aux yeux lorsque l'on jette un coup d'œil sur les indicateurs de qualité de vie (voir appendice). Le revenu par habitant est plus bas au Kerala qu'en Inde, mais il y est plus élevé qu'au Burkina Faso. Tandis qu'au Burkina Faso les gens doivent s'en sortir avec en moyenne moins d'un dollar par jour, le revenu moyen journalier est d'un peu plus d'un dollar au Kerala et il est même légèrement plus élevé dans l'Inde entière. Ceci est en conformité avec le fait que la majorité des enquêtés au Kerala vivent dans une sécurité sociale fragile, tandis que la majorité de ceux du Burkina Faso vivent dans la précarité, ce qui signifie que leur nourriture quotidienne n'est pas garantie.

D'énormes écarts se font jour en matière d'éducation et de santé, comme l'indiquent les taux d'alphabétisation et d'espérance de vie. Les taux d'alphabétisation pour les hommes et les femmes sont plus élevés au Kerala que dans le reste de l'Inde, mais comparés au Burkina Faso, ces chiffres sont deux fois plus élevés pour les hommes et cinq fois plus pour les femmes. L'espérance de vie dans les deux pays dénote aussi des différences considérables. La problématique du soutien des personnes âgées, en particulier des veuves, est par contre beaucoup plus urgente en Inde qu'au Burkina Faso qui est beaucoup plus confronté aux problèmes de base tels que l'alphabétisation et la santé de sa génération future.

Un autre contraste de taille est le fait qu'au Kerala, l'ethnicité est liée à la caste et à la religion, tandis qu'au Burkina Faso – qui compte plus de soixante groupes ethniques – la langue et d'autres critères culturels sont importants. D'autres différences se traduisent par les grands changements sociaux qui se sont produits au Kerala le siècle dernier. Ces changements sont le résultat des luttes menées à travers les mouvements sociaux et au sein des syndicats par la classe opprimée des sans-terre et des ouvriers agricoles, politiquement sensibilisés ; combats dirigés par la classe supérieure et les hauts dirigeants communistes des castes. Les Pulaya étaient particulièrement impliqués dans ces processus de changement. D'une part, les actions collectives, jointes à l'urgence du problème que pose le vieil âge, étaient favorables à la création d'une sorte d'État social au Kerala, dans le sens d'une « institution formelle de protection sociale envisagée comme responsabilité sociale » (Spicker 2000 : 145, traduction libre). En outre, une forte tradition de charité religieuse et de bienfaisance y existait déjà. Ces facteurs ont favorisé le logement, les « pensions » et les soins de santé pour les Pulaya âgés et ont permis le recours à la citoyenneté à une échelle plus large qu'au Burkina Faso.

D'autre part, comme nous l'avons évoqué dans le chapitre d'introduction sur le Kerala, avec la prise de conscience croissante de l'importance de la classe sociale, il s'est produit une rupture dans les relations de parenté, de caste et de localité. En ce qui concerne les relations de parenté, nous y avons également fait référence dans la partie précédente en élaborant des changements qualitatifs des relations filiales et conjugales en ce sens que les fils célibataires sont devenus plus importants pour les parents âgés en tant que donateurs de soutien et les liens entre époux se sont consolidés. Le système des castes a été transformé avec pour effet une mobilité géographique d'une part et une mobilité sociale vers le haut de l'autre pour les castes inférieures mais on note également une mobilité sociale vers le bas des foyers des castes supérieures, les Nayar à titre d'exemple. La localité a aussi été affecté en ce sens qu'à travers des mesures d'assistance sociale, les différences entre les villes et les régions rurales ont été neutralisées.

Enfin, les systèmes de parenté, y compris la composition du foyer et la façon de se marier diffèrent dans les deux sociétés. Même en assumant que les Pulaya ont un système de parenté patrilinéaire et non matrilinéaire,[1] il n'a ni le caractère ni la signification de la patrilinéarité comme on l'entend au Burkina Faso. Dans ce dernier contexte, la patrilinéarité correspond aux principes strictement observés du droit d'aînesse et de l'autorité des aînés du lignage, tout particulièrement dans le contexte rural. Ceci s'applique aussi plus ou moins aux femmes âgées et implique que les hommes plus jeunes tels les fils ou les neveux n'ont pas de pouvoir de décision sur les femmes âgées comme c'est le cas au Kerala.

---

[1] La règle de l'héritage de la maison dans la ligne de l'homme, par exemple, peut être considéré comme une indication que la descendance est aussi plutôt patrilinéaire.

La composition des familles varie aussi. Au Burkina Faso, conformément au système du lignage patrilinéaire, les familles étendues sont composées de groupes agnatiques de frères, leurs épouses, leurs enfants, et éventuellement d'autres parents patrilinéaires. En revanche, les foyers de famille étendue du Kerala sont généralement aujourd'hui composés de parents, d'un enfant marié, le plus souvent d'un fils et de son épouse et de leurs enfants ; alors que jadis, les frères mariés et leurs épouses, ou des sœurs mariées et leurs époux ainsi que leurs enfants en faisaient partie.

Au Burkina Faso, la polygamie est largement répandue, pas seulement en tant que valeur importante, mais aussi dans la pratique. Par exemple, au moins un tiers des enquêtés de la couche à bas revenus et de la couche à revenus moyens, en milieu rural comme en milieu urbain, sont dans ce régime de mariage. Ceci se traduit par la sécurité ou l'insécurité pour la femme, selon les circonstances, mais cela représente toujours la sécurité pour les hommes. De nos jours, le mariage est monogamique et a gagné en importance au Kerala, tandis que la polyandrie et la polygynie ont antérieurement existé, avec une forte prépondérance de la famille natale. En outre les dots, bien que légalement interdites depuis les années 1960, sont une « invention de la tradition » au Kerala depuis le siècle dernier, empruntée aux castes supérieures d'autres régions de l'Inde. Ce type de transactions matrimoniales met en péril la sécurité sociale dans le vieil âge des Pulaya démunis qui ont des filles. Au lieu de pouvoir épargner pour le vieil âge – un concept localement en usage et apprécié mais rarement appliqué à cause de la pauvreté – on épargne pour constituer des dots, en plus de la construction d'une maison, les deux étant d'une valeur équivalente en ville. Une maison en tuiles est un nouvel atout héréditaire important et peut être considérée comme garantie de sécurité pour le vieil âge. Les dots d'autre part contribuent à affaiblir les ressources de sécurité sociale des parents, spécialement des veuves âgées ayant des filles à marier. À part un hypothétique gain de statut social élevé et de droits à des provisions pour la fille en tant que femme au foyer dans son nouveau ménage – ce qui signifie un capital symbolique croissant pour la jeune génération de la fille et de son mari – les dots sont remises sans garantie d'une aide économique ou pratique en retour pour les donateurs, les parents démunis et d'autres membres de la parenté. Les dots et le fait d'être femme au foyer semblent se renforcer mutuellement au sein de la classe ouvrière pauvre et aboutit à affaiblir la responsabilisation (*disempowering*) des femmes dans le mariage, au lieu de la conforter (*empowering*). Nous pouvons donc affirmer que, chez les Pulaya, le mariage s'est davantage différencié selon le genre, avec des effets négatifs pour les femmes. Ces processus menacent en particulier la situation des veuves âgées pauvres et rendent probablement leur sécurité sociale encore plus incertaine dans l'avenir.

À côté de ces différences, nous discernons toutefois des similarités dans les deux sociétés, en l'occurrence l'accent important mis sur la solidarité familiale en matière de sécurité sociale dans le vieil âge. Mais comme l'illustrent les quatre cas d'étude, cette solidarité est limitée. Au Burkina Faso, la réciprocité généralisée est toujours valable comme un idéal, mais dans la pratique elle se limite aux relations entre parents et enfants. À cause des développements socio-économiques, le contrat implicite entre les générations s'est rétréci. Alors que l'obligation de s'occuper de la génération âgée incluait également les enfants des frères et sœurs tout comme ceux des coépouses, aujourd'hui seuls leurs propres enfants ont l'obligation de prendre en charge les parents âgés. Des cas où la « famille étendue » – notamment les enfants d'une coépouse – prend en charge une veuve démunie se rencontrent encore dans des villages comme à Kuila, mais ils sont de plus en plus rares. Au Kerala, le soutien financier venant exclusivement du fils pour ses parents âgés est un phénomène récent ; jadis, les propriétaires fonciers offraient eux aussi la sécurité sociale aux personnes âgées. Ceci n'est pas reconnu dans le discours ahistorique sur la piété filiale des institutions publiques indiennes ni dans celui de nombreux chercheurs en sciences sociales. Au Kerala comme au Burkina Faso, la prévoyance du vieil âge consistant à prendre bien soin des enfants déterminera largement plus tard la disposition des enfants à prendre en charge leur parents âgés. Le devoir des parents inclut l'obligation de donner une bonne formation aux enfants et de les marier, de construire une maison et d'épargner, exigences que les pauvres ne peuvent toutefois satisfaire que de façon fort restreinte.

À côté du soutien intergénérationnel fourni par les enfants, l'aide intergénérationnelle entre les époux est importante pour la sécurité sociale dans le vieil âge. Le caractère fondamental de la relation conjugale est semblable dans les deux régions. Le mariage est considéré comme un lien pour la vie durant lequel les époux peuvent mettre leurs revenus et leurs relations à leur profit mutuel. Le mari détient l'autorité et exerce hors du foyer, la femme fonctionne à l'intérieur du foyer. La responsabilité des femmes quant aux soins physiques des personnes âgées et des malades semble avoir un caractère universel (cf. Albert et Cattell 1994). Dans la pratique, la sécurité sociale de la femme âgée n'est assurée que si son mari remplit son devoir envers elle.

Dans les quatre sites de recherche, les veuves vivent dans la précarité, en partie à cause de la détérioration des conditions d'accès aux ressources pour le vieil âge tout au long de la vie, ce qui accentue la pauvreté. Le statut plus ou moins amélioré qu'elles ont acquis dans le vieil âge, selon le contexte social, ne peut pallier à cela. De plus, ces femmes ne possèdent généralement pas de maison ni d'épargnes (cf. aussi Cattell 2002).

Cependant, le soutien familial est, dans une certaine mesure, un mythe en ce sens que les relations de parenté dépendent des ressources économiques et symboliques exigées par différents membres de la parenté. Ceci rend même les relations intimes ambivalentes et incertaines. Pour les personnes âgées, il est important de disposer de ressources économiques pour avoir un pouvoir de négociation. Pour les enfants, ces ressources sont importantes car elles leur permettent de prendre en charge leurs parents âgés, tout comme leurs propres enfants et eux-mêmes. Les intérêts des parents et des enfants peuvent être divergents à cause des niveaux d'éducation et des besoins de consommation différents qui caractérisent la génération âgée et la génération plus jeune.

En ce qui concerne les relations de sécurité autres que celles entretenues avec les enfants, la réciprocité équilibrée au lieu de la réciprocité généralisée est importante du fait que les valeurs équivalentes sont échangées dans un laps de temps déterminé. Ceci s'applique également aux relations en dehors de la parenté : il n'y a pas d'échange ni de sécurité sociale sans un minimum de ressources économiques. Un autre facteur aggravant est le fait que la longévité augmente aussi la période de dépendance et le système de sécurité sociale s'en trouve saturé.

Le terme « voisinage étendu » émis par de Jong (dans ce volume) couvre les diverses relations de sécurité sociale des personnes âgées pauvres du Kerala urbain et rural qui comprennent et dépassent le cadre de la famille étendue. Au Burkina Faso, cela s'applique aussi à la couche moyenne. Ce qui distingue les deux groupes est la « redondance structurelle » (Elwert 1980) des relations de soutien. En milieu rural burkinabé, la famille étendue et le voisinage étendu sont identiques car tous les villageois sont apparentés soit par la famille natale soit par alliance.

Pour finir, les différences liées au genre dans le vieil âge au Kerala et au Burkina Faso peuvent se résumer comme suit. Dans les deux pays, le vieil âge est différencié selon le genre du fait que les femmes connaissent davantage d'insécurité dans le vieil âge. Pour ce qui a trait à la dimension politico-économique du genre, les femmes âgées pauvres du Burkina Faso, principalement en ville, semblent avoir la possibilité de faire de petits commerces, tandis qu'au Kerala les femmes âgées ont moins accès aux petits boulots, et on observe chez elles une forte tendance à se replier sur leur rôle de femmes au foyer. La situation économique des femmes âgées du Burkina Faso leur permet même, dans certains cas, de soutenir leurs enfants, au lieu de l'inverse comme c'est en général le cas. De surcroît, à cause de la forte valeur culturelle du droit d'aînesse au Burkina Faso, les jeunes hommes n'ont pas de pouvoir de décision sur les femmes âgées comme c'est le cas au Kerala, à moins qu'elles soient totalement infirmes.

Par leur pouvoir d'action (*agency*), au Kerala comme au Burkina Faso, les femmes essayent de s'adapter aux conditions du vieil âge afin de pouvoir joindre les deux bouts par leurs propres efforts, avec l'aide éventuelle de l'époux et des enfants, tout comme celle de leur voisinage. Elles demeurent actives en s'occupant du ménage et des soins aussi longtemps qu'elles le peuvent, à défaut, elles s'évertuent au moins à rester aimables dans leurs interactions avec leur parenté et les voisins. Les femmes protègent leurs maris contre la menace d'une éventuelle mauvaise réputation. Et notamment en milieu urbain burkinabé elles soutiennent des enfants qui ont en fait l'obligation de les protéger. Leurs filles les aident aussi tant qu'elles le peuvent. Alors que donner du soutien n'est pas très différencié selon le genre, en recevoir l'est d'autant plus.

Bien qu'au Kerala et au Burkina Faso les structures et les valeurs sont autrement différenciées selon le genre, tout comme la manière dont les personnes démunies font le genre diffère (*doing gender*), dans les deux sociétés, les femmes les plus pauvres vivent dans l'insécurité sociale. À cause des développements postcoloniaux différemment différenciés selon le genre au sein des deux sociétés, principalement en matière d'éducation et de santé, le degré d'insécurité que connaissent ces femmes varie cependant, tout comme le caractère de cette insécurité.

Développement communautaire : une nouvelle perspective sur la sécurité sociale dans le vieil âge

Les quatre études de cas fournissent une perspective nouvelle sur la sécurité sociale dans le vieil âge. En rapport avec le travail communautaire avec les personnes âgées et les politiques sociales qui y sont liées, nous estimons que les points suivants devraient être pris en considération :

– Avant tout, il importe d'envisager une approche prenant en compte les deux relations de soutien normatives et actuelles, qu'elles concernent une personne âgée ou jeune, une femme ou un homme, et de tenir compte aussi de la manière dont elles évoluent au cours de la vie d'un individu.
– Les personnes âgées ne devraient pas être considérées comme un groupe isolé et homogène. Leur hétérogénéité devrait être reconnue

et elles doivent être regardées en rapport avec les jeunes générations. De ce fait, le caractère spécifique des relations intergénérationnelles doit être compris en rapport avec l'âge et le genre, à la
fois dans la sphère de la parenté et de celle de la citoyenneté.

– La sécurité sociale dans le vieil âge est négociée dans un champ
conflictuel car les hiérarchie de l'âge et du genre évoluent suite aux
transformations sociétales, les ressources matérielles se font rares à
cause des développements économiques et les intérêts et les besoins des membres du foyer diffèrent généralement. La réciprocité
se négocie donc constamment selon l'âge, le genre et les moyens
individuels.

– La pauvreté dans le vieil âge, et l'insécurité qui en découle, ne peuvent s'expliquer par un réseau restreint de la parenté, mais plutôt
par le fait que être pauvre affecte la capacité de l'individu à participer aux échanges avec la parenté (et d'autres personnes) ce qui,
par ricochet, réduit son réseau de parenté et au-delà.

– La notion « voisinage étendu » proposée par de Jong met en lumière le fait que la famille étendue procurant du soutien est un
mythe, et met en même temps le doigt sur la diversité des relations
de sécurité, pas uniquement dans la famille, mais également en dehors.

– Le manque de ressources ne peut être compensé par le contrat implicite entre les générations ou par la piété filiale. La génération
plus jeune se paupérise davantage si elle s'applique à accomplir son
obligation, à savoir prendre en charge leurs parents âgés. D'autre
part, les personnes âgées s'appauvrissent encore plus si elles demeurent responsables de leurs enfants chômeurs et de leurs petits-
enfants. Dans ces cas, une aide extérieure financière et sociale
s'avère nécessaire.

– Dans un premier temps, il faudrait reconnaître et sensibiliser le
public aux bonnes actions des personnes âgées. À travers leurs efforts quotidiens et leur implication, elles apportent une contribution
à leur foyer, à la communauté et à l'État. Un débat sur ce sujet
pourrait générer des idées et des initiatives sur ces questions.

– Afin de faire avancer les questions relatives à la sécurité sociale, il s'avère primordial de créer continuellement des occasions de dialogue entre les chercheurs et les praticiens, opportunités qui permettraient aux deux parties de tirer avantage des expériences et des réflexions des uns et des autres et d'intégrer ainsi de nouvelles données et perspectives dans leurs travaux respectifs. Les partenariats de recherche Nord-Sud constituent une plate-forme favorable pour ce genre de dialogue.

Appendix / Appendice

Development Indicators[1]

	India	Kerala[2]	Burkina Faso
Income per capita	US$ 467	US$ 442	US$ 267
Literacy (above 14 years of age)	59.5 % M: 70.2 % F: 48.3 %	90.92 % M: 94.20 % F: 87.86 %	26.6 % M: 36.9 % F: 16.6 %
Life expectancy	M: 63 years old F: 64 years old	M: 69 (1998) F: 74 (1998)	M: 43 years old F: 46 years old[3]
Child mortality	59 of 1,000	15.6 of 1,000 (1998)	99 of 1,000
HIV/AIDS	0.8 % (2001)	0.08 % (2001)	6.5 % (2001)
Population 65+	4.8 %	60+: 10.84 % (2001)	2.9 %[4]

[1] The source of the figures on India and Burkina Faso is «WELT-IN-ZAHLEN.DE» which is based on the CIA World Factbook, 2004, if not noted otherwise. See www.welt-in-zahlen.de and www.cia.gov/cia/publications/factbook/.
[2] The source of the figures on Kerala in the first two lines is a website by the Government of Kerala, www.kerala.gov.in/ataglance/ataglance.htm; the source of the figures in the third and fourth line is another website by the Government of Kerala, www.prd.kerala.gov.in/prd2/hel/status.htm; the source of the figure in the fifth line is www.avert.org/indiaaids.htm; the figure in the last line is from «Ageing in Kerala» by K. G. Moli, in: Kerala Calling, August 2004, p. 10.
[3] Life expectancy in Burkina Faso is decreasing due to AIDS. In 1992, it was three years higher: for males 46 and for females 49 years of age.
[4] According to approximations by the Ministry of Social Action and National Solidarity (2001: 9, 10) in Burkina Faso, in 2005 the proportion of elderly (above the age of retirement of 55) of the total population will be 8.88 percent.

Indicateurs de développement[1]

	Inde	Kerala[2]	Burkina Faso
Revenu par habitant	467 US$	442 US$	267 US$
Taux d'alphabétisation (14 ans et plus)	59.5 % H: 70.2 % F: 48.3 %	90.92 % H: 94.20 % F: 87.86 %	26.6 % H: 36.9 % F: 16.6 %
Espérance de vie	H: 63 ans F: 64 ans	H: 69 (1998) F: 74 (1998)	H: 43 ans F: 46 ans[3]
Mortalité infantile	59 pour 1000	15.6 pour 1000 (1998)	99 pour 1000
VIH/sida	0.8 % (2001)	0.08 % (2001)	6.5 % (2001)
Population âgée de 65 ans et plus	4.8 %	60 ans et +: 10.84 % (2001)	2.9 %[4]

---

[1] Les données pour l'Inde et le Burkina Faso proviennent – si une autre source n'est pas indiquée – de « WELT-IN-ZAHLEN.DE » qui s'appuie à son tour aux données de la CIA World Factbook ; elles se rapportent à 2004, cf. http://www.welt-in-zahlen.de et http://www.cia.gov/cia/publications/factbook/.

[2] Les données pour le Kerala figurant aux deux premières lignes sont issues du site Internet du Gouvernement du Kerala www.kerala.gov.in/ataglance/ataglance.htm ; les données figurant aux lignes 3 et 4 sont quant à elles issues d'un autre site Internet du Gouvernement du Kerala, www.prd.kerala.gov.in/prd2/hel/status.htm ; les données de la ligne 5 ont pour source www.avert.org/indiaaids.htm ; les données de la dernière ligne sont tirées de «Ageing in Kerala» de K. G. Moli, dans : Kerala Calling, August 2004, p. 10.

[3] Au Burkina Faso, l'espérance de vie est de nouveau en baisse à cause du virus du sida. En 1992, elle était encore de trois ans plus élevée, à savoir 46 ans pour les hommes et 49 ans pour les femmes.

[4] D'après les estimations du Ministère de l'Action Sociale et de la Solidarité Nationale (2001 : 9-10) au Burkina Faso, la part des personnes âgées (définie d'après l'âge de la retraite de 55 ans) sera en 2005 de 8,88 % de l'ensemble de la population.

References / Bibliographie

Agarwal, Bina. 1991. Social Security and the Family: Coping with Seasonality and Calamity in Rural India. In: E. Ahmad et al. (eds.). *Social Security in Developing Countries*. Oxford: Clarendon Press. Pp. 171-244.

Albert, Steven M. and Maria G. Cattell. 1994. *Old Age in Global Perspective: Cross-cultural and Cross-national Views*. New. York: G. K. Hall.

Alexander, K. C. 1968. *Social Mobility in Kerala*. Poona: Deccan College, Postgraduate and Research Institute.

Anspach, Mark Rogin. 2002. *A charge de revanche – Figures élémentaires de la réciprocité*. Paris: Editions du Seuil, collection « La couleur des idées ».

Anthias, Floya. 2002. Beyond Feminism and Multiculturalism: Locating Difference and the Politics of Location. *Women's Studies International Forum* 25: 275-286.

Antoine, Philippe et al. 1998. (éds.). *Trois générations de citadins au Sahel. Trente ans d'histoire sociale à Dakar et à Bamako*. Paris: L'Harmattan.

Antoni, M. P. 1996. Village Development through People's Partnership. In: M. A. Taber, S. Batra (eds.). *Social Strains of Globalization in India: Case Examples*. New Delhi: New Concepts. Pp. 143-149.

Apt, Nana Araba. 1996. *Coping with Old Age in a Changing Africa. Social Change and the Elderly Ghanaian*. Aldershoot: Avebury.

Attias-Donfut, Claudine et al. 1994. La dynamique des générations. *Revue communications* 59, Générations et Filiation. Paris: Seuil. Pp. 5-12.

Attias-Donfut, Claudine et Léopold Rosenmayr (éds.). 1994. *Vieillir en Afrique*. Paris: PUF.

Baerends, Elsa. 1998. Changing Kinship: Family and Gender Relations in Sub-Saharan Africa. In: C. Risseeuw, K. Ganesh (eds.). *Negotiation and Social Space: A Gendered Analysis of Changing Kin and Security Networks in South Asia and Sub-Saharan Africa*. New Delhi, London: Sage Publications. Pp. 47-86.

Bailleul, Charles. 1996. *Dictionnaire Bambara-Français*. Bamako: Editions Donniya.

Bali, Arun P. 1997. Elderly Females: An Ignored Silent Majority. In: K. Bagchi (ed.). *Elderly Females in India, Their Status and Suffering*. New Delhi: Society for Gerontological Research and HelpAge India. Pp. 23-44.

Beck, Ulrich. 1986. *Die Risikogesellschaft: Auf den Weg in eine andere Moderne*. [Risk Society: Towards a New Modernity.] Frankfurt a. M.: Suhrkamp.

Benda-Beckmann, Franz von. 1988. Islamic Law and Social Security in an Ambonese Village. In: F. von Benda-Beckmann, K. von Benda-Beckmann, E. Casino, F. Hirtz, G. R. Woodman and H. F. Zacher (eds.). *Between Kinship and the State: Social Security and Law in Developing Countries.* Delft: Foris. Pp. 339-365.

Benda-Beckmann, Franz von and Keebet von Benda-Beckmann. 1998. Where Structures Merge: State and Off-state Involvement in Rural Social Security on Ambon, Eastern Indonesia. In: S. Pannell, F. von Benda-Beckmann (eds.). *Old World Places, New World Problems: Exploring Issues of Resource Management in Eastern Indonesia.* Canberra: Australian National University. Pp. 143-180.

Benda-Beckmann, Franz von and Keebet von Benda-Beckman. 2000 [1994]. Coping with Insecurity. In: F. and K. von Benda-Beckmann, H. Marks (eds.). *Coping with Insecurity: An "Underall" Perspective on Social Security in the Third World.* Yogyakarta: Pustaka Pelajar & Focaal Foundation. Pp. 7-31.

Benda-Beckmann, Franz von and Renate Kirsch. 1999. Informal Security Systems in Southern Africa and Approaches to Strengthen Them through Policy Measures. In: J. Freiberg-Strauss, K. Meyer (eds.). *The Real World of Social Policy. An Anthology of Project Experience.* Eschborn: Deutsche Gesellschaft für Technische Zusammenarbeit. Pp. 22-39.

Benda-Beckmann, Keebet von. 1988. Social Security and Small-Scale Enterprises in Islamic Ambon. In: F. von Benda-Beckmann et al. (eds.). *Between Kinship and the State: Social Security and Law in Developing Countries.* Delft: Foris. Pp. 451-471.

Benda-Beckmann, Keebet von. 1991. Developing Families: Moluccan Women and Changing Patterns of Social Security in the Netherlands. In: H. Claessen, M. van den Engel, D. Plantenga (eds.). *Het kweekbed ontkiemd.* Leiden: VENA. Pp. 35-60.

Benda-Beckmann, Keebet von. 2004. *An Inclusive Approach to Social Security: Changing Circles of Solidarity.* Proceedings of the Conference on "South-North Debates: Social Security Relations and Gender" in Ouagadougou, Burkina Faso in December 2003.

Benda-Beckmann, Keebet von and Francy Leatemia-Tomatala. 1992. *De emancipatie van Molukse vrouwen in Nederland.* [The Emancipation of Moluccan Women in the Netherlands]. Utrecht: van Arkel.

Benda-Beckmann, Franz von et al. 1988. Introduction: Between Kinship and the State. In: F. von Benda-Beckmann et al. (eds.). *Between Kinship and the State: Social Security and Law in Developing Countries.* Delft: Foris. Pp. 7-20.

Besana, Laura. 2001. *Les personnes âgées au Burkina Faso. Rapport de recherche.* Berne: Secrétariat suisse de la FAO.

Bhagyanath, Seema. 1998. *Ageing in India: A Sociological Inquiry.* Pune: Dept. of Sociology, University of Pune. Unpublished M. Phil. Dissertation.

Bhagyanath, Seema. 2003. *Old Age, Gender and Local Social Security in Rural Kerala.* Unpublished Final Report of the SNSF/SDC Project: No. 1270-059596.

Biezeveld, Renske. 2002. *Between Individualism and Mutual Help: Social Security and Natural Resources in a Minangkabau Village.* Delft: Eburon.

Böck, Monika and Aparna Rao. 2000. Introduction: Indigenous Models and Kinship Theories: An Introduction to a South Asia Perspective. In: M. Böck, A. Rao (eds.). *Culture, Creation, and Procreation: Concepts of Kinship in South Asian Practice.* New York: Berghahn. Pp. 1-49.

Bop, Codou. 1996. *Les femmes chefs de famille à Dakar.* In: J. Bisilliat (éd.). *Femmes du Sud, chefs de famille.* Paris: Karthala. Pp. 129-149.

Bose, Anil B. 1988. Policies and Programs for the Ageing in India. In: A. B. Bose, K.D. Gangrade (eds.). *The Ageing in India, Problems and Potentialities.* New Delhi: Abhinav Publications. Pp. 58-78.

Bourdieu, Pierre. 1977. *Outline of a Theory of Practice.* Cambridge, UK: Cambridge University Press.

Bourdieu, Pierre. 1990. *The Logic of Practice.* Stanford, CA: Stanford University Press.

Bourdieu, Pierre. 1996. On the Family as a Realized Category. *Theory, Culture and Society* 13: 19-26.

Bruijn, Mirjam de and Han van Dijk. 1994. A Pastoral Society in Crisis after the Droughts: Who cares for Social Security? In: S. Dittrich, J. Petersen-Thumser (eds.). *Social Security in Africa.* Berlin: German Foundation for International Development (DSE). Pp. 199-231.

Bruijn, Mirjam de and Han van Dijk. 1995. *Arid Ways. Cultural Understandings of Insecurity in Fulbe Society, Central Mali.* Amsterdam: Thela Publishers.

Busby, Cecilia. 2000. *The Performance of Gender: An Anthropology of Everyday Life in a South Indian Fishing Village.* London, New Brunswick, NJ: Athlone Press.

Cantor, Marjorie H. 1980. The Informal Support System: Its Relevance in the Lives of the Elderly. In: E. F. Borgatta, N. G. McCluskey (eds.). *Aging and Society: Current Research and Policy Perspectives.* Beverly Hills, London: Sage. Pp. 131-144.

Cattell, Maria. 1997. The Discourse of Neglect: Family Support for the Elderly in Samia. In: Th. Weisner et al. (eds.) *African Families and the Crisis of Social Change.* London: Begin & Garvey. Pp. 157-183.

Cattell, Maria. 2002. Holding up the Sky: Gender, Age and Work among the Abaluyia of Kenya. In: S. Makoni, K. Stroeken (eds.). *Ageing in Africa.* Aldershot: Ashgate. Pp. 155-175.

Central Statistical Organisation (CSO). 2000. *Elderly in India Profile and Pro-grammes 2000.* New Delhi: Ministry of Statistics and Programme Imple-mentation.

Chadha, N. K., V. Aggrawal, A. P. Mangla. 1992. Hopelessness, Alienation and Life-Satisfaction among Aged. *Indian Journal of Gerontology* 6: 82-92.

Chen, Martha Alter. 1998. Introduction. In: M. A. Chen (ed.). *Widows in India: So-cial Neglect and Public Action.* New Delhi, Thousand Oaks, London: Sage. Pp. 19-59.

Chowdhury, D. Paul. 1992. *Ageing and the Aged: A Source Book.* New Delhi: Inter-India Publications.

Cohen, Lawrence. 1994. Old Age: Cultural and Critical Perspectives. *Annual Review of Anthropology* 23: 137-158.

Cohen, Lawrence. 1998. *No Aging in India: Alzheimer's, the Bad Family, and Other Modern Things.* Berkeley, Los Angeles: University of California Press.

Collier, Jane, Rosaldo, Michelle Z. and Yanagisako, Sylvia. 1982. Is There a Fam-ily? New Anthropological Views. In: B. Thorne, M. Yalom (eds.). *Re-thinking the Family: Some Feminist Questions.* New York: Longman. Pp. 25-39.

Department of Economics and Statics. 1995. *Panchayat Level Statistic, Ernakulum.* Thiruvanathpuram: Government of Kerala.

Dittrich, Sabine and Jens Petersen-Thumser (eds.). 1994. *Social Security in Africa: Old Age, Accident and Unemployment. Proceedings of an International Conference held in Berlin 7–21 November 1993.* Berlin: German Founda-tion for International Development (DSE).

Drèze, Jean and Amartya Sen. 1991. Public Action for Social Security: Foundations and Strategy. In: E. Ahmad et al. (eds.). *Social Security in Developing Countries.* Oxford: Clarendon Press. Pp. 3-40.

Dube, Leela. 1997. *Women and Kinship: Comparative Perspectives on Gender in South and South-East Asia.* Tokyo, New York, Paris: United Nations Uni-versity Press.

Dube, Leela. 1998. Trends in Kinship Studies: Indian Material and Context. In: C. Risseeuw, K. Ganesh (eds.). 1998. *Negotiation and Social Space: A Gen-dered Analysis of Changing Kin and Security Networks in South Asia and Sub-Saharan Africa.* New Delhi, Thousand Oaks, London: Sage Press. Pp. 87-112.

Ela, Jean-Marc. 1994. *Quand l'Etat pénètre en brousse... Les ripostes paysannes à la crise.* Paris: Karthala.

Ela, Jean-Marc. 1994. *Afrique, l'interruption des pauvres: société contre ingérence, pouvoir et argent.* Paris: L'Harmattan.

Eloundou-Enyegue, Parfait Martial. 1992. *Solidarité dans la crise ou crise des soli-darités familiales au Cameroun.* Paris: Le dossier du CEPED N° 22.

Elwert, Georg. 1980. Die Elemente der traditionellen Solidarität. Eine Fallstudie in Westafrika. [Elements of Traditional Solidarity. A Case Study in West Africa.] *Kölner Zeitschrift für Soziologie und Sozialpsychologie* 32: 652-680.

Endeley, Joyce. 1998. Structural Adjustment and the Cameroonian Women's Lifeline: 1986 to 1995. In: C. Risseeuw, K. Ganesh (eds.). *Negotiation and Social Space: A Gendered Analysis of Changing Kin and Security Networks in South Asia and Sub-Saharan Africa.* New Delhi, London: Sage Publications. Pp. 226-255.

Faubion, James D. 2001. Introduction: Toward an Anthropology of the Ethics of Kinship. In: Faubion, James D. (ed.). *The Ethics of Kinship: Ethnographic Inquiries.* Lanham: Rowman and Littlefield. Pp. 1-28.

Finch, Janet and Jennifer Mason. 1993. *Negotiating Family Responsibilities.* London: Tavistock.

Foner, Nancy. 1984. *Ages in Conflict: A Cross-cultural Perspective on Inequality Between Old and Young.* New York: Columbia University Press.

Franke, Richard W. 1996. *Life Is a Little Better: Redistribution as a Development Strategy in Nadur Village, Kerala.* New Delhi: Promilla.

Franke, Richard W. and Barbara H. Chasin. 2000. Is the Kerala Model Sustainable? Lessons from the Past, Prospects for the Future. In: G. Parayil (ed.). *Kerala: The Development Experience – Reflections on Sustainability and Replicability.* London, New York: Zed. Pp. 16-39.

Frazer, Nancy. 1997. *Justice Interruptus. Critical Reflections on the "Postsocialist" Condition.* New York, London: Routledge.

Frazer, Nancy. 2000. After the Family Wage: A Postindustrial Thought Experiment. In: B. Hobson (ed.). 2000. *Gender and Citizenship in Transition.* Houndmills, London: Macmillan. Pp. 1-32.

Fuller, C. J. 1996. *The Nayars Today.* Cambridge: Cambridge University Press.

Fuller, C. J. 1997. Introduction: Caste Today. In: C.J. Fuller (ed.). *Caste Today.* Oxford: Oxford University Press. Pp. 1-31.

Ganesh, Kamala. 1998. Gender and Kinship Studies: Indian Material and Context. In: C. Risseeuw, K. Ganesh (eds.). 1998. *Negotiation and Social Space. A Gendered Analysis of Changing Kin and Security Networks in South Asia and Sub-Saharan Africa.* New Delhi, Thousand Oaks, London: Sage Press. Pp. 113-133.

Geest, Sjaak van der. 1997. Money and Respect: The Changing Value of Old Age in Rural Ghana. *Africa* 67 (4): 534-559.

Geest, Sjaak van der. 1998. The Social and Cultural Basis of Home Care to Elderly People in Ghana. In: A. Guerci (ed.). *Illness, Culture and Society.* Genova: Erga Edizioni. Pp. 461-480.

Geest, Sjaak van der. 2001. "No strength": Sex and Old Age in Ghana. *Social Science & Medicine* 53: 1383-1396.

Geest, Sjaak van der. 2002. Respect and Reciprocity: Care of Elderly People in Rural Ghana. *Journal of Cross-cultural Gerontology* 17: 3-31.

Ginneken, Wouter van. 2003. *Extending Social Security: Policies for Developing Countries*. ESS Paper No. 13. Geneva: ILO.

Glaser, Barney G. und Anselm L. Strauss. 1998 [1967]. *Grounded Theory. Strategien qualitativer Forschung* [Grounded Theory: Strategies of Qualitative Research]. Bern, Göttingen, Toronto, Seattle: Huber.

Gokhale, S.D., Ramamurthi, P.V., Pandit, Nirmala and Pendse, B.S. (eds.). *Ageing in India*. Mumbai, New Delhi: Somaiya Publications.

Gough, Kathleen. 1962. Nayar: Central Kerala; Nayar: North Kerala. In: D. Schneider, K. Gough (eds.). *Matrilineal Kinship*. Berkeley: University of California Press. Pp. 298-404.

Government of India (GOI). 1998. *The Aged in India: A Socio-Economic Profile. 1995-96*. Report No. 446.

Government of India (GOI). 1999. *National Policy on Older Persons*. New Delhi: Shastri Bhawan.

Gulati, I.S. and L. Gulati. 1995. Social Security for Widows. Experience in Kerala. *Economic and Political Weekly* 30 (34): 2451-2453.

Gulati, Leela. 1998. The Poor Widows of Kootam: A Study of Widows in a Squatter Settlement. In: M. A. Chen (ed.). *Widows in India. Social Neglect and Public Action*. New Delhi, Thousand Oaks, London: Sage. Pp. 347-360.

Gulati, Leela. 1990. Agricultural Workers' Pension in Kerala: An Experiment in Social Assistance. *Economic and Political Weekly* 25 (6): 339-343.

Gulati, I.S. and L. Gulati. 1998. Social Security for Widows: A Study of Schemes in Kerala. In: M. A. Chen (ed.). *Widows in India: Social Neglect and Public Action*. New Delhi, Thousand Oaks, London: Sage. Pp. 312-321.

Gulati, Leela, Ramalingam and I.S. Gulati. 1996. *Gender Profile Kerala*. New Delhi: Royal Netherlands Embassy.

Gurudoss, S. and T.R. Lakshminarayanan. 1989. A Study of Life-satisfaction in Relation to Marital Status among Aged. *Indian Journal of Social Work* 50: 236-238.

Hagberg, Sten. 2001. *Poverty in Burkina Faso: Representations and Realities*. Uppsala: Uppsala University.

Håkansson, N. Thomas and Robert LeVine. 1997. Gender and Life-Course Strategies among the Gusii. In: Th. Weisner et al. (eds.). *African Families and the Crisis of Social Change*. London: Begin & Garvry. Pp. 253-267.

Hirtz, Frank. 1995. *Managing Insecurity: State Social Policy and Family Networks in the Rural Philippines*. Saarbrücken: Breitenbach.

Hoffman, Barbara E. 2002. Gender Ideologie and Practice in Mande Societies and Mande Studies. *Mande Studies* 4: 1-20.

Holmes, Ellen Rhoads and Lowell D. Holmes. 1995. *Other Cultures, Elder Years*. Thousand Oaks, London, New Delhi: Sage.

INSD, Institut National de la Statistique et de la Démographie. 1998. *Résultats du recensement général de la population et de l'habitat au Burkina Faso de 1996*. Ouagadougou, INSD.

IRD, Institut de Recherche pour le Développement et al. 2000. *L'économie locale de Bobo-Dioulasso*, Ouagadougou, IRD, FaSEG/CEDRES.

Irudaya Rajan, S. 1999. Financial and Social Security in Old Age in India. *Social Change* 29: 90-125.

Irudaya Rajan, S., Mishra, U.S. and P. S. Sarma. 1999. *Elderly in India*. Delhi: Sage.

Irudaya Rajan, S. 1999. Ageing and Social Security. In: B.A. Prakash, (ed.). *Kerala's Economic Development: Issues and Problems*. New Delhi, Thousand Oaks, London: Sage. Pp. 49-71.

Irudaya Rajan, S. 2000. *Home Away from Home: A Survey of Old Age Homes and Inmates in Kerala*. Working Paper No. 306. Thiruvananthapuram: CDS.

Irudaya Rajan, S. 2001. Social Assistance for Poor Elderly: How Effective? *Economic and Political Weekly* 36: 613-61.

Irudaya Rajan, S., Mishra, U.S. and P. Sankara Sarma. 1999. *India's Elderly: Burden or Challenge?* New Delhi, Thousand Oaks, London: Sage Press.

Issac Thomas T.M. and Michael P.K. Tharakan. 1995. Kerala: Towards a New Agenda. *Economic and Political Weekly* August 5-12, 1993-2004.

Iyer, L. K. Anantha Krishna. 1981 [1909]. The Pulayans. In: L.K.A.K. Iyer. *The Tribes and Castes of Cochin*. Volume I. New Delhi: Cosmo. Pp. 87-127.

Iyer, L. K. Anantha Krishna. 1981 [1912]. The Nayars. In: L.K.A.K. Iyer. *The Tribes and Castes of Cochin*. Volume II. New Delhi: Cosmo. Pp. 1-102.

Jain, Shashi. 1999. Basis Social Security in India. In: W. van Ginneken (ed.). *Social Security for the Excluded Majority: Case Studies of Developing Countries*. Geneva: ILO. Pp. 37-67.

James, Wendy. 1978. Matrifocus on African Women. In: Shirley Ardener (ed.). *Defining Females: The Nature of Women in Society*. London: Croom Helm. Pp. 140-162.

Jeffrey, Robin. 1990. *Politics, Women and Well-being. How Kerala Became "a Mode"*. Houndmills, Basingstoke, Hampshire, London: Macmillan Press.

Jong, Willemijn de. 2001. Soziale Ganzheiten im Blickfeld ethnologischer Gender-Studien [Social Wholes in Anthropological Gender Studies.]. In: U. Davis-Sulikowski, H. Diemberger, A. Gingrich, J. Helbling (eds.). *Körper, Religion und Macht. Sozialanthropologie der Geschlechterbeziehungen* [Body, Religion and Power: The Social Anthropology of Gender Relationships.]. Frankfurt a. M.: Campus. Pp. 75-104.

Jong, Willemijn de. 2002. Forschungspartnerschaften aus der Sicht des Nordens – ethnologische Denkanstösse. [Research Partnerships from a Perspective of the North – Anthropological Reflections.] In: *Forschungspartnerschaften mit Entwicklungsländern: Ein Herausforderung für die Geistes- und Sozialwissenschaften*. [Research Partnerships with Developing Countries: A Challenge for the Humanities and the Social Sciences.] Tagungspublikation der SAGW und KFPE in Bern, 15. Juni 2001. [Conference Publication of the Swiss Academy of Humanities and Social Sciences and of the Swiss Commission for Research Partnerships with Developing Countries in Berne, 15th June, 2001.] Pp. 21–31.

Jong, Willemijn de. 2003. *Local Social Security and Gender in India and Burkina Faso. Social Security, Old Age and Gender in Urban Kerala*. Unpublished Final Report of the SNSF/SDC Project: No. 1270-059596.

Jong, Willemijn de. 2005. Anthropological Perspectives on Social Security. In: *Werkschau Afrikastudien 5 – Le forum suisse des africanistes 5*. Hamburg: Lit (forthcoming).

Kabeer, Naila. 2000. Social Exclusion, Poverty and Discrimination: Towards an Analytical Framework. *IDS Bulletin* 3: 83-97.

Kannan, K.P. and Shaji K. Francis. 2001. State-Assisted Social Security for Poverty Alleviation and Human Development: Kerala's Record and Its Lessons. In: S. Mahendra Dev, Piyush Antony, V. Gayathri and R.P. Mahajan (eds.). *Social and Economic Security in India*. New Delhi: Institute for Human Development. Pp. 411-438.

Kariyil, Antony. 1995. *Church and Society in Kerala: A Sociological Study*. New Delhi: Intercultural Publications.

Keesing, Robert M. and Andrew J. Strathern 1998. *Cultural Anthropology: A Contemporary Perspective*. Fort Worth: Harcourt Brace College Publishers.

Kinda, Fatoumata. 1998. *La pauvreté des femmes au Burkina Faso*. Ouagadougou: Ministère de l'Economie et des Finances du Burkina Faso, Direction de l'Orientations Economique et de la Prospective, UNICEF.

Kinda, Fatoumata. 2003. *La sécurité sociale locale, le vieil âge et le genre à Kuila, Burkina Faso*. Rapport final du projet SNSF/SDC: No. 1270-059596. Manuscript.

Koné, Kassim. 2002. When Male Becomes Female and Female Becomes Male in Mande. *Mande Studies* 4: 21-29.

Koning, Juliette and Frans Hüsken (eds.). 2005. *Reciprocity in Indonesia: Local Ways of Managing Insecurity*. Leiden, Singapore: Brill Academic Publishers / Times Academic Press (forthcoming).

Kumar, R. 1994. *Emerging Trends in Female Unemployment in Kerala: A Quantitative Analysis*. Paper presented at the International Congress of Kerala Studies, August 27-29, 1994. Session 17, ICKS-A, Vol. 2:73-74.

Kumar, S. V. 2000. Radical Change in Policy Needed to Reach the Old. *The Hindu*, 8th June, 2000.

Kurien, John. 2000. The Kerala Model: Its Central Tendency and the "Outlier". In: G. Parayil (ed.) 2000. *Kerala: The Development Experience – Reflections on Sustainability and Replicability.* London, New York: Zed. Pp. 178-197.

Kuruvilla, Theresiamma. 1989. *Plan for Thrikkakara-Kalamassery, a Peripheral Unit in Cochin.* Madras: Anna University, School of Architecture and Planning.

Lachaud, Jean-Pierre (éd). 1994. *Pauvreté et marché du travail urbain en Afrique subsaharienne: analyse comparative.* Genève: BIT.

Lachaud, Jean-Pierre. 1997. *Les femmes et le marché du travail urbain en Afrique subsaharienne.* Paris: L'Harmattan.

Lachenmann, Gudrun. 1994. Social Security in Developing Countries: the Gender Perspective. In: S. Dittrich, J. Petersen-Thumser (eds.). *Social Security in Africa.* Berlin. Pp. 127-150.

Lachenmann, Grudrun. 1997. Selbstorganisation sozialer Sicherheit von Frauen in Entwicklungsländern [Self-organization for Social Security of Women in Developing Countries]. In: M. Braig et al. (Hg.). *Begegnungen und Einmischungen.* [Encounters and Interferences.] Stuttgart: Verlag Hans-Dieter Heinz. Pp. 395-415.

Le Bris, Emile et al. 1987. *Famille et résidence dans les villes africaines. Dakar, Bamako, Saint-Louis, Lomé.* Paris: L'Harmattan.

Lejeal, Frédéric. 2002. *Le Burkina Faso.* Paris: Karthala.

Leliveld, André. 1994. *Social Security in Developing Countries: Operation and Dynamics of Social Security Mechanisms in Rural Swaziland.* Amsterdam: Thesis Publishers.

Leliveld, André. 2004. *Local Social Security Arrangements at Risk? A Case Study from Mbarara District, Uganda.* Proceedings of the Conference on "South-North Debates: Social Security Relations and Gender" in Ouagadougou, Burkina Faso in December 2003.

Mahajan, Anil. 1992. Social Dependency and Abuse of the Elderly. In: P. Krishnan, K. Mahadevan (eds.). *The Elderly Population in Developed and Developing World.* New Delhi: B. R. Publishing Corporation. Pp. 414-423.

Makoni, Sinfree and Koen Stroeken (eds.). 2002. *Ageing in Africa: Sociolinguistic and Anthropological Approaches.* Hampshire: Ashgate.

Marie, Alain (éd.). 1997. *L'Afrique des individus.* Paris: Karthala.

Marie, Alain. 1997a. Du sujet communautaire au sujet individuel. Une lecture anthropologique de la réalité africaine contemporaine. In: A. Marie (éd.). *L'Afrique des individus.* Paris: Karthala. Pp. 53-110.

Marie, Alain. 1997b. Conclusion. Individualisation : entre communauté et société, l'avènement du sujet. In: A. Marie (éd.). *L'Afrique des individus*. Paris: Karthala. Pp. 407-436.

Marulisiddiah, H. M. 1966. The Declining Authority of Old People. *Indian Journal of Social Work* 27: 175-185.

Mathew, P. M. 1999. The Industrial Stagnation of Kerala: Some Alternative Explanations. In: B. A. Prakash (ed.). *Kerala's Economic Development: Issues and Problems*. New Delhi, Thousand Oaks, London: Sage. Pp. 281-302.

Merlin, J. N. 1999. Elderly Abuse: A Study Among Urban-poor in Thiruvananthapuram. *Kerala Sociologist* 27: 50-75.

Ministère de l'Action Sociale et de la Solidarité Nationale. 2001. *Plan d'action national en faveur des personnes âgées au Burkina Faso*. Ouagadougou.

Ministère de l'Economie et du Développement. 2003. *Cadre stratégique de lutte contre la pauvreté*. Ouagadougou.

Ministère de l'Equipement (éd.). 1990. *Schéma de développement et d'aménagement urbain de Bobo-Dioulasso*. Mayenne (France): L'imprimerie de la nanutention.

Ministry of Social Welfare. 1987. The Aged in India: Policies and Programmes. In: M. L. Sharma and T. M. Dak (eds.). 1987. *Ageing in India – Challenge for the Society*. New Delhi: Ajanta Publications. Pp. 8-23.

Mohandas, M. 1999. Poverty, Food Intake and PDS in Kerala: Emerging Trends. In: B.A. Prakash (ed.). *Kerala's Economic Development: Issues and Problems*. New Delhi, Thousand Oaks, London: Sage. Pp. 72-93.

Mohanty, S. P. 1989. Demographic and Socio-Cultural Aspects of Ageing in India – Some Emerging Issues. In: R.N. Pati, B. Jena (eds.). *Aged in India. Sociodemographic Dimensions*. New Delhi: Ashish Publishing House. Pp. 37-45.

Moore, Henrietta. 1994. *A Passion for Difference: Essays in Anthropology and Gender*. Cambridge: Polity Press.

Nair, P. K. B. 1987. *Review and Analysis of Principle Social Welfare Schemes in Kerala State, India*. Unpublished Manuscript.

Neubert, Dieter. 1990. Von der traditionellen Solidarität zur Nicht-Regierungsorganisation: Eine steuerungstheoretische Analyse von Formen der Solidarität in Kenya. [From traditional solidarity to NGO: A Steering-oriented Analysis of Different Forms of Solidarity in Kenia.] In: K.-H. Kohl (Hg.). *Die Vielfalt der Kulturen*. [Plurality of Cultures.] Berlin: Reimer. S. 548-571.

Nioumou, Frédéric et al. 1997. *Genre et pauvreté au Burkina Faso*. Ouagadougou: INSD.

Nooteboom, Gerben. 2003. *A Matter of Style: Social Security and Livelihood in Upland East Java*. Rotterdam: Optima.

Nydegger, Corinne N. 1983. Family Ties of the Aged in Cross-cultural Perspective. *The Gerontologist* 23: 26-32.

Osella, Filippo and Caroline Osella. 2000. *Social Mobility in Kerala: Modernity and Identity in Conflict.* London: Pluto Press.

Palriwala, Rajni. 1994. *Changing Kinship, Family, and Gender Relations in South Asia: Processes, Trends and Issues.* Leiden: Women and Autonomy Centre.

Palriwala, Rajni. 2000. An Indian Fieldworker in the Netherlands: Reverse Anthropology. *IIAS Newsletter* 20: 17.

Palriwala, Rajni and Carla Risseeuw (eds.). 1996. *Shifting Circles of Support. Contextualizing Gender and Kinship in South Asia and Sub-Saharan Africa.* New Delhi, Thousand Oaks, London: Sage Press.

Panda, P. K. 1998. The Elderly in Rural Orissa: Alone in Distress. *Economic and Political Weekly* 33 (25): 1545-1550.

Parayil, Govindan (ed.) 2000. *Kerala: The Development Experience – Reflections on Sustainability and Replicability.* London, New York: Zed.

Peletz, Michael G. 2001. Ambivalence in Kinship since the 1940s. In: S. Franklin, S. McKinnon (eds.). *Relative Values: Reconfiguring Kinship Studies.* Durham, London: Duke University Press. Pp. 413-444.

Potts, Deborah. 1997. Urban Lives: Adopting New Strategies and Adapting Rural Links. In: C. Rakodi (ed.). *The Urban Challenge in Africa: Growth and Management of its Large Cities.* Tokyo, New York, Paris: United Nations University Press. Pp. 447-494.

Prakash, B. A. 1999. Economic Reforms and the Performance of Kerala's Economy. In: B. A. Prakash (ed.). *Kerala's Economic Development: Issues and Problems.* New Delhi, Thousand Oaks, London: Sage. Pp. 27-46.

Raj, B. and B. G. Prasad. 1971. Study of Rural Aged Persons in Social Profile. *Indian Journal of Social Work* 32: 155-162.

Rajagiri College of Social Sciences. 1991. *Socio-Economic Profile of Kothad Village.* Kalamassery: Rajagiri College.

Rajagiri College of Social Sciences. 1996. *Report of the Socio-economic Survey: Kalamassery Municipality.* Rajagiri Community Development Scheme (RCDS): Annual Report. Kalamassery: Unpublished mimeo. Appendix. Pp. 1-13.

Rajagiri College of Social Sciences. 1999. *An Assessment of the Kind of Support Required by Different Categories of the Elderly People.* Kalamassery, Kochi: Unpublished Research Report by the Rajagiri Research Institute.

Ramachandran V.K. 1995. *Kerala's Development Achievements: A Review.* Bombay: Indira Gandhi Institute of Development Research.

Ramachandran, V.K. 1997. On Kerala's Development Achievements. In: J. Drèze, A. Sen, (eds.). *Indian Development: Selected Regional Perspectives.* Delhi: Oxford University Press. Pp. 205-356.

Reddy, P. J. and D. Usha Rani. 1989. Status of the Elderly: A Case Study of Pensioners and Non-pensioners. *Journal of Social Research* 32: 70-81.

Renjini. D. 2000. *Nayar Women Today: Disintegration of Matrilineal System and the Status of Nayar Women in Kerala.* New Delhi: Classical Publishing Company.

Retnaraj, D. 1999. Patterns, Causes and Consequences of Urbanisation. In: B.A. Prakash (ed.). *Kerala's Economic Development: Issues and Problems.* New Delhi, Thousand Oaks, London: Sage. Pp. 150-163.

Risseeuw, Carla and Kamala Ganesh (eds.). 1998. *Negotiation and Social Space: A Gendered Analysis of Changing Kin and Security Networks in South Asia and Sub-Saharan Africa.* New Delhi, Thousand Oaks, London: Sage Press.

Risseeuw, Carla and Rajni Palriwala. 1996. Introduction: Shifting Circles of Support. In: R. Palriwala, C. Risseeuw (eds.). *Shifting Circles of Support: Contextualising Gender and Kinship in South Asia and Sub-Saharan Africa.* New Delhi, London: Sage Publications. Pp. 15-47.

Rogerson, Christian. 1997. Globalization or Informalization? African Urban Economies in the 1990s. In: C. Rakodi (ed.). *The Urban Challenge in Africa: Growth and Management of its Large Cities.* Tokyo: United Nations, University Press. Pp. 337-370.

Rondeau, Chantal. 1996. Femmes chefs de famille à Bamako. In: J. Bisilliat (éd.). *Femmes du Sud, chefs de famille.* Paris: Karthala. Pp. 151-170.

Roost Vischer, Lilo. 1997. *Mutter zwischen Herd und Markt. Das Verhältnis von Mutterschaft, sozialer Elternschaft und Frauenarbeit bei den Moose (Mossi) in Ouagadougou, Burkina Faso.* [Mothers between Home and the Market. Links between Maternity, Kinship and Women's Work among the Moose (Mossi) in Ouagadougou.] Basel: Wepf.

Rosenberg, Harriet. 1990. Complaint Discourse, Ageing and Caregiving among the !Kung San of Botswana. In: J. Sokolovsky (ed.). *The Cultural Context of Aging: Worldwide Perspectives.* Westport, CT: Bergin and Garvey. Pp. 19-41.

Rosenblatt, D. and M.P. Antoni. 2002. Elder Mistreatment. In: D.E. Rosenblatt, V.S. Natarajan (eds.). *Primer on Geriatric Care: A Clinical Approach to the Older Patient.* Cochin: Pixel Studio. Pp. 299-306.

Rosenmayr, Leopold. 2002. Zwischen Sippe und Modernität: Feldstudien zum Generationenkonflikt im Entwicklungsprozess Westafrikas. [Between Clan and Modernity: Studies on Intergenerational Conflict in the Process of Development in West Africa.] In: H. Marzi (Hg.). *Alter in Afrika: Tradition und Wandel.* [Old Age in Africa: Tradition and Change.] Mainz: Institut für Ethnologie und Afrika-Studien der Johannes-Gutenberg-Universität Mainz. Pp. 63-88.

Roth, Claudia. 1996. *La séparation des sexes au Burkina Faso.* Paris: L'Harmattan.

Roth, Claudia. 1998. Tee und Träume. Zum Generationenkonflikt der Männer in Bobo-Dioulasso [Tea and Dreams. The Intergenerational Conflict among Men in Bobo-Dioulasso]. *Ethnopsychoanalyse* Bd. 5, Jugend und Kulturwandel. [Youth and Cultural Change.] Frankfurt am Main: Brandes & Apsel. Pp. 153-166.

Roth, Claudia. 2003a. *Arrangements sociaux de protection et leurs limites: Recherche dans le quartier Koko à Bobo-Dioulasso, sur la protection sociale locale, le vieil âge et le genre.* Rapport final du project SNSF/SDC: No. 1270-059596. Manuscript.

Roth, Claudia. 2003b. Der mütterliche Schutz. Fünf Hypothesen zur sozialen Sicherheit in Burkina Faso [Maternal Protection. Five Hypothesis Concerning Social Security in Burkina Faso]. In: J. Schneider et al. (Hg.) *Werkschau Afrikastudien 4 – Le forum suisse des africanistes 4.* Hamburg: Lit. Pp. 113-132.

Rubinstein, Robert L. 1990. Nature, Culture, Gender, Age: A Critical Review. In: R. L. Rubinstein (ed.). *Anthropology and Aging: Comprehensive Reviews.* Dordrecht: Kluwer. Pp. 109-125.

Sahayam, M. D. 1988. Aged Females, the Most Deprived Among the Deprived. *Indian Journal of Social Work* 49: 261-269.

Sahlins, Marshall. 2004 [1965]. *Stone Age Economics.* London: Routledge.

Saradamoni, K. 1980. *Emergence of a Slave Caste: Pulayas of Kerala.* New Delhi: People's Publishing House.

Saradamoni, K. 1999. *Matriliny Transformed: Family, Law and Ideology in Twentieth Century Travancore.* New Delhi, Walnut Creek, London: Sage Press.

Sawadogo, Sita Malick et al. 2000. *Etude sur la pauvreté en milieu sémi-urbain : cas de Ouahigouya.* Ouagadougou: Coopération Suisse au Développement.

Schneider, David M. 1972. What is Kinship All About? In: P. Reining (ed.). *Kinship Studies in the Morgan Centennial Year.* Washington: Anthropological Society of Washington. Pp. 32-63.

Schott, Rüdiger. 1988. Traditional Systems of Social Security and their Present-day Crisis in West Africa. In: F. v. Benda-Beckmann et al. (eds.). *Between Kinship and the State.* Dordrecht: Foris Publications. Pp. 89-107.

Schoumaker, Bruno. 2000. Le vieillissement en Afrique subsaharienne. *Espace, populations, sociétés* 3: 379-390.

Shah, A. M. 1998. *The Family in India: Critical Essays.* New Delhi: Orient Longman.

Shah, A. M. 1999. Changed in the Family and the Elderly. *Economic and Political Weekly* 34 (20): 1179-1182.

Sokolovsky, Jay (ed.). 1990. *The Cultural Context of Aging: Worldwide Perspectives.* Westport, CT: Bergin and Garvey.

Sokolovsky, Jay. 1993. Images of Aging: A Cross-cultural Perspective. *Generations* 17: 51-54.

Somda, Prosper et Sita Malick Sawadogo. 2001. Le suivi de la pauvreté au Burkina Faso: instruments et contraintes. In: M. Koulibaly (éd.). *La pauvreté en Afrique de l'Ouest*. Paris, Dakar: Karthala, Codesria. Pp. 89-111.

Sooryamoorthy, R. 1997. *Consumption to Consumerism in the Context of Kerala*. New Delhi: Classical Publishing Company.

Spicker, Paul. 2000. *The Welfare State: A General Theory*. London: Sage.

Srinivas, M. N. 1997. *Caste: Its Twentieth Century Avatar*. New Delhi: Penguin.

Stahl, Claudia. 2001. *Lebenslauf und Altern in Entwicklungsgesellschaften: Das Fallbeispiel Kenia*. [Life-course and Ageing in Developing Societies: The Case Study of Kenia.] Frankfurt a. M.: Peter Lang.

Stivens, Maila. 1998a. Theorising Gender, Power and Modernity in Affluent Asia. In: K. Sen, M. Stivens (eds.). *Gender and Power in Affluent Asia*. London, New York: Routledge. Pp. 1-34.

Stivens, Maila. 1998b. *Gendering the Global and the Anti-Global: Asian Modernities, "Asian Values" and "the Asian Family"*. Paper for Transnationalism: An Exchange of Theoretical Perspectives from Latin American, Africanist and Asian Anthropology. ICCR International Conference. http://les1.man.ac.uk/sa/Transnationalism/stivensm.doc (September 2003).

Strauss, Anselm and Juliet Corbin. 1994. Grounded Theory Methodology. In: N.K. Denzin, Y.S. Lincoln (eds.). *Handbook of Qualitative Research*. Thousand Oaks, London, New Delhi: Sage Publication. Pp. 273-285.

Thomas Isaac with Franke, Richard W. 2000. *Local Democracy and Development: People's Campaign for Decentralized Planning in Kerala*. New Delhi: LeftWord.

Treas, J. 1975. Ageing and the Family. In: D. S. Woodruff, J. E. Birren (eds.). *Ageing: Scientific Perspectives and Social Issues*. New York: D. Van Nostrand Company. Pp. 92-108.

Uberoi, Patricia. 1993. Family, Household and Social Change. In: P. Uberoi (ed.). *Family, Marriage and Kinship in India*. Delhi: Oxford University Press. Pp. 383-393.

Udvardy, Monica and Maria Cattell. 1992. Gender, Ageing and Power in Sub-Saharan Africa: Challenges and Puzzles. *Journal of Cross-cultural Gerontology* 7: 275-288.

Ungerson, Clare. 2000. The Commodification of Care: Current Policies and Future Politics. In: B. Hobson (ed.). *Gender and Citizenship in Transition*. Houndmills, London: Macmillan. Pp. 173-200.

United Nations. 1994. *Ageing and the Family*. Proceedings of the United Nations International Conference on Ageing Populations in the Context of the Family. New York.

Uyl, Marion den. 1995. *Invisible Barriers: Gender, Caste and Kinship in a Southern Indian Village.* Utrecht: International Books.

Uyl, Marion den. 2000. Kinship and Gender Identity: Some Notes on *Marumakkathayam* in Kerala. In: M. Böck, A. Rao (eds.). *Culture, Creation, and Procreation: Concepts of Kinship in South Asian Practice.* New York: Berghahn. Pp. 177-197.

Willigen, J. van et al. 1996. Personal Networks of Older People in a Delhi Neighbourhood. *Indian Journal of Social Work* 57: 414-428.

Varghese, S. 1994. *Economic Activity Pattern of Women in Female-headed Households of Kerala.* Paper presented at the International Congress of Kerala Studies, August 27-29, 1994. Session 17, Vol. 3. Pp. 152-53.

Vatuk, Sylvia. 1980. Withdrawal and Disengagement as a Cultural Response to Aging in India. In C. L. Fry (ed.). *Ageing in Culture and Society: Comparative View Points and Strategies.* New York: Praeger Publications. Pp. 126-148.

Vatuk, Sylvia. 1990. To be a Burden on Others: Dependency Anxiety among the Elderly in India. In: O.W. Lynch (ed.). *Divine Passion: The Social Construction of Emotion in India.* Delhi: Oxford University Press. Pp 64-88.

Vel, Jaqueline. 1994. *The Uma-economy: Indigenous Economics and Development Work in Lawonda, Sumba (Eastern-Indonesia).* Wageningen: Ponsen and Looijen.

Veron, René. 2000. Sustainability and the "New" Kerala Model. In: G. Parayil (ed.). 2000. *Kerala: The Development Experience – Reflections on Sustainability and Replicability.* London, New York: Zed. Pp. 212-229.

Vidal, Claudine. 1994. La « solidarité africaine »: un mythe à revisiter. *Cahiers d'Etudes africaines* 136, xxxix-4: 687-691.

Vuarin, Robert. 1993. Quelles solidarités sociales peut-on mobiliser pour faire face au coût de la maladie ? In: J. Brunet-Jailly (éd.). *Se soigner au Mali.* Paris. Pp. 299-316.

Vuarin, Robert. 1994. L'argent et l'entregent. *Cahiers des Sciences Humaines* 30 (1–2): 255-273.

Vuarin, Robert. 2000. *Un système africain de protection sociale au temps de la mondialisation ou « Venez m'aider à tuer mon lion... ».* Paris: L'Harmattan.

Vuarin, Robert. 2004. *Tendances évolutives de la sociabilité protectrice à Bamako: clientèles, réseaux, mutuelles.* Compte rendu de la conférence « Débats Sud-Nord: Relations de sécurité sociale et genre », Ouagadougou, Burkina Faso, 15-16 décembre 2003.

Waerness, Kari. 1987. On the Rationality of Caring. In: A. S. Sassoon (ed.). *Women and the State: The Shifting Boundaries of Public and Private.* London: Hutchinson. Pp. 207-234.

Webster, John C. B. 1999. Who is a Dalit? In: S.M. Michael (ed.). *Dalits in Modern India: Vision and Values*. New Delhi: Vistar Publications. Pp. 68-79.

West, Candace and Don H. Zimmerman. 1987. Doing Gender. *Gender and Society* 1: 125-151.

World Bank. 1994. *A World Bank Policy Research Report. Averting The Old Age Crises. Policies to Protect the Old and Promote Growth*. New York: Oxford University Press.

World Bank. 2001. *Social Protection Sector Strategy: From Safety Net to Springboard*.

Yanagisako, Sylvia J. and Jane F. Collier. 1987. Toward a Unified Analysis of Gender and Kinship. In: J. Collier, S. Yanagisako (eds.). *Gender and Kinship: Essays Toward a Unified Analysis*. Stanford, California: Stanford University Press. Pp. 14-50.

Yuval-Davis, Nira. 1997. *Gender and Nation*. Thousand Oaks, London, New Delhi: Sage.

Zachariah, K. C., Kannan, K. P. and Rajan, S. Irudaya. 2002. *Kerala's Gulf Connection: CDS Studies on International Labour Migration from Kerala State in India*. Thiruvananthapuram: Centre for Development Studies.

Zimmermann, Francis. 1972. *La parenté*. Paris: PUF.

The Authors

Fatoumata Badini-Kinda
born in 1957, holds a Ph. D. in sociology, and is a lecturer ("maître-assistante") at the Faculty of Sociology at the University of Ouagadougou, Burkina Faso. She teaches on urban and industrial sociology, research methodologies and techniques, and gender and development analysis. Her research involves issues related to urbanisation, social security and old age, family migration, the situation of women and children, and especially poverty among women in Burkina Faso. Contact: fkinda_badini@univ-ouaga.bf

Seema Bhagyanath
born in 1971, is a Ph. D. candidate at the Department of Sociology, University of Pune, India. She is finishing a thesis on the empowerment of the elderly in organized settings in India for which she conducted fieldwork in the states of Maharashtra and Kerala. Her Ph. D. supervisor is Prof. Dr. Sujata Patel. Her M. Phil. dissertation is on ageing in India as well. She has also worked on small projects in the field of gender. Her current interests are care relations of the elderly, social security and empowerment. She joined the project on "Local Social Security and Gender in India and Burkina Faso" in the second year. Contact: bags22@rediffmail.com

Willemijn de Jong
born in 1949, is Associate Professor at the Institute of Social Anthropology, University of Zurich, Switzerland. She has conducted anthropological fieldwork in Indonesia since 1987 and in India since 2000. She has published on work, marriage and gender relationships as well as on rituals and social identity in Indonesia and on the anthropology of gender. Her current fields of interest are kinship, citizenship, gender, generations, body, social identities and social security. She was the head of the project on "Local Social Security and Gender in India and Burkina Faso". Contact: w.de.jong@access.unizh.ch

Claudia Roth
born in 1955, holds a Ph. D. in social anthropology, and is a researcher and lecturer at the Institute of Social Anthropology, University of Zurich, Switzerland. Her fields of interest include gender, old age, local social security, social change, urbanisation, anthropology of development and ethnopsychoanalysis. Since 1989, she has conducted regular research in Bobo-Dioulasso, Burkina Faso, and published about gender divisions, women in the informal sector, adolescence, intergenerational relationship, and methodological issues.
Contact: RothC@access.unizh.ch

Les auteurs

Fatoumata Badini-Kinda
née en 1957, docteur en sociologie, est Maître-assistante à la Faculté
de Sociologie de l'Université de Ouagadougou, Burkina Faso. Elle
enseigne la sociologie urbaine et industrielle, les méthodes et techniques de recherche, ainsi que l'analyse du genre et du développement.
Ses travaux de recherche traitent des questions d'urbanisation, de
sécurité sociale et du vieil âge, de migration de la famille, l'analyse de
la situation des femmes et des enfants, en particulier la pauvreté des
femmes au Burkina Faso.
Contact : fkinda_badini@univ-ouaga.bf

Seema Bhagyanath
née en 1971, est doctorante au Département de Sociologie de
l'Université de Pune, Inde. Elle est sur le point de terminer sa thèse
portant sur la responsabilisation (*empowerment*) des personnes âgées
au sein des groupes organisés en Inde. Pour sa thèse, elle a fait des
recherches de terrain dans les États du Maharashtra et du Kerala. Sa
directrice de thèse est le Prof. Dr Sujata Patel. Sa thèse porte aussi sur
le thème vieillir en Inde. Elle a également travaillé dans le domaine du
genre pour de petits projets. Actuellement, les relations de soins, la
sécurité sociale et la responsabilisation représentent ses centres
d'intérêt. Elle s'est jointe au projet sur la « Sécurité sociale et le genre
en Inde et au Burkina Faso » la deuxième année.
Contact : bags22@rediffmail.com

Willemijn de Jong
née en 1949, est professeur associé au Département d'Anthropologie
Sociale de l'Université de Zurich, Suisse. Elle a conduit des recherches anthropologiques en Indonésie depuis 1987 et en Inde depuis
2000. Elle a publié des travaux sur le mariage et les relations du genre,
les rites et l'identité sociale en Indonésie, ainsi que sur l'anthropologie
du genre. Ses domaines d'intérêt actuels sont la parenté, la citoyenneté, le genre, les générations, le corps, les identités sociales et la

sécurité sociale. Elle était la directrice du projet sur la « Sécurité sociale et le genre en Inde et au Burkina Faso ».
Contact : w.de.jong@access.unizh.ch

Claudia Roth
née en 1955, docteur en ethnologie. Elle est chercheur, enseignante et assistante au Département d'Anthropologie Sociale de l'Université de Zurich, Suisse. Ses domaines d'intérêt sont le genre, le vieil âge, la sécurité sociale, le changement social, l'urbanisation, l'anthropologie du développement et l'ethno-psychanalyse. Depuis 1989, elle a régulièrement conduit des recherches à Bobo-Dioulasso au Burkina Faso. Ses publications portent sur la séparation selon le genre, les femmes dans le secteur informel, l'adolescence, les relations intergénérationnelles et les questions de méthodologie.
Contact : RothC@access.unizh.ch

Schweizerische Afrikastudien – Etudes africaines suisses

hrsg. von der Schweizerischen Afrika-Gesellschaft (SAG)/édité par la Société suisse d'études africaines (SSEA)

Beat Sottas; Thomas Hammer; Lilo Roost Vischer; Anne Mayor (Hrsg./éd.)
Werkschau Afrikastudien – Le forum suisse des africanistes
Bd. 1, 1997, 392 S., 24,90 €, br.,
ISBN 3-8258-3506-5

Lilo Roost Vischer; Anne Mayor; Dag Henrichsen (Hrsg./éd.)
Brücken und Grenzen – Passages et frontières
Werkschau Afrikastudien 2 – Le forum suisse des africanistes 2
Bd. 2, 1999, 480 S., 25,90 €, br.,
ISBN 3-8258-4398-x

Yvan Droz; Anne Mayor; Lilo Roost Vischer (Hrsg./éd.)
Partenariats Nord-Sud/Forschungspartnerschaften
Werkschau Afrikastudien 3 – Le forum suisse des africanistes 3
Der dritte Band der Reihe "Le forum suisse des africanistes", herausgegeben von der Schweizerischen Afrika-Gesellschaft, ist dem Oberthema Forschungspartnerschaften zwischen dem Norden, hauptsächlich der Schweiz, und dem Süden, genauer Afrika, gewidmet. Die 23 zumeist jüngeren Autorinnen und Autoren unterschiedlicher Disziplinen befassen sich mit den Themenbereichen "Forschungspartnerschaften: Kontext und Beispiele", "Lokales Wissen und dauerhafte Entwicklung", "Gesundheit zwischen Verwaltung und lokaler Perzeption", "Fragen zur Politik" und "Grundlagenforschung zu Vergangenheit und Gegenwart". Hamady Bocoum, Direktor des "Patrimoine culturel du Sénégal", betont im Eingangsreferat den Zusammenhang zwischen wissenschaftlicher Partnerschaft und Globalisierung.
Bd. 3, 2001, 392 S., 30,90 €, br.,
ISBN 3-8258-5688-7

Jürg Schneider; Lilo Roost Vischer; Didier Péclard (Hg./éds.)
Werkschau Afrikastudien 4 – Le forum suisse des africanistes 4
Der vierte Band der Reihe „Schweizerische Afrikastudien", herausgegeben von der Schweizerischen Afrika-Gesellschaft/SAG, versammelt 16 überarbeitete und erweiterte Vorträge, die am 4. Forum Afrikastudien im Herbst 2002 in Basel gehalten wurden. Die Beiträge aus den Disziplinen Geschichte, Ethnologie, Literaturwissenschaften, Archäologie, Theologie, Geographie und Ökologie befassen sich mit einer breiten Palette von Themenbereichen und vermitteln dadurch eine gute Übersicht über die Forschungen des akademischen Nachwuchses mit Afrikabezug. Le quatrième volume de la série „Etudes africaines suisses" publié par la Société suisse d'études africaines regroupe 16 communications présentées lors du 4e forum suisse des africanistes à Bâle en octobre 2002. Les contributions, issues de disciplines aussi diverses que l'histoire, l'anthropologie, l'analyse littéraire, l'archéologie, la théologie, la géographie et l'écologie, se distinguent par la grande diversité des thèmes abordés. Elles donnent ainsi un bon aperçu des recherches menées en Suisse par une nouvelle génération d'africanistes.
Bd. 4, 2003, 344 S., 24,90 €, br.,
ISBN 3-8258-7208-4

Schriften der Vereinigung von Afrikanisten in Deutschland (VAD e. V.)

Heike Schmidt; Albert Wirz (Hg.)
Afrika und das Andere
Alterität und Innovation
Bd. 17, 1998, 408 S., 30,90 €, br.,
ISBN 3-8258-3395-x

LIT Verlag Münster – Berlin – Hamburg – London – Wien
Grevener Str./Fresnostr. 2 48159 Münster
Tel.: 0251 – 62 032 22 – Fax: 0251 – 23 19 72
e-Mail: vertrieb@lit-verlag.de – http://www.lit-verlag.de

Hans Peter Hahn; Gerd Spittler (Hg.)
Afrika und die Globalisierung
Aus dem Inhalt: Entwicklung, Wirtschaft
und Migration. Organisationskultur und
interkulturelles Management in Afrika,
Erika Dettmar; Cultural Environment,
Olukunle Iyanda; Wer ist dein Ndugu?
Verwandtschaftsbeziehungen in einer
tansanischen Fabrik, *Gundula Fischer;*
Konsum, Bedürfnisse und materielle Kultur,
Hans P. Hahn und Gerd Spittler; Kleidung,
Eleganz und Macht in Zentralafrika, *Anna-
Maria Brandstetter;* Das nubische Lehmhaus
in der Savanne Kordofans, *Gerhard Hesse;*
Mais-Insima und Milch – Ausdruck von
Freiheit und Modernität. Konsumvorlieben
in kultursoziologischer Interpretation, *Sabine
Tröger;* Zur Ethnologie des Krieges, *Trutz
von Trotha;* Genocidal Civil Wars and
the Construction of Mythical-Histories:
the View from the Great Lakes Region of
Africa, *René Lemarchand;* Afrikanische
Kriegsherren – Überlegungen zur Entstehung
von Gewaltmärkten im präkolonialen und
postkolonialen Afrika, *Michael Bollig;* Krieg
und Kriegserfahrung im Luwero-Dreieck,
Uganda, 1981-1986, *Frank Schubert;* Vom
Krieg zum Frieden im Norden von Mali,
Georg Klute
Bd. 18, 2000, 528 S., 30,90 €, br.,
ISBN 3-8258-4363-7

VAD-Script

Ulf Engel; Adam Jones; Robert Kappel
(Hg.)
Afrika 2000
CD-ROM
Auch wenn der Freundschaftsvertrag
zwischen Deutschland und Madagaskar schon
vor über einhundert Jahren unterzeichnet
worden ist, gehört Madagaskar nicht
zu den Ländern, die im Mittelpunkt der
deutschen Entwicklungspolitik stehen.
Die Hinwendung Deutschlands zu den
osteuropäischen Ländern nach 1999 hat
diese Tendenz noch verstärkt. Zu Unrecht;
denn Madagaskar ist ein kleiner Kontinent
für sich. Nirgendwo auf der Welt gibt es so
viele Tiere und Pflanzen, die endemisch sind,
das heißt, die nur auf Madagaskar und nicht
woanders vorkommen. Wirtschaftswachstum
und Bevölkerungsexplosion haben jedoch
dazu geführt, daß ein großer Teil dieser
einzigartigen Fauna und Flora bereits
ausgerottet ist oder vom Aussterben bedroht
ist. Im August 1998 trafen zum ersten Mal
deutsche und madagassische Wissenschaftler
in Madagaskar zusammen, um gemeinsam
Lösungsansätze zur Abwendung dieser
ökologischen Katastrophe zu erarbeiten. Das
Symposium unter dem Thema "Madagaskar:
Entwicklungsperspektiven – Bevölkerungs-
und Wirtschaftswachstum contra Erhalt der
natürlichen Umwelt" fand in Mahajanga an
der Nordwestküste Madagaskars statt. Die
teilnehmenden Wissenschaftler – Biologen,
Soziologen, Wirtschaftswissenschaftler,
Mediziner, Geologen u. a. – erörterten das
Thema aus dem Blickwinkel ihrer jeweiligen
Disziplinen.
Frühjahr 2005, ca. S., ca. 15,90 €, ,
ISBN 3-8258-5718-2

Politics and Economics in Africa
Series Editors: Robert Kappel
and Ulf Engel (Universität Leipzig)

Jedrzej Georg Frynas
Oil in Nigeria
Conflict and Litigation between Oil
Companies and Village Communities
"Oil in Nigeria is destined to become a
standard reference work on the Niger Delta
and a template for future legal studies.
Its relanvace extends beyond Nigeria and
it deserves a wide readership." (African
Affairs) "An important study of the interplay
among multinationals, local legal systems,
and activists for human rights and the
environment." (Foreign Affairs) "I would
highly recommend this book to everyone
interested in understanding the complex story
of the oil industry in Nigeria, the role of both
the state and the oil companies and the impact
of oil exploration on local communities
in the Niger Delta." (Journal of Modern

LIT Verlag Münster – Berlin – Hamburg – London – Wien
Grevener Str./Fresnostr. 2 48159 Münster
Tel.: 0251 – 62 032 22 – Fax: 0251 – 23 19 72
e-Mail: vertrieb@lit-verlag.de – http://www.lit-verlag.de

African Studies) "The autor's approach is lateral and the narratives made clear with illustrations and conclusions, are compelling and revealing." (Social & Legal Studies) "This carefully researched book ... is of interest not only to specialists in Nigeria, but to anyone seeking to understand how international relations of diplomacy and business have adapted to the brave new world of privatisation." (Stephen Ellis, African Studies Centre Leiden)
Bd. 1, 2000, 288 S., 25,90 €, br., ISBN 3-8258-3921-4

Ulf Engel
Die Afrikapolitik der Bundesrepublik Deutschland 1949 – 1999
Rollen und Identitäten
Gibt es angesichts der Vielschichtigkeit der afrikapolitischen Beziehungen Bonns eine übergreifende Klammer für die Interpretation der westdeutschen Afrikapolitik? Auf der Basis einer als "empirischer Konstruktivismus" bezeichneten Wissenschaftsmethode werden in dieser Arbeit vier Interpretationsdimensionen bemüht: Rollen, Normen, der Prozeß der Normenaneignung und das Verhältnis von Identität und Paradigmenwechsel. Dabei steht die Frage im Vordergrund, wie sich afrikapolitische Identitäten konstituieren, reproduzieren oder verändern. Einem Überblickskapitel zu den dominanten politischen Paradigmen der Bonner Afrikapolitik folgen Fallstudien zur Anwendung der Hallstein-Doktrin gegenüber Tanzania (1964 – 65), zur Beteiligung der Bundesrepublik an der UN-Sicherheitsratsinitiative 435 zur Lösung der Namibiafrage (1973 – 83), zur im Rahmen der Europäischen Politischen Zusammenarbeit betriebenen Sanktionspolitik gegenüber Südafrika (1985/86) sowie zur Politik in Zentral- und Westafrika unter den Vorzeichen regionaler französischer Hegemonie, mit besonderer Berücksichtigung von Togo (1956 – 67 bzw. 1991 – 94).
Bd. 2, 2001, 344 S., 25,90 €, br., ISBN 3-8258-4709-8

Barbara Praetorius
Power for the People
Die unvollendete Reform der Stromwirtschaft in Südafrika nach der Apartheid
Seit Anfang der 90er Jahre steht die südafrikanische Stromwirtschaft vor der Herausforderung, sich an die neuen gesellschaftlich-politischen Bedingungen am Kap anzupassen. Reformbedarf ergibt sich sowohl aus den historischen Ungerechtigkeiten als auch den exklusiven, von der Apartheid geprägten politisch-institutionellen Strukturen. Bereits frühzeitig begannen die neuen gesellschaftlichen Akteure mit breiten Konsultationsprozessen, in denen nach Lösungen für die Unterelektrifizierung, Strukturmängel und die fehlende Transparenz und Partizipation in der sektoralen Steuerung gesucht wurde. Die Autorin recherchierte diese Reformprozesse für die Zeit von 1990 bis 1999 während mehrerer Forschungsaufenthalte in Südafrika. Sie analysiert den Verlauf der sektoralen Koordinationsprozesse aus einer handlungstheoretischen Perspektive im Kontext des Systemwechsels zur Demokratie. Die Dynamik der sektoralen Verhandlungen lässt sich so aus dem Zusammenwirken von politisch-institutionellem Rahmen und dem strategischen Handeln politischer Akteure wie dem ANC, den Gewerkschaften, den Kommunen, den Regierungsinstitutionen und der Stromwirtschaft selbst erklären. Es zeigt sich, dass der zunächst formulierte Anspruch einer partizipatorischen und transparenten Entscheidungsfindung nur bedingt durchgehalten wird; er weicht vielmehr einer erneuten Zentralisierung der politischen Strukturen und Steuerungsmechanismen.
Bd. 3, 2000, 312 S., 25,90 €, br., ISBN 3-8258-4772-1

Wiebe Nauta
The Implications of Freedom
The changing role of land sector NGOs in a transforming South Africa
The term 'NGO' is so widely used nowadays that it has effectively lost its meaning.

LIT Verlag Münster – Berlin – Hamburg – London – Wien
Grevener Str./Fresnostr. 2 48159 Münster
Tel.: 0251 – 62 032 22 – Fax: 0251 – 23 19 72
e-Mail: vertrieb@lit-verlag.de – http://www.lit-verlag.de

Therefore, in order to put back flesh on what has become a very bare skeleton, this book attempts to portray a 'real' organization that originated during the anti-apartheid struggle in South Africa. By meticulously studying this land sector NGO over a prolonged period of time, much is revealed about its internal dynamics and the changing relationships with actors in the state, civil society and the market. This embedded tale (re-)introduces a historical, political and socio-economic dimension in the analysis of NGOs and shows that they are not as value-driven, autonomous, accountable and non-profit as is often claimed.

Bd. 6, 2004, 304 S., 29,90 €, br.,
ISBN 3-8258-7798-1

Afrikanische Studien

E. Adriaan B. van Rouveroy van Nieuwaal; Werner Zips (eds.)
Sovereignty, Legitimacy, and Power in West African Societies
Perspectives from Legal Anthropology
Africa has been given persistently the negative image of the lost continent: political turmoil, economic failures, hunger, disease, irresponsible and irrational warlords and corrupt regimes. Such a bias calls for a critique. The authors seek to analyse power divisions and struggles over sovereignty and legitimacy in African societies from a historical point of view. Possibilities for peaceful social relations are taken as much into account as internal frictions between state and "traditional authorities". In a striking difference to the legitimacy claims of single-rooted states, political legitimacy in many African states derives from two sources: the imposed European colonial states and the pre-colonial African polities. State and traditional authorities (systems of chieftaincy) depend on each other's contributions in striving towards the goals they both desire to achieve in the fields of development, stable *democratic* governance and human rights. "Indigenous" institutions are not necessarily inferior to state institutions. The opposite

might be true in view of the capacity of the traditional institutions not just to decide internal disputes, but actually to solve them and thus contribute to social cohesion. Such a perspective is highly relevant for a variety of concrete social relations of which gender relations are one important aspect.

Bd. 10, 1998, 264 S., 19,90 €, br.,
ISBN 3-8258-3036-5

Hans van den Breemer;
Bernhard Venema (eds.)
Towards Negotiated Co-management of Natural Resources in Africa
Within the field of management of natural resources, this book focuses on the various approaches of policy formulation and implementation. The question central to this book is how to co-operate with people, the various categories of residents as well as non-residents, in the rural areas: in a top-down, a participatory or a contractual (co-management) way. On the basis of a comparative analysis of 12 case studies in the book, these three approaches are thoroughly discussed and their internal and external constraints examined. The book starts with an editorial chapter, discussing the recent administrative and political developments in Africa as well as the new opportunities, which they offer for policies in the field of environment, and development. The question is brought up whether the recent processes of decentralization, democratization, and empowerment of local organizations have indeed created new opportunities or that they have only superficially changed the political culture of the countries concerned. In the concluding chapter of the book, the approaches are contrasted to each other as logical models, each with its own potentiality and limitations. Conclusions are formulated why the top down approach must result in improvization to escape from failure, and why the participatory approach risks to end up into a mixed balance. Special attention is given to the conditions and the prospects for the contractual or co-management approach, which has been introduced into Africa only

LIT Verlag Münster – Berlin – Hamburg – London – Wien
Grevener Str./Fresnostr. 2 48159 Münster
Tel.: 0251 – 62 032 22 – Fax: 0251 – 23 19 72
e-Mail: vertrieb@lit-verlag.de – http://www.lit-verlag.de

recently. Under certain conditions, this approach seems rather promising.
Bd. 12, 1999, 368 S., 25,90 €, br.,
ISBN 3-8258-3948-6

Fred Krüger; Georgia Rakelmann; Petra Schierholz (Hg.)
Botswana – Alltagswelten im Umbruch
Facettes of a Changing Society
Die Gesellschaft Botswanas verändert sich rapide. Dieses Buch greift damit verbundene aktuelle gesellschaftliche Prozesse auf und zeigt, wie facettenreich und von welchen Konflikten begleitet sich der rasche soziale Wandel vollzieht. Autorinnen und Autoren aus Botswana und Deutschland schlagen einen großen Bogen von dem sich verändernden Alltagsleben in Dörfern und Städten über die Entwicklung neuer kultureller und sprachlicher Identitäten hin zu den wachsenden Umweltproblemen im fragilen Ökosystem der Kalahari. Ihre dokumentarischen, erzählerischen und wissenschaftlichen Beiträge vermitteln schlaglichtartig einen tiefen und spannenden Einblick in gegenwärtige Lebenssituationen in diesem ungewöhnlichen afrikanischen Land.
Bd. 14, 2000, 224 S., 15,90 €, br.,
ISBN 3-8258-4671-7

Deutsch-Madagassische Gesellschaft e. V. (Hg.)
Madagascar: Perspectives de Développement
Croissance de la Population et Croissance Economique contre Sauvegarde de la Nature
Auch wenn der Freundschaftsvertrag zwischen Deutschland und Madagaskar schon vor über einhundert Jahren unterzeichnet worden ist, gehört Madagaskar nicht zu den Ländern, die im Mittelpunkt der deutschen Entwicklungspolitik stehen. Die Hinwendung Deutschlands zu den osteuropäischen Ländern nach 1999 hat diese Tendenz noch verstärkt. Zu Unrecht; denn Madagaskar ist ein kleiner Kontinent für sich. Nirgendwo auf der Welt gibt es so viele Tiere und Pflanzen, die endemisch sind, das heißt, die nur auf Madagaskar und nicht woanders vorkommen. Wirtschaftswachstum und Bevölkerungsexplosion haben jedoch dazu geführt, daß ein großer Teil dieser einzigartigen Fauna und Flora bereits ausgerottet ist oder vom Aussterben bedroht ist. Im August 1998 trafen zum ersten Mal deutsche und madagassische Wissenschaftler in Madagaskar zusammen, um gemeinsam Lösungsansätze zur Abwendung dieser ökologischen Katastrophe zu erarbeiten. Das Symposium unter dem Thema "Madagaskar: Entwicklungsperspektiven – Bevölkerungs- und Wirtschaftswachstum contra Erhalt der natürlichen Umwelt" fand in Mahajanga an der Nordwestküste Madagaskars statt. Die teilnehmenden Wissenschaftler – Biologen, Soziologen, Wirtschaftswissenschaftler, Mediziner, Geologen u. a. – erörterten das Thema aus dem Blickwinkel ihrer jeweiligen Disziplinen.
Bd. 15, 2000, 344 S., 20,90 €, br.,
ISBN 3-8258-4807-8

Joe L. P. Lugalla; Colleta G. Kibassa
Urban Life and Street Children's Health
Children's Accounts of Urban Hardships and Violence in Tanzania
The authors examine the dynamics of urban life and street children's health in the era of globalization and structural adjustments in Tanzania. They discuss the factors that push children out of their homes, how the children survive in streets, the hardships and violence they endure and how this affects their health. They argue that the impact of the legacy of colonial policies and some post-colonial development policies, the negative consequences of uncontrolled process of globalization, the impact of structural adjustments and the HIV/AIDS epidemic are simultaneously intensifying the situation of poverty in Tanzania. These processes are not only destroying families and communities that have for many years acted as safety nets for children in need, but are also manufacturing

LIT Verlag Münster – Berlin – Hamburg – London – Wien
Grevener Str./Fresnostr. 2 48159 Münster
Tel.: 0251 – 62 032 22 – Fax: 0251 – 23 19 72
e-Mail: vertrieb@lit-verlag.de – http://www.lit-verlag.de

poor, helpless and powerless children most of whom resort to street life.
Bd. 16, 2003, 176 S., 20,90 €, br.,
ISBN 3-8258-6690-4

Christoph Haferburg;
Jürgen Oßenbrügge (Eds.)
Ambiguous Restructurings of Post-Apartheid Cape Town
The Spatial Form of Socio-Political Change
What will tomorrow's Cape Town look like? This volume reflects a variety of aspects of urban development and restructuring efforts in Cape Town in the last years. A focus lies on the question if the "apartheid city" is reproducing itself. This leads to an evaluation whether current policies really counter societal imbalances. The essays presented here illuminate possible pathways towards the urban futures unfolding in a South African city in transition. Contributors: Jürgen Oßenbrügge, Patrick Bond, Vanessa Watson, Christoph Haferburg, Steven Robins, Marie Huchzermeyer, Antje Nahnsen, Edgar Pieters
Bd. 17, 2003, 200 S., 20,90 €, br.,
ISBN 3-8258-6699-8

Eva-Maria Bruchhaus (Ed.)
Hot Spot Horn of Africa
Between Integration and Disintegration
The volume includes most of the contributions to a meeting on recently completed or ongoing research projects concerning the "small" Horn of Africa, that is Ethiopia, Eritrea and Somalia, held in Hamburg in May 2002, as well as a few complementary articles. Contributions are widely diversified, as the Hamburg meeting had gathered young scholars from German universities working on extremely different themes. The subjects range widely from Agro-Anthropology to Political Science, with Sociology and Social Anthropology enjoying the strongest coverage.
Bd. 19, 2003, 208 S., 19,90 €, br.,
ISBN 3-8258-6835-4

Anne Schröder
Crossing Borders
Interdisciplinary Approaches to Africa
This book shows new approaches to the African continent and its various cultures, explores different facets of African cultures as they exist or undergo changes, and illustrates how and where African and European cultures come or have come into contact, interact, and create something new. The contributors are social, cultural and literary scientists, linguists, and artists of various cultural backgrounds who investigate topics on an African country and who use novel and often interdisciplinary methods. Their joint interest is a better understanding of the multifaceted character of the African continent, which is still often depicted as a cultural monolith, by exploring contemporary African literature, theatre, film, music and the use of linguistic methods as well as the experience of Africans in diasporas.
Bd. 23, 2004, 240 S., 19,90 €, br.,
ISBN 3-8258-7787-6

Jürgen Oßenbrügge;
Mechthild Reh (Eds.)
Social Spaces of African Societies
Applications and Critique of Concepts about "Transnational Social Spaces"
„Transnational social spaces" have emerged in recent years as a research area within migration and area studies. This volume is about African social spaces with examples of Central and Western Africa as well as of African - European relations. Authors from different disciplines like anthropology, geography, political and educational sciences outline their interpretations of transnational social spaces, based on theoretical and empirical work within a wider research project at the University of Hamburg about contemporary transformations of African societies.
Bd. 27, 2004, 256 S., 24,90 €, br.,
ISBN 3-8258-7850-3

LIT Verlag Münster – Berlin – Hamburg – London – Wien
Grevener Str./Fresnostr. 2 48159 Münster
Tel.: 0251 – 62 032 22 – Fax: 0251 – 23 19 72
e-Mail: vertrieb@lit-verlag.de – http://www.lit-verlag.de